337159

magCulture

new magazine design

INSTITUTE OF ART
UNIVERSI

29 OCT 2009

D1419267

magCulture

new magazine design

Edited and designed
by Jeremy Leslie

LAURENCE KING PUBLISHING

Published in 2003 by Laurence King Publishing Ltd
71 Great Russell Street
London WC1B 3BP
United Kingdom
Tel: +44 20 7430 8850
Fax: +44 20 7430 8880
e-mail: enquiries@laurenceking.co.uk
www.laurenceking.co.uk

Copyright © text and design 2003 Jeremy Leslie

All rights reserved. No part of this publication may be reproduced or transmitted in any form or by any means, electronic or mechanical, including photocopy, recording or any information storage and retrieval system, without prior permission in writing from the publisher.

A catalogue record for this book is available from the British Library

ISBN 1 85669 336 8

Designed by Jeremy Leslie

Typeface FF Atma

Printed in China

331159

741.652 LES

Contents

Introduction

6 Foreword
BY JEREMY LESLIE

8 Buy me...
DESIGNING MAGAZINES THAT SELL
AN INTERVIEW WITH ANDY COWLES

12 Take me...
MAGAZINES AS BRAND MESSENGERS
BY JEREMY LESLIE

15 Love me, hate me...
THE NEW WORLD OF THE MICROZINE
BY MICHAEL JACOVIDES

18 Download me...
CAN PRINT MAGAZINES WORK ONLINE?
BY PATRICK BURGOYNE

22 Lead me...
HOW NEWSPAPERS LEARN FROM MAGAZINES
BY MARK PORTER

The magazines

28 Format
52 Covers
86 Pace
108 Words
156 Pictures

174 Credits and Index

Foreword

BY JEREMY LESLIE

Magazines have always played a central role in our visual culture. A unique format, they represent a medium that combines a number of essential elements – portability, tactility, repetitiveness and a combination of text and images – that have enabled them to be continually renewable and relevant. These factors, combined with recent developments in production methods and the influence of new media, have enabled magazines to retain their position at the forefront of modern communication and continue to be a source of inspiration to graphic designers everywhere.

Magazines remain, at a most basic level, a combination of text and image created in a process of collaboration between editors and designers. The chemistry between these two disciplines is a central part of the process – a good magazine designer will always have a good grasp of journalism, a good editor will understand the importance of design. And within this broader issue, are the specific design elements: the page size, grid, typefaces and details, all of which contribute to the magazine's identity and visual impact.

Into this designed environment are added the other key elements that define a magazine. For example, it is the contrasting way in which two magazines will cover the same story that defines each magazine's philosophy and outlook – every component of the magazine, however small, has to be seen as part of the larger, ever-changing mass of magazines. The best, sharpest content will often spark the most interesting design in response.

Another key aspect of what makes a magazine's magazine-ness is that there will be another issue. For the magazine designer this means that he may be working on several issues at the same time, and that a new issue is often only half completed before the previous one comes back from the printer. A magazine is therefore an organic project that exists continually rather than in weekly/monthly/bi-monthly bites. This makes it easier to make gradual design changes rather than execute complete redesigns. This ability to continually develop and change without losing the central nature of the magazine is an essential part of good magazine design.

However, whereas once the use of the grid, a set of typefaces and other self-defined rules offered a one-off decision to aid the production process, the Apple Macintosh, now on every magazine designer's desk means that these basic rules can be set, reset, broken and adapted far more freely today. The designer now has more time to fulfil that desire for a unique identity, to question what does and doesn't work on the page. It is this positioning of the

traditional elements within this new cultural context that has created a surge, in recent years, in design-led and design-aware magazines.

And the repetitive nature of the magazine itself plays into the hands of the designer. Each new issue offers the chance to try something new, in reaction to the previous issues and to what other magazines (and other media) have been doing. It is this continuity that lends magazines the ability to both reflect and start graphic trends, as the examples selected for this book will demonstrate.

Today, there are more magazines than ever available, and more continue to be launched. But not all of them are relevant to *magCulture* – there are plenty of magazines being successfully published that are of little interest design-wise. Were an objective measure of quality magazine design possible, I believe the overall mean average would currently be higher than ever before. But here my concern is only with the magazines that are significantly above average in their design outlook.

It is no coincidence that Canadian magazine *Adbusters* features so prominently in this book. Published as a critique of consumerism, globalism and the state of the environment – some of the most challenging subjects of our time – the designers at *Adbusters* have responded with some of the strongest design statements currently being published. Designs such as the cover of the Design Anarchy Issue *(see page 84)* revel in the irony of using such a commercially orientated medium to criticize the very world in which these market forces dominate.

One of the themes of my earlier book, *Issues*, was that the computerization of magazine design had become the subject of magazine design. Magazines such as *Raygun* (US) had pushed the boundaries of early versions of layout software to create pages where design overtook content. Many magazine designers had responded to these experiments with completely neutral designs, almost 'non' designs. However, this has now changed. The shock of the computer is now over and technology is no big deal. The Apple Macintosh, QuarkXpress and Adobe Photoshop are taken for granted. Instead designers today see the technology simply as tools to achieve what they want.

magCulture looks at what magazine designers from around the world are trying to achieve today. One coherent theme that has surfaced is the reintroduction of 'handmade' techniques. Designers are eschewing the hi-tech and looking back to simple grids and blocks of text that recall pre-Macintosh typesetting; needlecraft is being used for illustration (*Dazed & Confused*, *Tank* [UK]); collage and handwriting have left the domain of secondary illustration and are being used to display the central content (*Adbusters*) and graffiti-style handwriting and marks are used to loosen otherwise tight layouts (*Nylon* [US], *Tank*, *Re-* [The Netherlands], *M-real* [International]). At first glance, these hand-drawn designs share *Raygun* art director David Carson's earlier disregard for content, but in fact the marks and doodles are more often used to enhance it, ironically through using technology.

Several magazines go further and adopt handmade styling for their physical format. *Mined* (UK) has made a virtue of roughly bound pages that rely on the reader tearing them to open them. *SexyMachinery* (UK) contains instructions on how to assemble loose elements into a bound magazine. In the process of reading, one becomes involved in its construction.

At the opposite end of the scale designers are using technology to experiment with new mixes of text, colour and image. A new flamboyance can be seen in magazines like *Frame* (The Netherlands), *Pop* (UK) and *Surface* (US). These designs mix text and image, applying Illustrator and Photoshop filters as necessary, to create integrated designs that owe as much to the influence of Japanese magazines as to websites.

Alongside the mechanics and creative processes of magazine design there are also wider issues at play, and *magCulture* explores these through a series of essays by prominent figures in this field. Such themes include a consideration of the commercial pressures surrounding a magazine's concept, as well as the processes involved in its actual construct and physical form, whether printed or available on the internet.

But above all, this book celebrates not just how the design of magazines has increased their influence on modern graphic design, but how the magazine format has increased its influence on other media too: newspapers are hiring magazine designers to help retain their relevance to readers who have access to real-time news on the internet; websites are looking to magazines for help in successfully combining words and images; advertisers are hiring magazine publishers to produce magazines that help communicate their brand messages, and, a new type of independent publisher is using modern production and distribution methods to create small-scale but influential 'microzines' that are unafraid to look to such famous US publications as *The New Yorker* and *National Geographic* for influence.

Today, magazines have fought off the challenge presented by other media and are now striding ahead of those same media, adapting new technology to further hone their ability to present content and design as one. Their visual influence is significant across newspapers, websites, marketing pieces and catalogues. Magazines have not only become a medium in their own right, they have also come to be defined by the way in which they define themselves. This is *magCulture*.

Buy me ...

DESIGNING MAGAZINES THAT SELL: AN INTERVIEW WITH ANDY COWLES

How did you first become involved in magazines?

I was involved through my school magazine, which, back in 1975 in the UK, we produced as a spoof of *The Sun* newspaper. We thought it was pretty funny, but when the headmaster saw it finally printed he ordered all copies to be burned, as he considered it to be nothing but sexist, puerile, sixth-form humour, which, frankly, it was. But a few copies were saved and entered into *The Sunday Times* school magazine competition, which it duly won, causing the biggest stink. The front page of the local paper screamed 'Blue Book Wins Prize'.

Our headmaster had to send back the prize money, and we were all nearly expelled.

I really enjoyed the whole thing – the power and subversive nature of magazines, how people get really upset or excited about them and how they can provoke strong debate. So when I left art school, I got a job as a magazine designer with Emap in the UK on *Horse & Pony* magazine. Which then led to being art editor of *Melody Maker* in 1982, followed by the launch of *Q* in '86, *Empire* in '89 and *Mojo* in 1993.

What changes have you seen in the industry in the past 20 years?

The biggest change has been, without question, the technology. The advent of the Apple Mac has allowed designers to have control over content and editors to have control over presentation. Design is no longer seen as some sort of repro function, a black art involving ancient language, a strange rubric and a lot of red film. The Mac has increased the level of magazine craft – the integration of words and pictures, box-outs, sidebars, captions, pull-quotes, subheads, lists and blobs – devices that attract a reader's attention.

The other huge change is that of celebrity and sex. This influences all magazines in every area, with the possible exception of specialist niche titles. You may not see a woman in a black brassiere on the front of a gardening title, but I bet publishers would do it if they thought it would sell more copies.

Have the commercial pressures changed since you started?

I don't think so. The need to sell has always been there. Circulation figures underscore everything you do on a consumer title. Advertising is more of a variable, depending on the nature of the readership. With *Wallpaper** (UK), for example, I would assume that, as long as the sales figures are adequate, they will sell a lot of space because of the very focused group of readers that they reach. Whereas a mass-market men's magazine like, say, *FHM* (UK), will need a big circulation to pull in the ads, as the readership is so broad-based.

Publishers are far more aware now that magazines can become

Maxim
(UK, November 2002)
220 x 285mm/8 3/4 x 11 1/4 inches
Art director *Damian Wilkinson*

(US, October 2002)
210 x 275mm/8 1/4 x 10 7/8 inches
Art director *David Hilton*

This magazine shook up the UK men's market with its diet of schoolboy humour and sex, before being successfully exported to the US and doing the same there.

brands. A magazine is more than just paper and ink – it's a set of values, a belief system. For sure it exists on paper, but can also appear in the form of websites, exhibitions, events, books and so on. The world's biggest magazines can spawn dozens of foreign editions. *Cosmopolitan* and *FHM* have a global presence similar to MacDonald's or Pepsi.

The key to making a magazine brand is consistency. It has to always be the same, yet also changing. The reader has to know what to expect, yet when the page turns they must be surprised.

Obviously, the level of design has increased enormously over the past 20 years. But it's still rare that a new consumer magazine comes along and shouts 'Bang! Look at me! This is different.' To be revolutionary is difficult. When a consumer magazine makes those moves, often the market will punish it. In terms of format and presentation, the market can reject things they haven't seen before, things that make the reader uncomfortable or that challenge them. But magazines can always succeed in finding new ways of packaging a story.

In the UK, *Loaded* was revolutionary because the moment it was invented you could talk about 'the *Loaded* reader' as a concept. *Q* magazine was revolutionary. It said 'You may be a sad, thirtysomething that enjoys listening to Phil Collins, but, actually, you're a power in the market place. You're our reader and we love you.' *LivingEtc* was revolutionary. It acknowledged that home magazines didn't have to be about paisley prints and how to repaint your kitchen. It just reflected a social trend, a distinct group of people, and packaged it perfectly. Likewise *Wallpaper**.

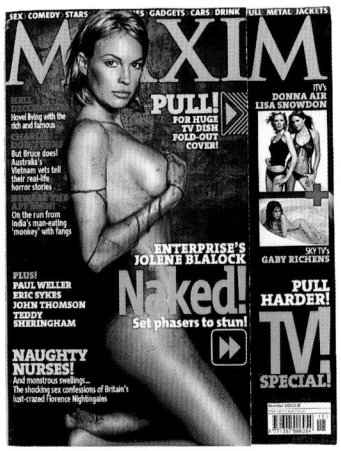

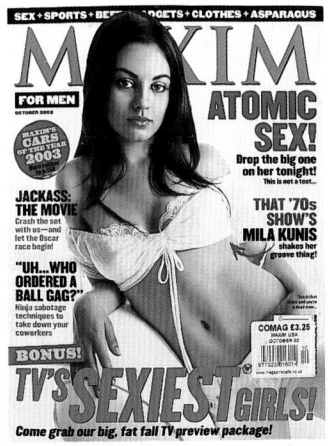

To make a mainstream magazine look revolutionary is next to impossible and probably not necessary. The really progressive, challenging work inevitably lies in magazines which people buy for that very fact. David Carson's *Raygun* (US) was a success because people bought it for the way it was presented.

However, taking those design values and merely applying them to another magazine does not work. For example, *Blah Blah Blah* (UK), a music magazine, attempted to use the *Raygun* look, but the magazine failed because readers need a certain functionality from a music magazine that is not required from a title that is understood to be an experimental pop cultural phenomenon. The *Blah Blah Blah* design was no less good than *Raygun*, but it didn't serve its purpose. Certain subject matter demands that text is read and subsequently a design that allows this to happen.

Yet *Raygun* has influenced the look of modern magazines to a considerable degree. It acknowledged that you could make the magazine look as if it had been created on a computer, as opposed to a replication of hot-metal setting, even if it's just in the details – a column rule touching a column of type, an invisible item pushing text over or even a transparent box.

Not all the magazines you mention were revolutionary design-wise. *Loaded* and *Wallpaper had design statements to make, but *LivingEtc* didn't.**
The look of *LivingEtc* isn't revolutionary but its design is, because in a consumer magazine, the design is all about the reader and making the link between content and presentation absolutely seamless. But *Loaded*, yeah, that was revolutionary because it looked like they were all off their heads when they were making up the pages. It was great because it reflected the editorial point of view and the needs of the readership. It would have been inappropriate for it to be slickly designed. Whereas *FHM* was a more conservative, black-white-and-red, safe, traditional style, which did not threaten or challenge a 20-year-old estate agent from the provinces.

Setting aside these successful magazines, can you identify any that were revolutionary, but which failed for their lack of commercial expertise?
Those magazines often tend to be great inside but have bad covers. *Neon* (UK), for example, was a wonderful, hip movie title, but with covers that didn't work because they didn't communicate the benefit of the magazine to the reader. So it never achieved the sales to keep it going.

Aside from that, most consumer magazines fail because they're not interesting enough to a big group of people. If they keep going in spite of that, then they are more of a vanity project, serving the needs of the owner or some other interested party, as opposed to the reader, such as Mohamed

LIBRARY & RESOURCE CENTRE, CAMPUS
THE SURREY INSTITUTE OF ART & DESIGN

Al Fayed's *Punch* or the *New Statesman* (UK).

On a pure design level, there are a lot of what you might call vanity publishing projects – *Raygun* was one of them – that inform other more commercial magazines and are important in that respect. This is true, though it's my suspicion that *Raygun* was profitable because there were enough design professionals who were interested in it, and enough brands like Levi's and Diesel that wanted to be associated with that kind of cutting-edge work to make it a viable proposition. It was clearly a very focused magazine.

I'm trying to think of magazines that were successful from an aesthetic point of view, yet commercially unsuccessful, and I find it hard to disengage the two. When I think of commercial I don't think of profit. I think of identity with the reader and their aspirations and desires. So if the design, the typography, the art direction, the page furniture, the colour and everything else communicates a certain feeling that I can clearly recognize – if I can see the reader – then it is successful. If I can't see who the reader is, the magazine confuses me.

What I'm thinking of here is design for designers. I'm thinking of magazines that ask questions about what a magazine is, what a magazine can be: magazines that are completely outside of the commercial world, that add to a discussion about what good design is.

Those kind of magazines aren't consumer magazines in the strictest sense. They are niche titles for people with an interest beyond the content: like a fashion magazine, but where the fashion is the very nature of print and ink. And fashion magazines, like *Raygun*, do influence mainstream consumer magazines, as did *The Face* when Neville Brody was there. It had an impact beyond its target market.

It's interesting you pair those two magazines. In both cases, the designers became superstars on the basis of their magazine design work.

Absolutely. The magazines were very high-profile vehicles for their own particular aesthetic. Both were great designers, though neither can necessarily say that those titles were their best work. My favourite Carson works are the surfing and snowboarding magazines before *Raygun*, such as *Beach Culture* (US). Here, they had to serve a practical purpose. They were niche leisure magazines, but with a very cool aesthetic to them. Those readers are demanding. I suspect surfers like their type in straight columns – they want to be able to read it. And so these pages created the sensibility of *Raygun*, but in a more practical context.

It is possible to be radical within a commercial context. UK *Vogue*'s redrawing of Gill two years ago was excellent. That was

The Face
(UK, Volume 3, Issue 64, May 2002)
220 x 300mm/8 3/4 x 11 7/8 inches
The 'original' style magazine is currently living up to its reputation for innovative design, which was earned during its '80s heyday under the art direction of Neville Brody.
Art director *Craig Tilford*

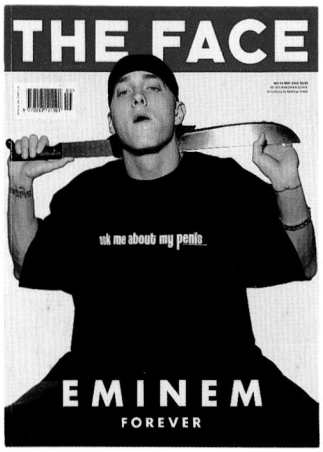

progressive – you don't mess with Eric Gill's work unless you're on sure ground. They did a wonderful job. They used all the type in black and white, and they had the production values to do it well.

It's interesting to see what *Harper's Bazaar* is doing in America now. They've gone back to the original logo and restored Fabien Baron's typography, the Bodoni, which seems the right thing to do. It's all very simple, black and white, following UK *Vogue*'s lead.

What are the differences between working in the UK and in the US?

There are so many! Two nations divided by a common language, and all that. The differences can be fundamental. Looking at their various magazines, the UK feels like a pagan country, and the US essentially a puritan country. Right now, Americans are conservative. Many publishers have trouble with sex on the covers of their magazines. They have difficulty with irony – they don't understand this form of humour. And the way in which they make their magazines is very traditional, using lots of separate departments. It is like the difference between American football and soccer. In American football, you have many people with their own job to do, and everything is controlled by one person at the top. Soccer teams are smaller – people take far more individual responsibility and work in each other's areas with greater fluency.

Overall, UK magazines have the edge in packaging – concepts, angles, box-outs, caption styles – whilst the US leads in terms of pure content – photography, writing, accuracy and so on. UK magazines can read poorly, measured against American titles, but they are funnier and make more opportunity to surprise the reader. The culture of perfectionism in US magazines can boil a lot of the fun out of the process.

The Americans like their market research. They put every detail of every issue to focus-group research and expect the editorial and design teams to respond immediately to the data.

For sure. The way the cover lines are written, the pose of the cover girl, the fashion styling, the colour palettes, can all be very controlled. Americans have the resources to put far more science into the process. They believe you can get results – sales – that way.

Is that because of the scale of the US publishing industry? Because so much more rides on success or failure?
Possibly. The numbers are so much larger, the circulations are enormous and the advertising figures are huge. Also, magazines are far more elevated products in the US. To be on the masthead of a magazine means something there. Magazines are considered more important than newspapers, whereas in the UK I suspect it's the other way round.

When you do get a European magazine breakthrough in the US, the results can be devastating. The enormous success of the US edition of *Maxim* demonstrates that. By US standards, *Maxim* looks really 'cutting-edge' because it is produced out of a mindset and a culture that are not their own. It looks radically different to American magazines because of the way it is made, not because of its 'design'. The thought process, production methods and its context are so different.

Staff working on American magazines refer to photographs as 'the art'. If you want to do a cut-out round someone's head in a photograph, you are interfering with 'the art'. This can trouble people, as in the US this technique is often considered that of a lower-class title. US magazines can take themselves very seriously. They like to separate the text and the pictures. They're designed so that the text is over here and 'the art' is over there. In the UK, magazines are less squeamish about developing the closest possible relationship between the text and pictures.

***Rolling Stone* is a good example of that tendency. Your predecessor, Fred Woodward, worked with some great photographers and designed some beautiful typographic layouts, but these two elements were always very separate.**
Fred's a brilliant typographer and a great art director. And his current work on American *GQ* continues to prove that. At *Rolling Stone* (US), the photography was always of the highest standard and likewise the typography. The two elements were always aesthetically balanced on the page, but there was not much integration of text and pictures. Caption-writing is not part of their culture, so, to this point, *Rolling Stone* has not developed these ways of communicating their points of view to their readership. There is a sense of expectation here that people will read. That's the American style. When you read a story in an US magazine, often the hook won't come until paragraph three. A feature may well start with two paragraphs of waffle. The English style is to start with a bang, straight in at the top, which is more of a newspaper style and approach. However, now that Ed Needham has been appointed as our new managing editor, all that could well change.

Do Americans read magazines in a different way?
I don't think so. We're all human. The success of a title like *Maxim* proves it. If there is a difference, it is that Americans have a little more reverence for magazines. They believe them to be important. The British perhaps consider them to be light entertainment.

You have an experience across a range of consumer magazines. Is there a particular area where your heart lies?
I enjoy magazines that are funny. I think that if you can make people laugh, then you make a relation with them that is stronger than almost any other. *Q* was, and still is, a funny magazine. Ironic, dry, well-informed, but funny. I love that. *Total Sport* (UK) was a funny magazine too, and I loved that as well. To do something where people are just entertained by the page is important.

> 'Looking at their various magazines, the UK feels like a pagan country and the US essentially a puritan country.'

What is the current state of consumer publishing?
Consumer publishing is always very dynamic. Magazines are such a spontaneous purchase. You're always living and dying by your next issue. Magazines can turn themselves around very quickly. They can go from being rubbish to brilliant in three issues. *The Face* still does that on a regular basis. New magazines launch all the time. Others are in slow and terminal decline, and will eventually disappear. It's always been so. The industry doesn't feel any different now to how it used to be, because it's always changing so fast.

On the one hand, it always seems to be more exciting, because you can do more with less, thanks to the technology. On the other, it's becoming more and more difficult to get access to celebrity. The power of the publicist is so big. And readers are also becoming so desensitized. Things that were considered shocking just five years ago are now the norm. Sex is no longer risqué, along with dozens of other things. Shocking people is a great function of a good consumer magazine. You should appal some people, yet truly delight the person who you really want – your reader.

Andy Cowles *is art director of Rolling Stone magazine*

Take me...

MAGAZINES AS BRAND MESSENGERS: BY JEREMY LESLIE

As I write this, the highest circulation magazines in the UK are *Sky* magazine, *O* magazine and the *AA magazine*. None of these titles are available on the newsstand, none are available by subscription. If you watch Sky television, use an Orange mobile phone or are a member of the AA car rescue service you will receive them. They will fall through your letter box delivering various degrees of brand- and sales-orientated messages mixed with lifestyle material. They are produced and distributed by publishers on behalf of commercial clients and are the clearest marker of the growth of customer publishing.

Magazines have always been vehicles for communicating with consumers – the income from advertising is a vital part of magazine economics (in the US it is *the* vital part). So it was perhaps inevitable that advertisers and marketers would eventually make the jump from buying advertising space in consumer magazines to publishing their own magazines.

The business model of the consumer magazine has become increasingly complex as publishers, advertisers and readers have become more sophisticated. What was once a simple financial exchange has become much more complicated. Today the advertiser is buying far more than just a page in a magazine. He is aligning the product or service he is selling with the rest of the content of the magazine – both the editorial and the other ads – and buying into a set of values and beliefs that the reader associates with the magazine. The advertiser is seeking to take advantage of the unique relationship between reader and magazine, a relationship unlike any created by other forms of media. As Kevin Roberts, CEO Worldwide of Saatchi and Saatchi has said, 'Great magazines are the ultimate interactive, tactile medium, they offer real emotional involvement.' The advertiser is hoping that some of the magic of that involvement will rub off on his product. The reverse happens too. A magazine will happily offer a discounted page to

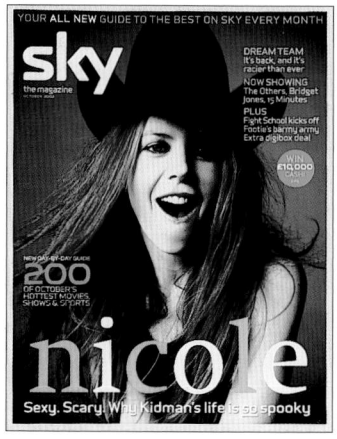

Sky Magazine
(UK, October 2002)
210 x 265mm/8 1/4 x 10 1/2 inches
The UK's highest circulation magazine promotes movies and sports coverage to satellite television viewers.
Art direction *Chris Parker and David Grenham*

Sony Style
(US, Autumn 2000)
228 x 275mm/9 x 10 7/8 inches
Sony produce a wide range of consumer electronics and use this magazine, which is sold on the newsstand, to cross-sell their products by combining them with lifestyle content, presented using a clean modern design.
Creative director *Terry Koppel*

an advertiser with the right 'fit'. You want your magazine to look hip? Do whatever you have to do to get Prada to buy a page.

And research has shown that readers expect advertising in their magazines – take away 'their' advertising and they complain.

Such research is endless. The sheer economic scale of the mainstream magazine industry today has led to extended research into every element of the publishing process. Major US publishers routinely focus group each page of every magazine and expect the creative teams to respond urgently to the opinions generated, while advertisers invest in tracking research to check the efficacy of their ads. Publishers and advertisers know increasing amounts about how the relationship between their respective interests is perceived by the reader.

Publishers have long been using the language now favoured by brand specialists to describe the character of their magazines. But it is only recently that magazines have come to be overtly regarded as brands. Visit the website of the National Magazine Company – the UK arm of publisher Hearst – and you'll find their magazines listed under the heading 'Our Brands'.

Front covers, content, and advertising all have to fit the brand. The celebrity on the cover has to be on-brand, to reflect the right values. Like advertising this is a two-way process. An editor might want Tom Cruise on his front cover,

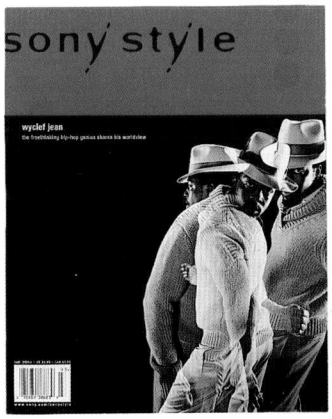

but will Tom Cruise's marketing team want him to appear on it? Does his brand fit your brand?

The cachet held by longstanding, successful brands such as *Vogue* and *Cosmopolitan* has been used to launch local editions across the world, and is now being used to create new titles – *Vogue Teen* and *Cosmo Girl* (US) – seeking to attract younger readers to the core brands and help ensure their future. Men's magazines spin off titles such as *Maxim Fashion*(US), and *Loaded Fashion*(UK), built around potentially lucrative ad sales. Such titles have a level of brand recognition that many owners of consumer products would kill for. Without realizing it, magazine designers have become brand experts, responsible for many of the strongest brands around today.

It is against this background that advertisers and their clients began to explore new relationships with publishers. Why pay a publisher to include a page of your message in their magazine when you could publish your own magazine full of your message(s)? Why not produce a magazine actually about, rather than merely featuring, your brand? Thus customer publishing was born.

Over the past 20 years customer publishing has grown from being a rather murky world of cheaply produced give-away magazines that were little better than glorified catalogues (for which the miserable word magalogue was coined) to encompass not only the biggest magazines in the UK, but also some of the best-designed publications. Titles such as *Volvo* (International), *Army* (UK), and *M-real* (International) regularly win awards for their design, and an increasing number of high-profile magazine designers are being attracted to this field of design.

For the designer, customer publishing can be a refreshing alternative to the pressures of the consumer magazine world. All magazines designers have to work within a commercial environment, but for consumer magazines this means just one thing - they have to sell. To help them achieve this singular aim there is a single business model, based on the same distribution channels and sales outlets as your competitors. Consumer magazines are generally monthly, carry ads and have to conform to a page size that is easily distributed via the news trade.

When launching a new customer magazine, however, the designer is more likely to start with a blank sheet of paper. How often will it be published? What format can it be? As Rami Lippa, creative director of Redwood, one of the major UK customer publishing agencies, says, 'The challenge for the customer magazine designer is striking the right balance between "pure" editorial values and the brand environment they need to express.' Gone are the deliberations over whether the magazine cover will stand out on the newsstand against its competitors. Instead, the concern is whether the cover fulfils the client's brief.

That brief is different for each project. The client may want to increase product sales or emphasize a brand message. They may want to improve or adjust their relationship with their customers,

'Magazine designers have become brand experts, responsible for some of the strongest brands around today.'

Volvo Magazine
(International, Autumn/Winter 2002)
220 x 284mm/8 3/4 x 11 1/4 inches
Ten different language editions of this magazine are mailed to Volvo owners in 30 countries. It sets out to express the spirit of the Volvo brand while keeping customers up to date with the company's range of cars.
Art director *Lynn Watt*

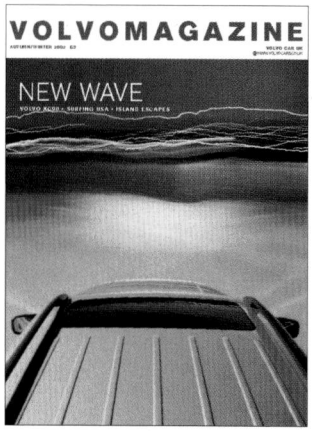

or perhaps even reach a new group of customers altogether.

One magazine that successfully combines these three functions is *Waitrose Food Illustrated (UK),* published on behalf of Waitrose supermarkets. The magazine is Waitrose's chosen method of communicating to its customers that they are about quality food above cheaper prices. It uses commissioned photography and restrained, modern typography to create an upmarket, glossy magazine that reflects the clients' brand values and successfully communicates the quality message. The magazine also acts as a loyalty reward, being free to holders of a Waitrose account card. Finally, it also has a direct effect on sales; items highlighted on the cover and in major features regularly see increases in sales instore.

Other customer magazines are purely brand-orientated. Finnish paper company M-real publish a bi-annual magazine of the same name in the UK, targeting magazine creatives, a group to whom paper manufacturers would not normally address their marketing. The magazine is printed on the product it promotes, allowing the content to avoid the hard sell. Instead it concentrates on being a must-read/look publication, changing its design each issue in response to the issue's theme, building up a loyal readership, winning awards and generally garnering attention on behalf of the client.

Customer magazines have to be thought of as part of the wider marketing effort by both client and publisher. Alongside the magazine, M-real also sponsor various magazine awards and run client workshops, the aim being to position their paper brands at the heart of the publishing industry.

But as the broader marketing imperatives change, the magazine must change too. This can present the designer with a challenge way beyond the normal redesign.

When *IKEA Room* (UK) was launched in 1997 the brief was to move customer perception of the furniture store away from 'cheap and cheerful' toward ' the source of good, modern design at low prices'. The magazine was launched as a large, square-format lifestyle magazine full of room sets featuring good-looking, young people enjoying life. In 2001 when the marketing direction changed the magazine was relaunched at a smaller page size giving a more pluralist vision of IKEA providing solutions to the issues facing modern society: extended families, lack of living space, the degrading of the environment. It was a reinvention on a scale a consumer magazine could never risk for fear of alienating its paying readers.

Occupying the top three positions in the audited circulation figures is one sign of the scale of the UK customer publishing industry. Another is that after initial disdain for this new area of publishing, consumer publishers are now moving into customer publishing themselves. Both Condé Nast and National Magazines have recently set up such publishing divisions.

Meanwhile, most of the major UK customer publishers have been taken over by the global marketing conglomerates. Despite this international interest, the market for customer publishing outside the UK remains relatively small and creatively uninteresting. London and New York remain the twin centres of western magazine publishing, but the US industry has been slow to pick up on customer publishing, with the post 9/11 fallout slowing it down further. Examples that stand out include *A&F Quarterly* from fashion company Abercrombie & Fitch, which caught a lot of attention with its 'Back to School' issue featuring pictures of high-school-age models in sexually provocative poses, while Sony have created a lifestyle title around its electronics ranges with its well-designed but editorially unfocused *Sony Style*.

One exception to this UK/US axis is the German title *Statements*. Like *M-real*, this is essentially a niche title, published on behalf of bathroom equipment manufacturer Dornbracht on a smaller scale than many of the projects discussed here. Aimed at a very precise group of opinion formers, *Statements* publishes artists' interpretations of 'bathroom culture', and each issue comes in a different form, a recent example being a leather-bound book.

But whatever the scale of the project, it is the brand itself that defines the magazine: combine a strong brand, a strong creative team and a magazine-literate client and you will get a powerful magazine. But magazines are unapologetic messengers. Start with a brand weakened by lack of clarity and the magazine can only reflect that.

All the magazines discussed above are part of broader marketing strategies carried out on behalf of clients with well-defined messages to convey. They are strong brands that have engendered equally strong magazines. For the designer, translating such brands into the language of magazines is a highly satisfying creative challenge.

And as the design-led titles such as *M-real* and *Statements* reveal, no customer magazine can succeed without good design. In the world of the multi-million circulation magazine, *Sky*, *O* and *AA* magazines are highly sophisticated, design-conscious projects that belie their mass circulation status.

Love me, hate me...

THE NEW WORLD OF THE MICROZINE: BY MICHAEL JACOVIDES

Big, Wish You Were Here, Neo2, Viewpoint, Deliciae Vitae ('Do you have the first issue?'), *Carl's Cars*, *Tank, Mined*, *Nice Magazine* ('This is just a block of wood, man!'), *Street Fashion*, *Lab, Oyster* ('C'est nouveau!'), *10*, *Putt*, *Nest*, *Dutch*, *Self Service*, *Nylon* ('A bit mainstream. Try Borders.'), *Surface*, *032c*, *Magazine*, *List* ('We're not sure if they're still going.'), *Coupe*, *Re-*, *AM7*, *Spector*, *Very*, *Catalogue*, *The Illustrated Ape*, *Another Magazine* ('Sorry, madam. It's a magazine. Once they've sold out, they don't print any more.'), *Intersection* ('I'd like it in hardback.'), *Archis*, *Adbusters*, *Visionaire* ('How much?!'), *Doing Bird*, *Exit*, *Shift!* ('But I sold my VCR.').

A bookshop somewhere in London (though it could easily be in Paris, New York, Milan, Barcelona or Stockholm). It's an early Tuesday evening, and the small retail space is crammed full of people jockeying for elbow room around the one wall of the shop that is dedicated to selling magazines.

The titles on the shelves are more than a little fashionable-looking, but Italian *Vogue*, *The Face* and *Wallpaper** (UK) are absent. In place of the familiar are scores of magazines that make up a newsstand from a parallel universe. Some look like huge steroid-injected versions of *Harper's Bazaar* (US), others like bohemian journals put together by Jean Cocteau. One of them comes with its own light box, another is just an A4-sized block of wood. One isn't printed at all, but comes on video tape. Some of the titles are indulgent, difficult, elitist and esoteric, others conservative. But whatever category they fall into, they're getting the customers excited, as they discuss them, and importantly, there is a queue at the till.

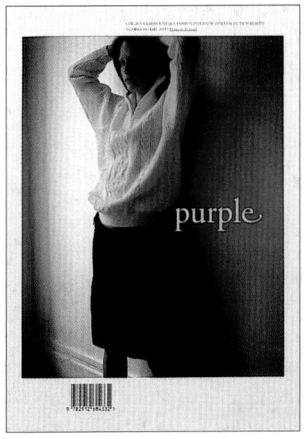

Purple
(France, Issue 13, Autumn 2002)
200 x 270mm/7 7/8 x 10 5/8 inches
This is one of the original microzines.
Art director *Makoto Ohrui*

Something is happening in the world of magazines. For the past few years, a new strain of independent publishing has emerged and evolved into what is sometimes called the 'microzine'. Vibrant, iconoclastic, stylish and innovative, microzines are beginning to show the rest of the magazines on the rack just what you can do if you've got a little

‘There is an emerging trend within the microzine to question the very nature of what a magazine is.’

imagination and are prepared to challenge the status quo. Not since the post-Punk explosion of independent record labels in the late 1970s have different creative tycoons come together to provide alternatives to the mainstream.

Like those independent record labels, microzines are inspired by the ‘do-it-yourself’ ethic, and share a disillusionment with the prevalent commercial sector. Anti-commercial, cut-and-paste zines they are not, however. Talking to the art directors and editors of microzines for this piece the same influences are cited again and again: *The Face, The New Yorker, Harper's Bazaar, National Geographic*. Microzines are, on the whole, produced by individuals who have loved or been greatly influenced by, mainstream titles. Their defining characteristics are high production values, a lavish use of photography, an emphasis on design – in a word, slickness.

It's surprising, actually, just how ‘slick’ or conservative in design microzines are. As they are published independently, you might expect rampant Carson-ogenics from art directors given free reign, but, on the whole, a new simplicity can be found. Many microzines like London-based *10* or *Self Service* in Paris, for instance, keep text and images well apart. Indeed, to all practical ends, words and pictures are given their own sections, as is the case with *Tank* (UK), again from London. Photography is almost always presented full-bleed. With these magazines, you're either reading text or reading images – they represent two distinct modes. It makes for a pleasurable pace, after the visual information overload frequently found in most mainstream titles.

It would be encouraging to think that the mainstream could adopt some of the rethinking microzines have brought to magazine design, and they can, to an extent. Yet one should bear in mind that the microzine's freedom to stray from accepted norms is down to the entirely different economic model by which it exists.

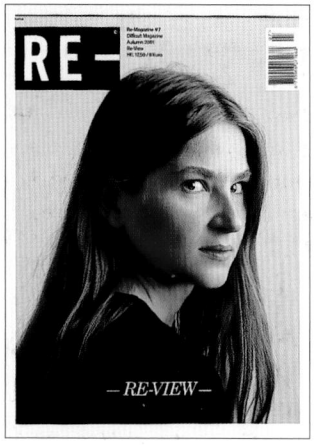

Re-
(The Netherlands, Issue 7, Autumn 2001)
218 x 297mm/8 5/8 x 11 3/4 inches
Every issue of this magazine asks questions about what a magazine can or should be.
Designer *Jop van Bennekom*

Microzines have micro-niches. They sell in small numbers to a relatively affluent, international and visually sophisticated readership. Outlets for microzines are restricted to design-oriented bookshops, designer clothes shops and the occasional switched-on newsagent (invariably located in the centre of large cosmopolitan cities). It's this market that defines the look of the microzine.

Cover lines are largely absent on the fronts of microzines because they don't have to compete on the newsstand. A microzine reader appreciates the absence – it is cleaner, so it will look better on their coffee table.

Also, the appearance of advertisements is minimal. Microzines usually survive through a combination of sponsorship and high cover prices. Perhaps the best example of this would be the New York-based *über*-fashion title *Visionaire*. Published quarterly, it distinguishes itself by its variation in format and presentation. No two issues look the same. Recent examples would be the issue that came with its own light box to view the images supplied, and another sponsored by Fendi, which came boxed with its own Fendi kid-leather neck-warmer. But *Visionaire* carries no advertising. It receives sponsorship from luxury brands (eager to be associated with such a hip product) and has a luxury cover price too – a subscription for four issues costs $675 (about £480).

Perhaps, though, the major contributing factor to the design of the microzine is the determination and maverick nature of their creators. Magazines like the recently-arrived-on-the-scene *Deliciae Vitae* (France), or the more established, and very successful, New York-based *Nest* magazine, are distinguished by the singular visions of their founders.

Edited and designed by its creator Joseph Holtzman, *Nest* has a very distinct take on the world of interiors, one that eschews the dominant vogue for urban modernism in favour of an aesthetic that embraces the idea of using sculpted forms, colour and pattern. This philosophy directly informs the design of the magazine. Some issues are shaped or die-cut to produce a carved or sculptural effect. Others are fastened with ribbon. White space is noticeable by its absence. Instead, images are surrounded, decorated even, by blocks of colour pattern and textures that interact with the images. The more conservative magazine professional might say that *Nest* breaks every rule.

‘I didn't learn the rules, so you can't say I set out to break them,’ says Holtzman. ‘When I started, I didn't know about magazine design and really didn't want to.

Shift!
(Germany, Issue 13, 2002)
214 x 260mm/8 ½ x 10 ¼ inches
This issue consists solely of advertisements created and contributed by artists and designers from across the world.
Art director *Anja Lutz*

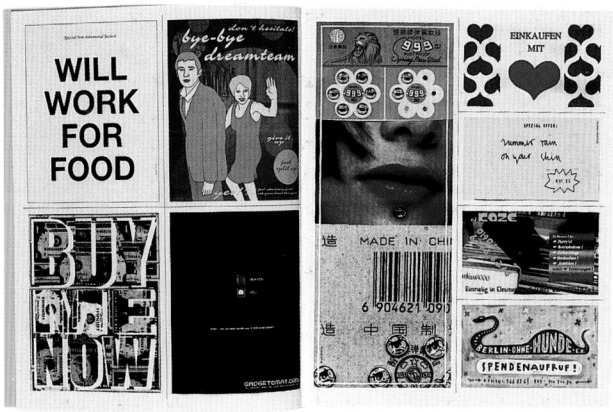

Established people in publishing were telling me you couldn't do this and you couldn't do that – but I've done all those things.'

Similarly, the editor and publisher of the luxuriantly sexy and decadent *Deliciae Vitae* manages any commercial considerations that might interfere with the design of his magazine. 'I say no to many lucrative advertising deals, because I don't want bad images – I pick and choose what I want,' says Kinder Aggugini. Of course, the producers of microzines are well able to take these risks. There are no large publishing houses watching the bottom line or throwing results from research surveys or focus groups at them.

Despite the discrete, privileged position of the microzine, their influence on the mainstream is beginning to surface. This is most notable in fashion magazines, an area of publishing that can't be seen to be standing still, whose raison d'être is responding to and setting trends. Andreas Laeufer, art director of Tank Publications explains: 'The larger fashion magazines have loads of little images and text boxes to draw readers in, but if you look at the layout of *Another Magazine* or *Pop* (UK), I think things are changing. It's all full-bleed images and lone pages of text. Which is all great, because it's changing the rhythm of magazines. It's not only about fashion photography either, but fine art photography... *Another Magazine* has photo journalism, still-life and city photography, giving photographers loads of space. I think all these changes to more commercial publications are down to magazines like *Tank*.'

It would be wrong to claim that microzines are trying to establish a new design language for the mass-market magazine, however. Microzines want to do things on their own terms. Yes, there's unexpected conservatism about their design, but that, in itself, presents an alternative. The alternative is not always the avant-garde. Having said that, there is an emerging trend within the microzine to question the very nature of what a magazine is, how it works, or how it could work. In short, microzines are developing self-reflective tendencies.

Two recent covers of the Canadian anti-brand microzine, *Adbusters,* express this development. One cover has a standard portrait of an attractive model, only she is obscured by thick, black marker scribble. The second simply has the word 'Magazine' printed on a blank background. Both covers show an awareness of the medium. Even mainstream independent titles, like *Dazed & Confused* (UK), have been deconstructing the magazine. Recent issues contained articles with sub marks and corrections.

Perhaps two of the most interesting microzines to have questioned the magazine format have both come from the creators of the fashion-centric title *Tank*. Published quarterly, *Mined* (UK) blurs the boundaries between magazines and books. Printed without a cover its bound sections are clearly visible. The paper is thick, its rough edges forcing you to cut the pages to open it. *Tank*'s art director, Andreas Laeufer, explains: '*Mined* is essentially an unfinished product. What we do with *Mined* is question everything we do with *Tank*, a high-gloss coffee-table magazine... *Mined* is really a book with the pace of a magazine. Reading a book is much slower than reading a magazine, and with *Mined* the challenge was to introduce a magazine speed. It has features that run over 20 pages, but then speed is picked up with things like fashion spreads. But then you have to cut the pages, which makes the journey last longer than the ten minutes it takes to flick through *The Face*.'

Where this experimentation with the magazine will lead is perhaps a fruitless question to ask. Some of it may well be assimilated into the mainstream. What it does show is that the magazine is coming of age. It is finally moving beyond its function as vehicle for disseminating information about that which exists outside of itself – what we call journalism. Perhaps the most exciting realization for magazine creatives is that their titles could actually aspire to being art, existing for no other reason beyond their existence.

One new microzine certainly comes close to being an artwork. Or maybe its aim was to undercut such pretensions. *Nice Magazine* (UK) consists of an A4-sized block of wood. On the 'cover' is the title – *Nice Magazine*. On the 'back page' is an ad for Evisu jeans. That's it. And its price is £7.50. A situationist gag? A statement about the ecological resources magazines devour? A call to action to take the raw material and create your own microzine? Like true artists, the creators of *Nice Magazine* were unavailable for comment.

Michael Jacovides *is director of the Fifty One magazine consultancy*

Download me...

CAN PRINT MAGAZINES WORK ONLINE? BY PATRICK BURGOYNE

Remember the dot.com boom? Suddenly, everyone had to have a website. Why, they weren't entirely sure, but they knew they couldn't be left stalled on the on-ramp of the information superhighway. Magazine publishers were no different. Convinced of the Web's opportunities and scared to death that their competitors would exploit them first, publishers rushed to the Web, with very mixed results.

In spite of the well-publicized calamities that followed, as major publishing houses lost millions in ill-thought-out online adventures, the Web continues to offer tempting possibilities to anyone publishing or intending to publish a magazine.

By definition, the World Wide Web is a global medium, whereas it is very difficult to reach an international audience with a printed magazine. Organizing effective distribution overseas is a logistical headache; launching overseas requires large financial risk, while the compromise of a franchise model involves inevitable loss of control over your cherished brand. But with a website, a magazine can reach the world without ever having to leave home.

The marketing opportunities are massive, but the advantages of the Web go beyond revenue generation. For a start, a title can publish as often as it likes – a boon for monthlies frustrated by their rigid schedule. Content can be presented online in a manner that would be impossible in print – particularly valuable for magazines concerning film or audio.

Many publishers who took the online plunge early on, however, found the medium far less straightforward than they had thought. The Web is a different world, demanding different skills and different revenue models. Many publishers failed to answer the most fundamental question – how do we make money from our website? But even today, magazine art directors who are translating a print magazine to the Web, still face a tricky set of problems.

Print magazines work. They never crash, their batteries don't run out and they don't need plug-ins. They are portable, light (well, light-ish) and everyone knows how to use them. Moreover, the mechanics of creating a magazine brand are tried and tested. Art directors know how to use paper stock, repro and print quality, the pacing of layouts, choices of typography and covers to embody the aspirations and values of their magazine. But how to translate those values online? For art directors of print magazines this has proved a major challenge, especially for upmarket titles.

Many have learned the hard way, that there is far more to producing a magazine online than putting up a slideshow of the printed version. You may have thought dealing with printers and repro houses was tough, now you've got programmers and hosting companies to wrestle with.

The limited resolution and image sizes available online will probably not do justice to your expensive fashion story. Neither will your spectacular typographic feature openers look so glorious

when rendered at 400x355 pixels on a dodgy monitor in a brightly lit room. But there are tools at the designer's disposal that can create a complementary look and feel for a magazine's website. The tactility of the printed product can be mirrored by the feel of a site's design elements – the way a button reacts when it is rolled over, the speed at which elements load or the way in which they behave on the screen. If a magazine has a youthful, fun appeal, this can be achieved through appropriate sound effects, animations, audio and colours, just as the same tools can be used to create a more serious, hi-style aesthetic.

Not all magazines have explored these possibilities. Some have opted for a simple treatment online, staying visually faithful to their paper-based parent. Swedish lifestyle title *Stockholm New* (www.stockholmnew.com) takes this approach, presenting spreads from the magazine in an elegant Flash-based slideshow. The only alteration to the printed version is a larger point size on headlines and captions to aid legibility.

UK style title, *SleazeNation* (www.sleazenation.co.uk), was more adventurous. With a reputation for powerful covers, strong typographical treatments and innovative photography, *SleazeNation* initially set up its website (in June 2000) to give the magazine an international presence and to experiment with content unsuitable for the printed version.

At first, articles placed on the site were replicas of the printed version, but, with the arrival of designers Alex Smith and Nemone Caldwell six months after the site launched, a more appropriate strategy was introduced. 'We were interested in creating something a little different, using the capabilities of the Web to make the whole experience more involving for the viewer,' Caldwell says. 'Whereas previously the articles stuck to a more or less rigid formula (title at the top, image to the side, text along the length, with a crooked line under the title), we have tried to experiment a bit more within the 400x355 pixel space that we have to work in.'

Reflecting its relative importance to the publishers, each issue of the printed magazine was completed first. Then, Smith and Caldwell would receive the Quark files for the issue and work out which articles would work best on the internet. 'Usually, we chose an article which a) was more likely to appeal to a web-using audience, b) we could play around with visually and c) one which we ourselves are interested in. We tried to avoid articles with large amounts of text, as these are memory-heavy and the site wasn't really designed for easily reading huge chunks (one of the main problems with adapting the magazine). We were also keen to put stuff on the website that wasn't in the magazine. For example, once we did a feature on a graphic novel and animated certain scenes from it. Generally, the magazine experiments with print and words a lot more, whereas we tended to be more visual.'

The core content of the site was driven by the printed magazine, but additional material appeared on the site only, such as a news section updated weekly, a gallery and competitions, as well as a selection of different music tracks each month. In Caldwell's view, however, the website was never likely to threaten the primacy of the print magazine: 'The website will never take over the print version. The whole thing about a magazine is the actual physicality of it. Something you can hold in your hand, rip pages out of and doodle on, or whatever. A website is transient, it comes and it goes, it changes constantly. It's never something you can "have" in the same way as with a magazine. But, that's exactly why the website is important – because it provides the user with a different kind of experience.'

The alternative functionality of websites, therefore, offers added value to the reader of a print magazine and a means for the publisher to enhance the package to be sold to subscribers, but not the only means. Websites are still not great at displaying video or large amounts of detailed images. Magazines that rely on a great deal of this content, such as *Creative Review* (UK), turned to CD-Rom and then DVD to deliver a high-quality experience to a specialist readership. And where content is purely text-based, email provides an alternative publishing medium to the website: music industry gossip sheet *Popbitch* has created a

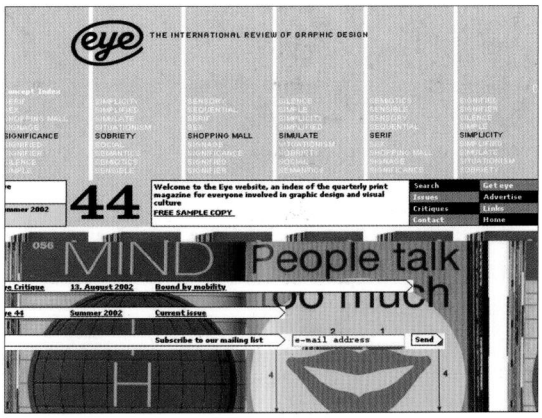

Eye
This site acts as both search engine and online advertisement for the printed magazine *Eye*. Its design was conceived at the same time as the latest redesign of the printed magazine and the two media share many common elements.
Design *Nick Bell and Artificial Environments*

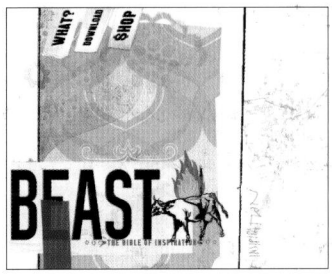

Beast
This magazine is distributed as PDFs from its own website.
Design *Thomas Schostok*

Hint
Available solely online, this fashion magazine uses the immediacy and animation possibilities of the Web to create a different type of magazine in an overcrowded market.
Design *Deanne Cheuk @ Neomu*

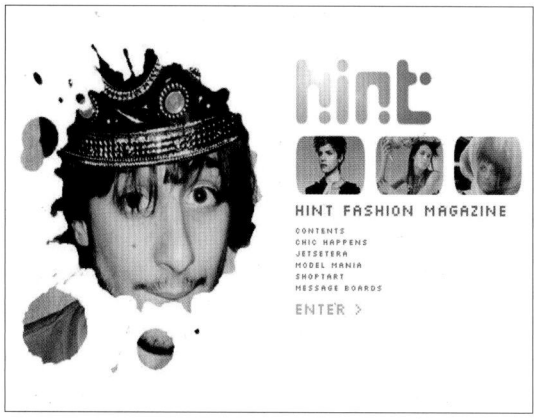

major following for its scurrilous email service, which delivers salacious titbits to subscribers. *Beast*, on the other hand, is produced as a downloadable set of PDFs (www.ths.nu/beast).

One area in which the Web does offer leadership is in managing and retrieving data. Graphic design quarterly *Eye* (UK) is a visually led magazine, but its website does not feature pictorial content. The site 'was never intended to be a magazine itself – its role is to complement and to serve as an index to the printed quarterly,' wrote *Eye* editor John L Walters, when announcing the launch of the site in Issue 43, Spring 2002. It takes an innovative approach to archiving – a list of concept words on the homepage can be dragged to the active area and a list of issues that dealt with that concept is revealed.

Another innovation with *Eye* is that both website and magazine were designed together. With the print magazine undergoing a redesign at the same time as the development of the website, it was possible to work with both in mind, providing an unusually harmonious marriage of the two media. 'Some editorial elements of *Eye*'s new design were intended for both media, for example the key words and phrases at the start of each feature,' writes Walters. 'They're both a means with which to explore the website and a quick way to communicate some of the content of the article.'

SleazeNation and *Eye* represent two of the happier translations of a print magazine to the online environment, from an aesthetic point of view. However, they remain subordinate to their printed parent and their content reflects that. Stand-alone Web magazines must work harder online, but they can do so free of some of the restrictions faced by their print peers.

For anyone who has an idea for a new magazine, the Web offers a genuine alternative publishing medium. After all, a magazine is about conveying information, which is not dependent on putting ink to paper. *This is a Magazine* (www.thisisamagazine.com), a monthly online magazine based in Milan, is very much in the tradition of independent fashion/style magazines, but turns convention on its head by publishing primarily on the Web, with a printed spin-off produced every three months.

And when photographer Nick Knight and graphic designer Peter Saville decided to start *ShowStudio* (www.showstudio.com), a publishing vehicle for new fashion imagery, they rejected print in favour of a website. '*ShowStudio* can get away from corporate politics and broadcast to the world,' explained Knight in an interview with New York-based online fashion magazine *Hint* (www.hintmag.com). 'It's a global audience, global distribution. Even the big magazines can't do that.'

Going online allowed *ShowStudio* to look at fashion in a way that would not have been possible in print: 'There are things a magazine can't do,' Knight noted. 'I've always considered fashion, how it's represented in print, to be a little disadvantaged. There's been a compromise because photographers have to sum it up in one moment. I always felt motion imagery would benefit fashion. If the dress can move, it's better for the dress.'

Hint is an online fashion magazine that is providing an alternative to its glossy print counterparts. Founder and creative director Lee Carter recognized those same freedoms mentioned by Knight: '*Hint* began as a means of circumventing the politics, power-plays and petrified hierarchy of the cut-throat industry of fashion magazines,' he says. 'When I started *Hint* in 1998, I felt I didn't want to waste years of my life in that kind of thankless arena. With an indie like *Hint*, I could avoid the pitfalls of investor backing and parent-company paranoia, since the costs of a web server pale in comparison to the crippling expense of print publishing and distribution. And there was (and is) nothing like *Hint* on the Web, whereas there are many newsstand publications devoted to avant-garde fashion. That said, I have begun to think seriously about a *Hint*-to-print expansion, but it would probably mean a biannual magazine or a book of photos, not a monthly.'

Though broadly similar in content to printed fashion magazines, *Hint* exploits the Web to provide an experience that print cannot. 'The moving image is very important in *Hint*'s photo shoots,' says Carter. 'I always include Flash motion of some kind. Then I add snippets of music, usually a preview of an upcoming CD, to make it fully robust experience, more so than print magazines can provide. One of the more successful of these was the first shoot we ran since 9/11. Called

"Hidden Places", it was a very personal and sombre series of photos to which Björk added bits of music from her Vespertine CD, which had not yet hit stores.'

Where the Web would appear to be at a disadvantage for a fashion publication is in its reproduction of photography, but Carter insists that this is not a major problem on *Hint*: 'Occasionally, I meet a photographer or stylist who hasn't yet opened up to the internet, but once they take a look at the motion effects and funky music of *Hint*'s photos shoots, they're eager to try it out. Since *Hint* has a higher circulation than most print fashion magazines, they usually score big gigs immediately after their work goes live. *Hint* has become a sort of launchpad for new talent. Plus, since *Hint* won last year's Webby Award for Best Fashion Website, the word really got out that *Hint* is as viable a place as print magazines to appear in.

'Obviously, websites can't offer the tactile experience that glossies can, but glossies can't compete with the enhancing effects of light from a computer screen,' Carter continues. 'I found that colour and shape have more impact in Web shoots, simply because of the bright glow of a monitor.'

The Web offers great creative possibilities, but designers do face increasing restrictions, thanks in part to the rise of usability theory. Usability experts assess sites according to the ease with which users may carry out a variety of tasks. Though well-intentioned, the result of putting their findings into practice is often to make all sites look the same, with contents listed down the left-hand side, all links underlined in blue and so on. To some extent, of course, all print magazines follow familiar conventions in order to aid readers, but, online, this homogeneity reaches new levels, due, in the main, to it being such a new medium.

Bob Watts, art director of US news site *Salon* (www.salon.com), says that, for him, 'Usability drives just about all design decisions. The primary nod is to readability – typeface, size and variety were all decided with the reader in mind.' But the site is still visually interesting. 'We want the reader to have complete ease of use and a pleasant experience. So far, the readers have indicated that illustration and various design elements are part of that complete experience.'

> 'Websites can't offer the tactile experience that glossies can, but glossies can't compete with the enhancing effects of light from a screen.'

Salon is one of the few sites to have successfully switched to charging subscribers, and herein lies the big problem for magazines on the Web. In many ways, reading or 'using' a magazine online can be a far richer experience than anything offered by print, but examples of financially viable magazines online are few and far between. Of the other titles discussed here, which are some of the most highly thought of on the Web in terms of design, *ShowStudio* relies largely on Nick Knight's own finances to keep it going while, despite winning Best Magazine Website at the UK's 2001 Magazine Design Awards, while *SleazeNation* made Smith and Caldwell redundant, shortly after conducting the interview for this piece. At the time of writing, the future of the site is uncertain.

It would be harsh to blame designers for this situation. Publishing houses have so far found no mechanism for bringing in revenue from websites to match the print models of page advertising, newsstand sales and subscriptions. No matter how beautiful their design, websites were seen by many publishers as a luxury add-on to the core product and, as such, they were the first to go when times got hard. Web-only magazines arguably face even greater pressures, having no print parent to subsidize and promote them (although, at least, the independent ones don't have to fulfil the voracious appetite for profit of a major publisher).

Despite the current gloom surrounding the Web, the opportunities that so excited publishers initially do still exist. The potential of this digital, networked world has only begun to be explored. At the start, it was assumed that the website would be the chief vehicle for distributing information on these networks, but, in the future, what we now think of as 'online' publishing may take many different forms. Already, email is used as an alternative to news-based sites and SMS, mobile phones and devices and interactive television offer more alternatives. And with better technology, the Web will improve in quality and speed.

The challenge for designers is to take these opportunities and use them to create products that are as useful and compelling to readers as those of their print antecedents.

Patrick Burgoyne *is editor of Creative Review and author of Browser: the Internet Design Project, Reload and Used*

Lead me ...

HOW NEWSPAPERS LEARN FROM MAGAZINES: BY MARK PORTER

For most of their history, newspapers have remained largely untouched by what would nowadays be recognizable as 'design'. Typefaces were traditionally chosen to fit as many words as possible on a page, while maintaining a minimum legibility. When photography was introduced pictures were scaled, as much to ensure that faces remained recognizable through a coarse half-tone screen as to create drama and impact.

Design was part of the journalist's job, and if any attention was paid to the overall aesthetic, it would often take the form of a gentlemanly request to a respected typographer to cast an eye over the pages.

But the last quarter of the 20th century saw a revolution. Increasing demand from advertisers for colour sites forced newspapers to improve their printing. Most went from letterpress machines in the basement, using a technology which had changed little in hundreds of years, to sophisticated offset plants, which approach the depth of colour and crispness of magazine printing.

A similar transformation occurred in page production, from hot metal and photocomposition to desktop typesetting and make-up. Many PC-based newspaper systems are principally designed for efficient database and object management, and seem absurdly restricting to QuarkXpress-trained magazine designers. But when formatted pages produced on such systems are combined with Macintosh elements – from small panels and graphics to whole pages – almost anything is possible.

Technological progress reflects a more demanding commercial environment. Newspapers, as news providers, now face powerful competition from an expanding television sector and from the internet. Consumers who have lived through a design explosion have high expectations, and newspaper owners now seek a design that helps them achieve a clear positioning in the marketplace. More advertising demands editorial that reflects the products being advertised (cars, fashion, travel and food). Fierce competition has forced papers to add new sections, in an attempt to improve their offering to both readers and advertisers.

Newspapers now have more pages, with higher production values, and face stronger competition than ever before. How has design responded?

'Ten years ago, intellectuals would settle for text,' says consultant Mario Garcia, whose firm is involved in around 15 newspaper redesigns every year. 'Right now, even the most intellectual elite like some eye popcorn. That's a real shift for graphic designers.'

Newspapers have indeed had to learn some lessons from magazines, television and the internet. The 1982 launch of *USA Today* was dramatic evidence of the impact of other media on the newspaper world. Its design was heavily influenced by magazines such as *Time* and *Newsweek* (US), and most of all by television (an early advertising slogan described it as a paper 'for readers who grew up as viewers'). Colourful graphics and photography were an integral part

of the news presentation, along with a telegraphic approach to writing, which anticipated some of the forms of news delivery on the Web. The result was a seductive formula which has made *USA Today* America's biggest-selling newspaper, and which is likely to be adopted by more and more papers chasing younger readers and the ever-growing commuter market. Even the 115-year-old *San Francisco Chronicle* recently crossed the great divide by relaunching as a tabloid, with a poppy, colourful design that reflects a breathless, net-influenced approach to reporting.

Serious papers shun such 'dumbing-down', but still reveal the influence of other media. The growth of infographics, used along with sidebars and feature-length stories, in complex 'packages', has its roots in the weekly news magazines (as well as the Sunday papers of the 1970s). Magazine coverlines – punchy, alluring, but often flippant tasters of the content – are reborn in newspaper teaser panels, a sure sign of increased competition. But the influence of magazines on modern news design is probably clearest in the use of images. Many editors are now happy to respond to a major news event with a dramatic use of photographs. On September 12, 2001, many of the British papers were swathed in wrap-around photographic posters. Tabloids and broadsheets all over the world cleared their front pages for massive images, and even Germany's ultra-conservative *Frankfurter Allgemeine* published photographs on the front page – reportedly for the first time.

But despite greater use of colour and an awareness that design can no longer be ignored, news and comment sections (which editors – and many readers – consider the heart and soul of a newspaper) tend to retain traditional values. The involvement of the art director in these areas is limited by pressures of time and space, and often by a suspicion that strong design will compromise the character of the paper. Designers clearly have a role to play in establishing an overall style and in training, but their involvement usually takes the form of giving the journalists a toolbox to produce the paper — in most cases, pages will be laid out by sub-editors rather than graphic designers. Whatever their expertise, the art director's voice will be just one amongst many in the newsroom; editors, news editors, picture editors and section editors all have strong opinions, and decisions on presentation have traditionally been their responsibility. Typographic skills can be learnt relatively easily, but news values and newsroom culture can only be grasped with experience, which is perhaps why many of the most successful newspaper designers trained as journalists. And as editions are changed during the night, the art director may not even be in the building to offer an opinion.

Die Woche
(Germany, 12 March 1999)
320 x 475mm/12 5/8 x 18 3/4 inches
This newspaper combines classic newspaper devices – the line drawing of Pegusus within the masthead – with modern editorial use of type and colour.
Design *Lo Breier*

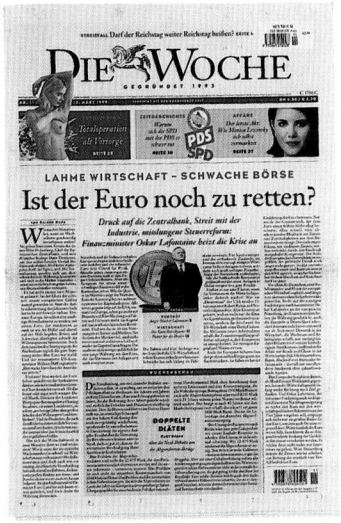
DIE WOCHE

LAHME WIRTSCHAFT – SCHWACHE BÖRSE

Ist der Euro noch zu retten?

Druck auf die Zentralbank, Streit mit der Industrie, misslungene Steuerreform: Finanzminister Oskar Lafontaine bringt die Krise an

DOPPELTE DIÄTEN

But modern newspapers are not just about news. As recently as 1986, *The Guardian* (UK) published one 16-page broadsheet daily. It now publishes – in an average week – a daily news broadsheet, two daily tabloid features sections, a glossy magazine, five Saturday tabloids and a listings magazine, as well as frequent one-offs and specials. The proliferation of sections (most in the area of 'features' – arts, entertainment, lifestyle, celebrities, travel and personal finance) has created new design opportunities.

The first newspaper magazines appeared in America in the late 19th century, and the *Boston Globe*, *Chicago Tribune*, *Philadelphia Inquirer* and Canada's *National Post* continue the tradition with thoughtfully designed supplements on Sundays. The UK's *The Sunday Times Magazine* was launched in 1962. By the late 1960s and early 1970s, under art director Michael Rand and art editor Dave King, it was taking advantage of its lavish budgets to break new ground in journalistically driven design. Although often best remembered for its photojournalism, such as Don McCullin's powerful dispatches from Biafra, Vietnam and Cambodia, the magazine developed a new graphic language which King called 'creating visual features'.

Possibly the most original and beautiful use of the format was Germany's *Frankfurter Allgemeine Magazin*. It thrived in the 1980s under Willy Fleckhaus, who had made his name at *Twen* in the 1960s and was returning to magazines after ten years of teaching and book design. Fleckhaus's solution to the problem of reflecting the intellectual weight of the newspaper in a colour magazine was to create sequences of lavish spreads with rigorous type, dramatically scaled photography and daring illustration, followed by unadorned pages of solid text. The beautifully composed covers had an unvarying black background. After Fleckhaus's death in 1983, he was succeeded by his pupil Hans-Georg Pospischil, who continued until the magazine was closed.

The colour supplement was reinvented again in Britain in September 1992 when *The Guardian* turned its *Weekend* section into a tabloid magazine. The design was by David Hillman at Pentagram, who had redesigned the newspaper four years earlier. Printed heat-set

Tentaciones
(Spain, 18 January 2002)
295 x 405mm/11 3/4 x 16 inches
Design *Fernando Gutierrez*

D
(Italy, December 1998)
210 x 276mm/8 1/4 x 10 7/8 inches
Art director *Joel Berg*

These are two examples of newspaper magazines that have been designed by magazine designers.

offset on enhanced newsprint, *Weekend* was a low-cost option for *The Guardian* (it was designed by sub-editors, used staff photographers and had low paper costs). The production economies were not lost on *The Guardian*'s rivals, and, for a few years in the early 1990s, the style was enthusiastically embraced by many other British newspapers. Thereafter, it was slowly abandoned in favour of more conventional magazine formats (*Weekend*, like many of its rivals, is now printed gravure on glossy paper), though it still survives in other markets.

Most magazines have a well-defined audience and can focus content accordingly. Newspaper readerships tend to be much broader, but in theory, the lack of sales pressure on the newsstand gives colour supplements greater opportunities to experiment. However, many editors still insist on imitating paid-for magazines, and the majority of newspaper magazines resemble newsstand titles in design and editorial. Supplements have occasionally been a medium for serious, groundbreaking content, for example, Tibor Kalman and Jenny Holzer's chilling collaboration for the *Süddeutsche Zeitung Magazin* in 1993, in which Holzer's texts about rape were written on women's bodies in ball-point pen, and the cover had a tip-on card printed with ink containing real blood. But the tendency is towards a formula of celebrity interviews, leavened by

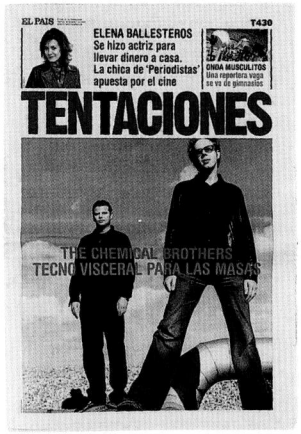

culture and (more rarely) serious reportage in the front half, and fashion, lifestyle, interiors, food and health at the back. Design is often no more adventurous than that of more commercially driven, paid-for titles, but the most accomplished are certainly amongst the best-designed titles in the magazine world. Regular award-winners include the ever-impressive *Süddeutsche Zeitung Magazin*, *Guardian Weekend*, *D* (the lavish monthly fashion magazine from *La Repubblica*), *El Mundo*'s *Metropoli* and the venerable *New York Times Magazine*, currently stronger than ever under art director Janet Froelich. Even business newspapers can now produce powerful magazines, like the *FT*'s *The Business* (UK) (launch design by the prolific Vince Frost, who also gained acclaim for *The Independent Magazine* in the UK) and *Estampa* from Brazil's *Valor* (designed by Simon Esterson).

But magazines are expensive to produce and are usually only

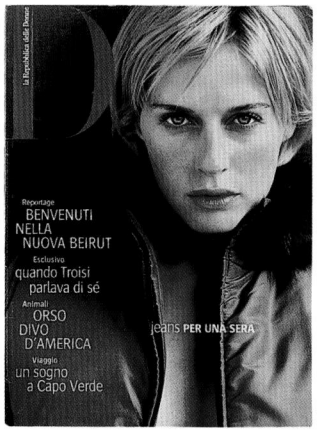

published at the weekend. Modern papers can have a range of other sections that lie somewhere between traditional newspapers and magazines in design and content. Indeed, many papers, particularly in Germany and Switzerland, have now abandoned their magazines for more newsprint sections. The multi-section paper was pioneered by *The New York Times*, which introduced the Weekend, Science Times, Sports Monday, Home and Living sections under design director and managing editor Lou Silverstein in the late 1970s. They used large illustrations and photographs to create magazine-influenced pages, which lent the sections an identity very different from the sobriety of *The Times*, and which enriched the vocabulary of newspaper design.

A design approach that would not be tolerated at the heart of many papers is now considered acceptable – and even desirable – in features sections, which are often intended to attract readers who may not be interested in hard news. (For most newspaper publishers this means young people and women.) The result is that some of these sections – like many weekend magazines – have a design which is totally unrelated to the parent paper, and the art directors who produce them (many from the magazine world) may never have met the editor, or attended a news conference. They have proved fruitful environments for experimentation. *Tentaciones*, the entertainment section of Spanish *El País*, designed by Fernando Gutierrez, set new standards of sophistication for tabloid supplements. In Sweden, *Dagens Nyheter*'s two tabloids, *På Stan* and *LördagSöndag*, put many magazines to shame. In Britain, *The Guardian*'s daily features tabloid, *G2* (another Hillman design, redesigned several times since), has been imitated by its rivals (*The Times*'s *T2*, *The Scotsman*'s *S2* and *The Independent Review*).

Europe also has weekly newspapers that avoid hard news and concentrate on features and analysis, and whose relaxed deadlines allow a strong influence from magazine design. The late, lamented *Die Woche*, which closed in 2002, had full colour on every editorial page and combined elegant newspaper typography with powerful infographics and a thoughtful, witty use of photography. *Dimanche.ch*, the Web-influenced Lausanne Sunday designed by Barcelona's Antoni

Cases Asociats, takes this language to a new level, using colour, type, images and complex panels and page furniture to create an intensity on the page that only the most hyperactive consumer magazines can match. Germany's *Die Zeit* is at the other extreme, sober and correct, but still clearly influenced by magazine culture.

Magazine designers tend to value execution over establishing a format. Art directors from Brodovitch to Baron have become famous by producing great sequences of pages, but the world's most celebrated newspaper designers do not make their reputations by doing layouts. Designing a modern newspaper goes far beyond typography – it requires a deep knowledge of journalism, an understanding of the architecture of a multi-section publication, and an awareness of branding and market positioning. The expertise to accomplish these tasks, and to communicate with editors and publishers and gain their confidence, is the preserve of very few. Hence the rise of the elite international newspaper designer. Consultants such as Mario Garcia, Roger Black, Antoni Cases and Ally Palmer travel the world to advise newspapers in every territory.

As in so many other areas, globalization can lead to a degree of cultural homogenization. The basic forms and techniques of the modern newspaper – teaser panels, indexes, bold section fronts and fonts from a handful of star type-designers (often chosen because of their range of weights rather than any intrinsic relationship to the character of the paper) – are increasingly formulaic.

> 'The most accomplished newspaper supplements are certainly amongst the best-designed magazines in the world.'

But, for the moment, many cultural differences do persist. Formats vary from country to country. Tabloid design travels best and seems to be a more universal language, but in middle-market and serious papers there is still a wide range of approaches. The hispanic world (South America, in particular, is a vast and thriving newspaper market) tends towards textured pages heavy with boxes and panels and baroque rulework, with vibrant colour palettes. Many serious papers in the German-speaking countries, like the *Frankfurter Allgemeine* or *Neue Zürcher Zeitung*, shun modish styles and remain confidently austere and soberly black and white. European papers tend to maintain a fairly consistent pace throughout, while North and South America often prefer dramatic, set-piece sections fronts, which can seem absurdly over-designed to European eyes. Even the work of the super-consultants reflects this. Roger Black's rich mix of internet-age sophistication and American vernacular is wildly exuberant in Mexico City's *Reforma*, but stripped-down and relatively cool in Zürich's *Tages Anzeiger*. 'Shed your assumptions,' says Black. 'If you don't start at zero and learn a culture, the design will never work.'

This is a key moment for design in the contemporary newspaper. Many have only recently acquired substantial art departments and ex-magazine art directors. On a magazine, everybody knows what an art director is, and most have an idea of what they should be doing.

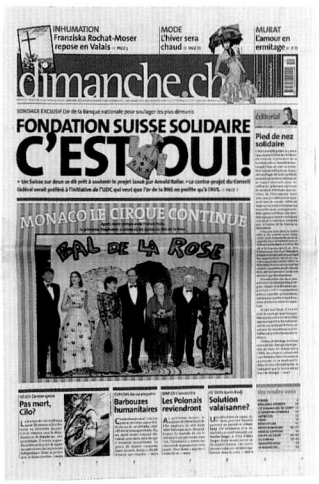

dimanche.ch
(Switzerland, 17 March 1999)
320 x 475mm/12 3/4 x 18 3/4 inches
This newspaper is heavily influenced by both magazines and the Web.
Design *Antoni Cases*

But, on a newspaper, things are not so clear, and designers coming from magazines must adapt. They can expect a lot of involvement – and a great deal of freedom – in magazines and features sections; they will be kept busy with special projects and redesigns; but they may not have much influence over tomorrow's front page. *The Guardian*'s September 12, 2001 Issue *(see page 157)*, which won a silver medal in New York's SPD awards, the first ever for a newspaper news section, probably owed more to the efforts of the journalists than it did to the art director. But the form of the paper that produced that edition owes as much to the graphic designers who shaped it over the past 15 years.

Design (and designers) have gained a foothold in the newspaper world in magazines and peripheral sections. But they will inevitably become indispensable in every part of the paper. Most print newspapers already have a symbiotic relationship with their online counterparts, and websites as well as magazines will continue to influence newspaper presentation. A new generation of editors, the rise of marketing departments, and inevitable price increases will all lead to a desire for more intensively designed newspapers. We must ensure that they are not just more designed, but better designed.

Mark Porter *is creative director of The Guardian newspaper*

The magazines

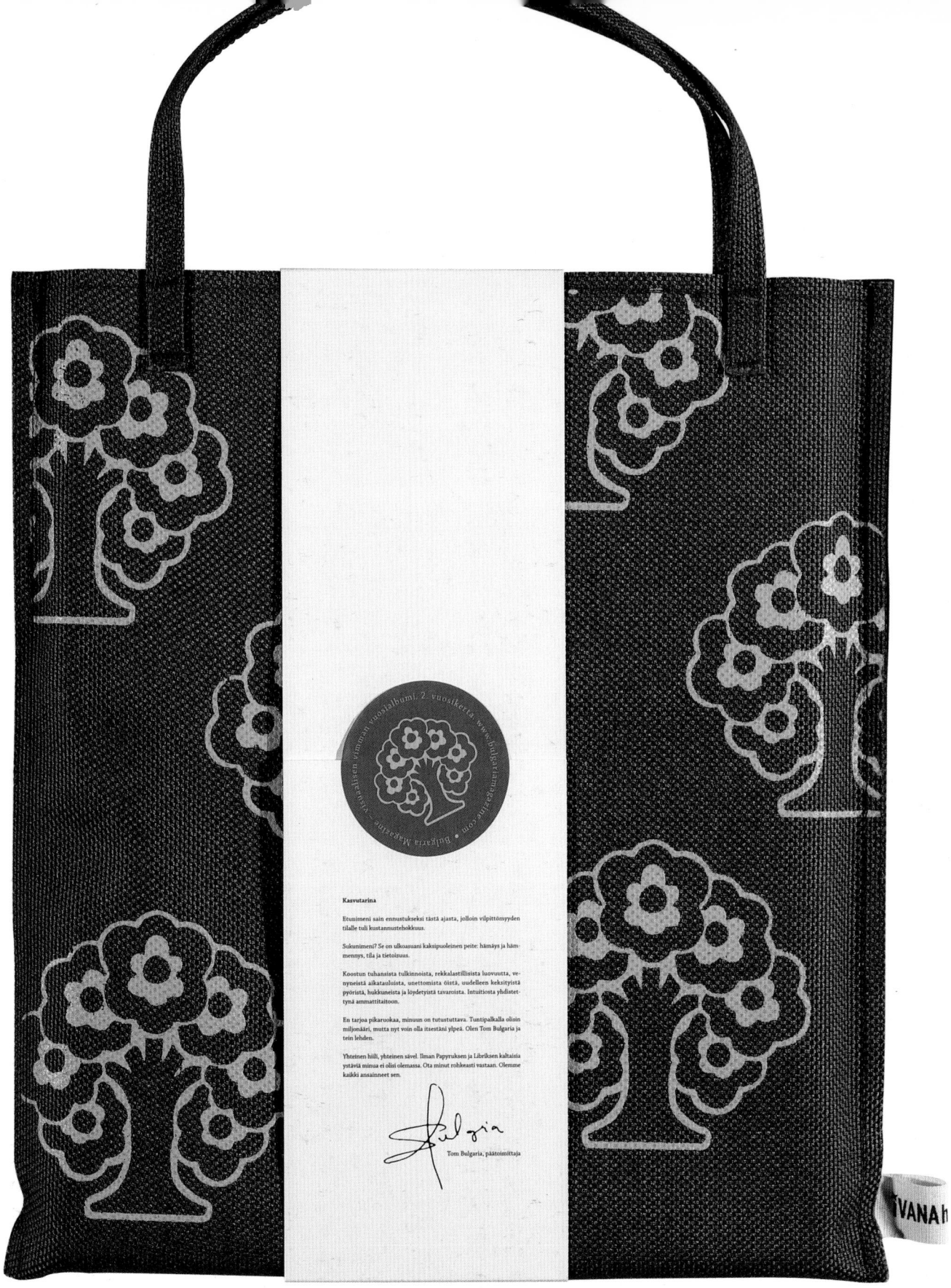
Bulgaria Magazine – suomalisen ylimmän uusialbumi. 2. vuosikerta www.bulgariamagazine.com
Kasvutarina
Etunimeni sain ennustukseksi tästä ajasta, jolloin vilpittömyyden tilalle tuli kustannustehokkuus.
Sukunimeni? Se on ulkoasuani kaksipuoleinen peite: hämäys ja hämmennys, tila ja tietoisuus.
Koostun tuhansista tulkinnoista, rekkalastillisista luovuutta, venyneistä aikatauluista, unettomista öistä, uudelleen keksityistä pyöristä, hukkuneista ja löydetyistä tavaroista. Intuitiosta yhdistettynä ammattitaitoon.
En tarjoa pikaruokaa, minuun on tutustuttava. Tuntipalkalla olisin miljonääri, mutta nyt voin olla itsestäni ylpeä. Olen Tom Bulgaria ja tein lehden.
Yhteinen hiili, yhteinen sävel. Ilman Papyruksen ja Libriksen kaltaisia ystävä minua ei olisi olemassa. Ota minut rohkeasti vastaan. Olemme kaikki ansainneet sen.
Tom Bulgaria, päätoimittaja

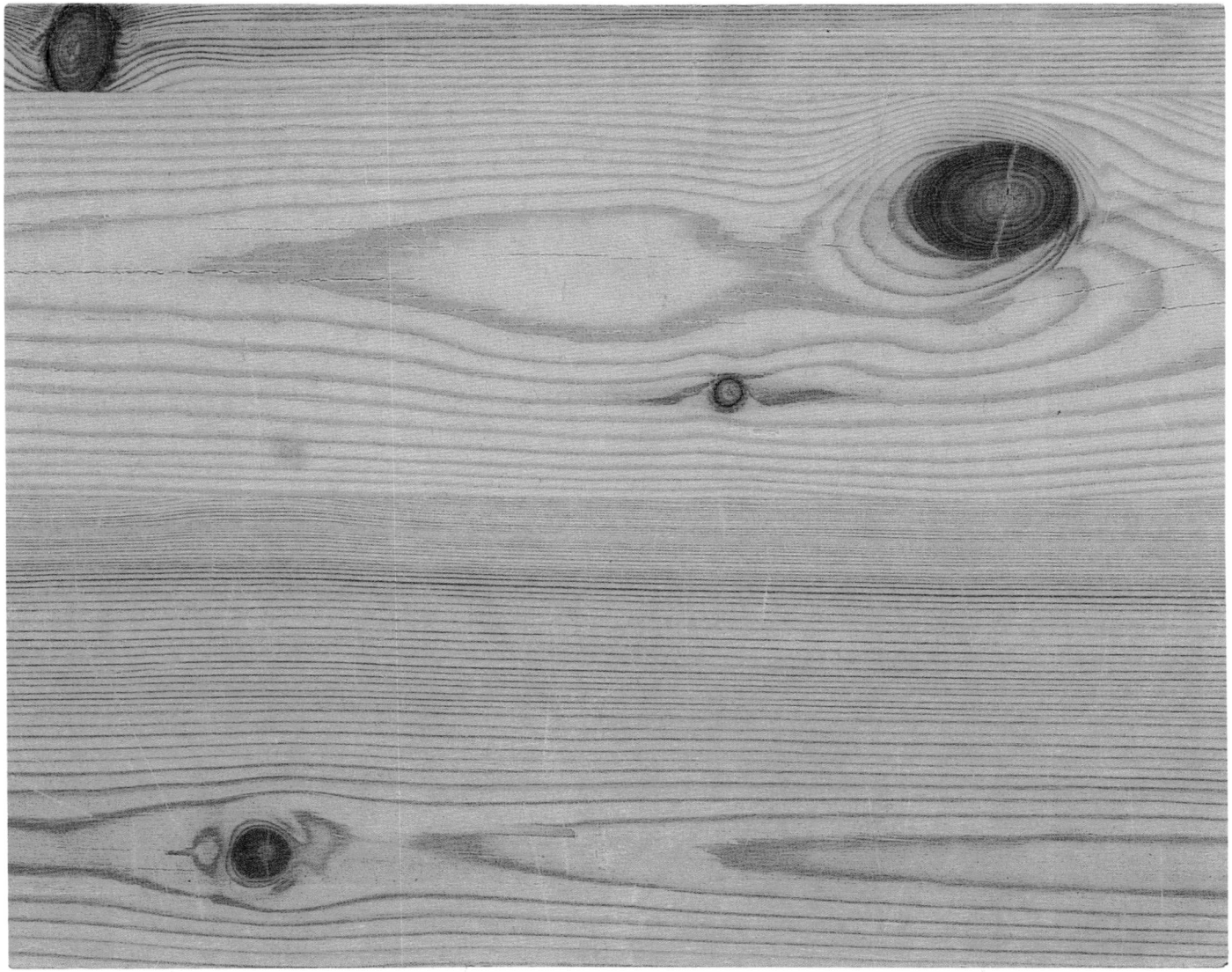

Bulgaria *(Finland, Issue 2, Summer 2002) 225 x 277mm/8 7/8 x 10 7/8 inches*
Launched to give young Finnish visual and literary talents space to demonstrate their skills in a non-commerical environment, this magazine has a deliberately obtuse name to confound expectation. This issue comes in a cloth bag (OPPOSITE) featuring a motif – co-designed by Finnish fashion designer Paola Suhonen – that symbolizes the forests which surround and protect Finland and its people. The cover (THIS PAGE) continues this idea, having the appearance of wood.
Art director *Tom Bulgaria*

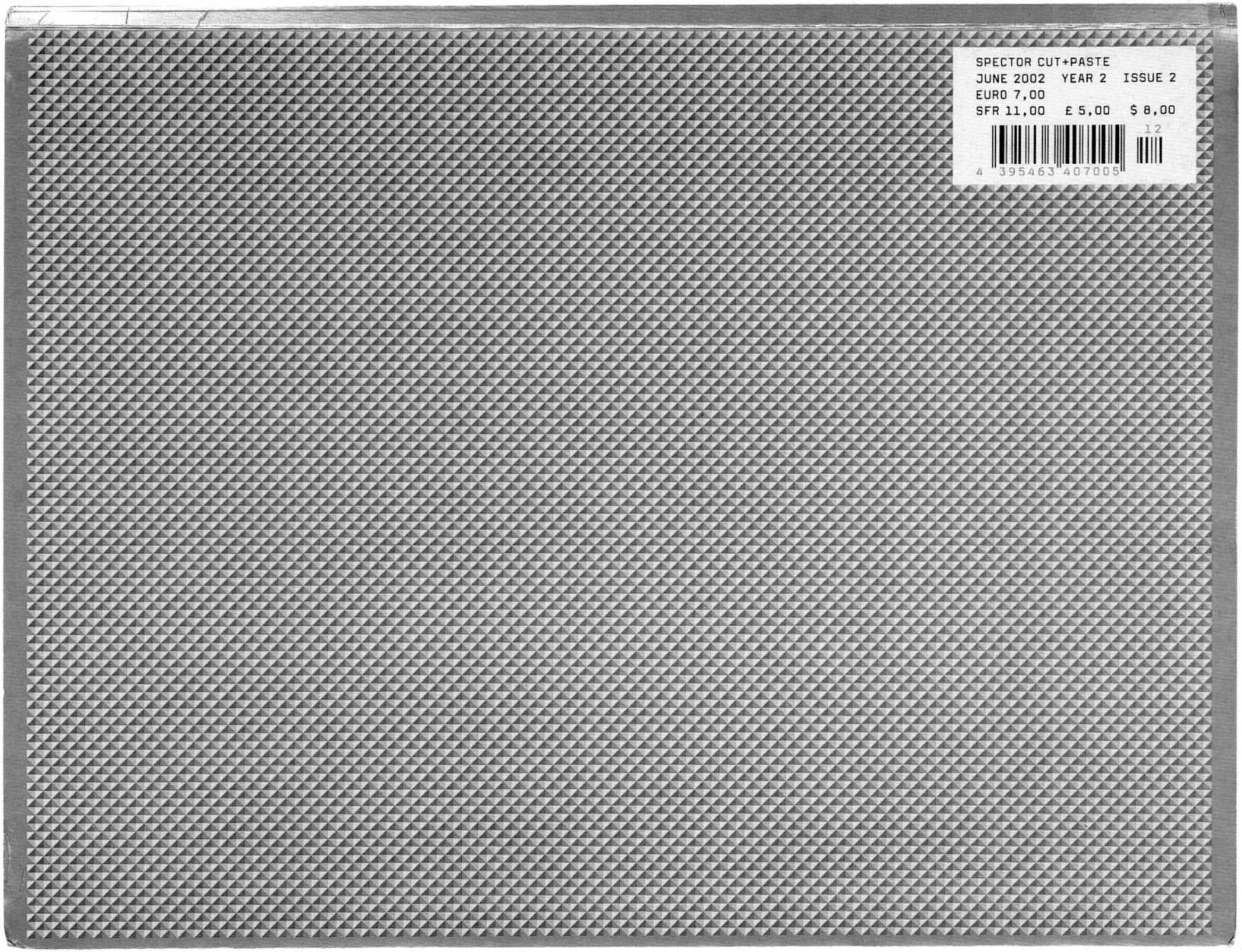
SPECTOR CUT+PASTE
JUNE 2002 YEAR 2 ISSUE 2
EURO 7,00
SFR 11,00 £ 5,00 $ 8,00
12
4 395463 407005

A
B
C
D
E
F
G
H
I
J
K
L
M
N
O
6
PRESS FOR LONG TIME
POST CARD
SHELLEY FOX 11
autumn / winter 2001 collection
showing from 14th - 20th March
from 9.30am - 6.00pm
2M DESIGN STUDIO
33, Rue des Blancs Manteaux
75004 PARIS
tel : 00 33 1 40 27 00 14
fax : 00 33 1 40 27 00 15
mobile : 00 44 958 459 491
SHELLEY FOX 11
POST CARD
but when I really
want to talk
say complete
sentences I
only have
fragments.
SHELLEY FOX 9
THE COMMA HALL
15 NEC LON SQUARE
LONDON WC2
LONDON TUBE: 2 MIN WALK
15TH FEBRUARY @ 12 NOON
I LOOK AT YOU, YOU LOOK LIKE ME
Issue SM05, an architectural production
Summer 2002
£8.75 / €13.99
Portrait... problem of recognition,
therefore fundamental problem of
meaning, always-already, however,
fatal difficulty of the motif of 'inner life'...
window to the psyche of psychologists
(of which the most beautiful example is
the madman of Gericault) rather than to
the psyche of the theologians or ancient
philosophers, which moves in precisely
the opposite direction... hence portrait
as the thematics of loneliness, city as
'portrait' (embodiment) of collective life,
the 'incarnation' of the anonymous class
of 'city' - solidarity (without salvation)...
Peter Carl
sexymachineny
there are ideas in feelings
E 8-75

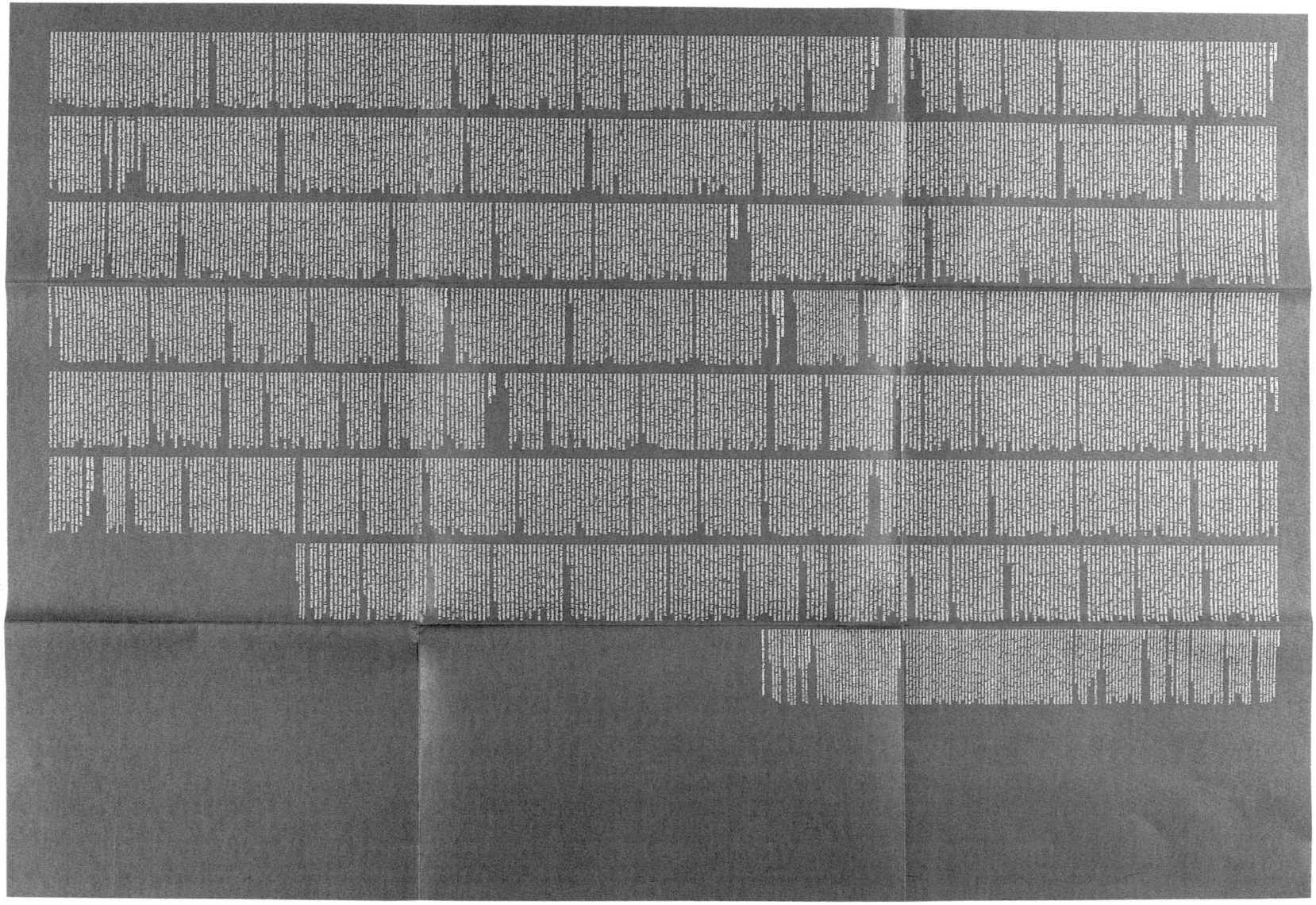

Typographic *(UK, Issue 58, 2002) 210 x 297mm/8 1/4 x 11 3/4 inches*
The Journal of the International Society of Typographic Designers is designed by a guest designer each issue. This issue, subtitled 'Too Much Noise Not Enough Time', consisted of an A4 magazine wrapped in an A1 sheet of grey paper. All the text of the issue was printed on the inside of the wrapper (THIS PAGE), the magazine itself being a series of flat-colour pages (OPPOSITE). In a typically iconoclastic statement, the designers defined the magazine as 'conveying everything we felt needs to be said about typography'.
Designers *The Designers Republic*

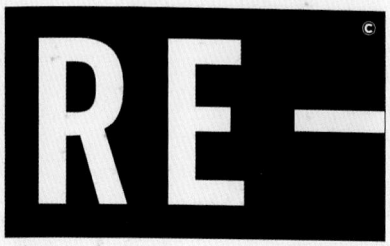

Re-Magazine #23
Spring 2007

Re-Magazine
Established 1997

NL/B/D - € 9,00
F - € 9,50
UK - £5.95

IT'S SPRING
TWO THOUSAND SEVEN

(2007)

Re– *(The Netherlands, Issue 23, Spring 2007)*
220 x 300mm/8 3/4 x 11 7/8 inches
Published in 2002, but with every date reference including copyright details stating 2007, this issue deals with time, looking back at the present from the future. It is made up of a set of 440 x 300mm (17 1/4 x 11 7/8 inches) sheets folded once and bound together by a rubber band where the spine would normally be. There are several picture stories that require the reader to remove the rubber band and separate the pages to see the full image at once. The series of portraits of men in t-shirts, 'We', by Anuschka Blommers and Niels Schumm, make best use of this unusual format. The way the individual sheets come together when bound means that pages opposite each other have similar but different images. Only the centre spread has one complete image. The rubber band is visible across this spread.
Designer *Jop van Bennekom*

Museo-Teo *(Italy, Issue 16, November 1999)*
300 x 210mm/11 7/8 x 8 1/4 inches
Themed as 'On the Edge', this issue of this art fanzine was spiral bound on each edge and perforated in the middle. Readers had to tear open the perforated edge to access the pages. Once opened, the magazine became divided into two halves, which had to be read together.
Design *Pigeon*

STATEMENTS V

★ ★ ★ ★ ★

Statements *(Germany, Issue 5, Summer 2002) 225 x 277mm/8 7/8 x 10 7/8 inches*
Previous issues of this magazine, published in celebration of 'bathroom culture' by German bathroom equipment manufacturer, Dornbracht, have taken the form of a tabloid newspaper, a glossy spiral-bound volume, a videotape and a gallery exhibition. This issue is a white leather-bound book containing work by artists/designers Veronique Branquinho, Jeremy Scott, Raf Simons and Bernhard Willhelm.
Art director *Mike Meiré*

Mined *(UK, Issue 1, May 2001) 160 x 240mm/6 1/4 x 9 1/2 inches*
Sponsored by Levi's (its name is 'denim' backwards), this 512-page combination of essays, profiles, photography and illustration is published in an unfinished, bound format. It comes untrimmed, meaning the reader has to tear or cut open the edges of each 32-page section to access the individual pages.
Art director *Andreas Laeufer*

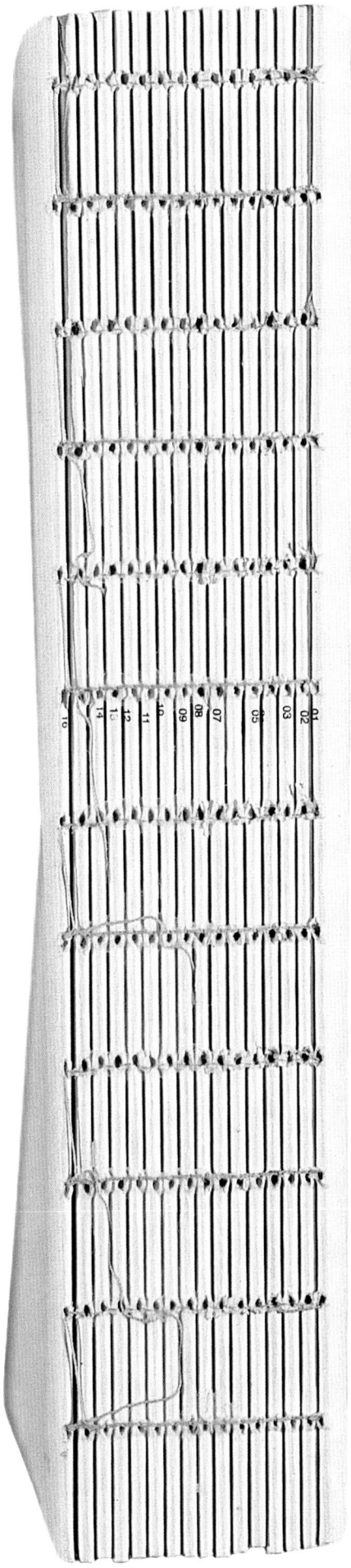

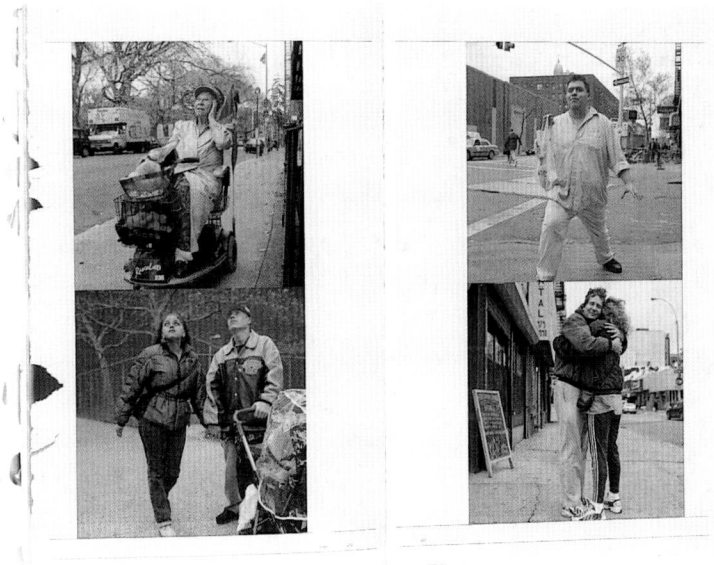

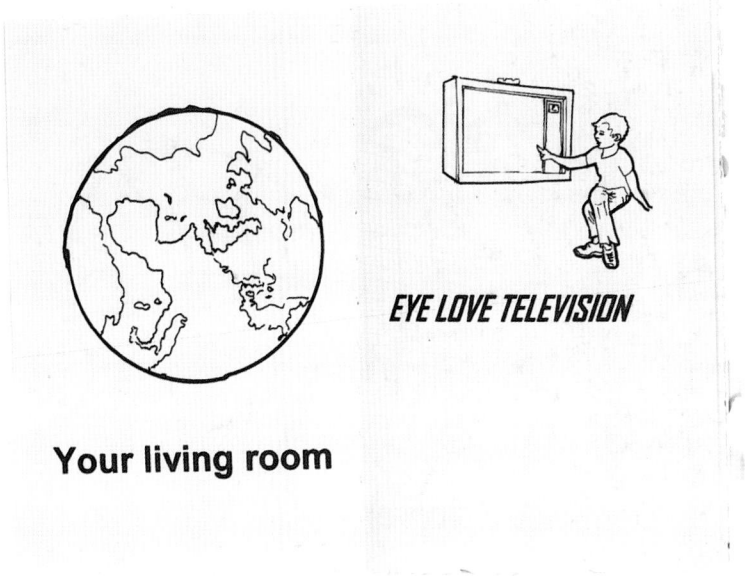

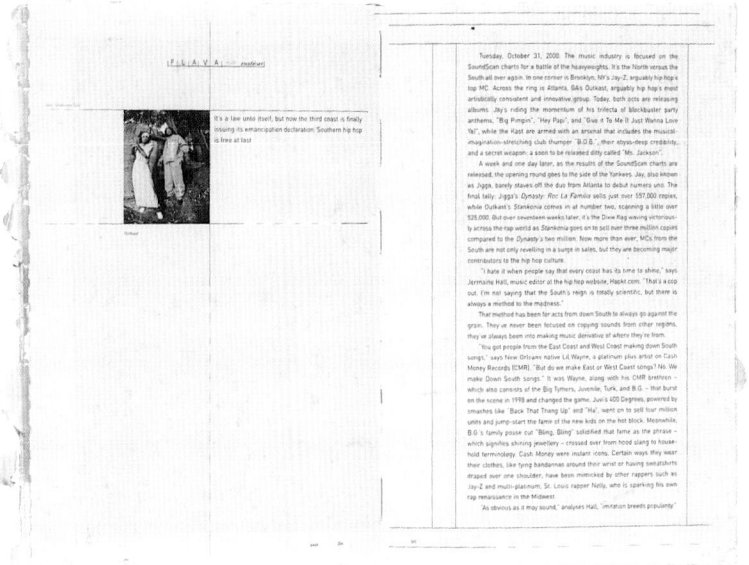

Tuesday, October 31, 2000. The music industry is focused on the SoundScan charts for a battle of the heavyweights. It's the North versus the South all over again. In one corner is Brooklyn, NY's Jay-Z, arguably hip-hop's top MC. Across the ring is Atlanta, GA's Outkast, arguably hip hop's most artistically consistent and innovative group. Today, both acts are releasing albums. Jay's riding the momentum of his trilecta of blockbuster party anthems, "Big Pimpin'", "Hey Papi", and "Guess If Ya Me'll Just Wanna Love Ya", while the Kast are armed with an arsenal that includes the musical-imagination-stretching club thumper "B.O.B.", their abyss-deep credibility, and a secret weapon: a soon to be released ditty called "Ms. Jackson".

A week and one day later, as the results of the SoundScan charts are released, the opening round goes to the side of the Yankees. Jay, also known as Jigga, barely staves off the duo from Atlanta to debut numero uno. The final tally: *Jigga's Dynasty: Roc La Familia* sells just over 557,000 copies, while Outkast's *Stankonia* comes in at number two, scanning a little over 528,000. But over seventeen weeks later, it's the Dow Rag waving victoriously across the rap world as *Stankonia* goes on to sell over three million copies compared to the *Dynasty*'s two million. Now more than ever, MCs from the South are not only revelling in a surge in sales, but they are becoming major contributors to the hip hop culture.

"I hate it when people say that every coast has its time to shine," says Jermaine Hall, music editor at the hip hop website, Hiphop.com. "That's a cop out. I'm not saying that the South's reign is totally scientific, but there is always a method to the madness."

That method has been for acts from down South to always go against the grain. They've never been focused on copying sounds from other regions, they've always been into making music derivative of where they're from.

"You got people from the East Coast and West Coast making down South songs," says New Orleans native Lil Wayne, a platinum plus artist on Cash Money Records (CMR). "But do we make East or West Coast songs? No. We make Down South songs." It was Wayne, along with his CMR brethren – which also consists of the Big Tymers, Juvenile, Turk, and B.G. – that burst on the scene in 1998 and changed the game. Juvi's 400 Degrees, powered by smashes like "Back That Thang Up" and "Ha", went on to sell four million units and jump-start the fame of the new kids on the hot block. Meanwhile, B.G.'s family posse cut "Bling, Bling" solidified that fame as the phrase – which signifies shining jewellery – crossed over from hood slang to household terminology. Cash Money were instant icons. Certain ways they wear their clothes, like tying bandannas around their wrist or having sweatshirts draped over one shoulder, have been mimicked by other rappers such as Jay-Z and multi-platinum, St. Louis rapper Nelly, who is sparking his own rap renaissance in the Midwest.

"As obvious as it may sound," analyses Hall, "imitation breeds popularity."

Home, *Sculpture Park, Museum Boijmans van Beuningen, Rotterdam*

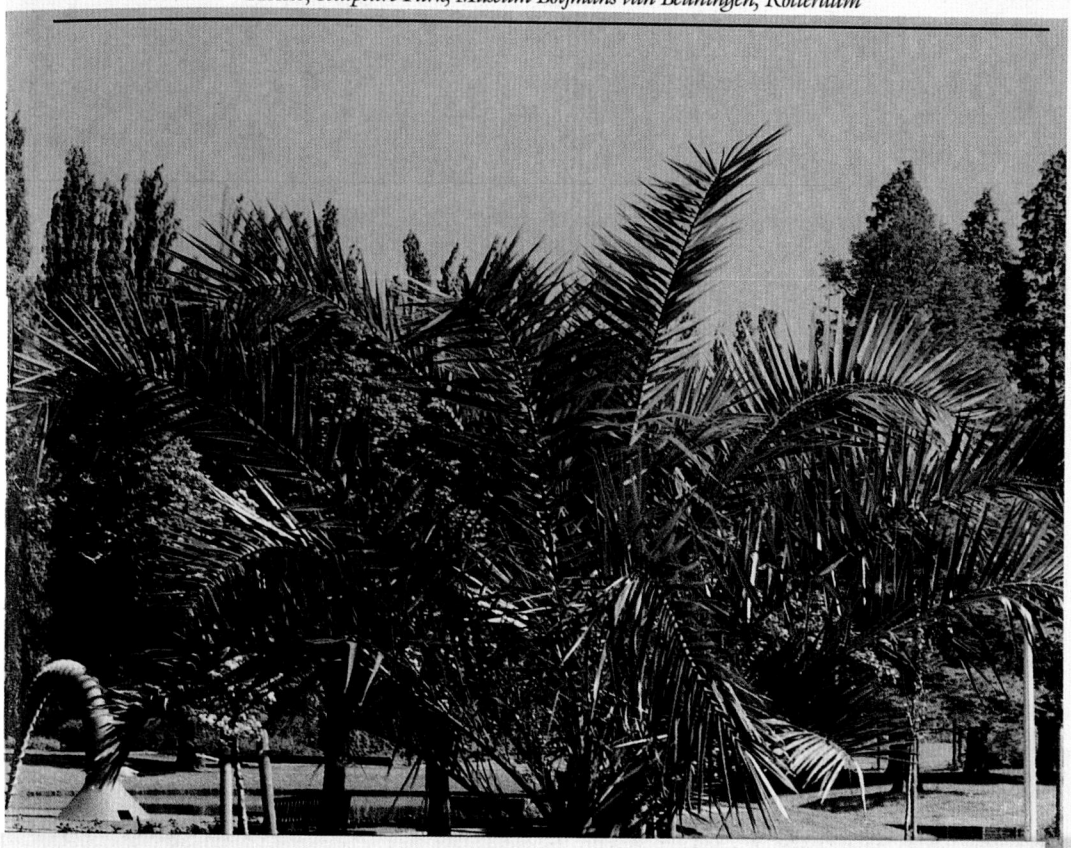

No! I don't know what I'm missing!

(see the back of this card to find out more)

PORT
BETAALD
AMSTERDAM

YES! I do/*NO!* I don't* realise that *Catalogue* is a new magazine.
YES! I would/*NO!* I wouldn't* like to know more.
YES! I do/*NO!* I don't* agree that art should lose the capital A.
YES! I do/*NO!* I don't* agree that change brings discussion.
YES! I like/*NO!* I hate* the idea of a guest editor for every issue.
YES! I do/*NO!* I don't* think this could introduce fresh perspectives.
YES! I would/*NO!* I wouldn't* like to be considered as a guest editor.
YES! I do/*NO!* I don't* realise that by doing so I have the freedom to feature one or more artists, whom I feel deserve that much attention for what they have been doing or saying recently.
YES! I do/*NO!* I don't* realise that 'that much attention' is 48 pages.
YES! I do/*NO!* I don't* realise that artist is a vague term.
YES! I do/*NO!* I don't* realise that I must invite others to comment.
YES! I do/*NO!* I don't* realise that all commentary will be published.
YES! I do/*NO!* I don't* have an opinion.
YES! I do/*NO!* I don't* respect everyone else's.

(*delete do's and don'ts)

Catalogue

NieuwezijdsVoorburgwal 96
1012 SG Amsterdam
The Netherlands

(ref: Cat.001. Spring 2001)

Issue 1, Spring 2001

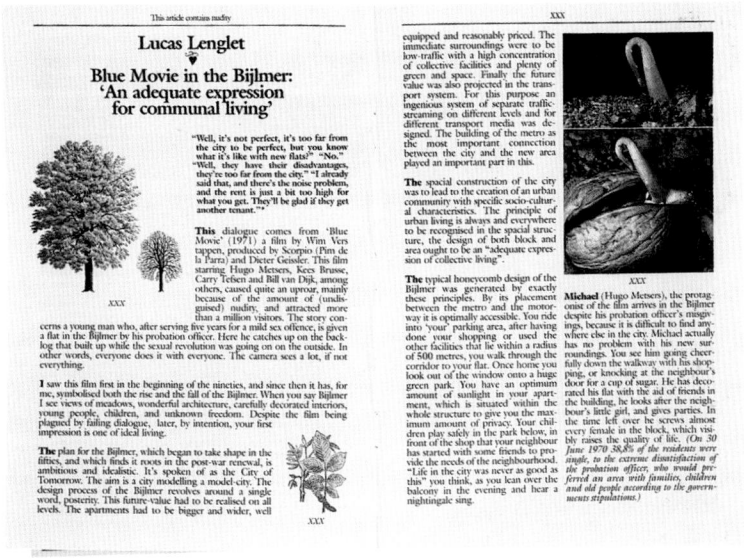

This article contains nudity

Lucas Lenglet

Blue Movie in the Bijlmer: 'An adequate expression for communal living'

"Well, it's not perfect, it's too far from the city to be perfect, but you know what it's like with new flats?" -No." "Well, they have their disadvantages, they're too far from the city." "I already said that, and there's the noise problem, and the rent is just a bit too high for what you get. They'll be glad if they get another tenant."*

This dialogue comes from 'Blue Movie' (1971) a film by Wim Vers tappen, produced by Scorpio (Pim de la Parra) and Dieter Geissler. This film starring Hugo Metsers, Kees Brusse, Carry Tefsen and Bill van Dijk, among others, caused quite an uproar, mainly because of the amount of (undisguised) nudity, and attracted more than a million visitors. The story concerns a young man who, after serving five years for a mild sex offence, is given a flat in the Bijlmer by his probation officer. Here he catches up on the backlog that built up while the sexual revolution was going on on the outside. In other words, everyone does it with everyone. The camera sees a lot, if not everything.

XXX

I saw this film first in the beginning of the nineties, and since then it has, for me, symbolised both the rise and the fall of the Bijlmer. When you see Bijlmer I see views of meadows, wonderful architecture, carefully decorated interiors, young people, children, and unknown freedom. Despite the film being plagued by failing dialogue, later, by intention, your first impression is one of ideal living.

The plan for the Bijlmer, which began to take shape in the fifties, and which finds it roots in the post-war renewal, is ambitious and idealistic. It's spoken of as the City of Tomorrow. The aim is a city modelling a model-city. The design process of the Bijlmer revolves around a single word, posterity. This future-value had to be realised on all levels. The apartments had to be bigger and wider, well

XXX

XXX

equipped and reasonably priced. The immediate surroundings were to be low-traffic with a high concentration of collective facilities and plenty of green and space. Finally the future value was also projected in the transport system. For this purpose an ingenious system of separate traffic-streaming on different levels and for different transport media was designed. The building of the metro as the most important connection between the city and the new area played an important part in this.

The spacial construction of the city was to lead to the creation of an urban community with specific socio-cultural characteristics. The principle of urban living is always and everywhere to be recognised in the spacial structure, the design of both block and area ought to be an "adequate expression of collective living".

The typical honeycomb design of the Bijlmer was generated by exactly these principles. By its placement between the metro and the motorway it is optimally accessible. You ride into 'your' parking area, after having done your shopping or used the other facilities that lie within a radius of 500 metres, you walk through the corridor to your flat. Once home you look out of the window onto a huge green park. You have an optimum amount of sunlight in your apartment, which is situated within the whole structure to give you the maximum amount of privacy. Your children play safely in the park below, in front of the shop that your neighbour has started with some friends to provide the needs of the neighbourhood. "Life in the city was never as good as this" you think, as you lean over the balcony in the evening and hear a nightingale sing.

XXX

Michael (Hugo Metsers), the protagonist of the film arrives in the Bijlmer despite his probation officer's misgivings, because it is difficult to find anywhere else in the city. Michael actually has no problem with his new surroundings. You see him going cheerfully down the walkway with his shopping, or knocking at the neighbour's door for a cup of sugar. He has decorated his flat with the aid of friends in the building, he looks after the neighbour's little girl, and gives parties. In the time left over he screws almost every female in the block, which visibly raises the quality of life. *(On 30 June 1970 38,8% of the residents were single, to the extreme dissatisfaction of the probation officer, who would preferred an area with families, children and old people according to the governmental stipulations.)*

Issue 2, Spring 2001

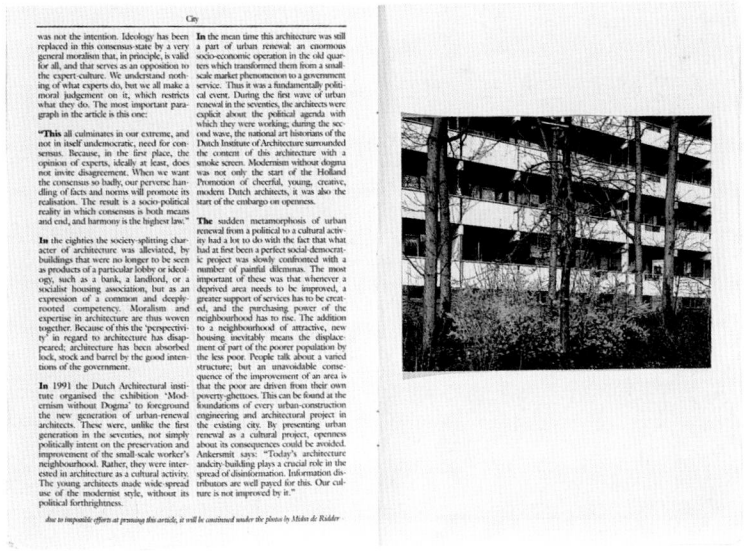

City

was not the intention. Ideology has been replaced in this consensus-state by a very general moralism that, in principle, is valid for all, and that serves as an opposition to the expert-culture. We understand nothing of what experts do, but we all make a moral judgement on it, which restricts what they do. The most important paragraph in the article is this one:

"This all culminates in our extreme, and not in itself undemocratic, need for consensus. Because, in the first place, the opinion of experts, ideally at least, does not invite disagreement. When we want the consensus so badly, our perverse handling of facts and norms will promote its realisation. The result is a socio-political reality in which consensus is both means and end, and harmony is the highest law."

In the eighties the society-splitting character of architecture was alleviated, by buildings that were no longer to be seen as products of a particular lobby or ideology, such as a bank, a landlord, or a socialist housing association, but as an expression of a common and deeply-rooted competency. Moralism and expertise in architecture are thus woven together. Because of this the 'perspectivity' in regard to architecture has disappeared; architecture has been absorbed lock, stock and barrel by the good intentions of the government.

In 1991 the Dutch Architectural institute organised the exhibition 'Modernism without Dogma' to foreground the new generation of urban-renewal architects. These were, unlike the first generation in the seventies, not simply politically intent on the preservation and improvement of the small-scale worker's neighbourhood. Rather, they were interested in architecture as a cultural activity. The young architects made wide-spread use of the modernist style, without its political forthrightness.

due to impossible efforts at pruning this article, it will be continued under the photos by Mishe de Ridder

In the mean time this architecture was still a part of urban renewal: an enormous socio-economic operation in the old quarters which transformed them from a small-scale market phenomenon to a government service. Thus it was a fundamentally political event. During the first wave of urban renewal in the seventies, the architects were explicit about the political agenda with which they were working; during the second wave, the national art historians of the Dutch Institute of Architecture surrounded the content of this architecture with a smoke screen. Modernism without dogma was not only the start of the Holland Promotion of cheerful, young, creative, modern Dutch architects, it was also the start of the embargo on openness.

The sudden metamorphosis of urban renewal from a political to a cultural activity had a lot to do with the fact that what had at first been a perfect social-democratic project was slowly confronted with a number of painful dilemmas. The most important of these was that whenever a deprived area needs to be improved, a greater support of services has to be created, and the purchasing power of the neighbourhood has to rise. The addition to a neighbourhood of attractive, new housing inevitably means the displacement of part of the poorer population by the less poor. People talk about a varied structure; but an unavoidable consequence of the improvement of an area is that the poor are driven from their own poverty-ghettoes. This can be found at the foundations of every urban-construction engineering and architectural project in the existing city. By presenting urban renewal as a cultural project, openness about its consequences could be avoided. Ankersmit says: "Today's architecture ancity-building plays a crucial role in the spread of disinformation. Information distributors are well payed for this. Our culture is not improved by it."

Issue 2, Spring 2001

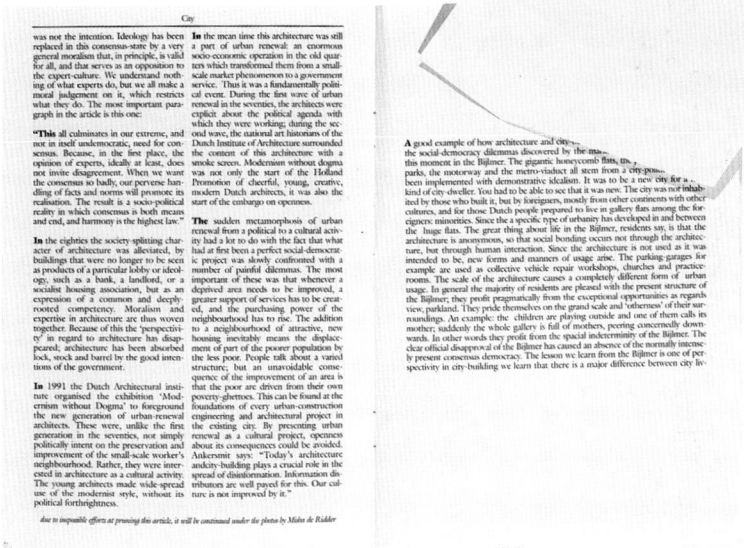

City

was not the intention. Ideology has been replaced in this consensus-state by a very general moralism that, in principle, is valid for all, and that serves as an opposition to the expert-culture. We understand nothing of what experts do, but we all make a moral judgement on it, which restricts what they do. The most important paragraph in the article is this one:

"This all culminates in our extreme, and not in itself undemocratic, need for consensus. Because, in the first place, the opinion of experts, ideally at least, does not invite disagreement. When we want the consensus so badly, our perverse handling of facts and norms will promote its realisation. The result is a socio-political reality in which consensus is both means and end, and harmony is the highest law."

In the eighties the society-splitting character of architecture was alleviated, by buildings that were no longer to be seen as products of a particular lobby or ideology, such as a bank, a landlord, or a socialist housing association, but as an expression of a common and deeply-rooted competency. Moralism and expertise in architecture are thus woven together. Because of this the 'perspectivity' in regard to architecture has disappeared; architecture has been absorbed lock, stock and barrel by the good intentions of the government.

In 1991 the Dutch Architectural institute organised the exhibition 'Modernism without Dogma' to foreground the new generation of urban-renewal architects. These were, unlike the first generation in the seventies, not simply politically intent on the preservation and improvement of the small-scale worker's neighbourhood. Rather, they were interested in architecture as a cultural activity. The young architects made wide-spread use of the modernist style, without its political forthrightness.

due to impossible efforts at pruning this article, it will be continued under the photos by Mishe de Ridder

In the mean time this architecture was still a part of urban renewal: an enormous socio-economic operation in the old quarters which transformed them from a small-scale market phenomenon to a government service. Thus it was a fundamentally political event. During the first wave of urban renewal in the seventies, the architects were explicit about the political agenda with which they were working; during the second wave, the national art historians of the Dutch Institute of Architecture surrounded the content of this architecture with a smoke screen. Modernism without dogma was not only the start of the Holland Promotion of cheerful, young, creative, modern Dutch architects, it was also the start of the embargo on openness.

The sudden metamorphosis of urban renewal from a political to a cultural activity had a lot to do with the fact that what had at first been a perfect social-democratic project was slowly confronted with a number of painful dilemmas. The most important of these was that whenever a deprived area needs to be improved, a greater support of services has to be created, and the purchasing power of the neighbourhood has to rise. The addition to a neighbourhood of attractive, new housing inevitably means the displacement of part of the poorer population by the less poor. People talk about a varied structure; but an unavoidable consequence of the improvement of an area is that the poor are driven from their own poverty-ghettoes. This can be found at the foundations of every urban-construction engineering and architectural project in the existing city. By presenting urban renewal as a cultural project, openness about its consequences could be avoided. Ankersmit says: "Today's architecture ancity-building plays a crucial role in the spread of disinformation. Information distributors are well payed for this. Our culture is not improved by it."

A good example of how architecture and city ...
the social-democracy dilemmas discovered by the ma...
this moment in the Bijlmer. The gigantic honeycomb flats, the ...
parks, the motorway and the metro-viaduct all stem from a city-pos...
been implemented with demonstrative idealism. It was to be a new city for a ...
kind of city-dweller. You had to be able to see that it was new. The city was not inhabited by those who built it, but by foreigners, mostly from other continents with other cultures, and for those Dutch people prepared to live in gallery flats among the foreigners: minorities. Since the a specific type of urbanity has developed in and between the huge flats. The great thing about life in the Bijlmer, residents say, is that the architecture is anonymous, so that social bonding occurs not through the architecture, but through human interaction. Since the architecture is not used as it was intended to be, new forms and manners of usage arise. The parking garages for example are used as collective vehicle repair workshops, churches and practice-rooms. The scale of the architecture causes a completely different form of urban usage. In general the majority of residents are pleased with the present structure of the Bijlmer; they profit pragmatically from the exceptional opportunities as regards view, parkland. They pride themselves on the grand scale and 'otherness' of their surroundings. An example: the children are playing outside and one of them calls its mother; suddenly the whole gallery is full of mothers, peering concernedly downwards. In other words they profit from the spacial indeterminity of the Bijlmer. The clear official disapproval of the Bijlmer has caused an absence of the normally intensely present consensus democracy. The lesson we learn from the Bijlmer is one of perspectivity in city-building we learn that there is a major difference between city liv-

Issue 2, Spring 2001

Catalogue *(The Netherlands) 148 x 210mm/5 7/8 x 8 1/4 inches*
The relatively low print-run of around 1500 copies enables this magazine to add a different extra element every issue. Issue 1 (OPPOSITE) included pull-out posters, while issue 2 (THIS PAGE) had colour pictures stapled in by hand. Design *Goodwill*

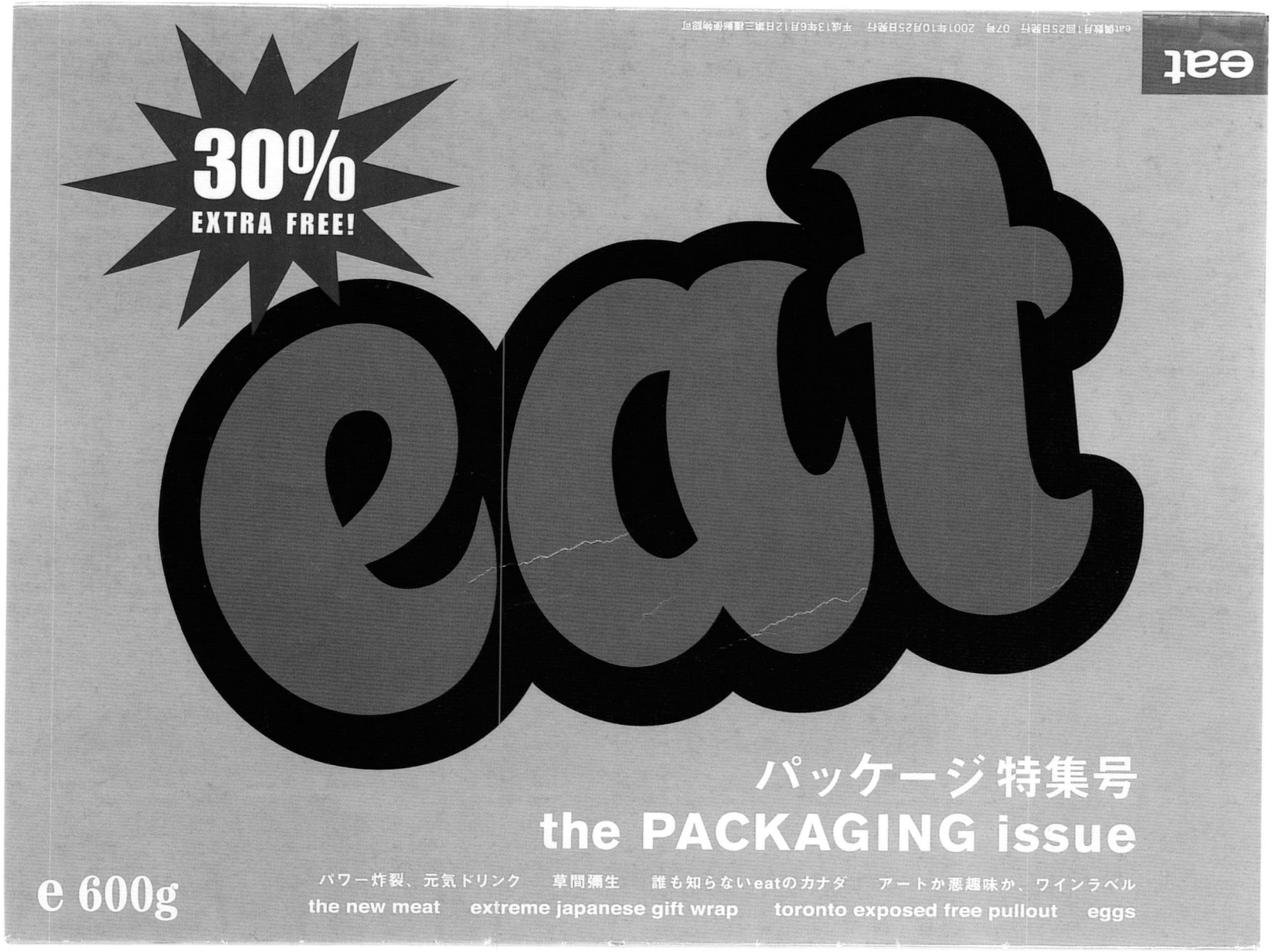
eat
eat雑誌月1回25日発行 07号 2001年10月25日発行 平成13年6月12日第三種郵便物認可
30%
EXTRA FREE!
eat
パッケージ特集号
the PACKAGING issue
e 600g
パワー炸裂、元気ドリンク 草間彌生 誰も知らないeatのカナダ アートか悪趣味か、ワインラベル
the new meat extreme japanese gift wrap toronto exposed free pullout eggs

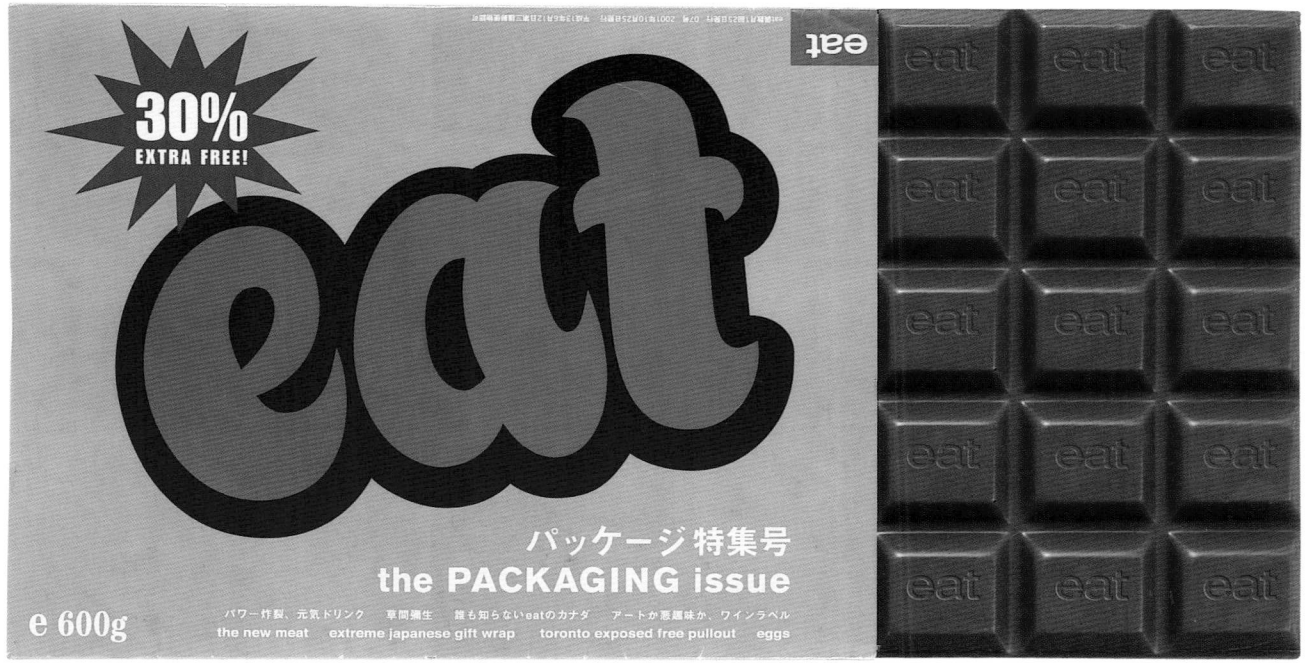

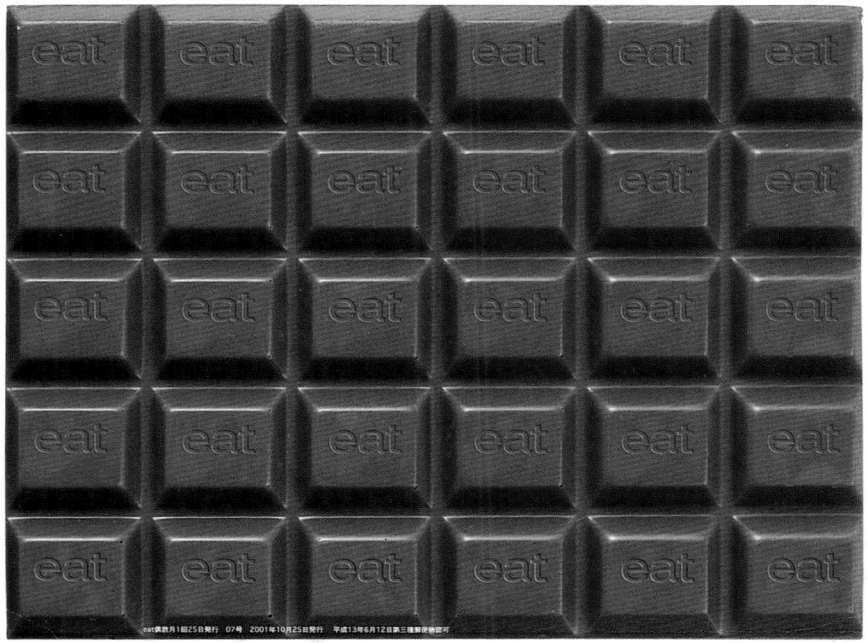

Eat *(Japan, Issue 7, November/December 2001)*
225 x 277mm/8 3/4 x 10 7/8 inches
A special 'Packaging' issue of this Anglo-Japanese food magazine came with a chocolate-style wrapper that slipped off to reveal a photograph of chocolate on the front cover.
Art director *Tin Brown*

THIS PAGE **Domus** *(Italy, Issue 849, June 2002) 245 x 320mm/9 3/4 x 12 3/4 inches*
This architecture magazine comes shrinkwrapped in plastic with bold coverlines printed on it: ideal for the sales shelf (LEFT). Remove the plastic and you have a plain pictorial front cover that will look appropriate in the reception area of all architects' practices (RIGHT).
Art director *Simon Esterson*

OPPOSITE **No. A/B/C...** *(Belgium, Issue A, Summer 2001) 230 x 297mm/9 x 11 7/8 inches*
Each issue of this fashion magazine is titled a single letter and overseen by a different editor, in this case Dirk Van Saene. The issue has no cover: instead it starts with the contents page and is wrapped in plastic printed with its title, 'A'.
Art direction *Paul Boudens and Madelaine Wermenbol*

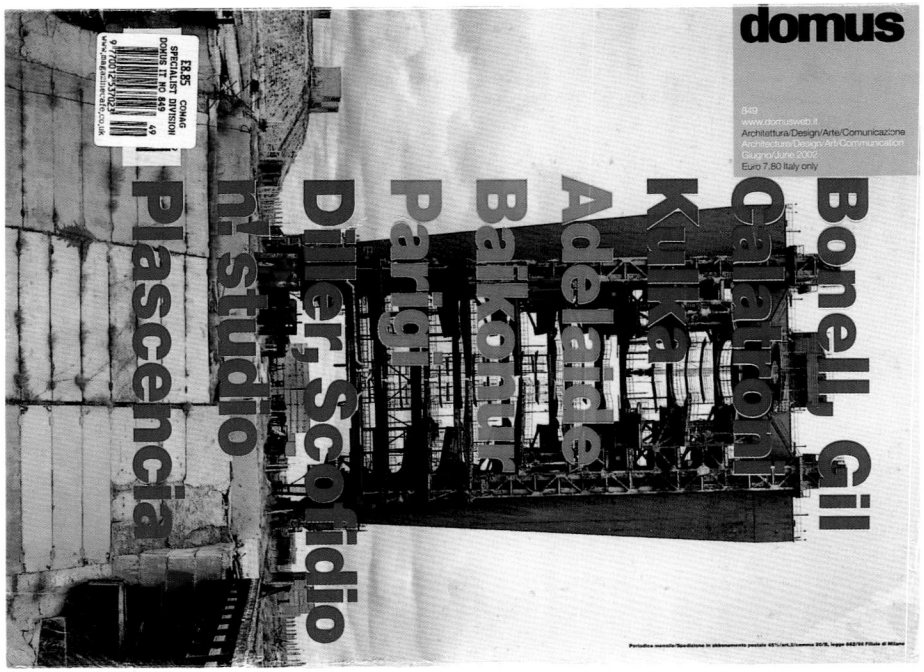

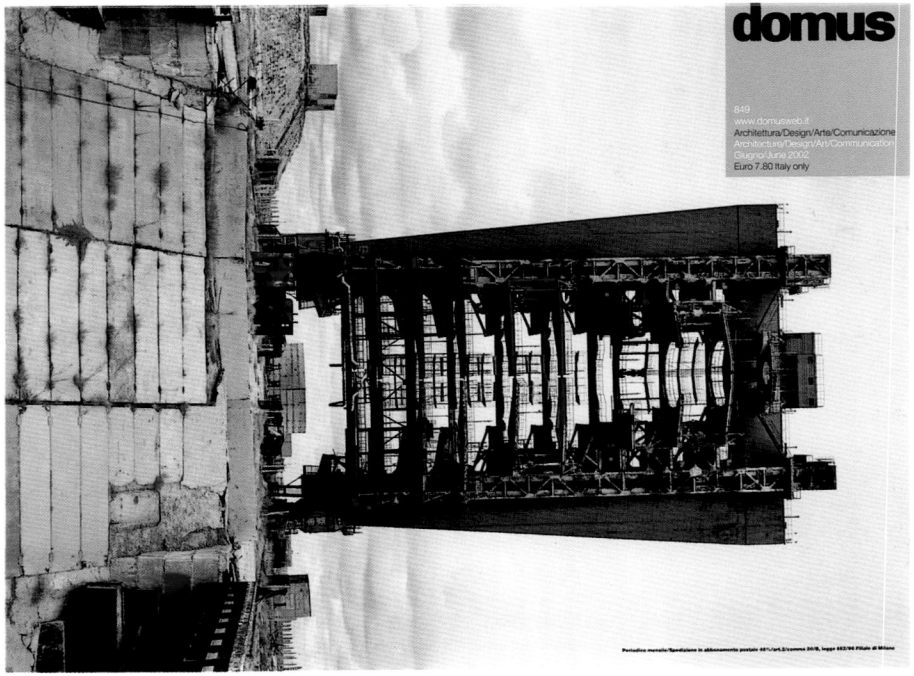

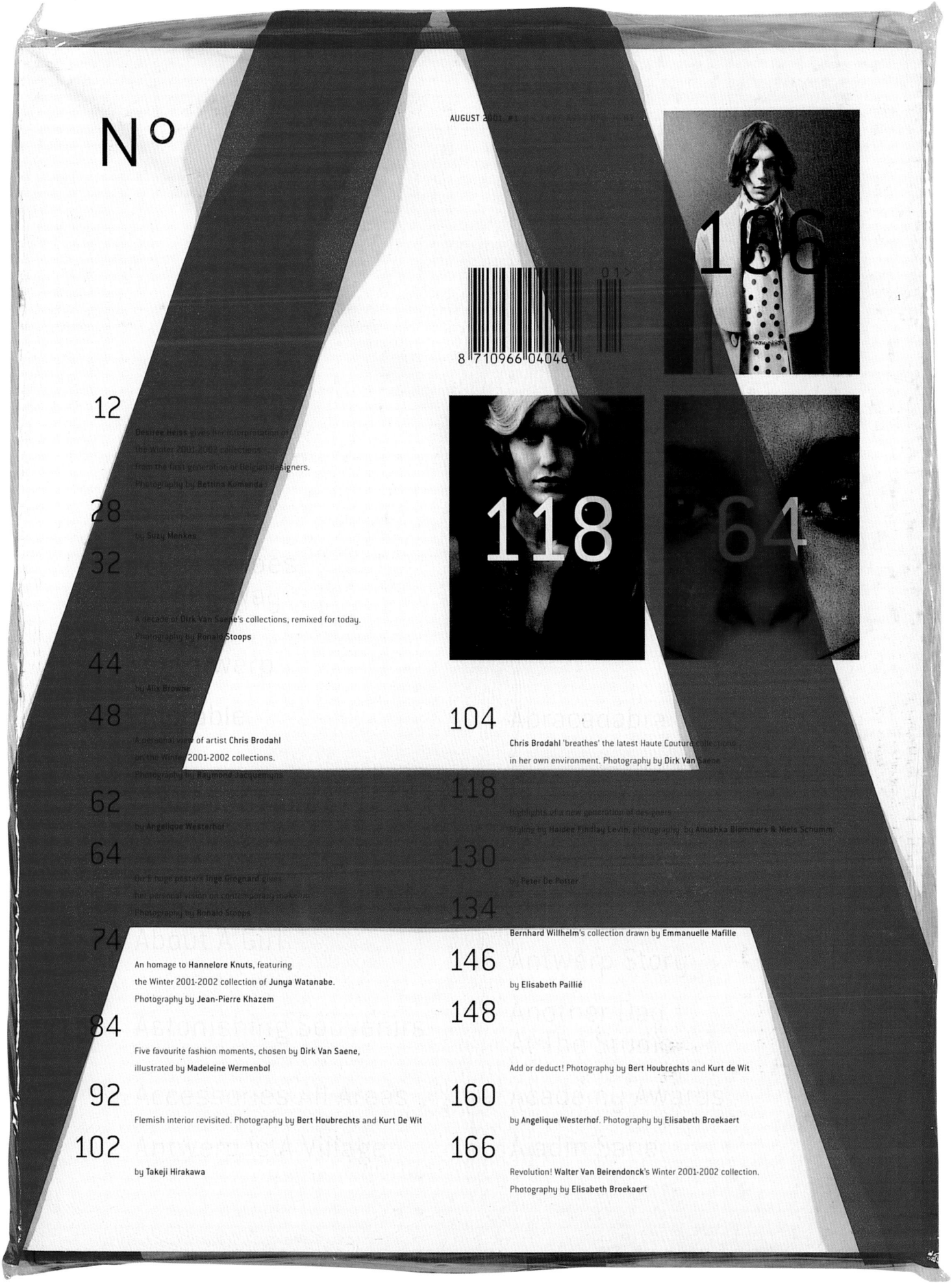

N°

AUGUST 2001 #1

8 710966 040461 01>

12

Desiree Heiss gives her interpretation of the Winter 2001-2002 collections from the last generation of Belgian designers. Photography by Bettina Komanda

28

by Suzy Menkes

32

A decade of Dirk Van Saene's collections, remixed for today. Photography by Ronald Stoops

44

by Alix Browne

48

A personal view of artist Chris Brodahl on the Winter 2001-2002 collections. Photography by Raymond Jacquemyns

62

by Angelique Westerhof

64

Dirk's nude pastels Inge Grognard gives her personal vision on contemporary nakedness. Photography by Ronald Stoops

74

An homage to Hannelore Knuts, featuring the Winter 2001-2002 collection of Junya Watanabe. Photography by Jean-Pierre Khazem

84

Five favourite fashion moments, chosen by Dirk Van Saene, illustrated by Madeleine Wermenbol

92

Flemish interior revisited. Photography by Bert Houbrechts and Kurt De Wit

102

by Takeji Hirakawa

104

Chris Brodahl 'breathes' the latest Haute Couture collections in her own environment. Photography by Dirk Van Saene

118

Highlights of a new generation of designers. Styling by Haidee Findlay Levin, photography by Anushka Blommers & Niels Schumm

130

by Peter De Potter

134

Bernhard Willhelm's collection drawn by Emmanuelle Mafille

146

by Elisabeth Paillié

148

Add or deduct! Photography by Bert Houbrechts and Kurt de Wit

160

by Angelique Westerhof. Photography by Elisabeth Broekaert

166

Revolution! Walter Van Beirendonck's Winter 2001-2002 collection. Photography by Elisabeth Broekaert

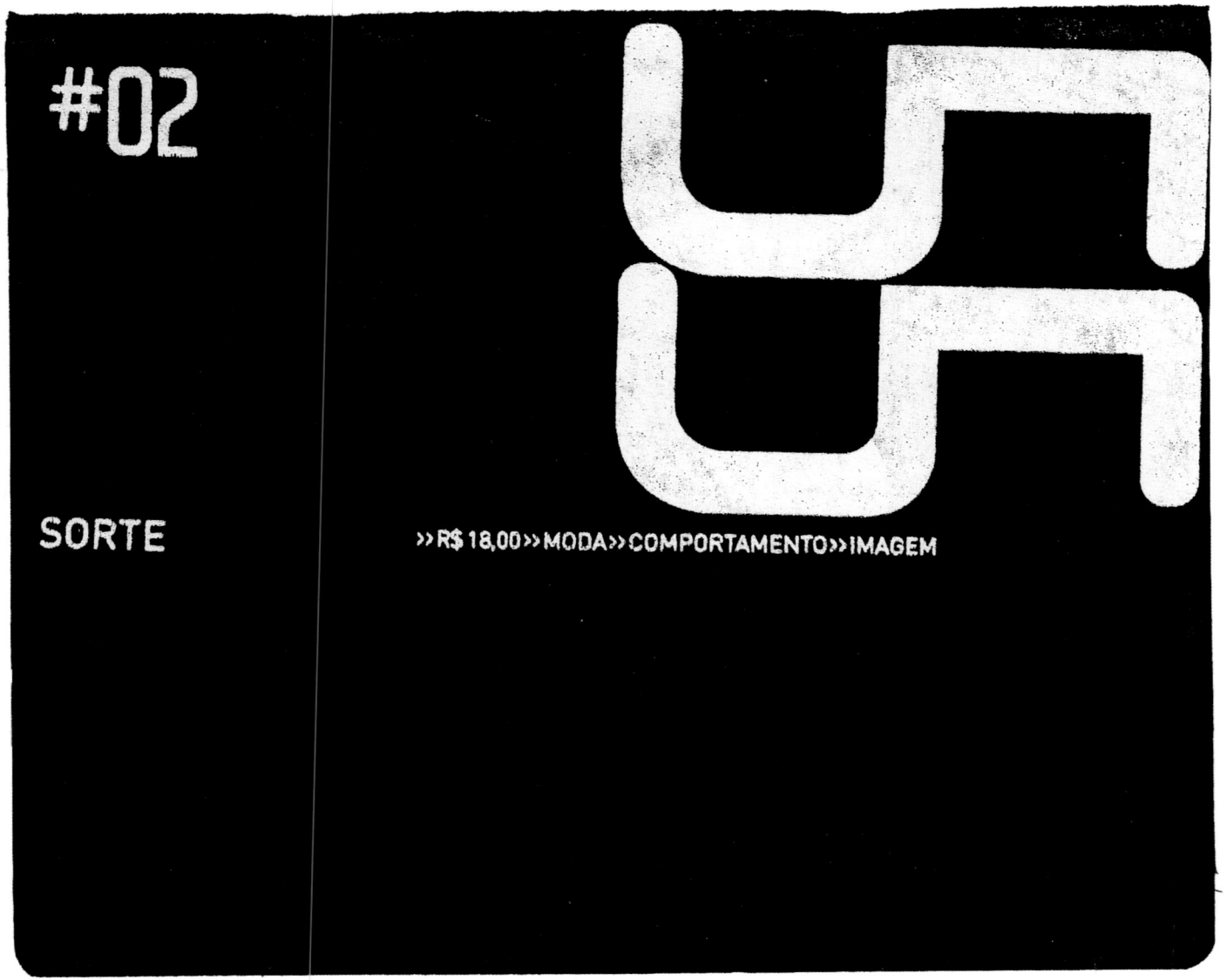

THIS PAGE **55** *(Brazil, Issue 2, 2002) 254 x 303mm/10 x 12 inches*
This fashion magazine retains its size but changes its cover material every issue. The first issue had a transparent plastic sleeve around it, while this issue is bound in fake suede with the type screenprinted on.
Art director *Helio Rosas*

OPPOSITE **Nice Magazine** *(UK, Issue 1, Spring 2002) 230 x 300mm/9 x 11 7/8 inches*
The ultimate experiment in magazine format? At first glance it's the same size, thickness and weight as a standard consumer magazine, and has its title printed clearly on the front. But pick it up and it's a solid piece of wood. Is this an artful joke about the state of magazines or a serious comment about the destruction of forests for paper? Either way, it's been a bestseller at all stores selling it.
Designer *Unknown*

nice magazine

LIBRARY & RESOURCE CENTRE CAMPUS
THE SURREY INSTITUTE OF ART & DESIGN

Issue 1, Autumn/Winter 2000

Issue 2, Spring/Summer 2001

Issue 3, Autumn/Winter 2001

Issue 4, Spring/Summer 2002

Issue 1, Winter 2000/01

Issue 2, Summer 2001

Issue 3, Winter 2001/02

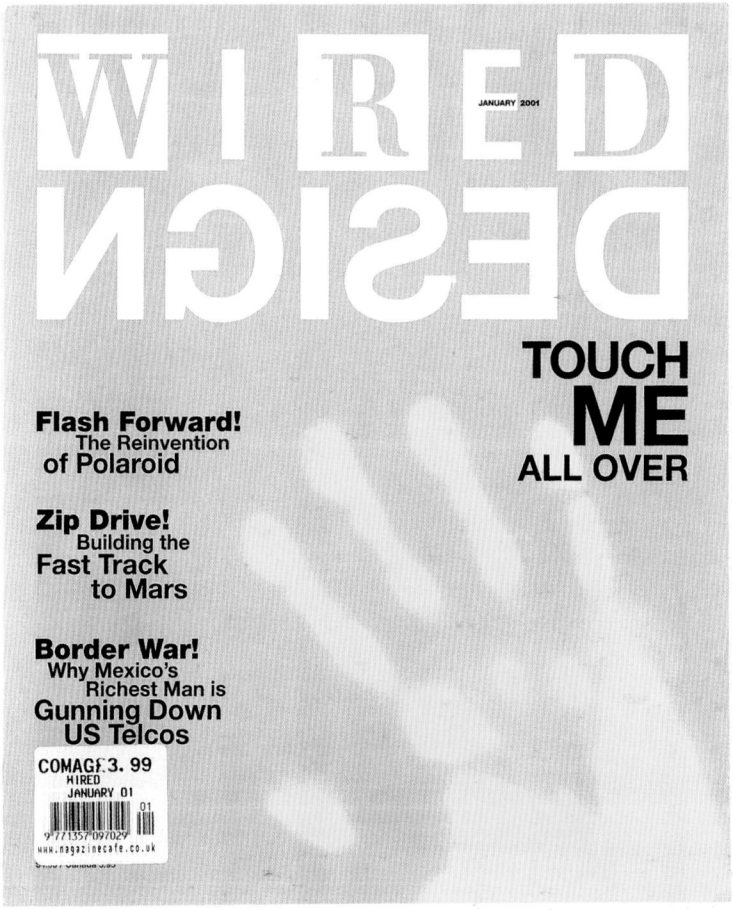

OPPOSITE **Exit** *(UK) 230 x 315mm/9 x 12 ½ inches*
Commercially, the complete absence on the cover of information about the contents of this fashion magazine may seem perverse but in fact these minimalist covers stand out well against the manic shouting of so many other magazines.
Art director *Mark Juber*

THIS PAGE **032c** *(Germany) 230 x 315mm/9 x 12 ½ inches*
A biannual fanzine produced by art/design/event studio, 032c, it takes its name from the Pantone colour reference for a bright red. The covers always take the form of a large swatch of the Pantone red, only the details at the bottom left change from issue to issue.
Art director *Vladimir Llovet Casademont*

Wired *(USA, Issue 9.01, January 2001) 230 x 273mm/9 x 10 ¾ inches*
This blank cover changes when touched by the reader. Heat-sensitive ink reacts to the the reader's hand, representing a feature in the issue about design being human- and not technology-led.
Design director *Daniel Carter*

ADBUSTERS

Magazine

220 g $5.75

US/CAN $5.75 UK £3.95 ¥1200

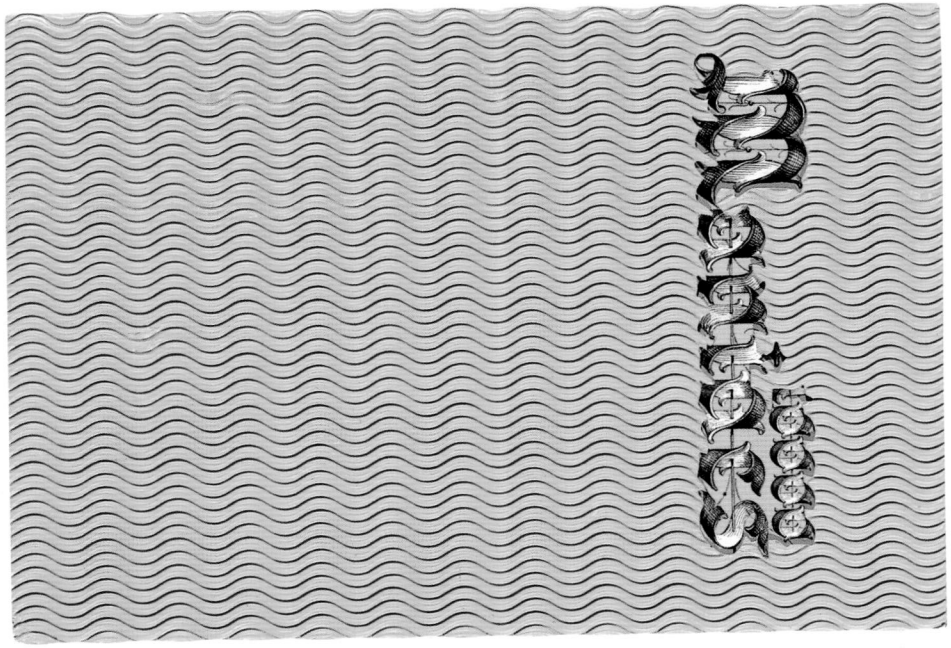

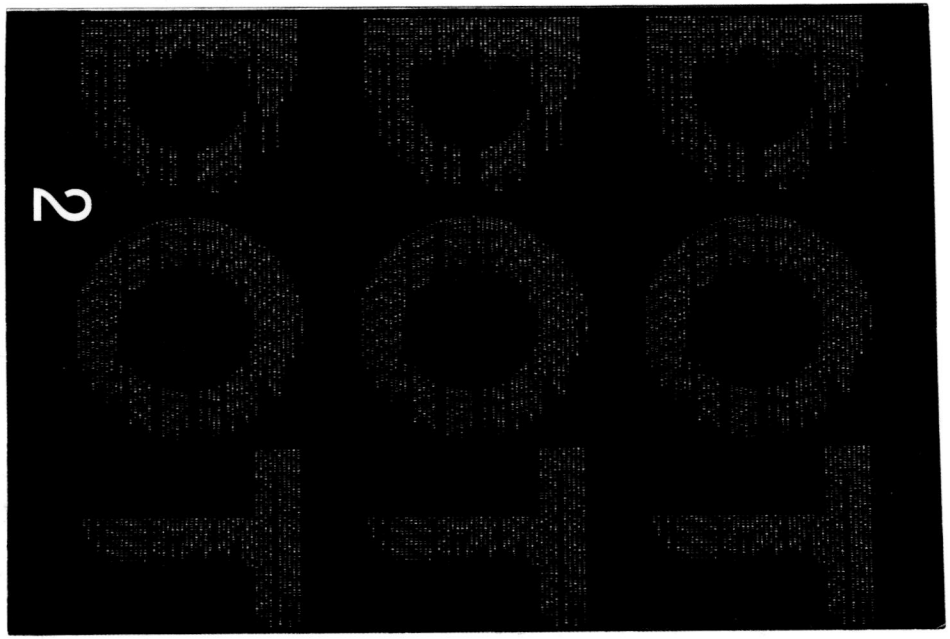

OPPOSITE **Adbusters** *(Canada, Issue 29, Spring 2000)*
230 x 272mm/9 x 10 3/4 inches
The label 'Magazine' is bolder than the magazine's own name on this cover, to acknowledge the role of magazines as product.
Art director *Chris Dixon*

THIS PAGE **10,000 Maniacs** *(Italy, Issue 3)*
210 x 297mm/8 1/4 x 11 3/4 inches
This edition of the graffiti magazine features a textured cover paper with a die-cut hole through which the title is visible.
Art director *Cristian*

Dot Dot Dot *(UK, Issue 2, Winter 2000)*
165 x 234mm/6 1/2 x 9 1/4 inches
The title on the cover of this design journal is written using characters constructed from their own postscript code.
Design *Jurgen Albrecht, Stuart Bailey, Peter Bilak and Tom Unverzagt*

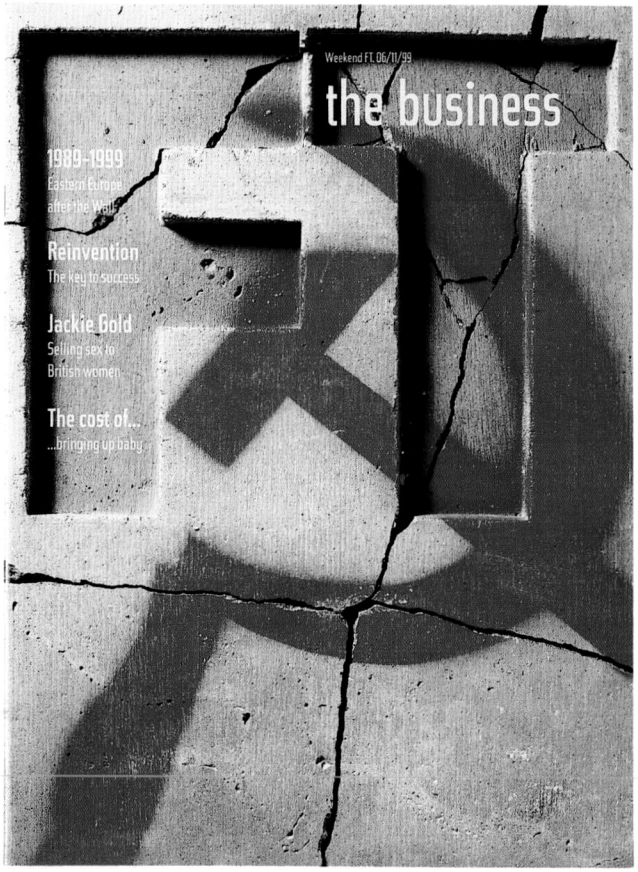

6 November 1999

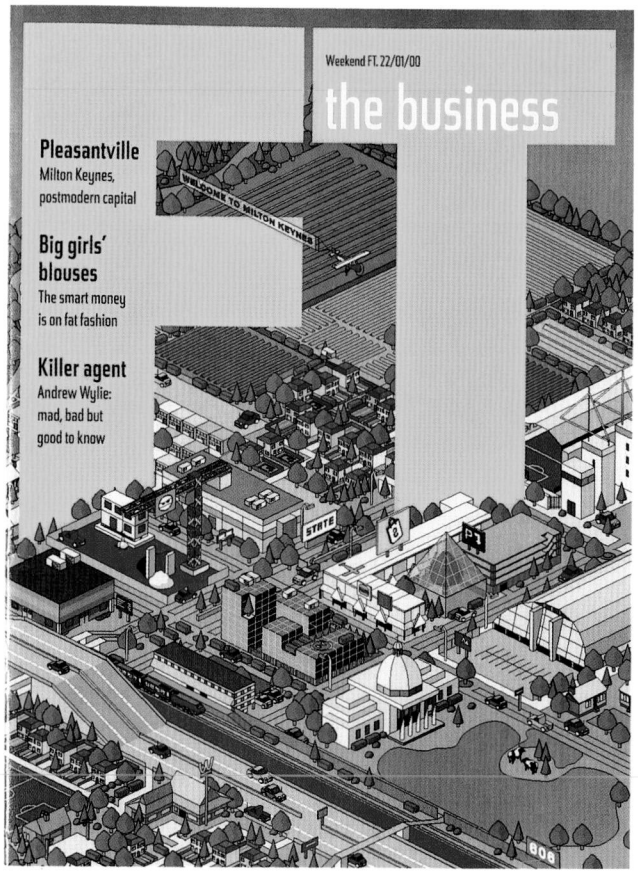

22 January 2000

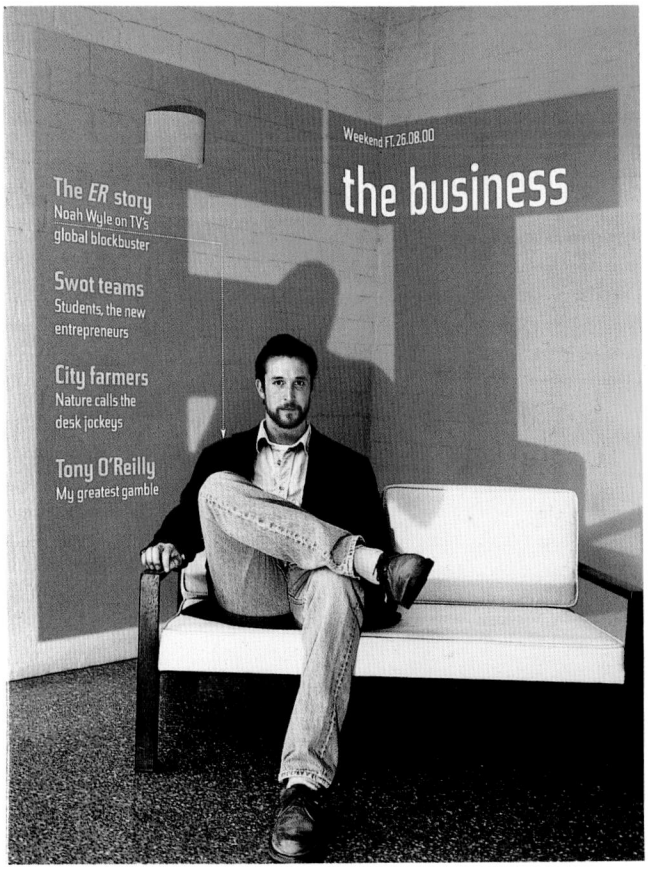

26 August 2000

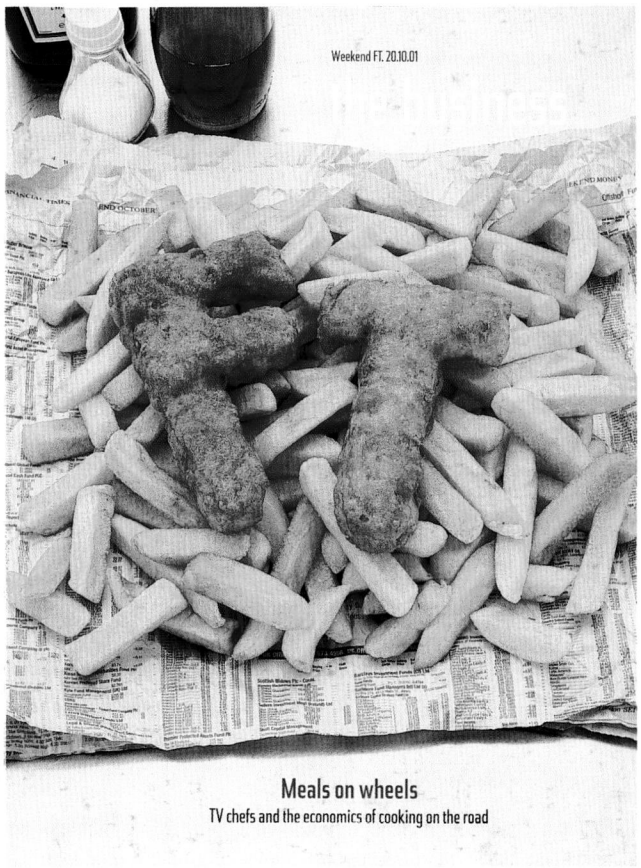

20 October 2001

FT: The Business *(UK)*
165 x 234mm/6 ½ x 9 ¼ inches
In this supplement, the letters of the main title *FT* were used as a movable graphic element that worked as part of the image, the execution of which changed each week.
Art director *Gary Cook*

THIS PAGE **Taxi** *(UK, Issue 1, Summer 2002)*
240 x 320mm/9 1/2 x 12 3/4 inches
Published internationally by the GettyImages picture library as an editorialized image catalogue, this magazine not only relegates its name to the bottom of the cover, but uses different hand-written versions of the name for different issues. This first issue included an appeal to readers to send in their version of the name in their handwriting.
Design director *Chris Ashworth*

Hot Rod *(Norway)*
165 x 210mm/6 1/2 x 8 1/4 inches
This microzine is published in Oslo and is the personal project of its publisher/editor/designer. The baroque logo design on the top two examples gives nothing away about the content: the bottom example doesn't even include the logo.
Designer *Jan Walaker*

OPPOSITE **Coupe** *(Canada)*
245 x 294mm/9 3/4 x 11 3/4 inches
This uses the magazine format to take a close look at the 'wonders of the modern electronic age'. It does so through busy collages of text and image, following none of the rules of magazine design. Rules are avoided on these covers too: all that links them together is the page size. Issue 5 features the magazine's name in spot varnish only, which is invisible in this reproduction.
Art direction *The Bang*

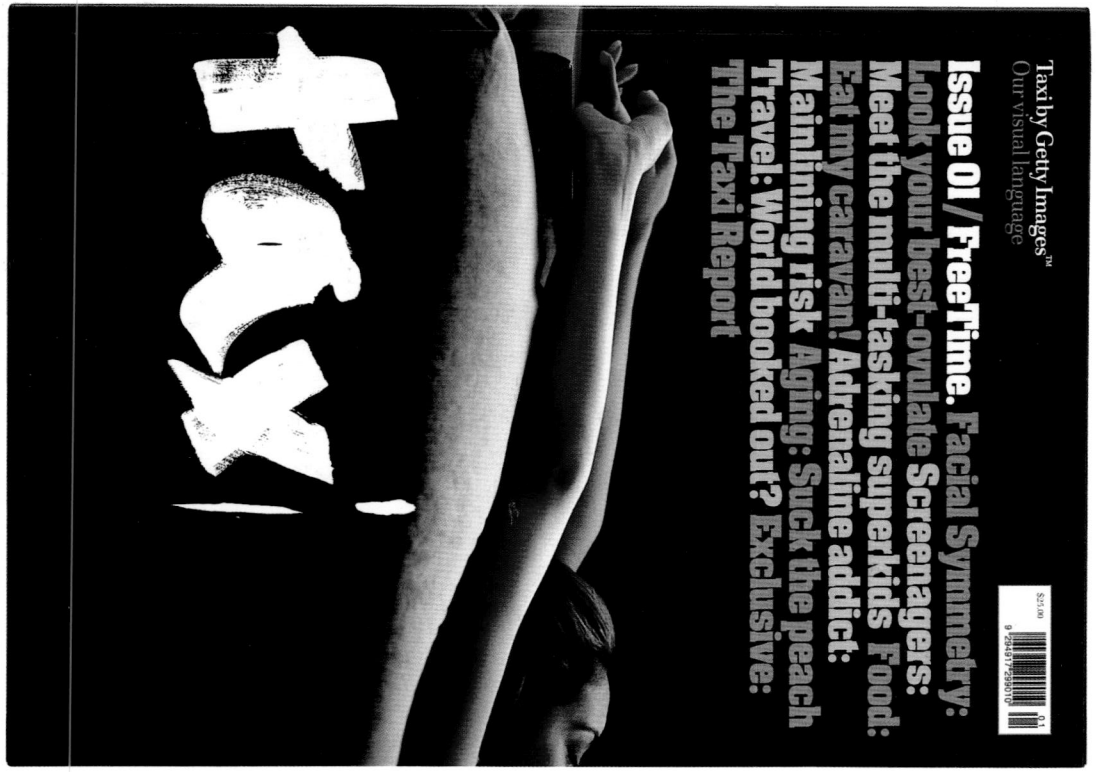

Issue 10

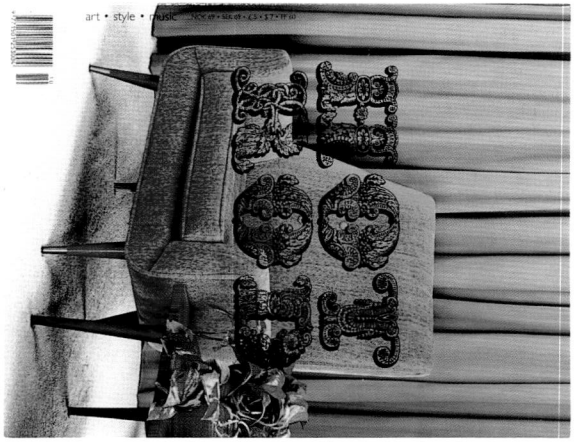

Issue 14

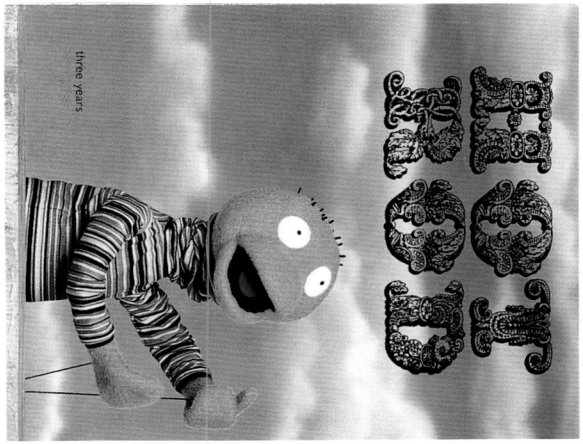

Issue 15

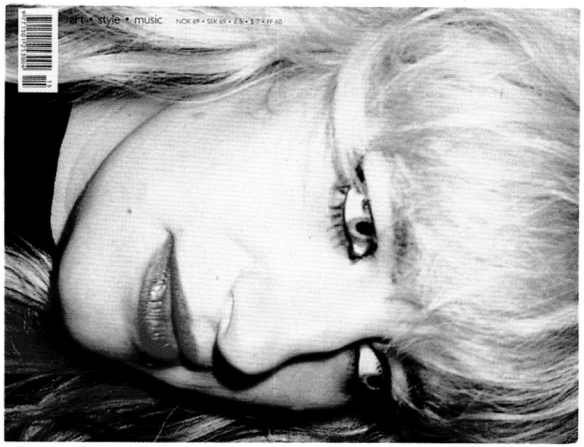

Issue 1, 1999

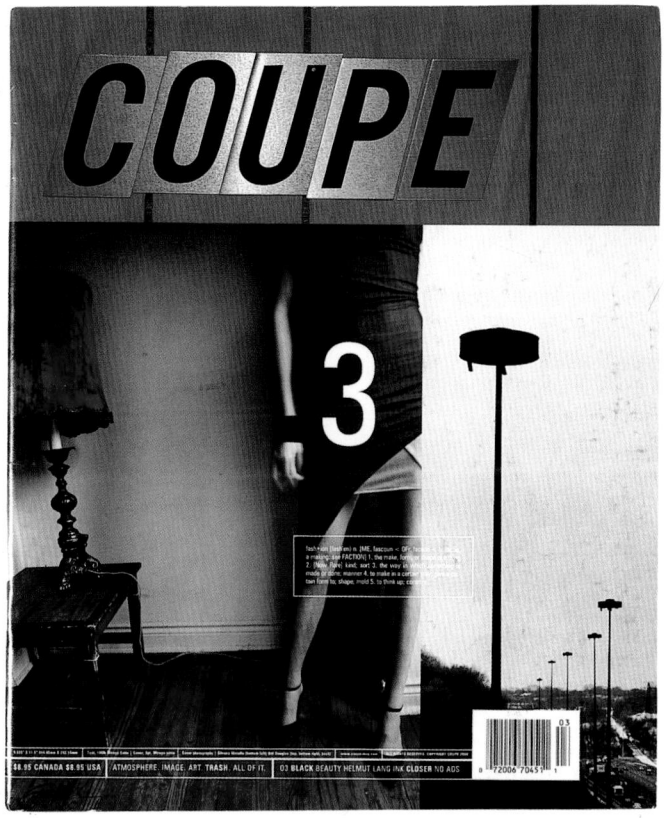

Issue 3, 2000

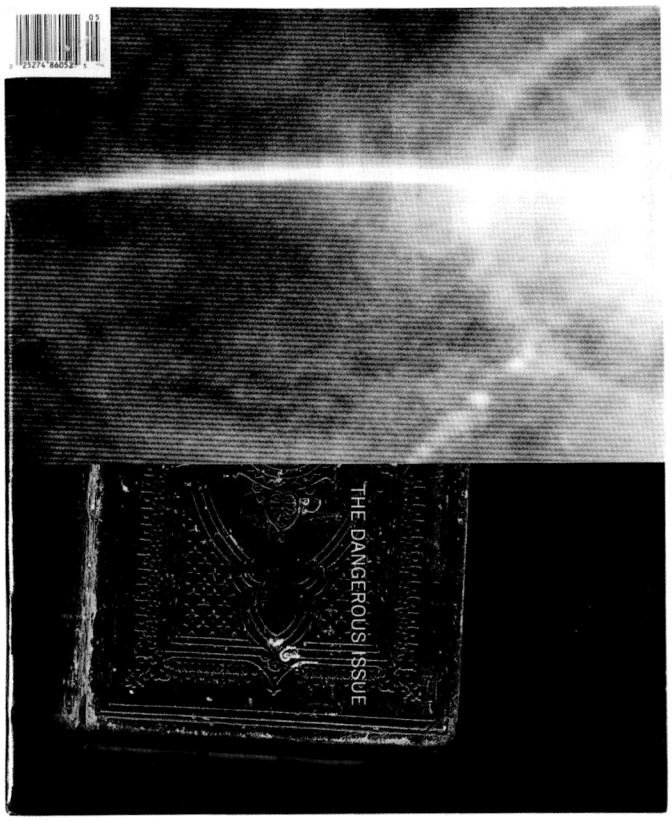

Issue 5, 2001

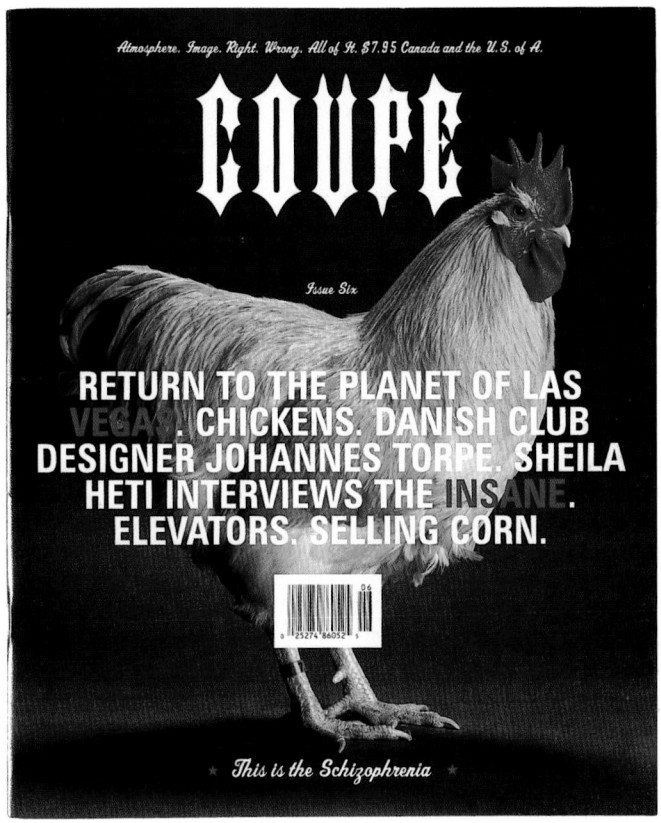

Issue 6, 2001

THIS PAGE **Stockholm New** *(Sweden, Issue 12, 2002)*
218 x 280mm/8 3/4 x 11 inches
The title, issue number and theme become a single graphic entity.
Art director *Joel Berg*

Young Blood *(France, Issue 8, June 2001)*
230 x 297mm/9 x 11 3/4 inches
The name takes second place to the issue number, the bitmapped numbers serving as the recognizable logo element of the cover.
Art director *Pierre Henri Brunel*

Moving Pictures *(UK, Issue 4, December 2000)*
225 x 275mm/8 7/8 x 10 3/4 inches
Magazines with long names are always awkward for the designer. Here, the problem is solved by using the name to frame the cover image.
Art director *Michael Booth*

OPPOSITE **BEople** *(Belgium, Issue 2, February/March/April 2002)*
230 x 305mm/9 x 12 inches
Each issue of this magazine about Belgium features a person obliterated by the title in a white circle, rendering the individual irrelevant and emphasizing the generic nature of its name.
Art direction *Base Design*

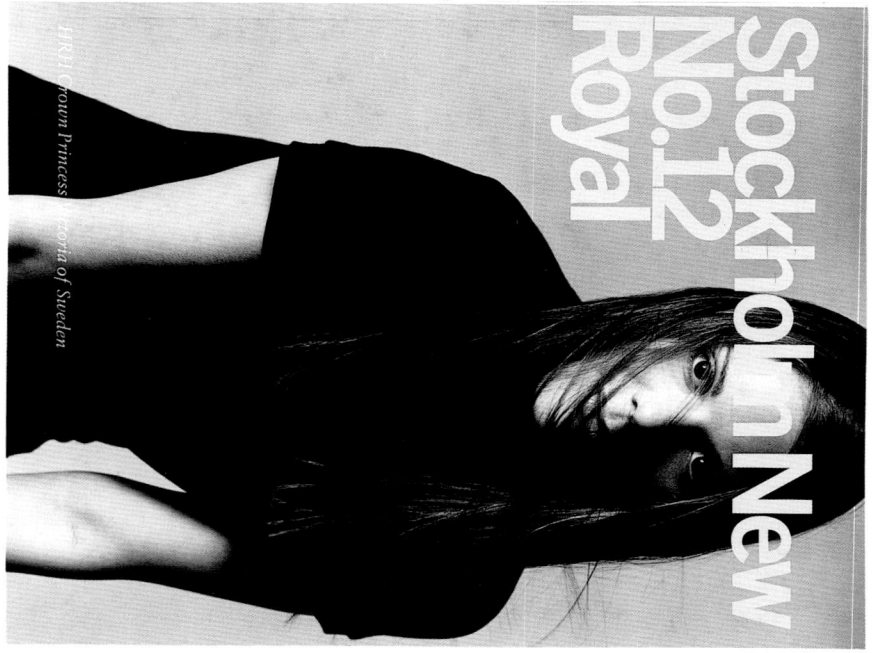

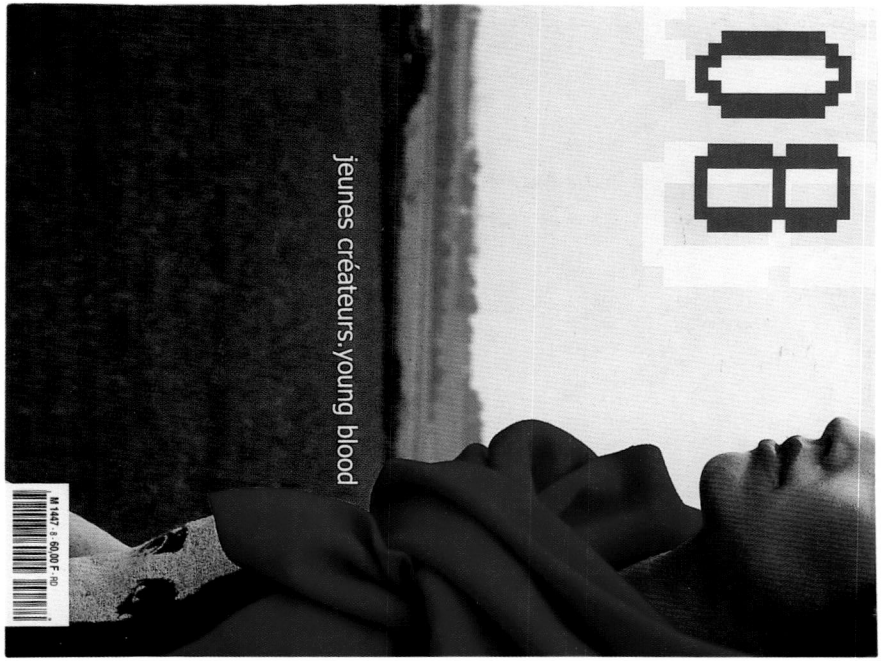

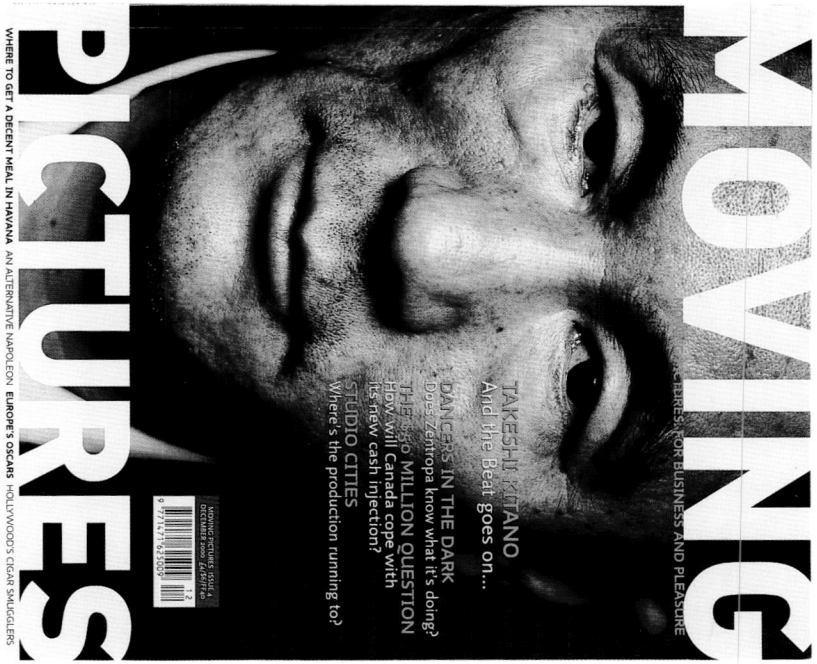

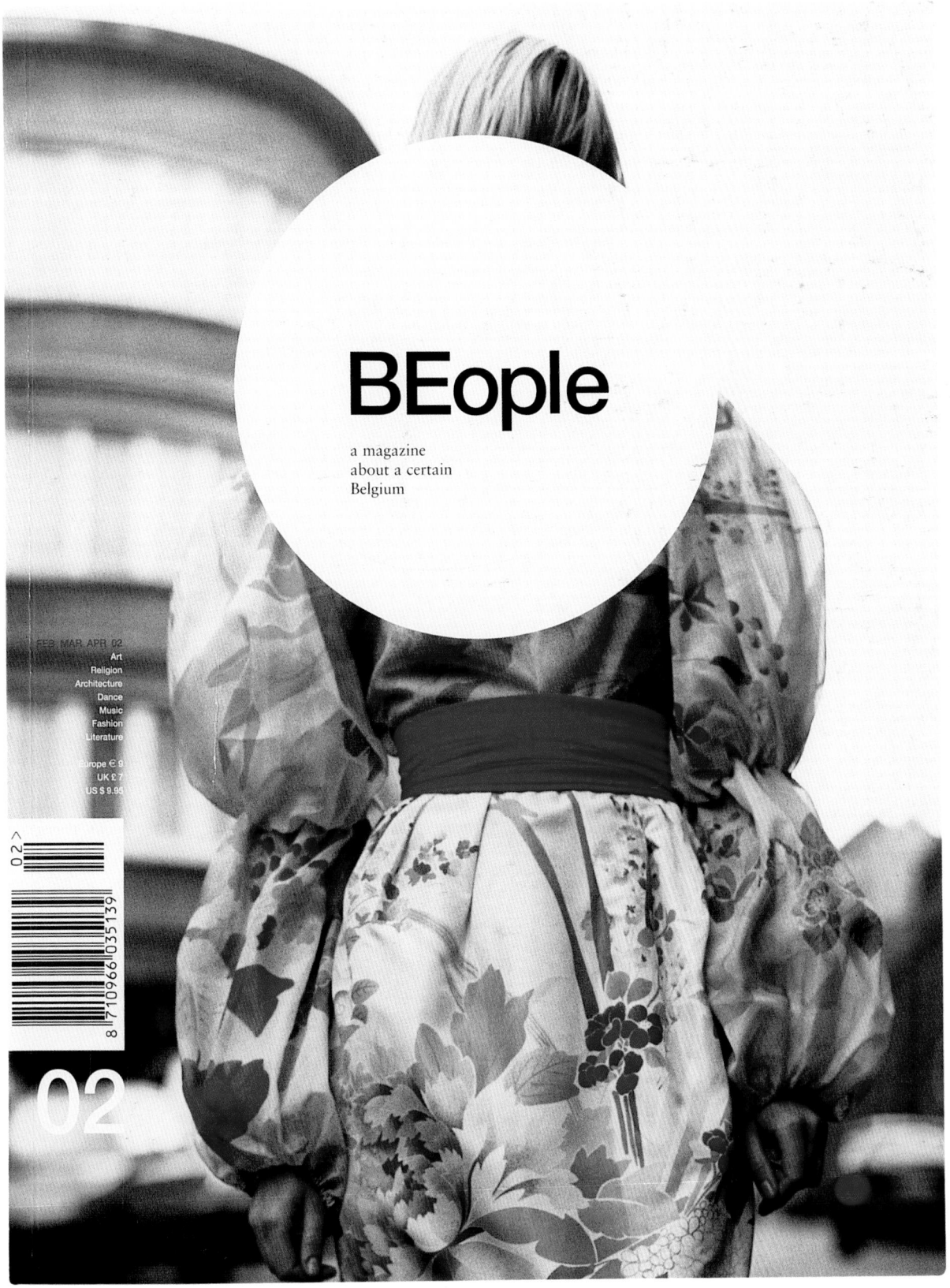
BEople
a magazine
about a certain
Belgium
FEB MAR APR 02
Art
Religion
Architecture
Dance
Music
Fashion
Literature
Europe € 9
UK £ 7
US $ 9.95
02>
8 710966 035139
02

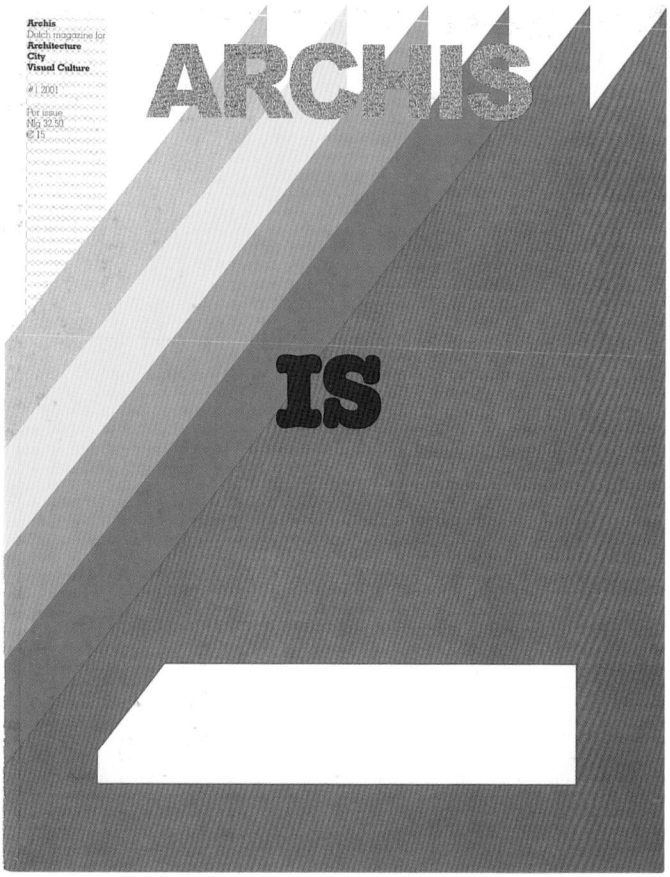

Issue 1, 2001

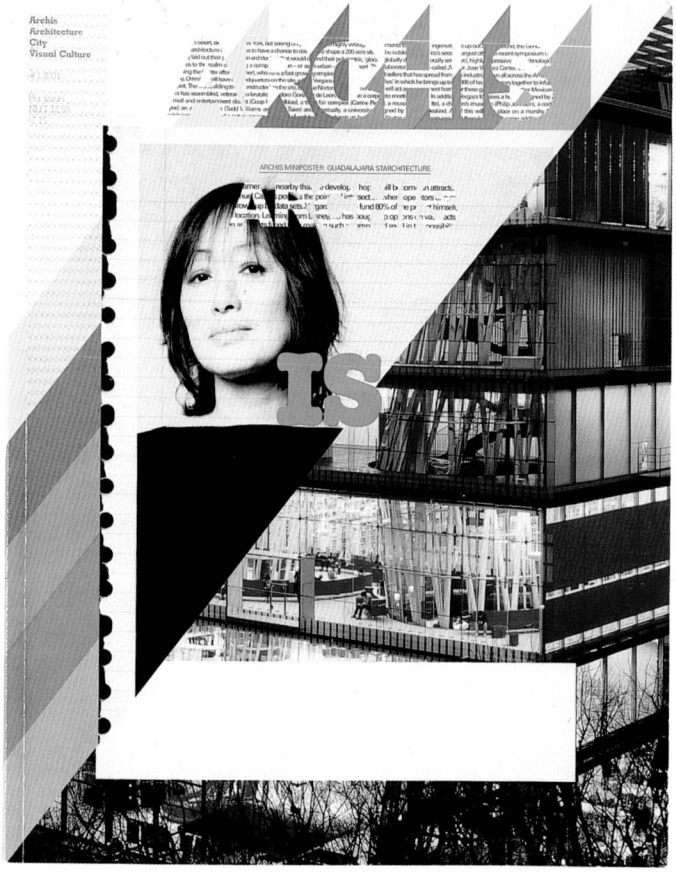

Issue 2, 2001

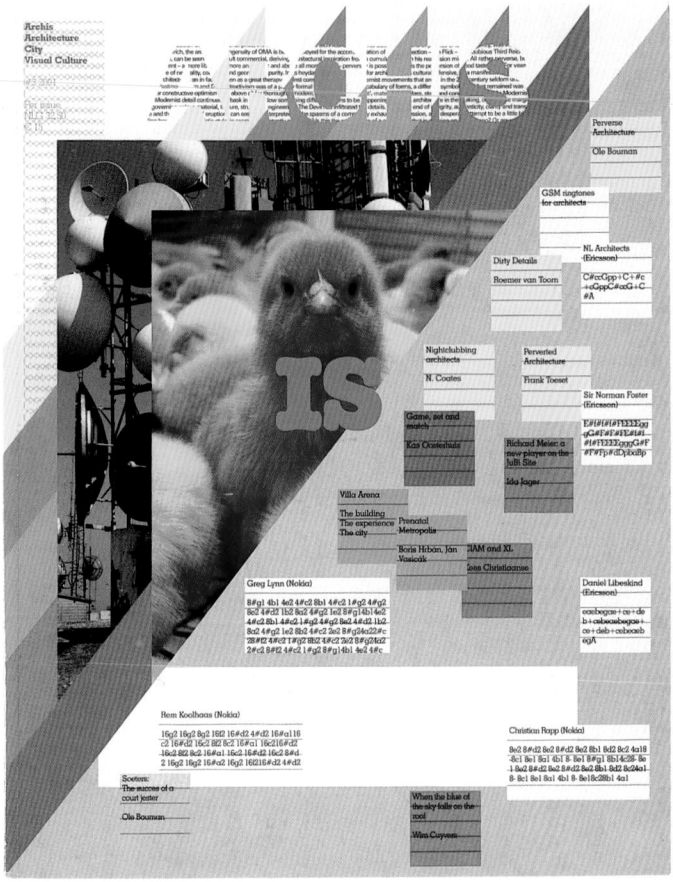

Issue 3, 2001

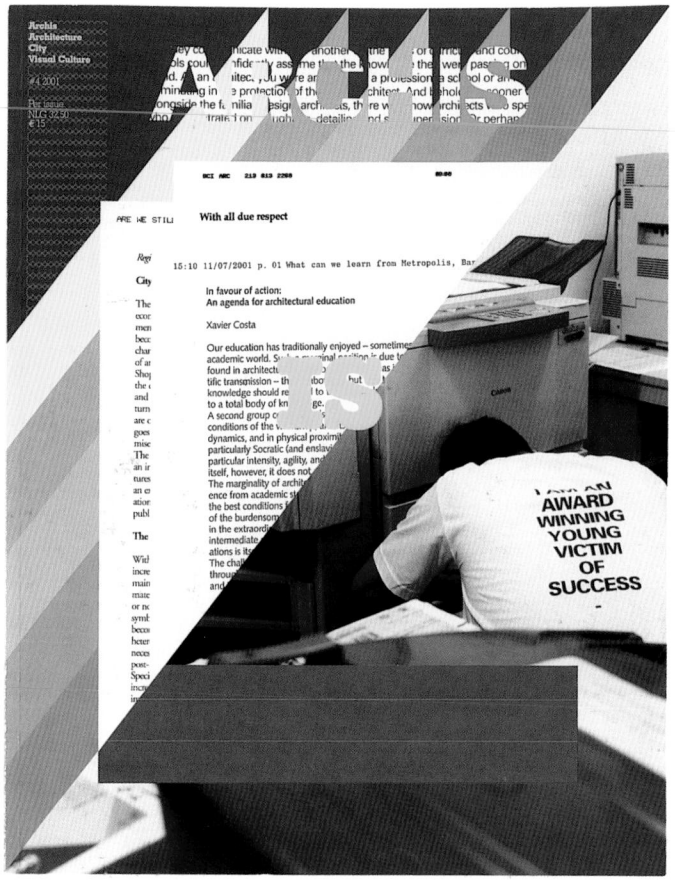

Issue 4, 2001

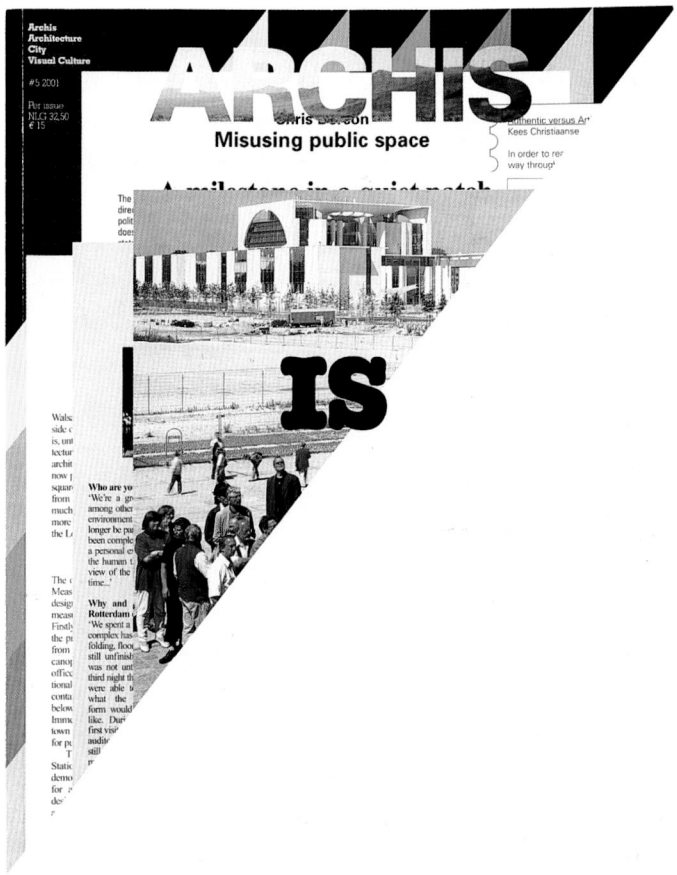

Issue 5, 2001

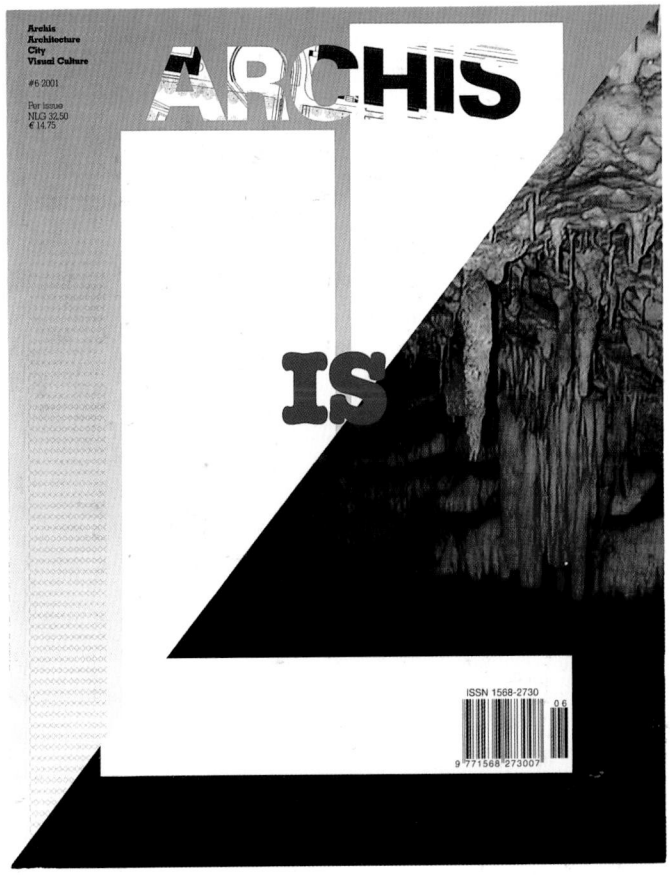

Issue 6, 2001

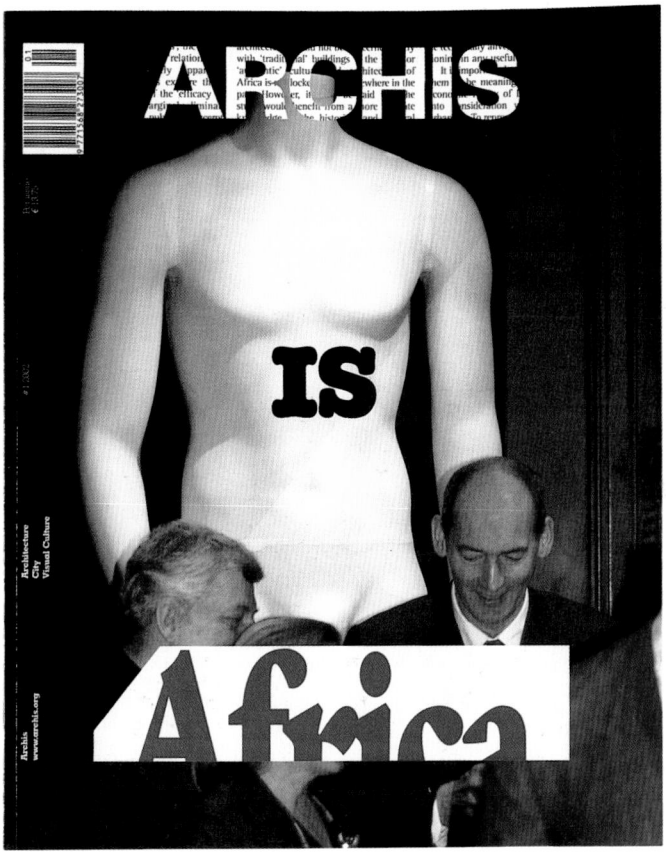

Issue 1, 2002

Archis *(The Netherlands) 230 x 275mm/9 x 10 7/8 inches*
This series of front covers ignores all the rules of cover design, instead relying on a strong visual identity featuring a multi-layered mix of samples from each issue's content – both text and image – and a pattern of stripes created from the colour codings used for sections inside; mundane colours inspired by office filing systems.
Art direction *Maureen Mooren and Daniel van der Velden*

AM7

AKADEMISCHE MITTEILUNGEN SIEBEN

EIN MONOTHEMATISCHES MAGAZIN
ZUM THEMA KOMMUNIKATION
ENTSTANDEN AN DER ADBK STUTTGART

AM7 SEITE [02] BIS [43]

INHALT AM7
EDITORIAL
AMSIEBENLOVESAG
DEUTSCHE FLUGSICHERUNG
TELEFON
SPACE INVADER
WWW.VECTORAMA.ORG
WAS SOLL ICH ANZIEHEN?

AM7 SEITE [44] BIS [99]

THE SUN YEARS
FARBEN IN EUROPA
TRANSIT GRAFIK
MAIL ART
FILE EXCHANGE
DIE LETZTE SMS
SINUTYPE™
DANK UND IMPRESSUM

PRINTED IN EUROPE

WWW.AMSIEBEN.COM

07>

2 112000 102001

K1/K2/K4

STENCIL [ACAMONCHI]
POSTER [THE SUN YEARS]
STICKER [TRANSIT GRAFIK]

K5 UND K3

TRANSFER [FILE EXCHANGE]

ESB/NYC [FARBEN IN NYC]

GENERAL NOTICE

FOR ADDITIONAL INFORMATION
PLEASE VISIT OUR URL
WWWDOTAMSIEBENDOTCOM

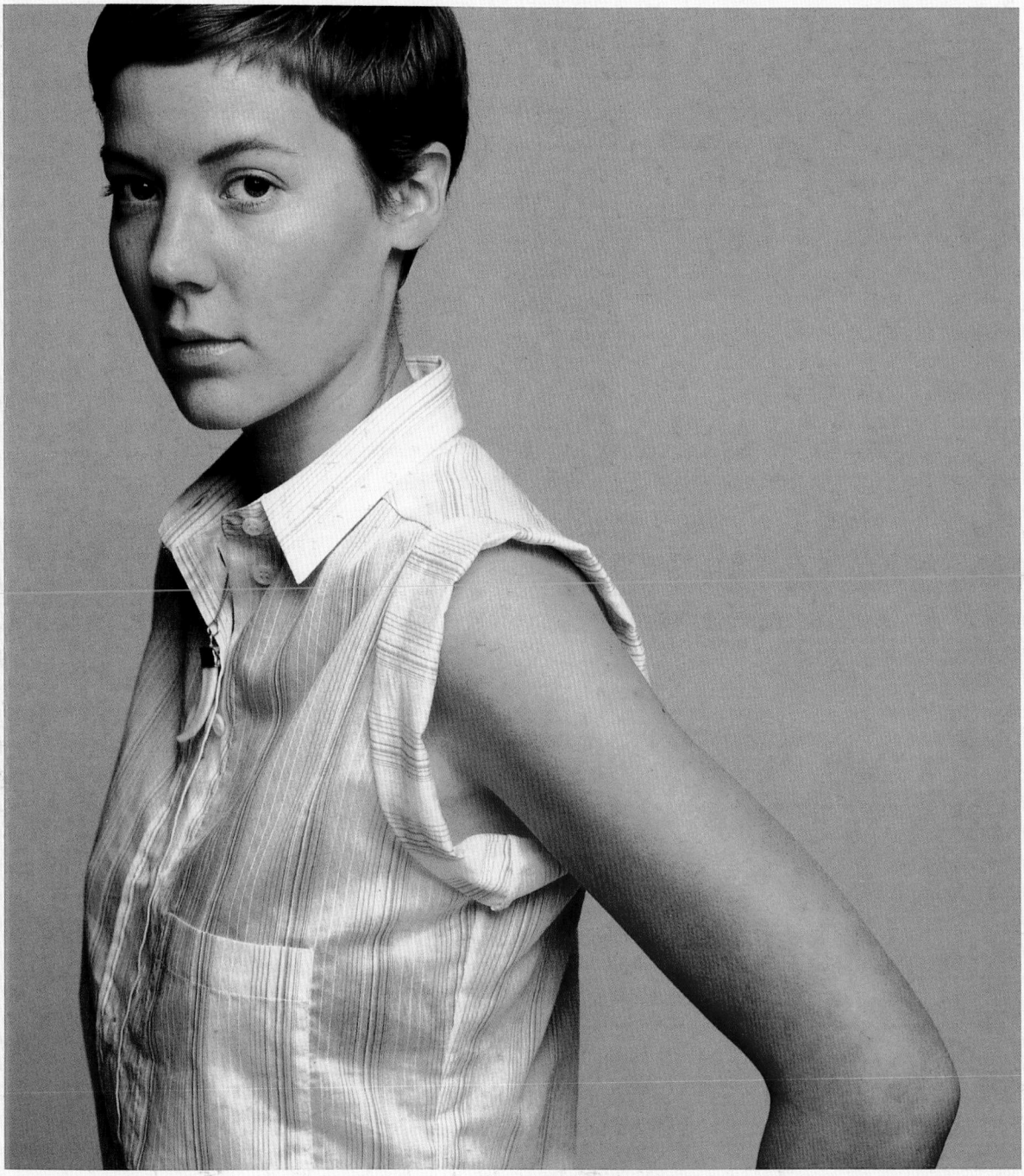

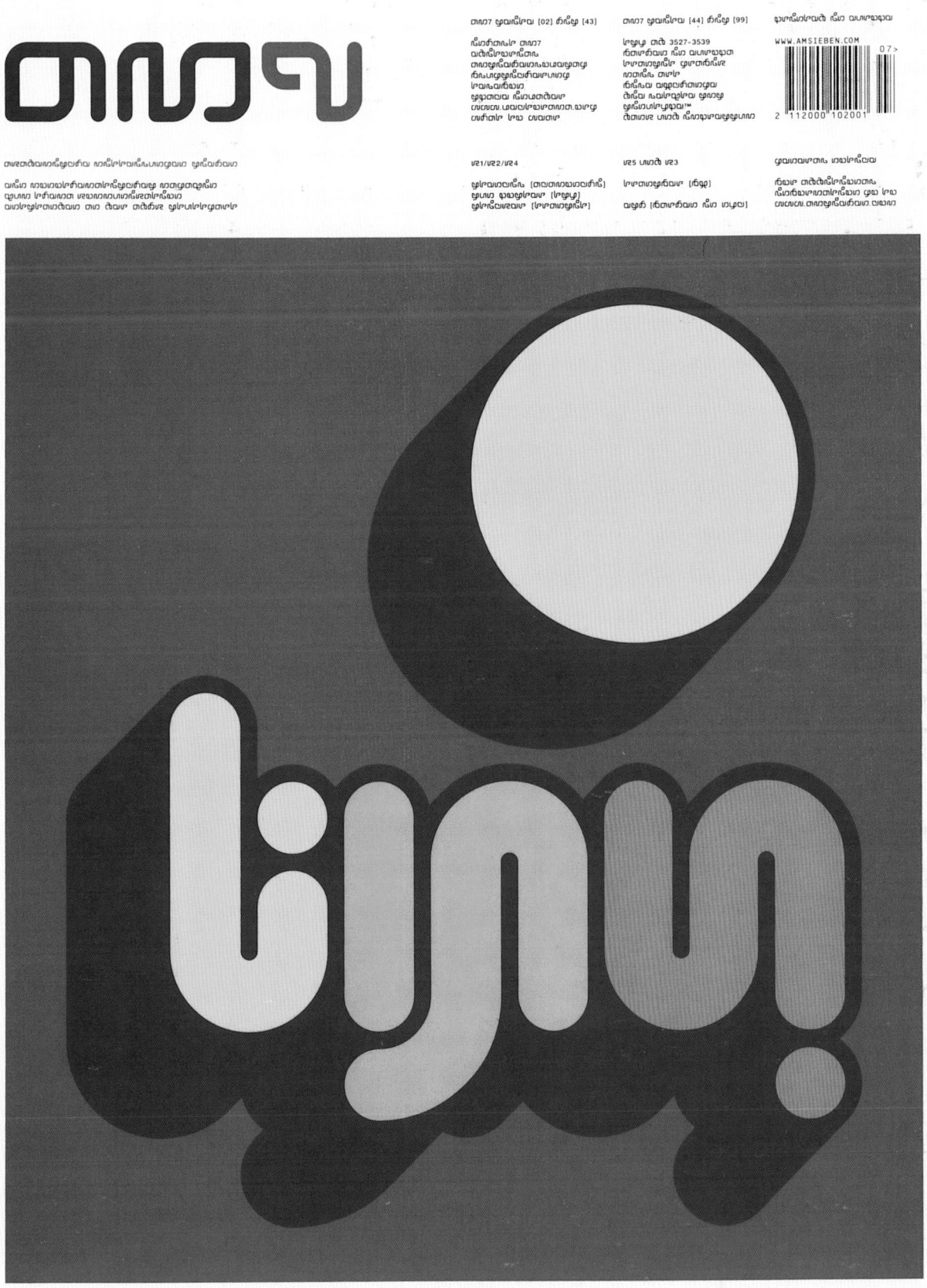

AM7 (*Germany, Issue 1, Summer 2002*) *230 x 290mm/9 x 11 ½ inches*
A choice of covers: the front cover (OPPOSITE) and back cover (THIS PAGE) of this magazine about communication give very different levels of legibility.
Design *Daniel Fritz and Maik Stapleberg*

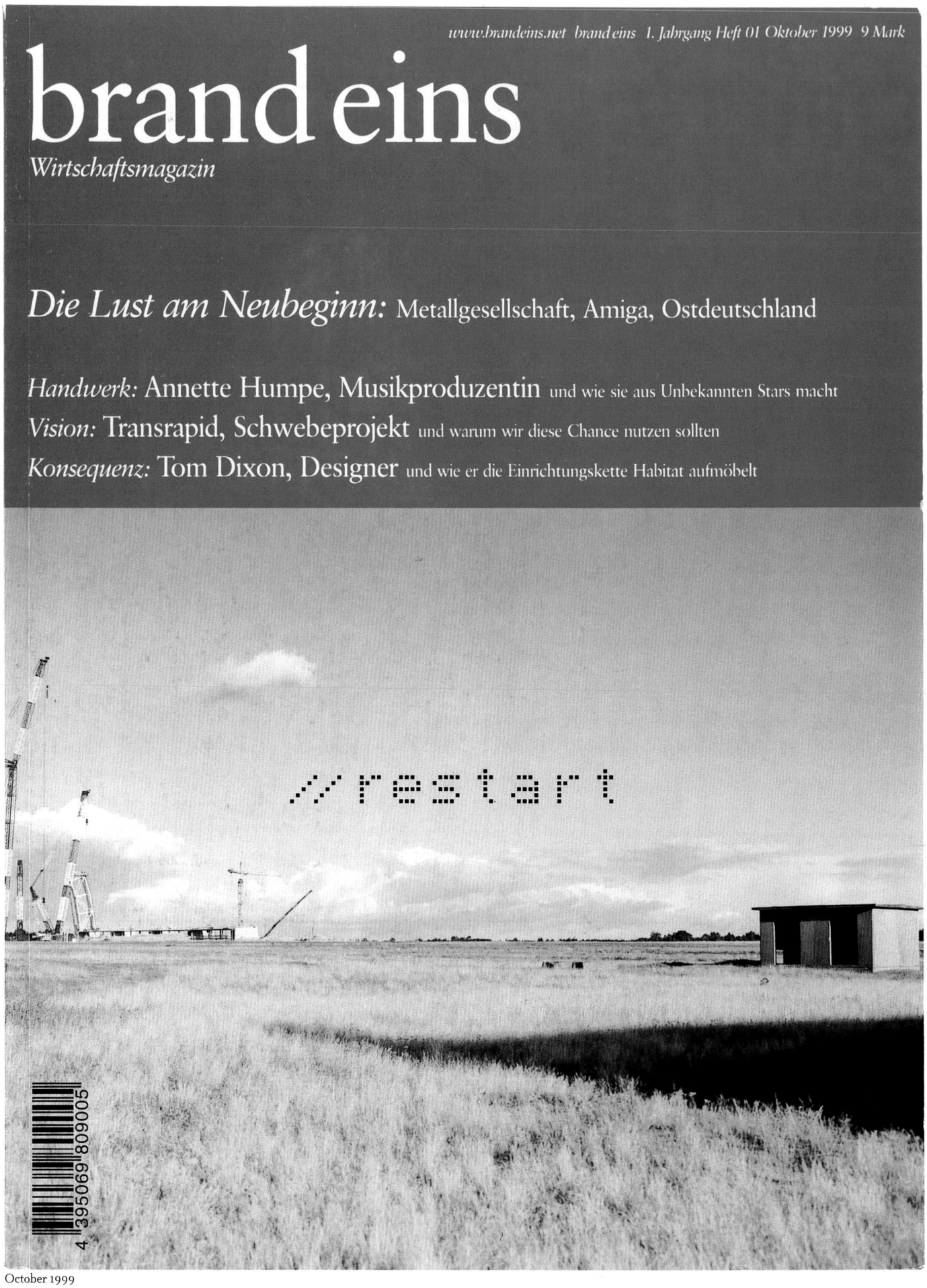

October 1999

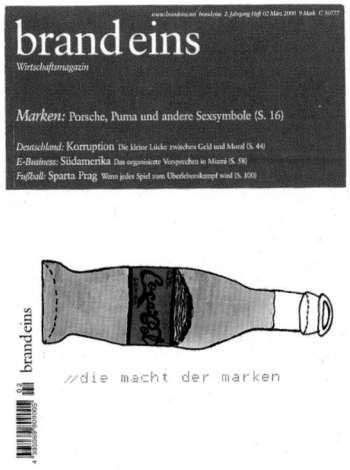

March 2000

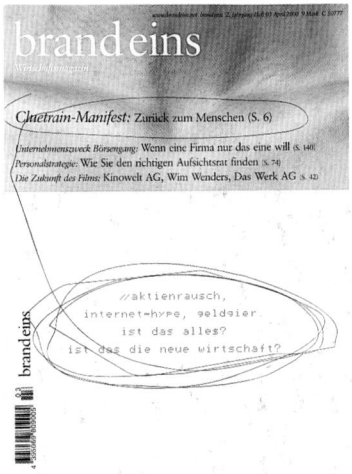

April 2000

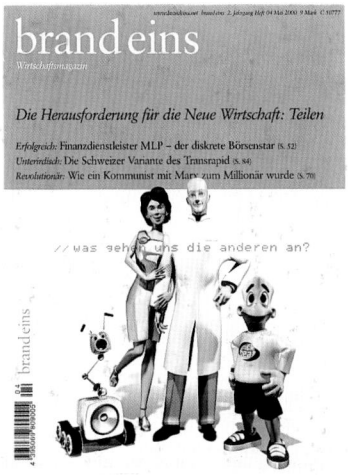

May 2000

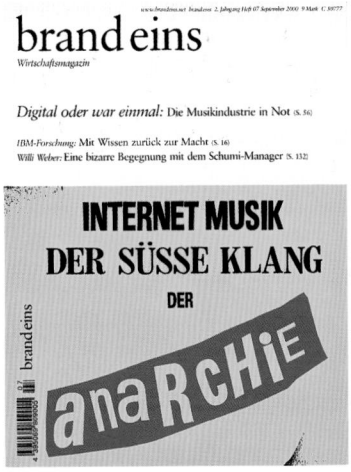

September 2000

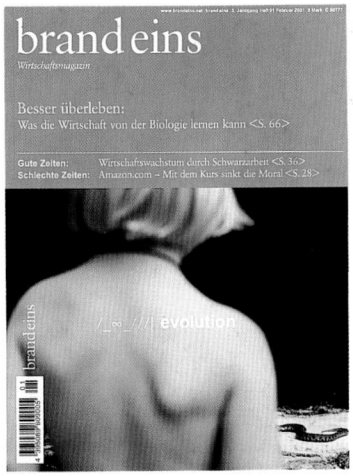

February 2001

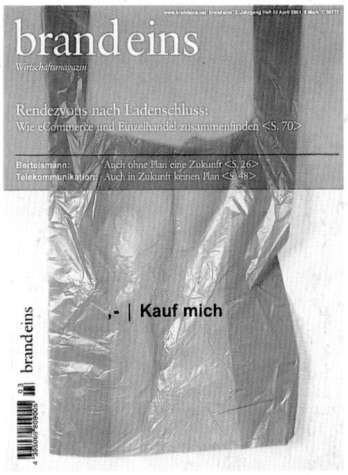

April 2001

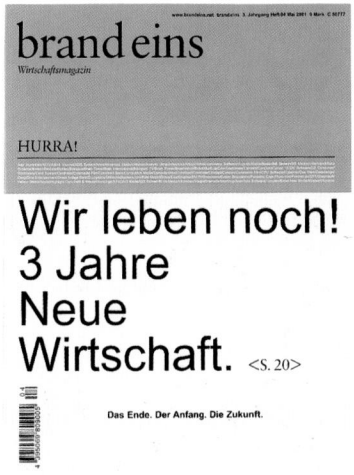

May 2001

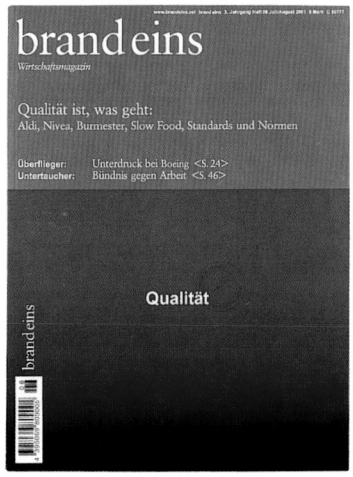

July/August 2001

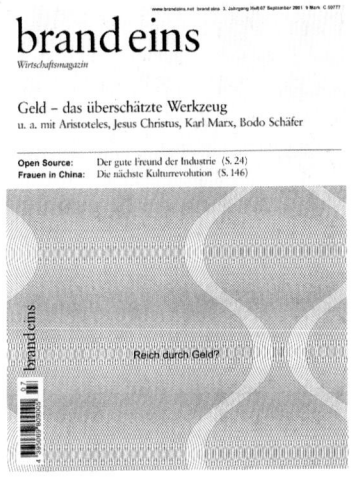

September 2001

Brand Eins *(Germany) 210 x 280mm/8 ¼ x 11 inches*
Despite working to a tightly formatted design, these covers display a variety of solutions to potentially dull business subjects. Typography, photography, illustration and colour are all used to vary the end result.
Art director *Mike Meiré*

[100分で日本の深層を読む!]
the info-ninja magazine [才蔵]
http://www.ultracyzo.com/
定価690円

人気ギョーカイ最前線　転職・就職もこれでバッチリ!

サイゾー

5分で"ムネオ騒動"のすべてがわかる
鈴木宗男と愉快な仲間たち
永久保存版・宗男スキャンダル大全

ペルー公邸人質事件・5年目の真実
告発! ムネオハウスだけではない 新たなるODA疑惑があった
フジモリ元大統領をかくまう小泉政権の闇

イームズ大ブームの「インテリア業界」を大解剖
声に出して読みたくない「イヤミなギョーカイ用語」
ジャニーズ・ドラマとそごう倒産の奇妙な一致
仰天!「裏原宿ファッション」のソックリ商品ビジネス

[人気連載]
爆笑問題「日本原論」
宮台真司×宮崎哲弥「M2 われらの時代に」
決死の北朝鮮潜入ルポ

april 2002 4

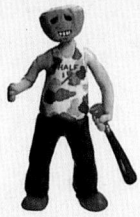
ファッション業界
「裏原、まだまだオイシイぜ」

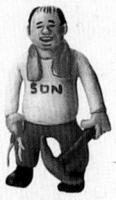
IT業界
「今度はコレやります」

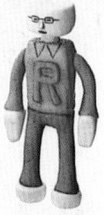
マンガ業界
「へのつっぱりはいらんですよ」

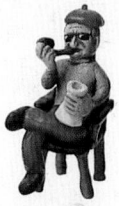
映画業界
「なんで「アメリ」が!」

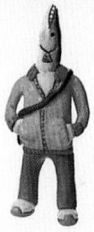
中目黒業界
「業界人で大賑わいナリ」

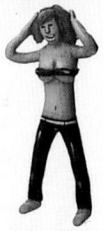
カフェ業界
「古いよ、もう」

あなたの業界は あと2年もちますか?

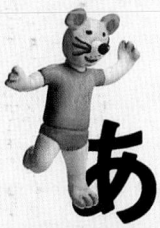
おもちゃ業界
「一寸先は闇でチュー」

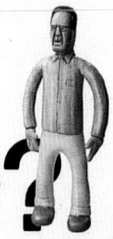
インテリア業界
「コレいい感じじゃない♥」

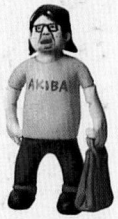
出版業界
「ワァオ、西和彦だぁ」

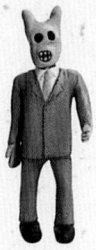
永田町業界
「マキコがいぬ間に……」

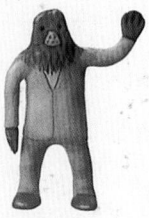
流通業界
「悪い癖には慣れました」

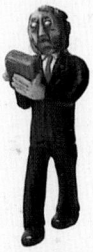
金融業界
「こっちがカネ借りたいよ」

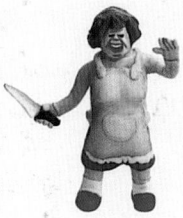
料理業界
「薬原はるみになるワ」

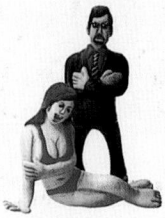
芸能界
「ワシが有名にしたる」

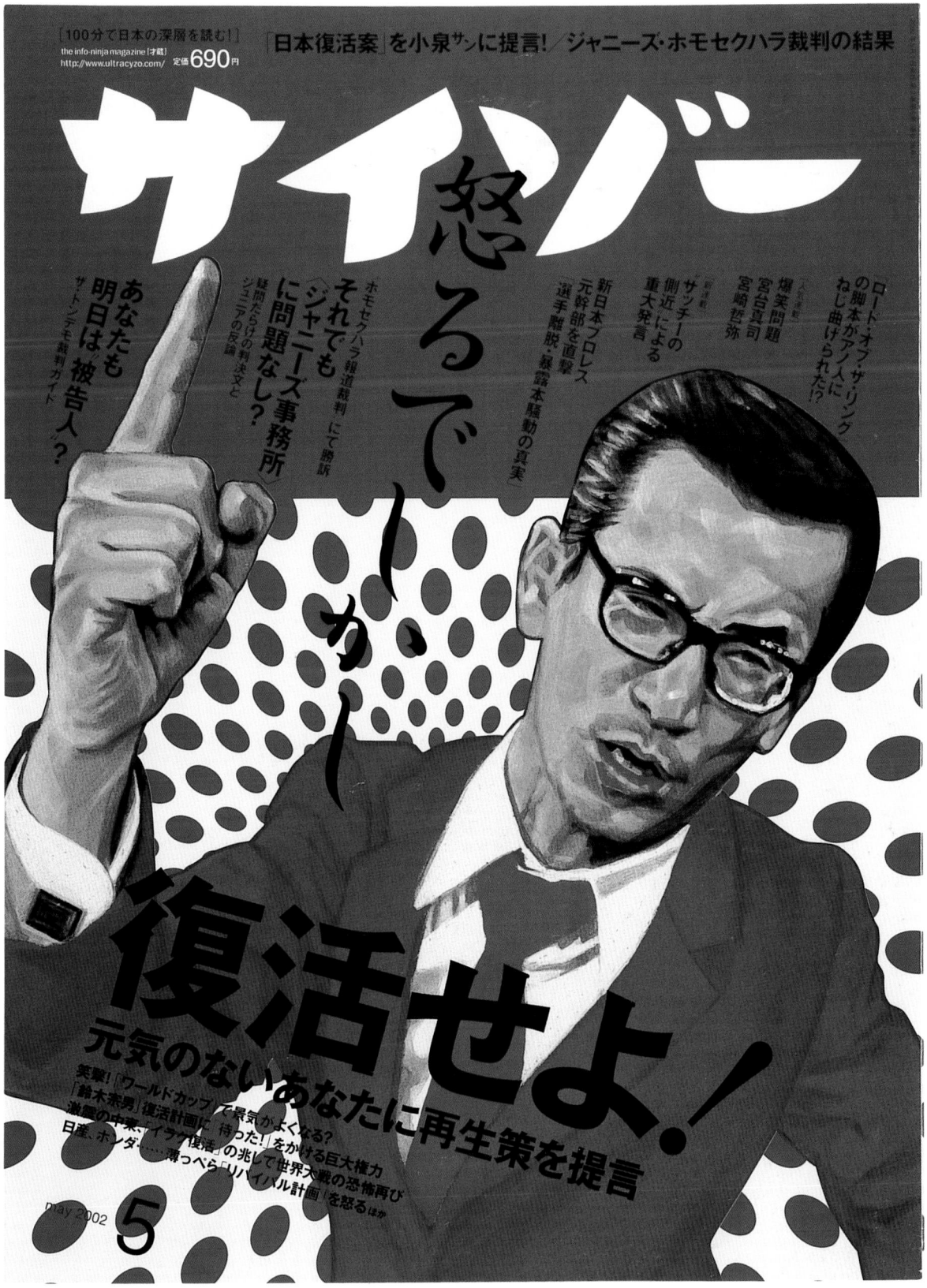

Cyzo *(Japan) 210 x 283mm/8 1/4 x 11 1/4 inches*
Started as an alternative to the Japanese edition of *Wired*, this 'info-ninja' magazine acts as a controversy-attracting critique of the Japanese economy, and in particular of its new technology sector. Its covers feature a mix of western and Japanese influences: the bold red-and-white logo reflects the very direct approach of western magazine mastheads, while the pictorial catalogue (OPPOSITE) and the cut-out image on a graphic background (THIS PAGE) are typically Japanese in their approach.
Art director *Kobahen*

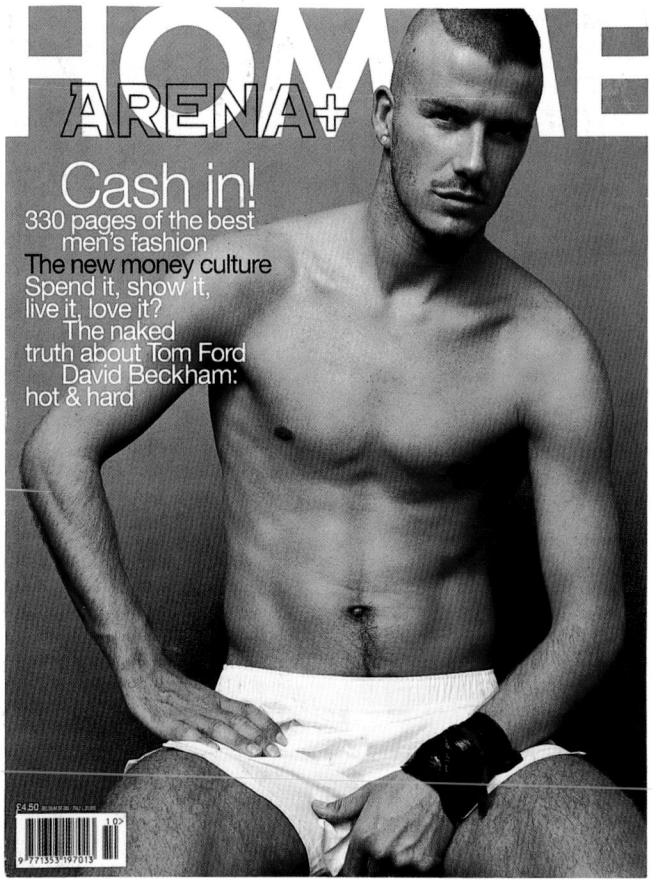

Issue 14, Autumn/Winter 2000/01

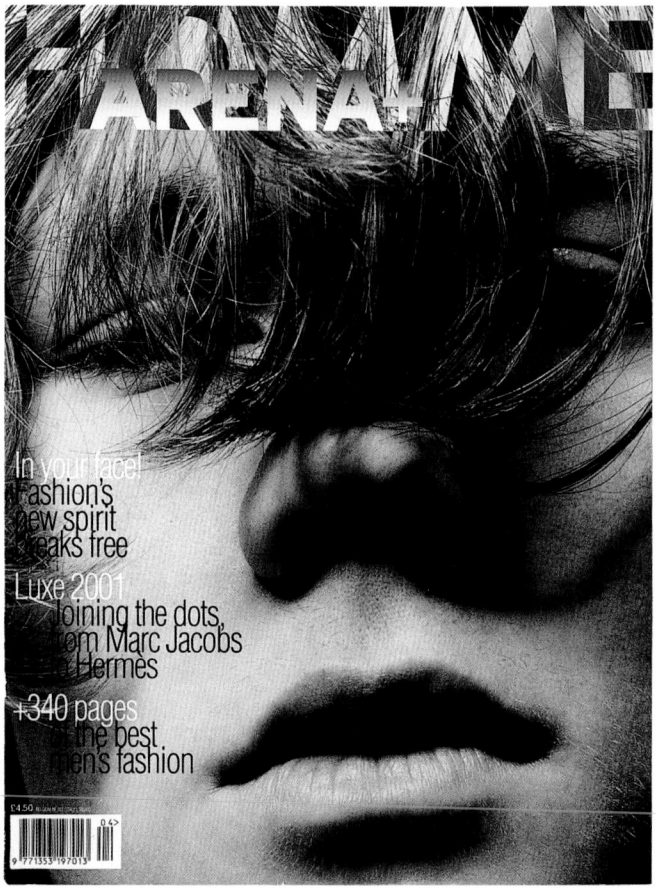

Issue 15, Spring/Summer 2001

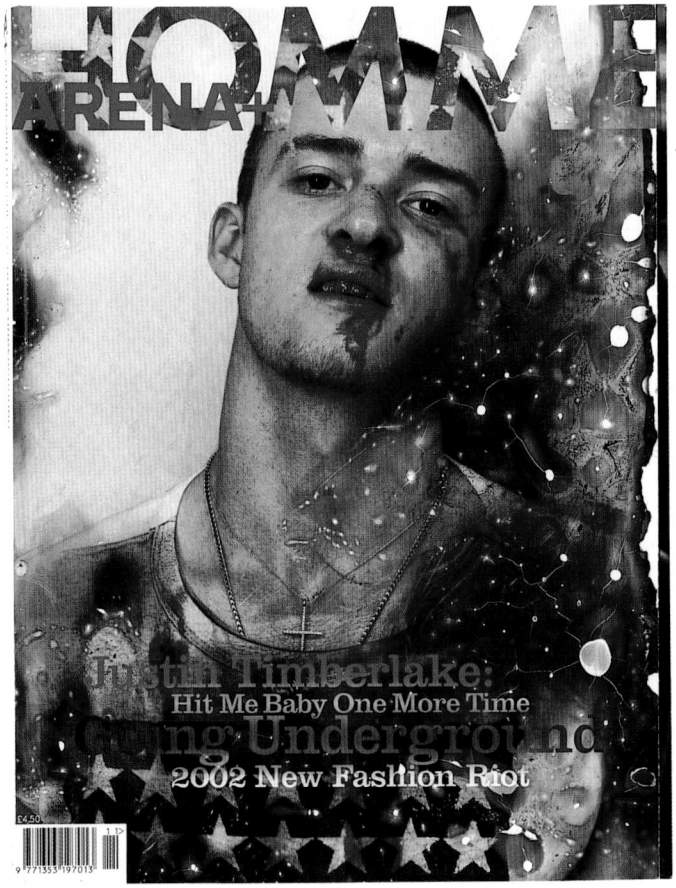

Issue 16, Autumn/Winter 2001/02

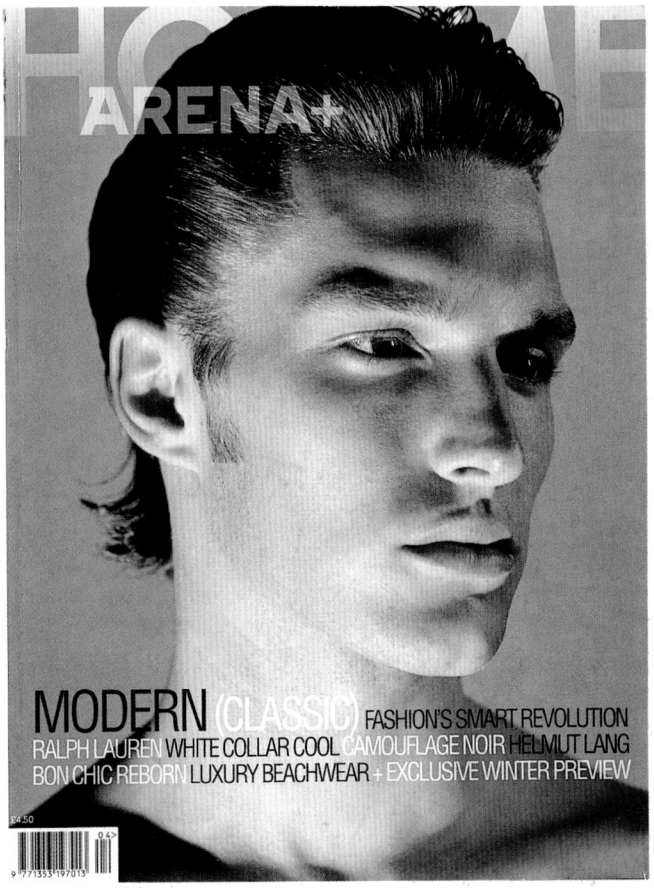

Issue 17, Spring/Summer 2002

Arena Homme Plus *(UK)*
230 x 300mm/9 x 11 7/8 inches
The magazine logo and cover image blur together. On issue 14 (OPPOSITE, LEFT) the logo is clearly visible; by issue 17 it has almost disappeared. Despite this, the strength of the photography and styling mean the covers maintain their identity. Art direction *Joseph Logan and Tim McIntyre (Baron & Baron)*

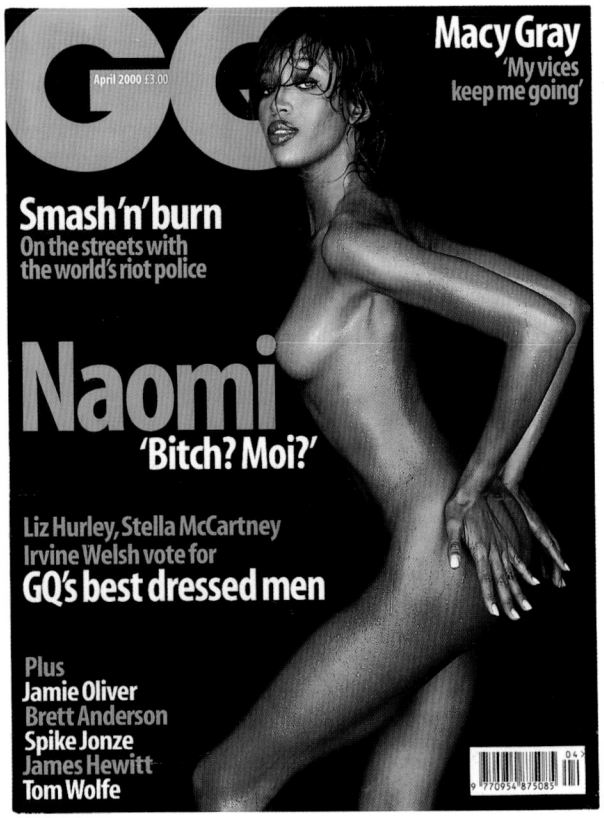

April 2000

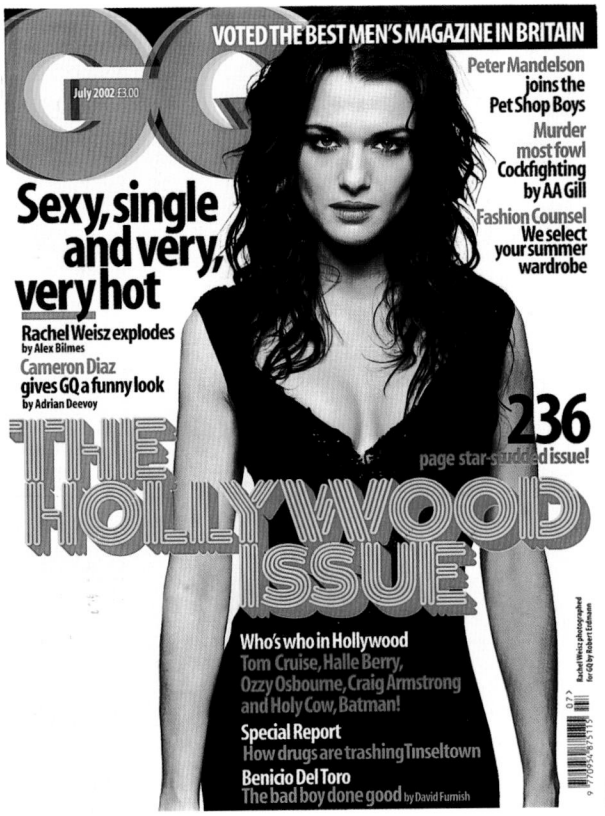

July 2001

gone back to our core values to make sure we don't lose the advertising. Before that we had gone a bit more mad [he points to the Pamela Anderson cover], which I liked but I know a lot of people hated. They didn't get the irony. Pammy is mental – she's the most extraordinary, pop-culture, sexual being. We did our best, using playful lettering and stuff. It's fun. But some people didn't get that and some advertisers couldn't see the difference between that and a *Loaded* cover with a badly photographed Jo Guest. I've always thought that with the branding of *GQ* and Condé Nast behind us we could get away with more, like when *Vogue* put the Spice Girls on their cover. Maybe that's just wishful thinking. But now we've gone a bit more upmarket again.

There are still women in bikinis though...

'Libido' is the word the editor always uses. That's what British *Esquire* has lost. I admire their attempt to rise above it (featuring only men on their covers), and I'd rather put men on our covers, or at least half men to women. It's easier to cover men. It's hard showing sexy – the Pamela cover was easy because she can be sexy – but so many of the other cover stars don't want to appear sexy, only to promote a movie.

But it's a difficult balance to get right and I think we've gone too far sometimes. What happened with the Pamela cover was that a competitor, *Esquire*, went into full PR mode, attacking our cover to the advertisers. I believe that cover was good – if you're going to do a girl in a bikini then do it properly; it's far more honest. But if the opposition are going to the fashion advertisers in Milan and saying drop *GQ*, advertise with us instead, we have to respond. We're British, we've got a bit of tongue-in-cheek but the head of Armani won't necessarily understand that. He'll say 'I don't want my ad in that...'. You want to push it a bit, have a bit of personality but in the mass market it's difficult.

The Chairman of Condé Nast, Jonathan Newhouse, described *GQ* as a magician's act. You've got to communicate one thing to the reader – that it's a great read with lots of football, girls and booze. And you've got to tell a completely different thing to the advertisers – that we hang out with Richard James and Oliver Peyton and we wear Cartier watches. We have to produce a magazine that does both. I'm lucky in that it's the look that is talking to Richard James and Cartier. It's the content that has to provide the football and girls. Even when we were flirting with being more populist, the look was the thing – the content could push the taste barriers but the look was upmarket because Gucci, Prada and Armani wanted that.

It's interesting, we're not talking much about design.

It's all relevant though. As a magazine designer you have to have empathy with the editor, publisher and advertising sales teams. You can't let them think you're just some aesthete who wants to use pink for the sake of it. That's rubbish, and you'll be told to do it red or run along.

Any art director is only as good as the editor and publisher. I have been very fortunate, the three editors I have had at *GQ* have all been very different but they've all had the correct relationship with me as art director; they've trusted me to do my side of the job. I'll always argue for what I think is right and that instils confidence.

On many magazines there isn't that good relationship and it shows, where the editor puts too much pressure on them about how they see the magazine should evolve. That's become more common in the past ten years. It's bred a generation of art directors who are really good designers possibly but they're not having the input and the overview that they should. No magazine can be successful under those circumstances.

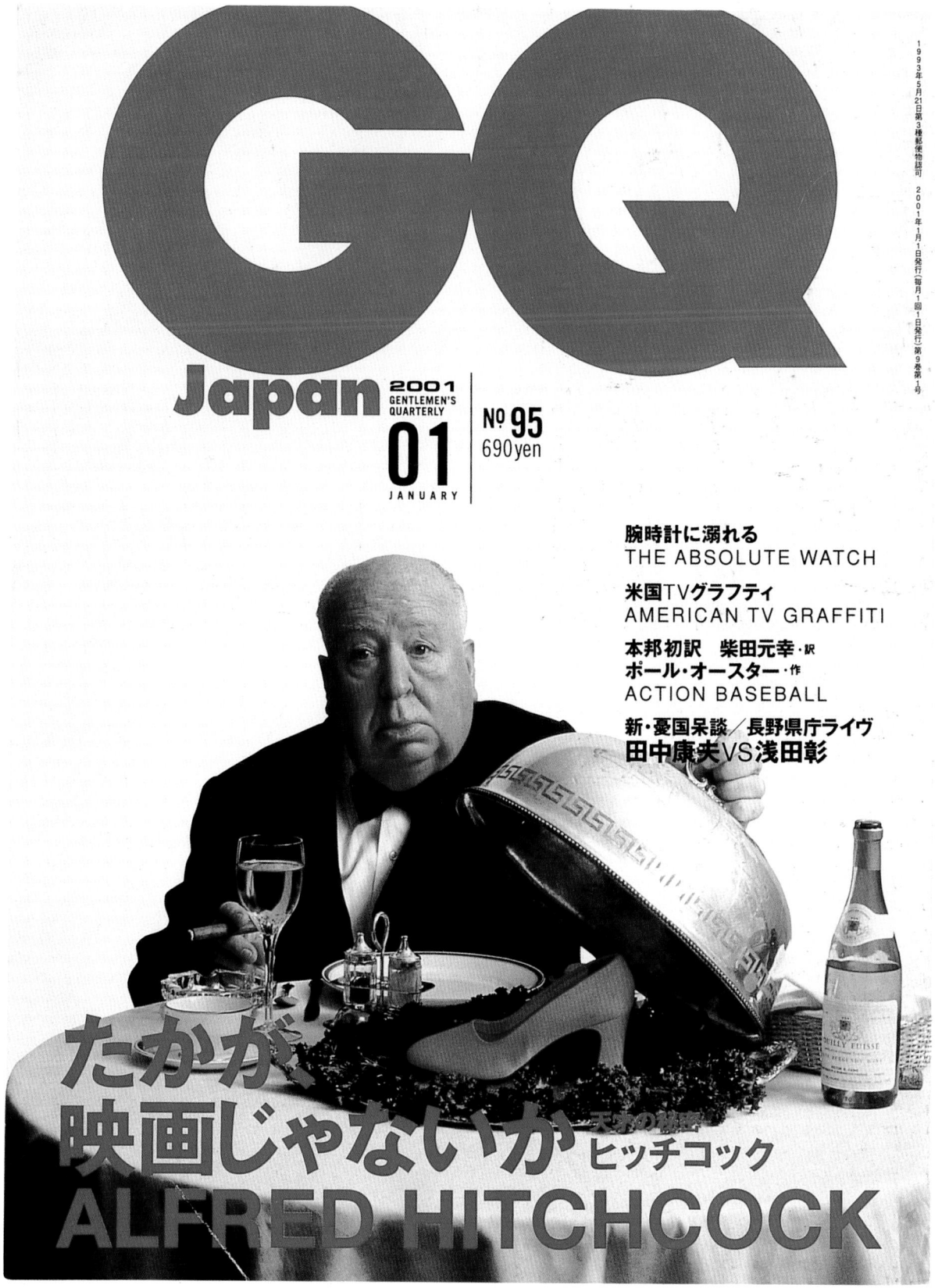

GQ *(Japan, Issue 95, January 2001) 207 x 275mm/8 1/8 x 10 7/8 inches*
Aside from the immediate difference in the way the *GQ* logo is used, a different market means a different approach to the content of covers. In Japan *GQ* uses its western roots to sell itself, featuring icons such as Marilyn Monroe, Andy Warhol, The Beatles and Alfred Hitchcock.
Art directors *Shoukon Paik and Takahito Noguchi*

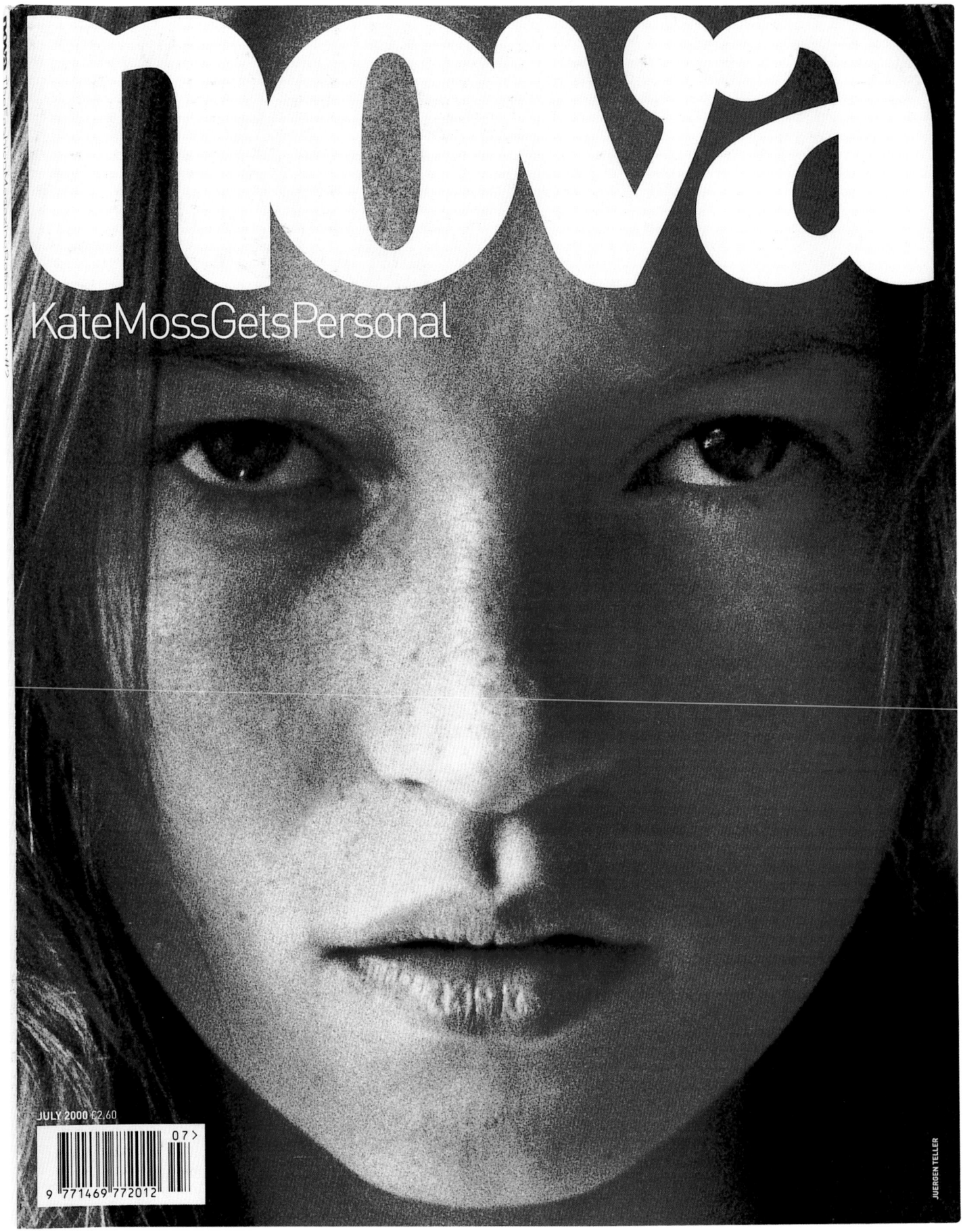
nova
KateMossGetsPersonal
JULY 2000 £2.60
07>
9 771469 772012
JUERGEN TELLER

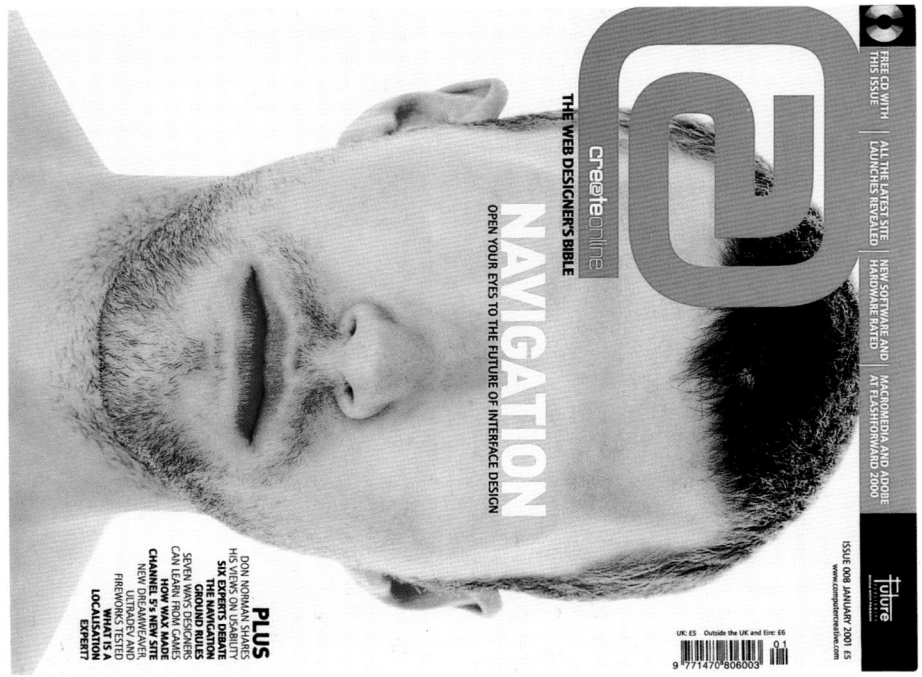

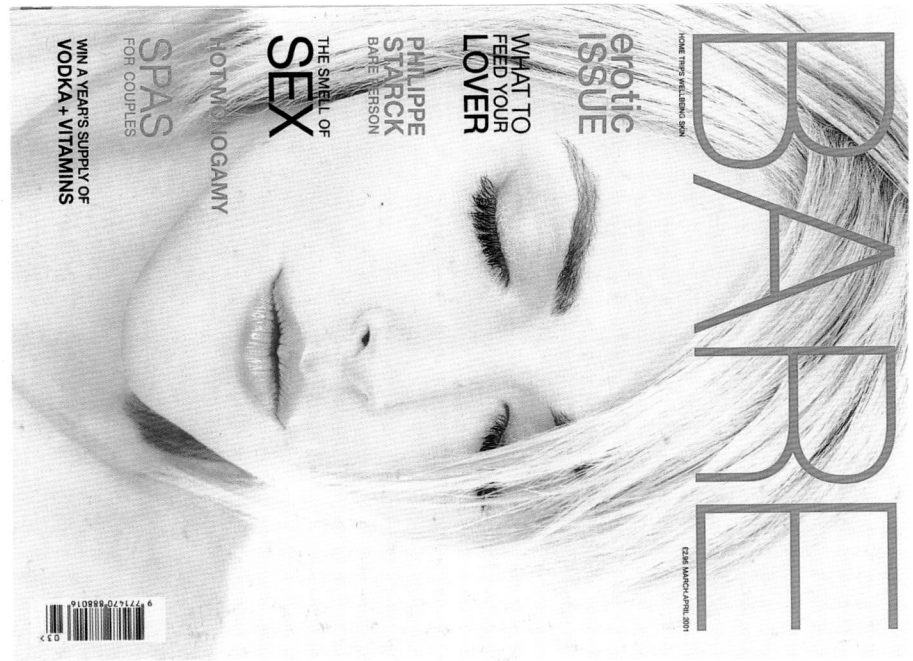

OPPOSITE **Nova** *(UK, Issue 2, July 2000)*
230 x 284mm/9 x 11 1/8 inches
Eye contact on covers is regarded as essential to attract readers. This example takes full advantage of Kate Moss's celebrity status, her larger-than-life face staring out at the reader.
Art director *Gerard Saint*

THIS PAGE **Cre@te** *(UK, Issue 8, January 2001)*
210 x 280mm/8 1/4 x 11 inches
Here, Photoshopping out the eyes creates a disturbingly engaging image.
Art director *Paul Kurzeja*

Bare *(UK, Issue 4, March/April 2001)*
230 x 300mm/9 x 11 7/8 inches
Sophie Dahl's closed eyes exude relaxation and calm.
Art director *Kirsten Willey*

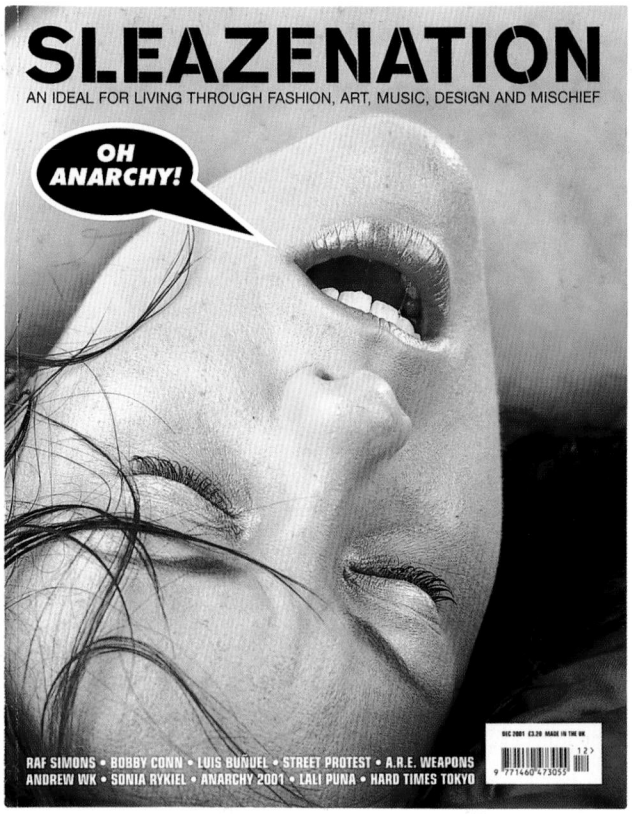

February 2001

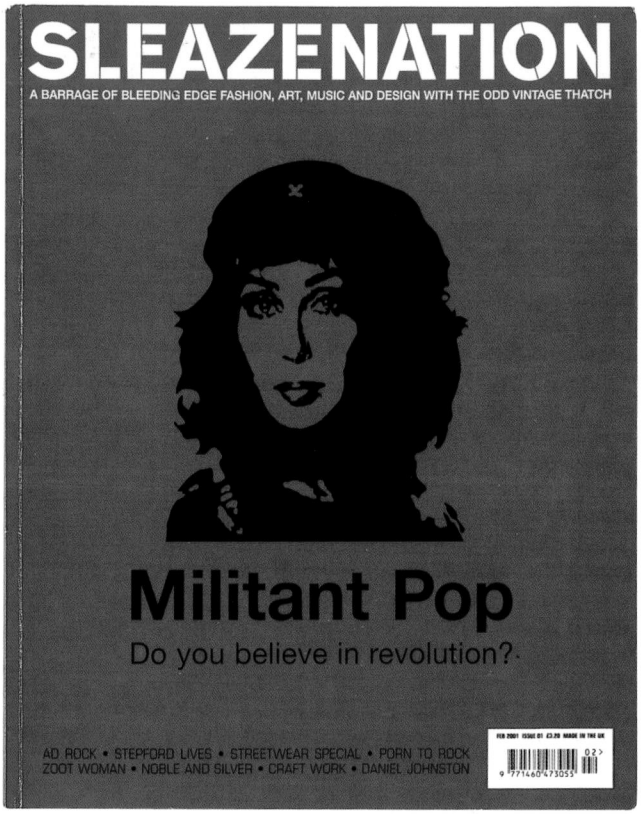

November 2001

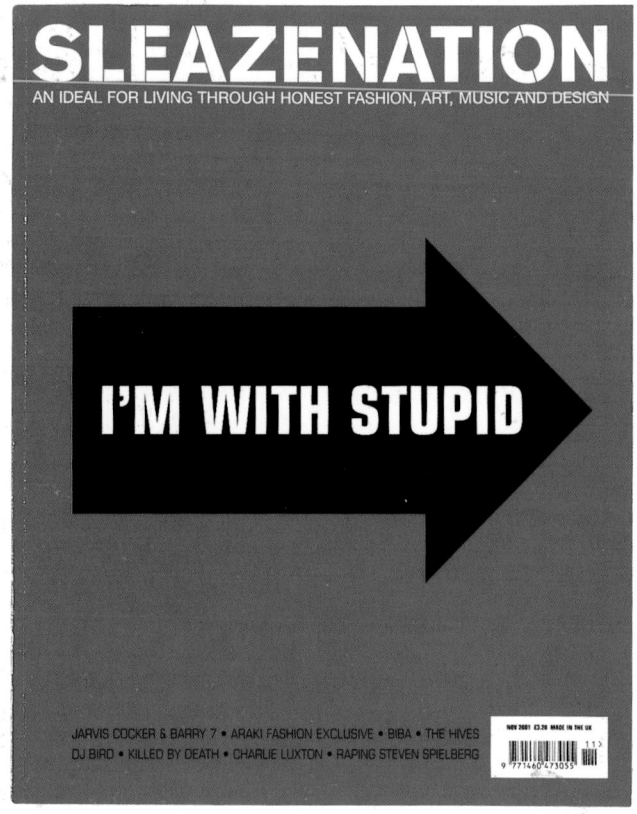

December 2001

SleazeNation *(UK) 230 x 285mm/9 x 11 1/4 inches*
Experimenting with very direct single messages on its front cover, this style magazine's approach ranges from the subtle mimickry of 'Militant Pop' to the in-your-face directness (stupidity?) of 'I'm With Stupid', itself mimicking a t-shirt slogan. The two photographic examples are subtler but still very direct. 'Oh Anarchy!' uses an ironic combination of picture and text that illustrates a feature inside the issue, which asks why anarchy is sexy. The cover opposite pushes irony a step further, taking the standard components of a glossy cover – pouting model, screaming headline and fluorescent fifth colour – and subverting them through the wording of the headline.
Creative director *Scott King*

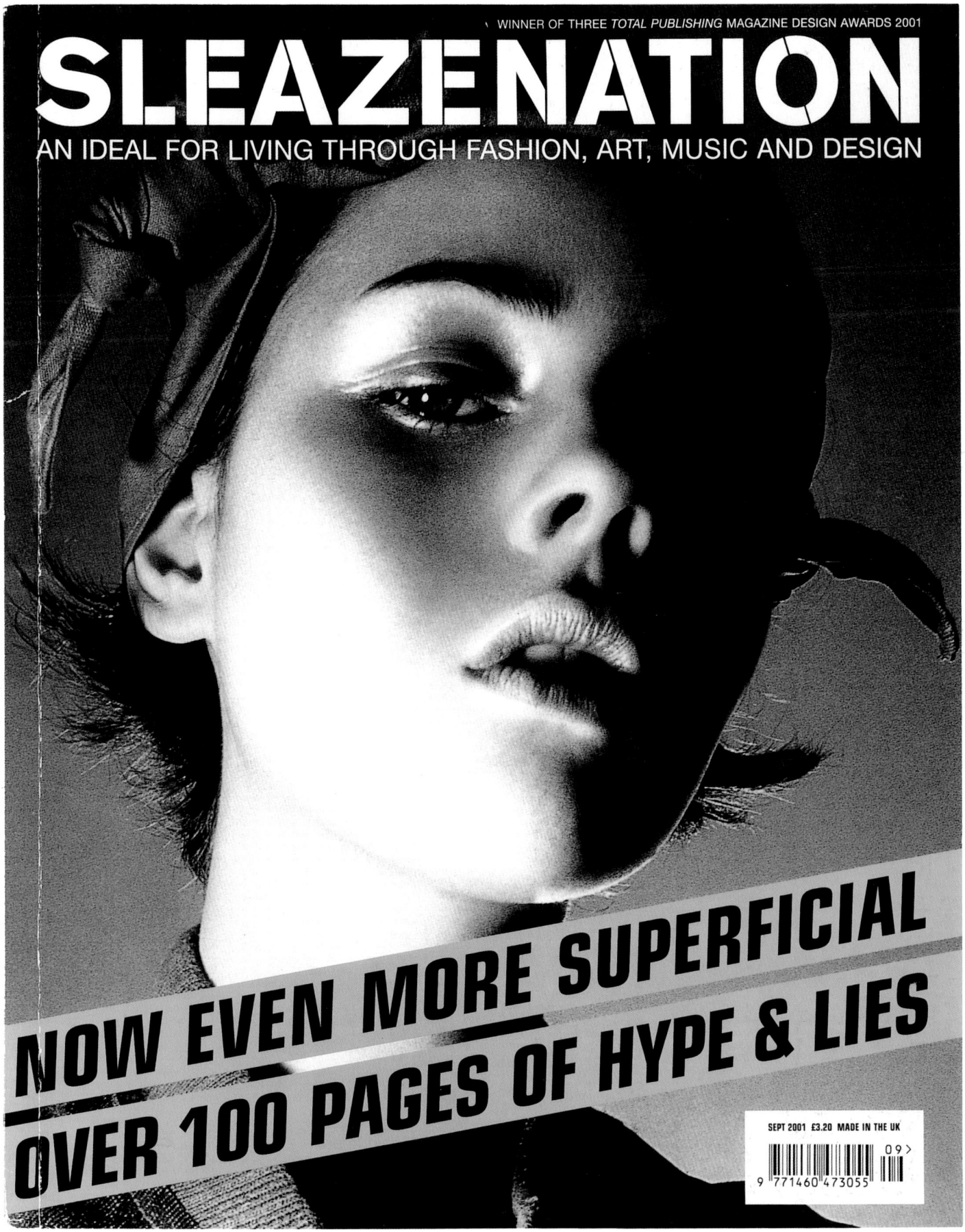

September 2001

THIS PAGE **Eat** *(Japan, Issue 11, September 2002)*
230 x 297mm/9 x 11 3/4 inches
The subject of fast food is announced by a large removable sticker that mimics the lid of a pot noodle container, which when peeled off reveals a photograph of the noodles inside the pot.
Art director *Tin Brown*

OPPOSITE **Time Out** *(UK, Issue 1595, March 14–21 2001)*
215 x 300mm/8 1/2 x 11 7/8 inches
At first glance, it looks like the butcher's knife has cut some fresh, bloody meat: a closer look reveals it has cut some tomatoes; a visual trick that neatly introduces the subject of vegetarianism while not excluding carnivores.
Art director *Balwant Ahira*

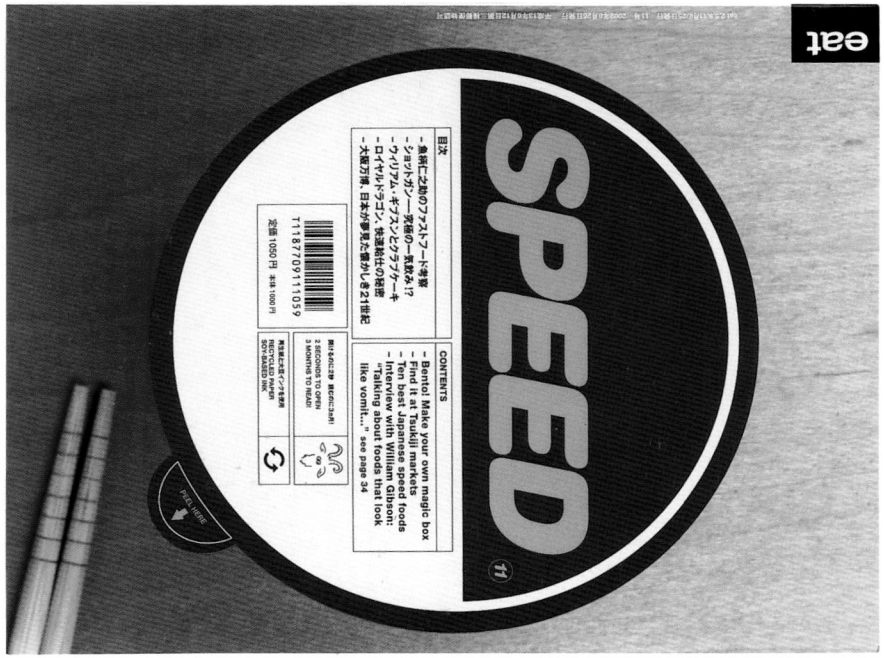

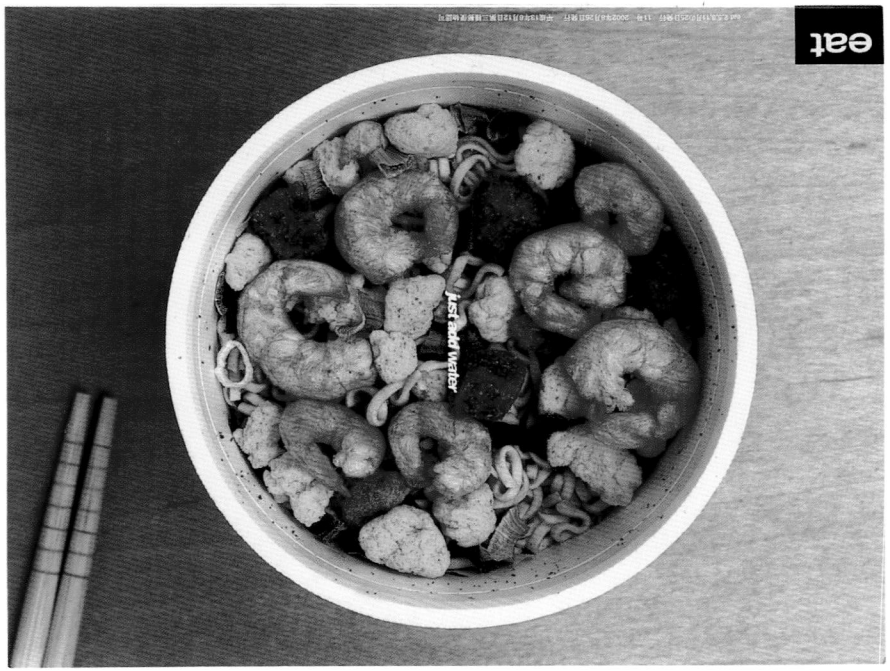

Time Out

London's living guide
March 14-21 2001 No.1595 £2.20

TIM BUCKLEY
FUN LOVIN' CRIMINALS
LAURA LINNEY
THE PRISONER
CITIBANK PHOTO PRIZE
36-PAGE TV SECTION

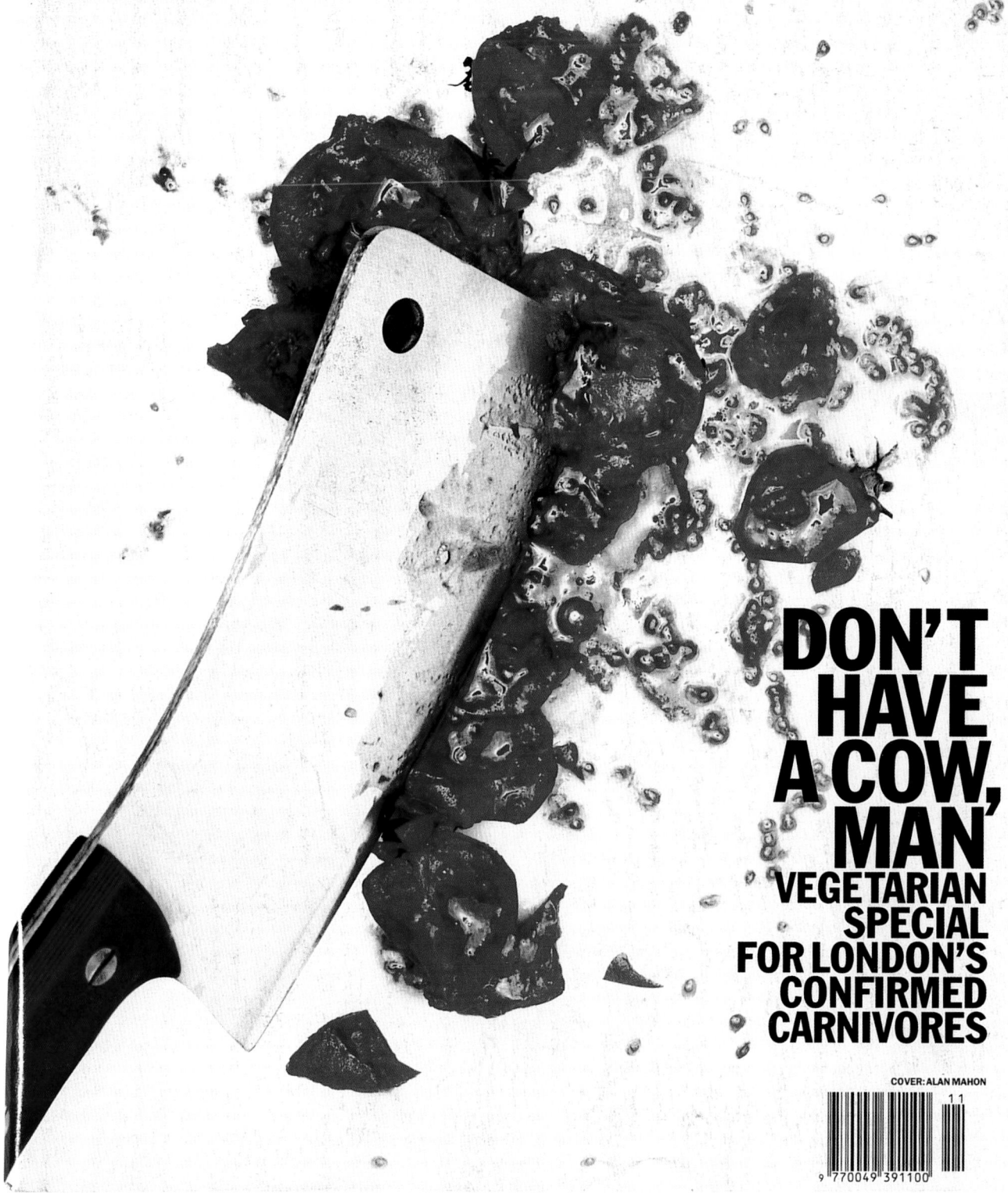

DON'T HAVE A COW, MAN

VEGETARIAN SPECIAL FOR LONDON'S CONFIRMED CARNIVORES

COVER: ALAN MAHON

11
9 770049 391100

THIS PAGE **Hot Air** *(UK, Issue 75, October–December 2001) 228 x 300mm/9 x 11 7/8 inches*
The illustration commissioned for this cover is used to describe the theme of the issue – Happiness – rather than any specfic story inside.
Art director *Warren Jackson* Illustration *James Jarvis*

Relax *(Japan, April 2002) 210 x 297mm/8 1/4 x 11 3/4 inches*
Same illustrator, different message. This time the work featured relates to a review in the magazine of a book of the illustrator's work.
Art direction *NANA* Illustration *James Jarvis*

OPPOSITE **M-real** *(International, Issue 4, November 2001) 280 x 2800mm/11 x 110 1/4 inches*
The cover of this magazine with no name (it is published on behalf of a Finnish paper company and aimed at magazine creatives) changes to reflect the theme of the issue, in this case, 'Response'. This illustration relates to a piece in the magazine about the ideal components for a succesful magazine cover.
Art director *Jeremy Leslie* Illustration *Austin @ New Studio*

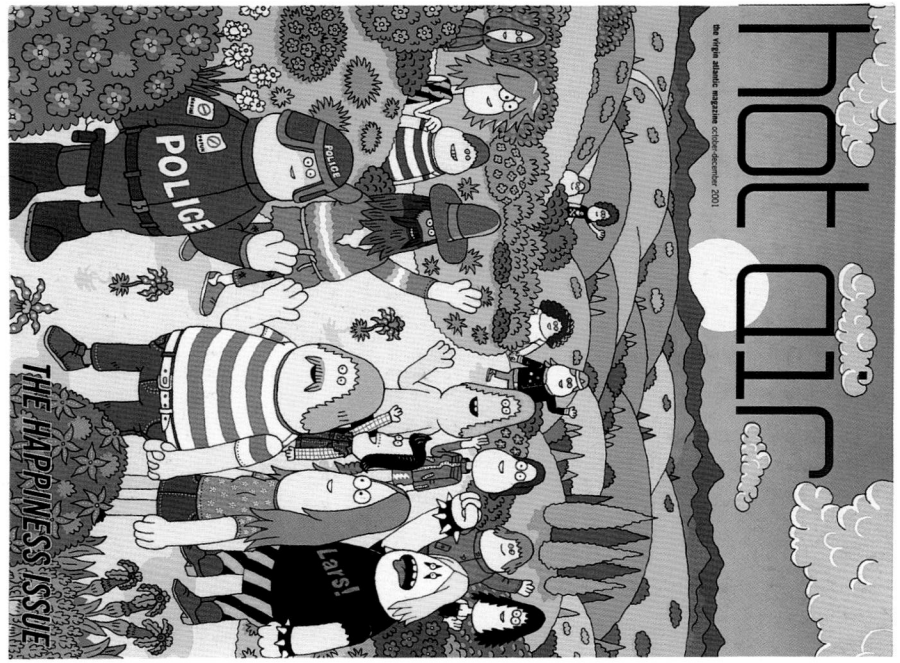

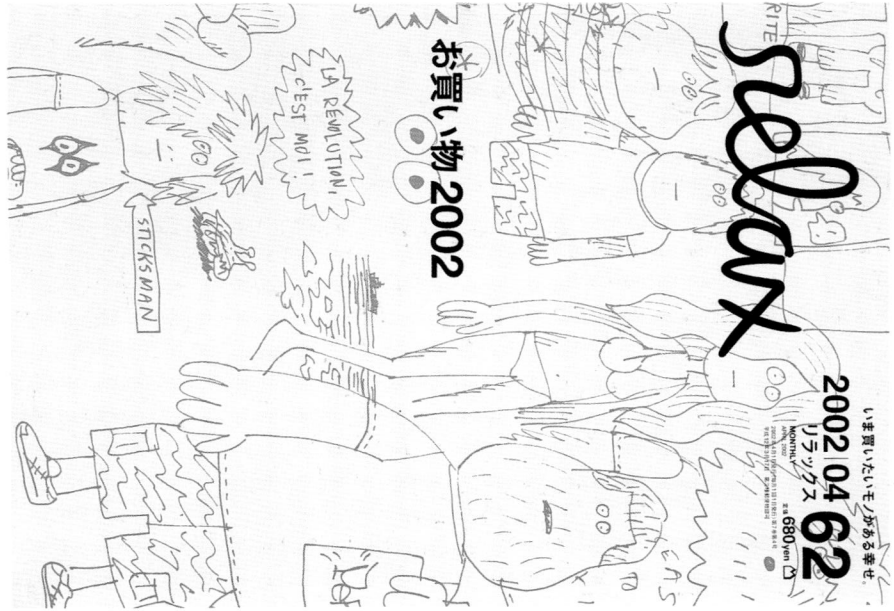

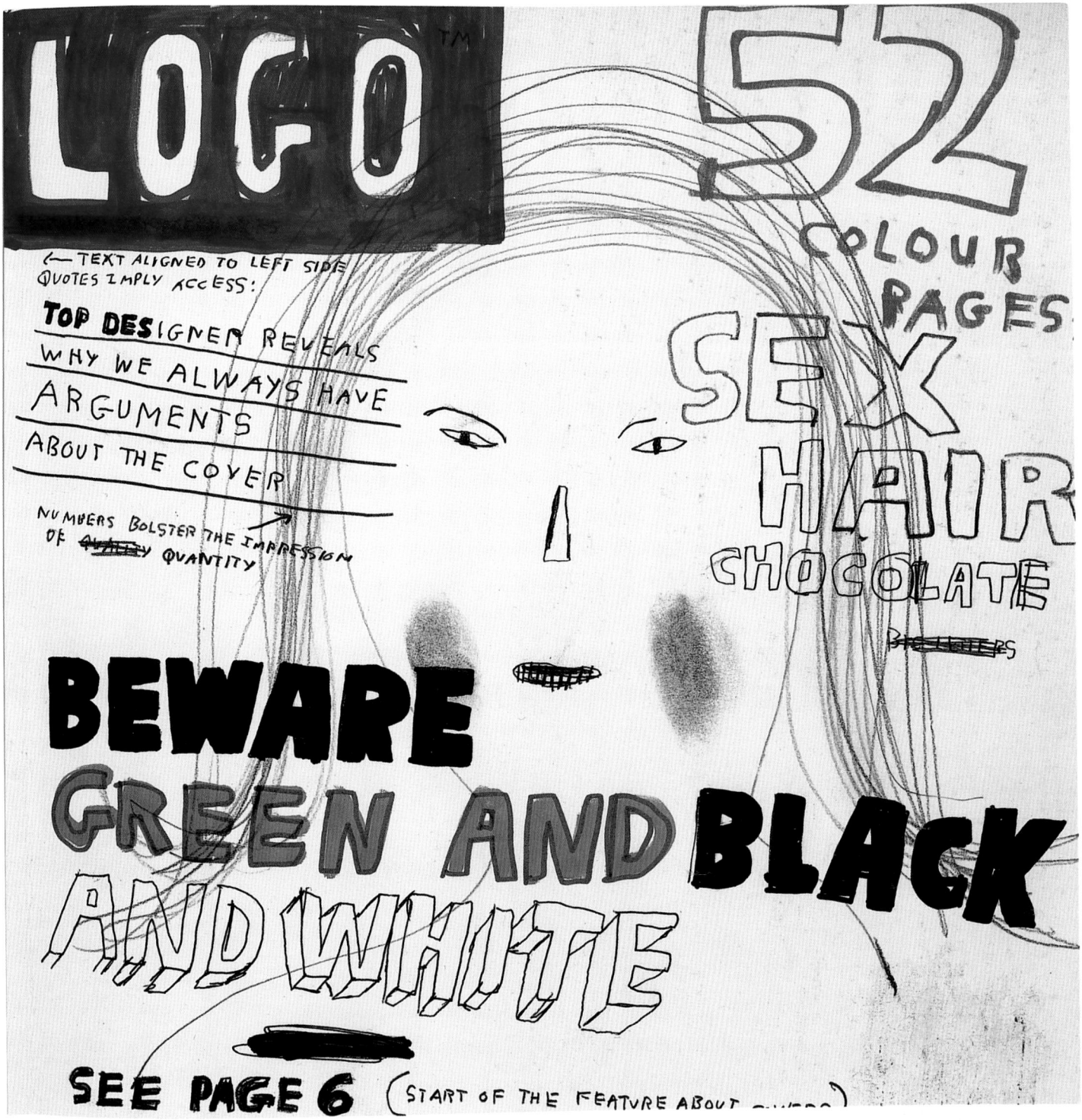
LOGO
52
COLOUR
PAGES
SEX
HAIR
CHOCOLATE
← TEXT ALIGNED TO LEFT SIDE
QUOTES IMPLY ACCESS:
TOP DESIGNER REVEALS
WHY WE ALWAYS HAVE
ARGUMENTS
ABOUT THE COVER
NUMBERS BOLSTER THE IMPRESSION
OF QUANTITY
BEWARE
GREEN AND BLACK
AND WHITE
SEE PAGE 6
(START OF THE FEATURE ABOUT

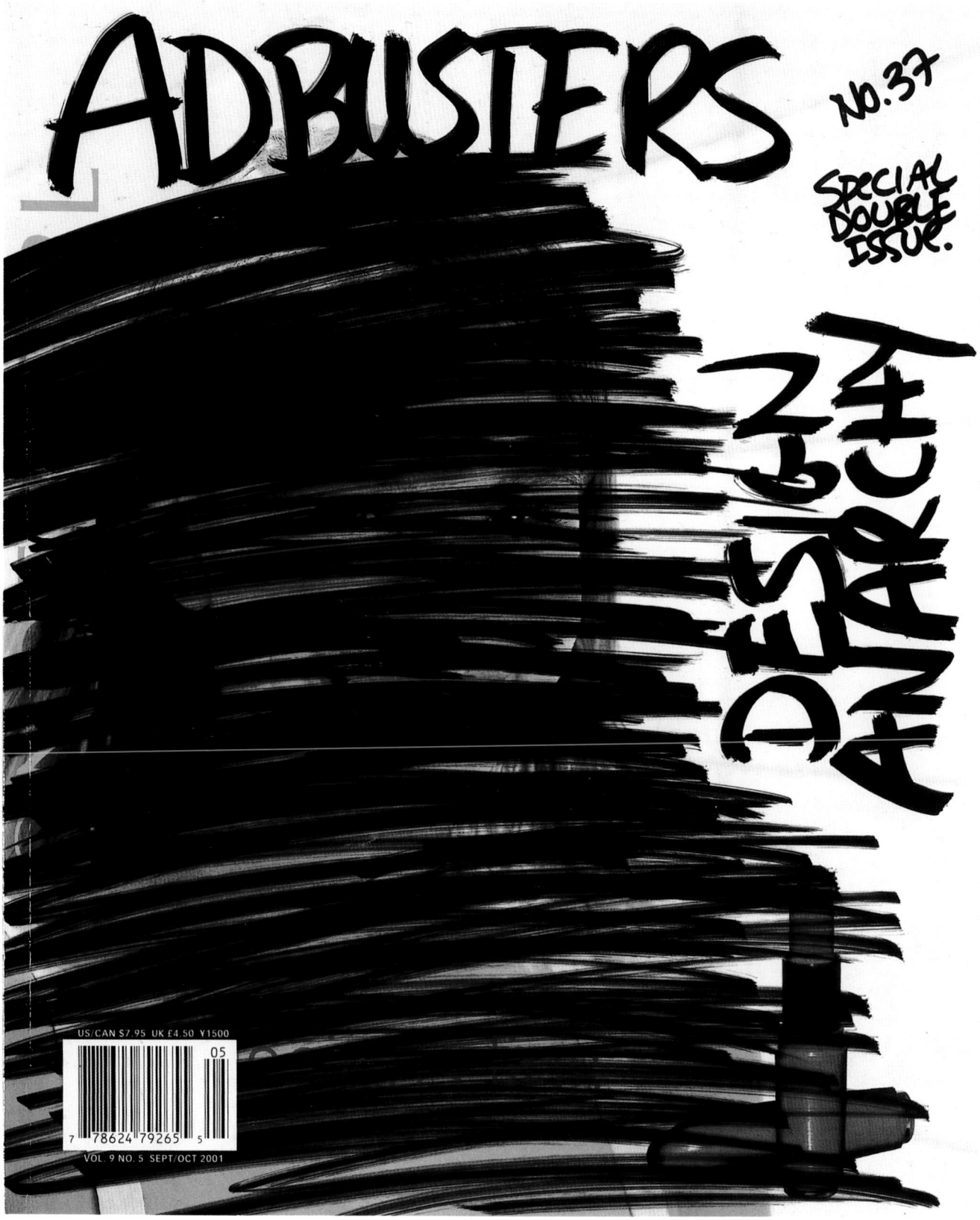

Adbusters *(Canada, Issue 37, September/October 2001) 228 x 274mm/9 x 10 7/8 inches*
This cover features heavy black marker pen scrawled over a glossy lipstick ad to announce its 'Design Anarchy' theme.
Guest art director *Jonathan Barnbrook*

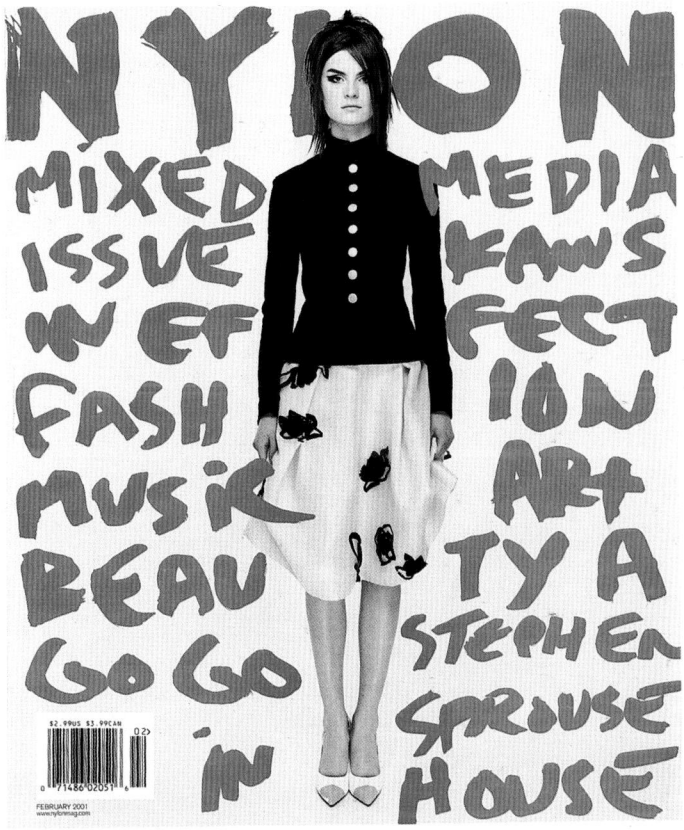

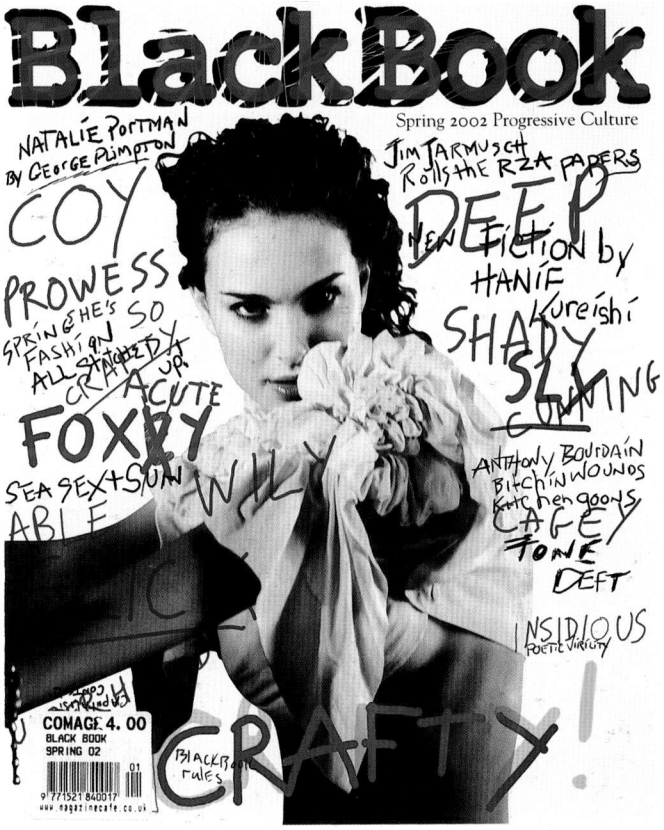

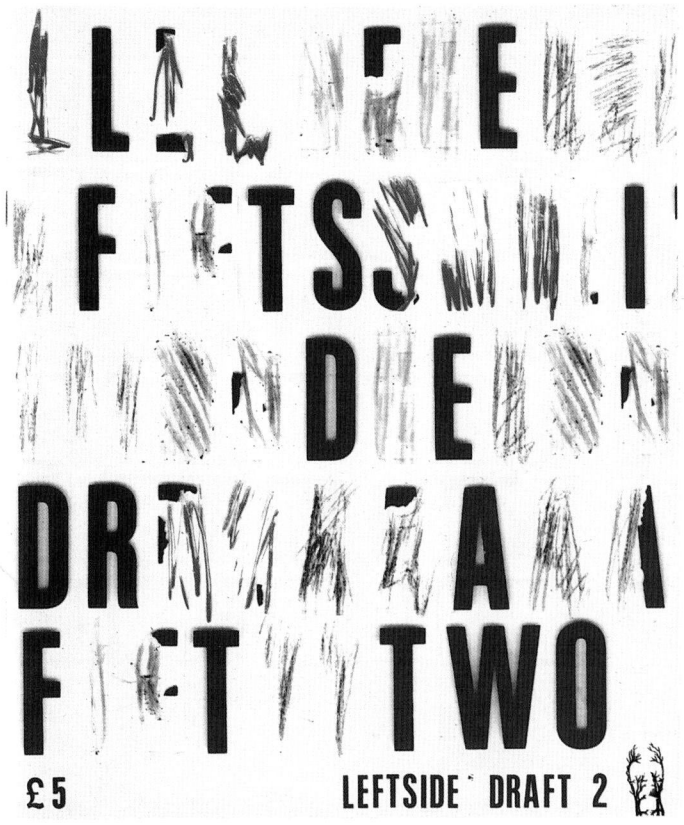

Nylon *(USA, February 2001) 230 x 274mm/9 x 10 7/8 inches*
Art director *Lina Kutsovskaya*
Black Book *(USA, Issue 22, Spring 2002) 228 x 274mm/9 x 10 7/8 inches*
Art director *Paul Che Ritter*
Two glossy fashion magazines use handwritten covers to state their independence from the mainstream.

Leftfield *(UK, Issue 2, November 2001) 280 x 280mm/11 x 11 inches*
Rubdown lettering is used to give a rough-and-ready impresssion on the cover of this independent magazine, which is a college project.
Design *Cai Taylor and Kyn Taylor*

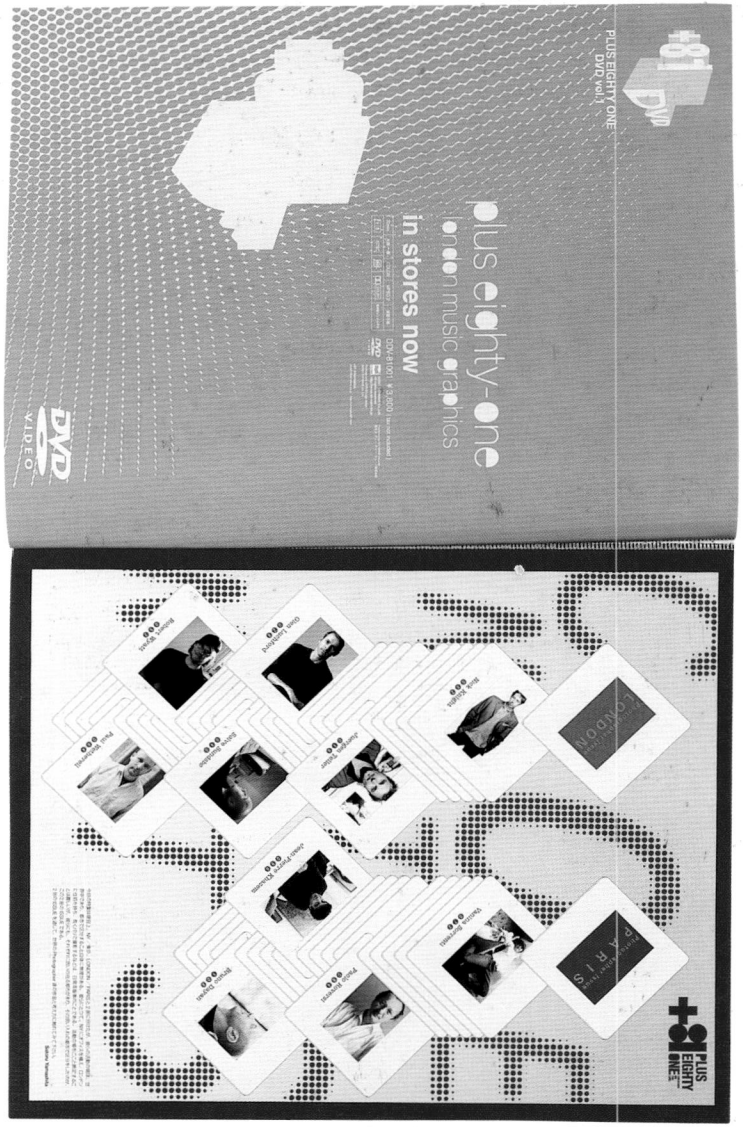

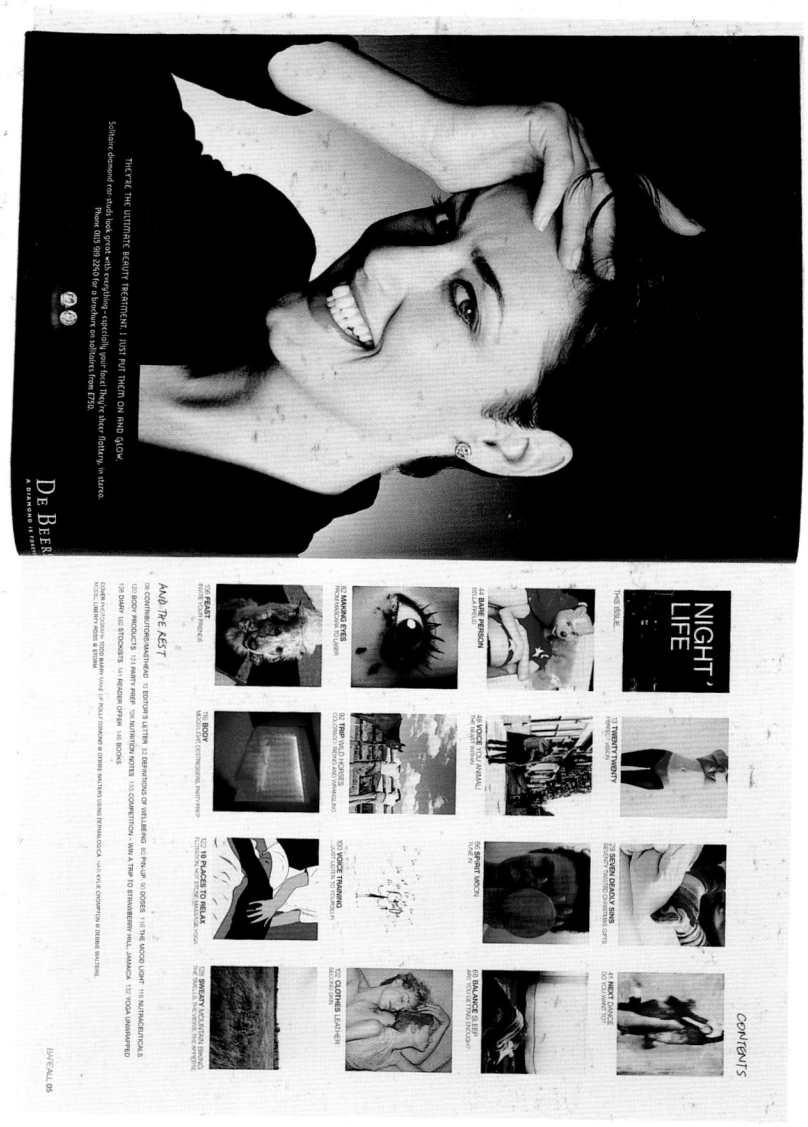

Bare *(UK, Issue 2, November/December 2000) 230 x 300mm/9 x 11 7/8 inches*
The contents page is the first place the reader goes to for information on content and navigation. In this example a clean grid of annotated images acts as contents page.
Art director *Kirsten Willey*

Plus Eighty One *(Japan, New Year 2002) 225 x 270mm/8 7/8 x 10 3/4 inches*
This special 'Photographers Issue' of this Asian creative arts magazine used portraits of the photographers set in stylized slideholders on its contents page.
Art director *Kazunari Nomoto*

021 contents

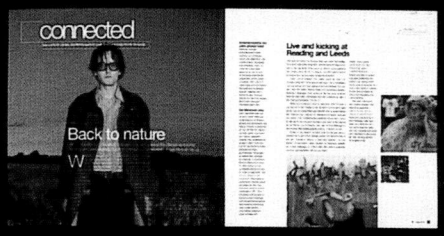

06 **Connected**
Jarvis Cocker gets in festival mood, Orange Prize for Fiction winner Ann Patchett waxes lyrical, plus the latest Orange news

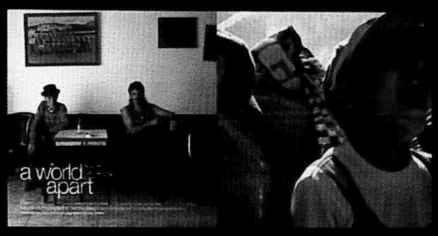

18 **Portugal calling**
Are you seeking splendid isolation or a cosmopolitan buzz? Take your Orange phone to Portugal and enjoy the best of both

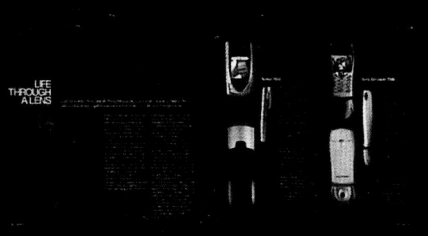

26 **Photo messaging**
Share the experience by sending a photo of that special moment from your Orange phone, available soon

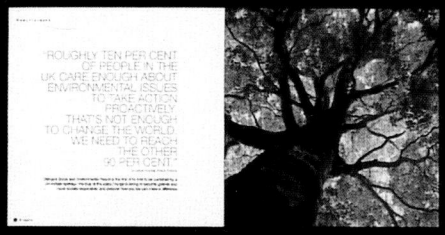

28 **Environment**
With its first Social and Environmental Report, Orange confirms its commitment to staying green

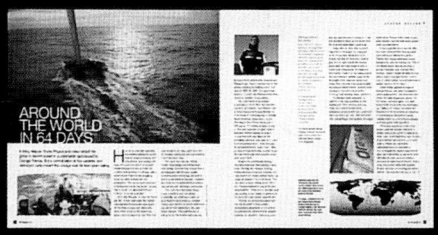

32 **Orange abroad**
Bruno Peyron and his crew set a world record when they sailed round the world in 64 days in the Orange catamaran

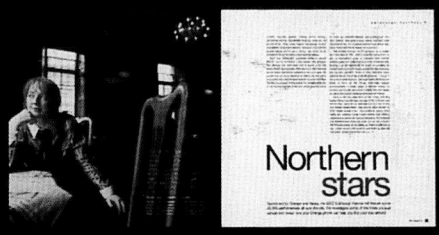

34 **Edinburgh Festival**
This year's Orange-sponsored Edinburgh Festival has its share of unusual venues. Let Orange be your guide

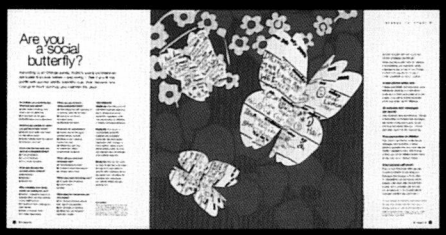

40 **Orange In Front**
Always burning the candle at both ends? Get organised with Orange's great new package, Orange In Front

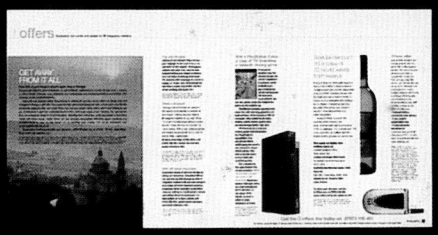

44 **Offers**
Win a PlayStation 2, save on a case of quality world wines, and enjoy a discount on a holiday to Spain, Italy or Portugal

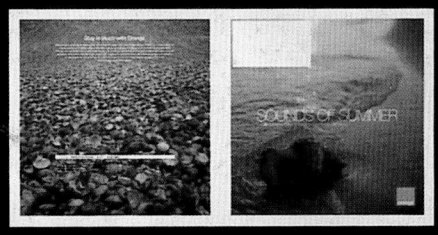

Your Orange European music guide
Tune in to the best of the summer's music events around Europe with your fold-out Orange festival guide

PLUS 43 **Competition** Win a stylish Piaggio scooter 47 **Orange Editions** Lie back and relax, take shelter or keep your picnic cool with the latest products selected for you by Orange 48 **Accessories** Get an exclusive ten per cent off funky covers for your Orange phone 49 **Mailbox** Your comments and queries about Orange 50 **Textlife** Award-winning comedienne Francesca Martinez talks by text message about her new solo show at the Edinburgh Festival 51 **Orange Directory** A guide to Orange contact numbers, information and call charges

O *(UK, Issue 21, Summer 2002)*
260 x 260mm/10 ¼ x 10 ¼ inches
Miniatures of page layouts are used on the contents page of this customer magazine for Orange mobile phone users, to announce a redesign and encourage the reader to enter the new-look magazine.
Art director *Simon Robinson*

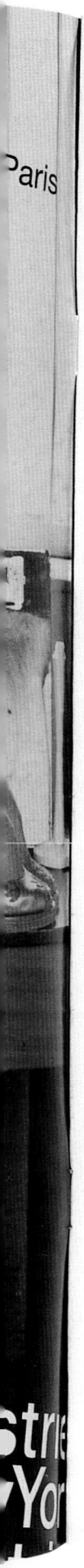

art	SOUS LA BANNIERE ETOILEE	12
couture	L'AVANT-GARDE NEW-YORKAISE	18
dream	L'AMERIQUE DES PODIUMS	28
écran	LE CINEMA INDEPENDANT, DEAD OR ALIVE ?	30
enquête	AMERICAN MANUFACTURING	34
extérieur	LAST EXIT TO BROOKLYN	36
icône	CHLOE, CHAN ET RITA	40
interview	LOVE / HATE	52
life	DOWN SOUTH	54
people	DESTROY ALL MONSTERS	62
politique	TIMES SQUARE INQUIETUDE	68
série	LES ANGES	74
sport	INDOOR	85
stéréo	MEGALOPOLES SONIQUES	90
street	UNITED COLORS OF AMERICA	92
zéro	MES AMERIQUES	96

Liberation Style *(France, Issue 7, Summer 2002) 240 x 330mm/9 ½ x 13 inches*
This contents page leads with generic subject headings, only including more specific information as a secondary element alongside the page numbers. By doing this, the page becomes a signifier of what the magazine represents, rather than a precise piece of navigation.
Art direction *Andreas Bozajic and Fredrika Jacobsson*

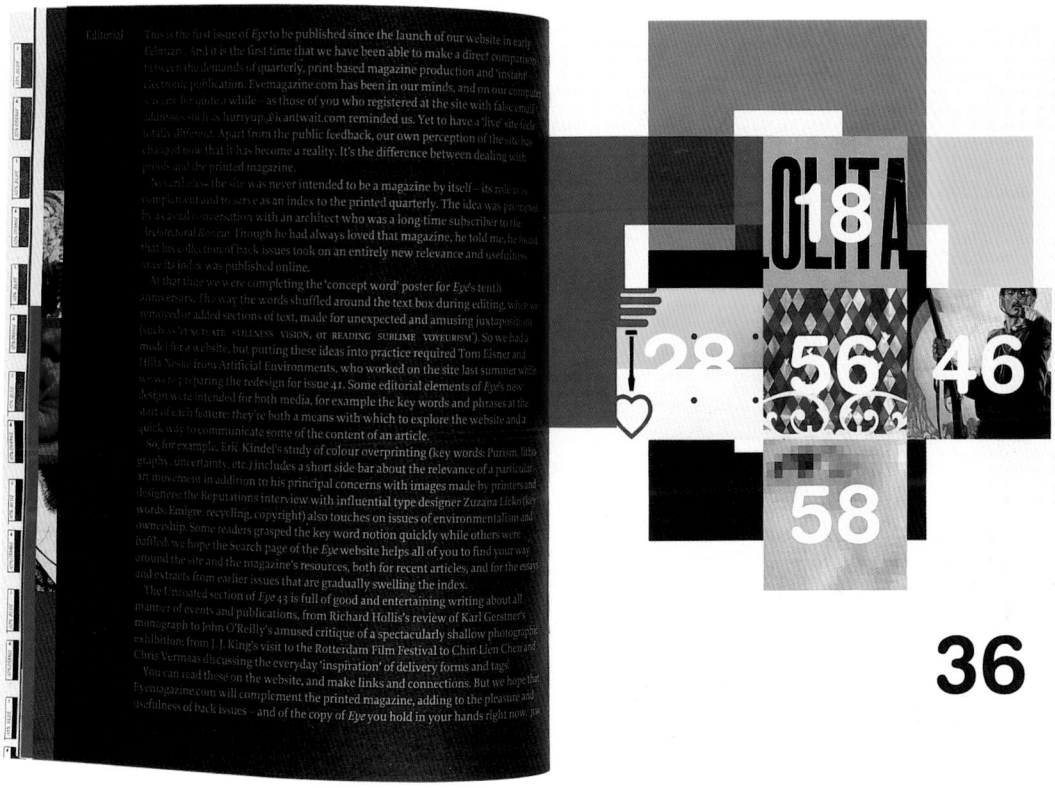

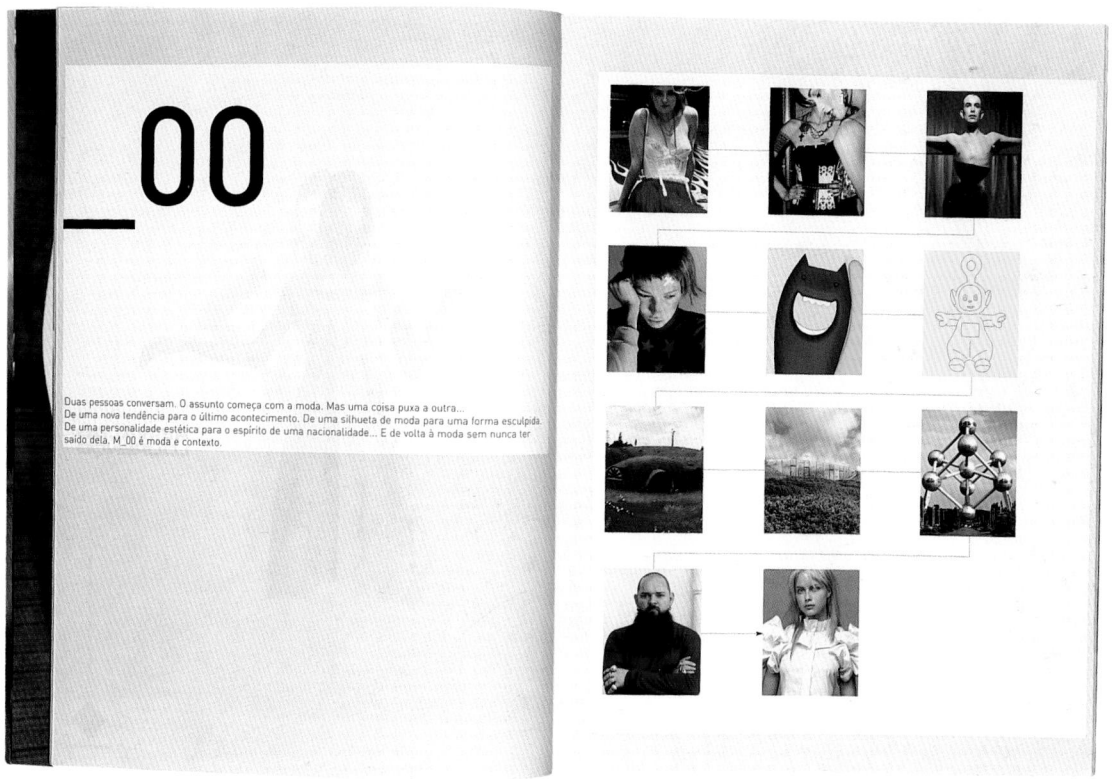

Eye *(UK, Issue 32, Spring 2002) 235 x 297mm/9 1/4 x 11 3/4 inches*
In addition to a brief written list of contents, which appears elsewhere, this design magazine also runs this abstract visual contents list opposite the drily presented editor's letter.
Art director *Nick Bell*

M *(Brazil, Pilot Issue, 2001) 228 x 297mm/9 x 11 3/4 inches*
This is a purely visual contents page: there are no text or page numbers, just pictures presented as a flow diagram.
Art direction *Roberto Cipolla and Helio Rosas*

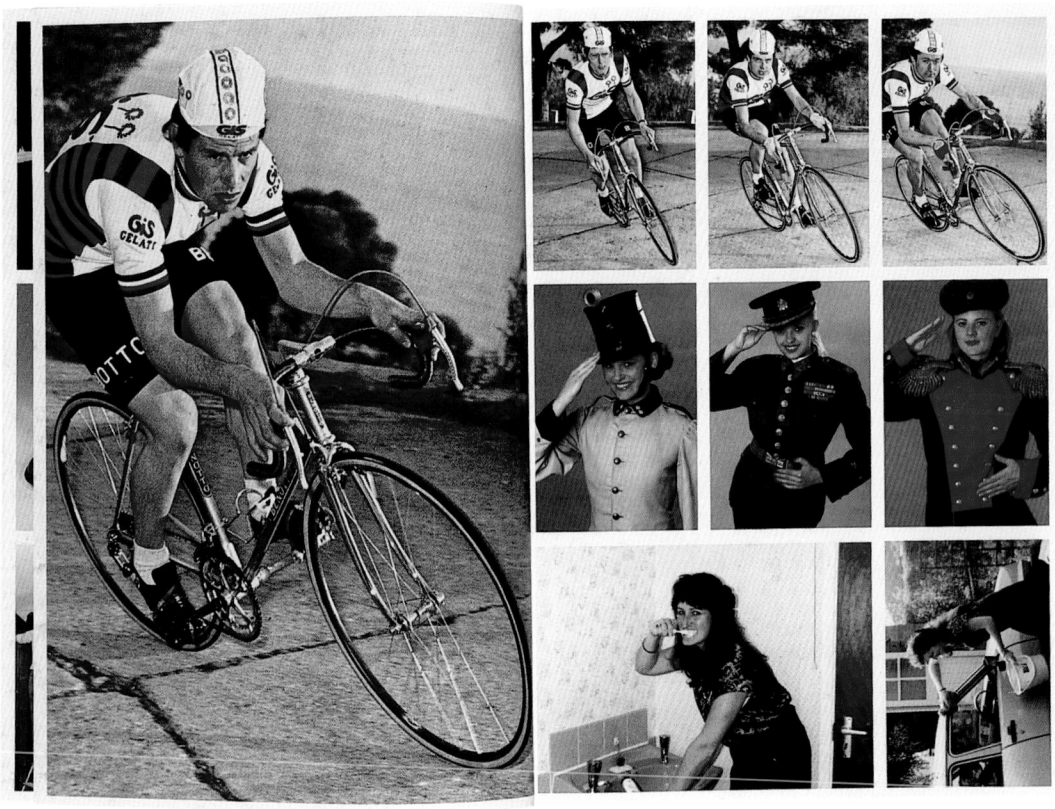
GiS
GELATI

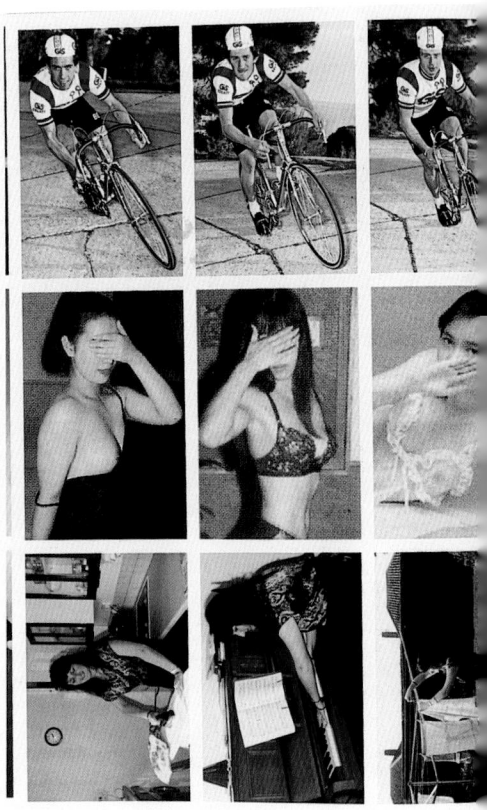

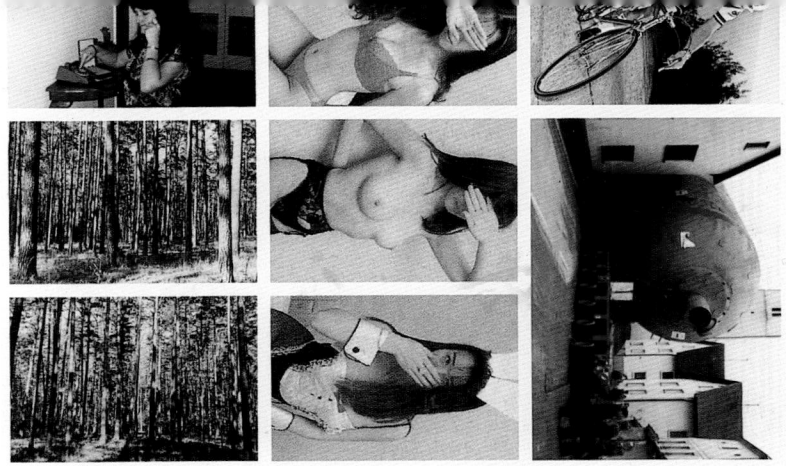

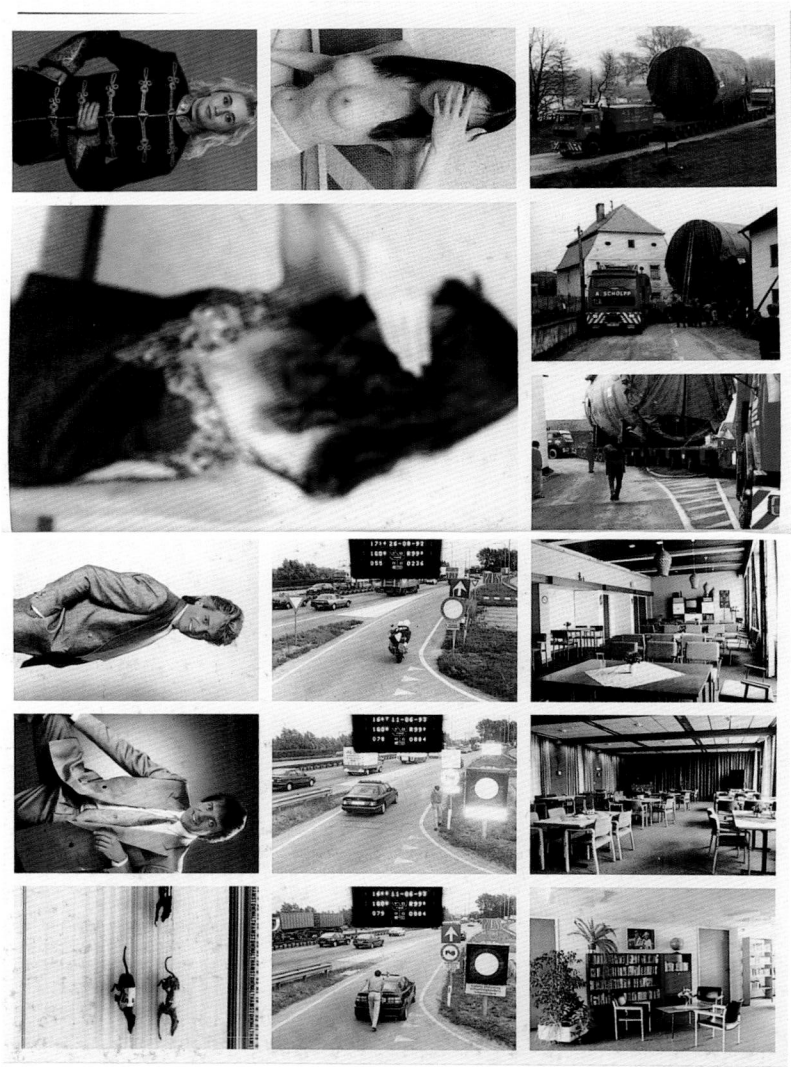

Useful Photography *(The Netherlands, Issue 1, 2001)*
210 x 297mm/8 1/4 x 11 3/4 inches
A collection of random, found, photographs are featured here, edited together to form a gently paced series of gridded layouts that flow from page to page. A number of repetitive/series pictures continue from one page to another, inviting the reader to apply a narrative of their own.
Design *Hans Aarsman, Claudie de Cleen, Julian Germain, Erik Kessels and Hans van der Meer*

DARREN ALMOND

INTERVIEWED BY PHIL HEBBLETHWAITE

British artist Darren Almond addresses an obsession with time, space and their respective relationships with man-made forms. BIG spoke with him about his latest piece - a transatlantic adventure.

Phil Hebblethwaite: *Tell me about the piece.*

Darren Almond: At the end of August 2001, my installation piece entitled Meantime was activated – it is basically a continuously running clock powered by an internal generator - and set to Greenwich Mean Time. The piece was put on the back of a truck and driven down to the port city of Southampton on the south coast of England. The shipping company P&O Nedlloyd agreed to transport the piece, and kindly allowed myself and Richard Dawson to make the transatlantic journey with it and document the journey photographically. The photographs in turn became part of the work itself, which was to be exhibited at a gallery in New York. The installation, the process, the journey of the piece in space and time itself would ultimately be the subject of the exhibit, which will continue around the world in a succession of spaces. We started our six day journey to New York in early September. The shipping company loaded the container so that as we set sail the digits of the clock were facing the city of Southampton. The container itself was designed in the United States. It is 40 feet long and can carry 40 tons of cargo. The transport of containers around the world is very often not a simple transaction. Shipping containers are like units of currency travelling the world, sometimes never arriving at an assigned destination. The whole mass of container units are like a floating stock market. Containers can stay afloat for years at a time with the produce intact, get turned away and sit idle in stock yards.

PH: *What type of clock is the installation?*

DA: It's an electro-magnetic clock so the readout is similar to the read-out of a Casio watch, but it's a mechanical version of that. You always see them in British railway stations, usually broken down. It shows seconds so it develops its own sense of rhythm, which the container itself amplifies when closed. One part of the second display has already turned over nearly a million times in its short life. You need to spend some time with it to get into the repeated cycle of the rhythm. It can be quite meditative. Or, if you are in front of it for a while, the sound can slip into the subconscious and disappear and become silent, as most sounds can. The clock is a huge object in human terms, but in relative terms it isn't that big. You can't tell what time it is when you stand in front of it. The numbers only appear clearly when you get some perspective.

PH: *How is this piece related to your other work?*

DA: The journey of the installation from London to New York is, in a way, a counterpoint to the films that I make. The films generally have an association to railways and have tended to follow an easterly route. I was born and grew up in the seventies in England, so I was part of the cold war generation. Yet I seemed to be very much on the fence between the two sides of the war. I grew up on the cusp of what I imagined to be the East and the West, the new and the old.

PH: *You've been to New York before, but only by air. How did the experience of travelling by boat compare to simply boarding a plane?*

DA: To travel to the States via the ocean is a totally different experience to flying. There's much more room for contemplation. Twenty-four hours after you leave Southampton you're not even past the most westerly point of England. Early on it was beautiful - very calm in the Channel and the sun was shining. I was down at the bow of the boat and there was no breeze - there was a wind pocket, because of the design of the ship. On a plane, the oxygen is removed from you. Any sense of taste is removed from you. And any sense of speed and temperature and connection is removed from you. You are vacuum-sealed, alienated from time and motion. When I was on the boat, the occasional plane would fly overhead. I would look up and think that those people were missing out on so much. There is a tangible sense of moving through space and time which passengers on modern airliners are deprived of. You gain an hour of sleep each night of the crossing so one doesn't experience jet-lag and the familiar sense of dislocation that you experience when you arrive in New York. But mostly, as you travel, it is far easier to get your head around the scale of the journey and the distance and how that effects things culturally. This must be exaggerated with the even greater oceans, greater distances.

PH: *So you gain a different perspective on the earth itself?*

DA: The deck of the ship is a vantage point – you are relatively high in relation to the surface of the ocean. With this perspective you can actually experience the curvature of the earth. It becomes clear that we are on a huge globe, moving through space. The sciences that, as a child, I thought were courageous acts of mental ability all of a sudden appeared to be visual reactions to quite natural existence.

PH: Was there a feeling of sensory deprivation whilst on the ocean?

DA: It was strange. The route we took is the busiest shipping route in the world but we only saw one other vessel during the whole journey. We could just about see it with our binoculars in the distance. Occasionally you get dolphins at the bow jumping over the waves and large seagulls and albatresses floating around. We also saw a couple of whales. Other than that we were left looking at the weather, which is a beautiful thing to sit and watch in itself. You look at the sky not the sea because you are in the sea - you're in the present moment - and you're concerned about what is going to be in front of you. You can see storms and you can look through storms and see that a clear patch is behind. The captain of the ship was able to navigate his way across using the installation. With Greenwich Mean Time and knowing what time that you left the dock you work out your relative position. And then you use the stars to work out your other co-ordinates.

PH: Did sailing with this clock give you a heightened sense of time?

DA: No, but arriving in New York itself did. I'd spent six days in an extremely calm environment, despite the fact that we crossed the Flemish Cap - a submerged mountain off Newfoundland. Out there the sea goes from being a couple of kilometres deep to being a hundred metres shallow. This affects the weather patterns above. The water is warmer and three weather fronts can sometimes collide. We experienced extremely violent seas - the boat was bending, which it is designed to do, and disappearing into waves. The clock could have been washed off - something I was unaware of. Ships sometimes lose containers. But being on the boat meant that I became unused to the verticality of a city like New York. The horizon had become the norm. It was quite confrontational. The clock took a bit of a battering during the course of the journey - more so in New York than it did on the boat. It's going to get fixed there and then it's going to move on. The idea is to put it on a train across the desert to the West Coast, then on a ship across the Pacific until, eventually, it'll do a whole revolution. All along it will show Greenwich Mean Time so it can work out where it is.

PHOTOGRAPHY: RICHARD DAWSON

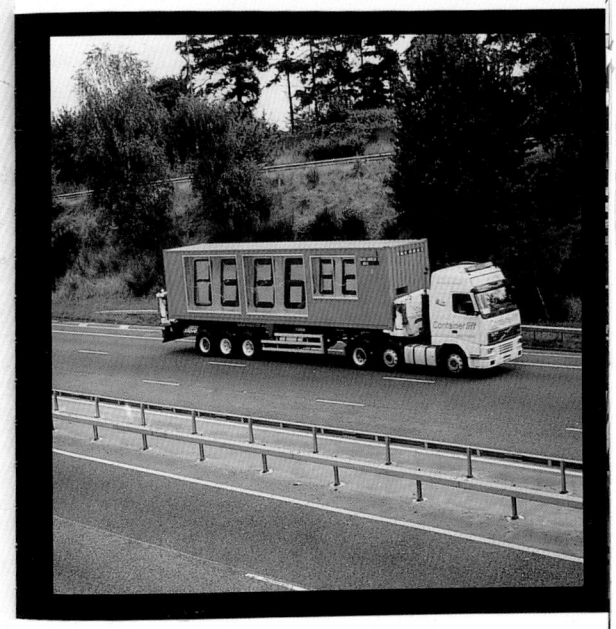

Above: The London Orbital, M25.

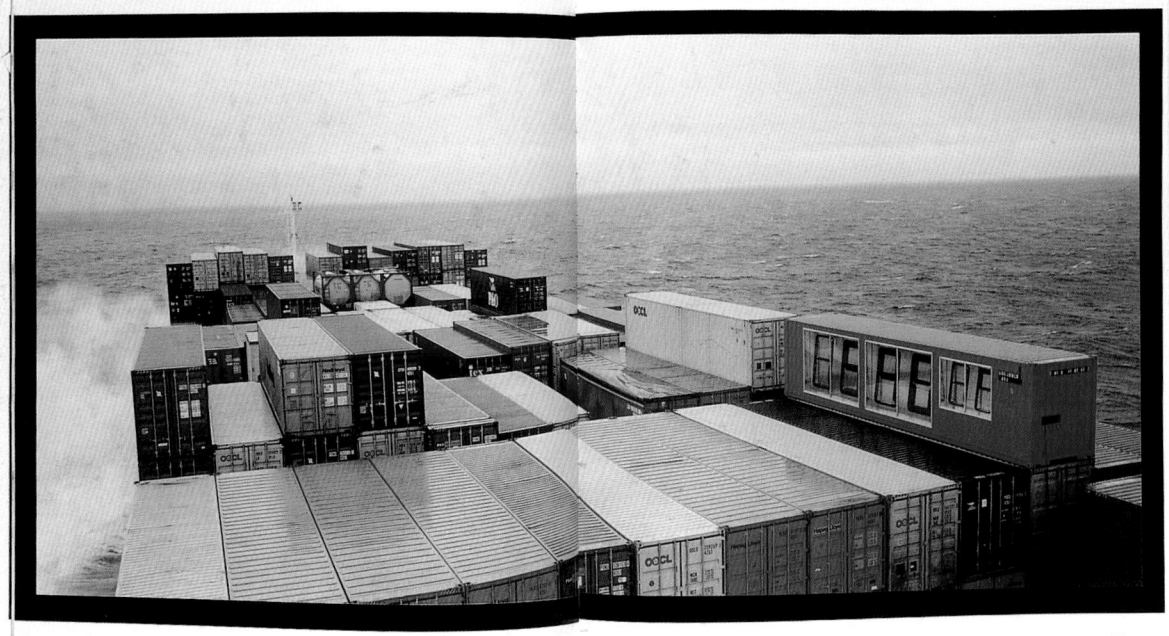

Above: Mid Atlantic.

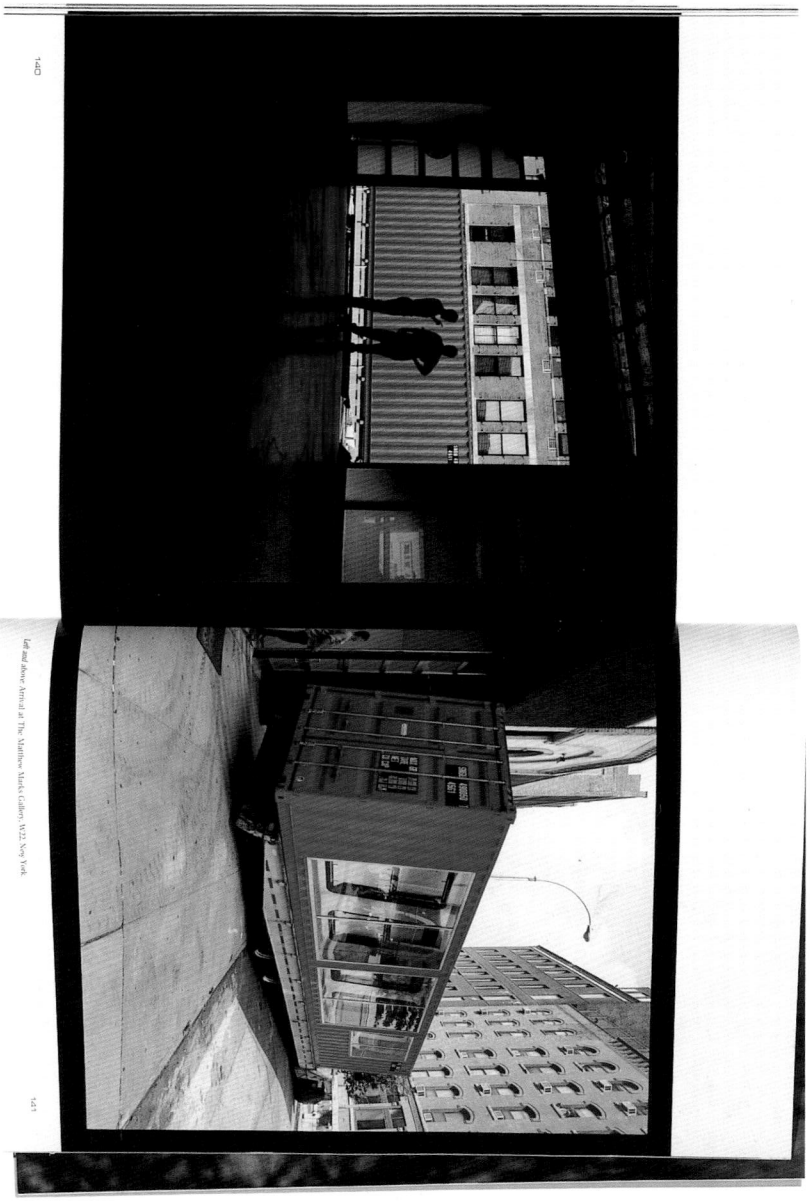

140

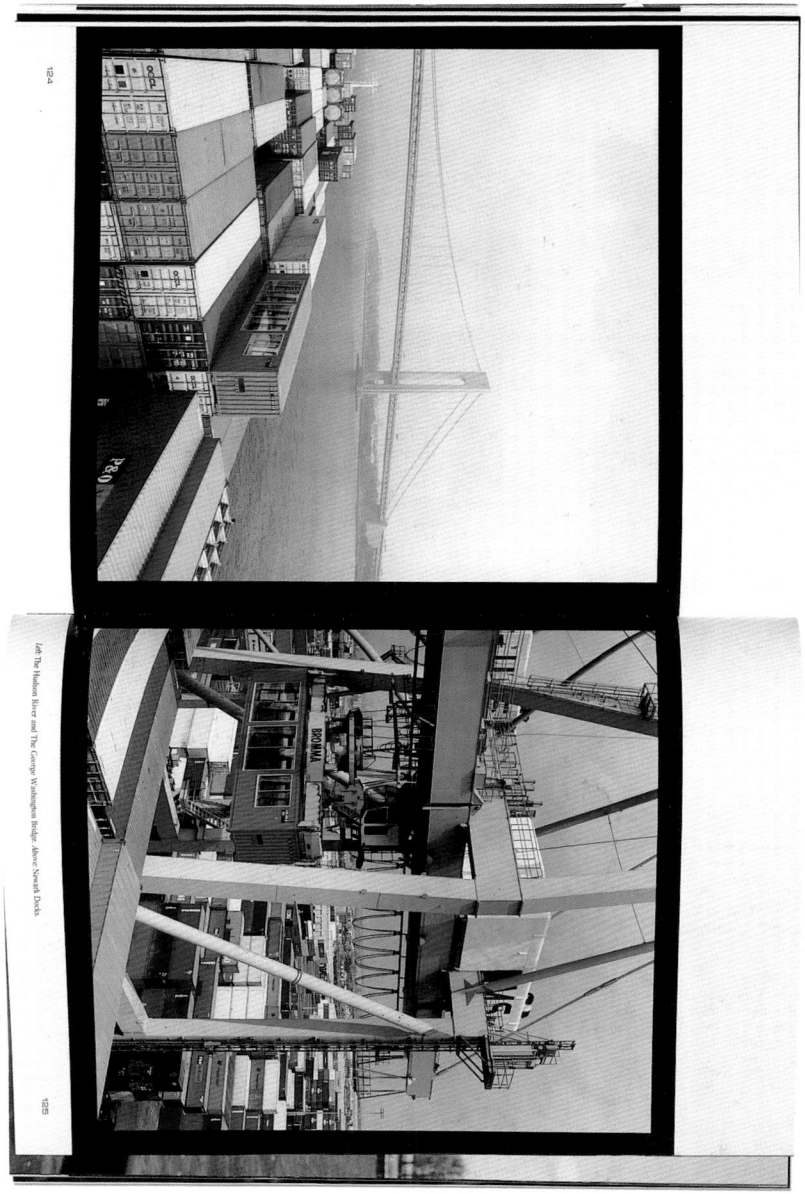

124

left and above Arrival at The Matthew Marks Gallery, W22, New York.

141

left The Hudson River and The George Washington Bridge, above Newark Docks

125

Big *(USA, Issue 41 The Transatlantic Issue, 2002) 235 x 297mm/9 1/4 x 11 3/4 inches*
Artist Darren Almond's installation piece, 'Meantime', featured a large digital clock set into a freight container. The container was transported from Almond's studio to Southampton Docks and then by sea to New York where it was exhibited in a gallery. The project was photographed by Richard Dawson and his pictures later ran in this Transatlantic Issue of the magazine. The pictures were published in chronological order but spread throughout the issue, bringing an awareness of time to the readers' experience of the project.
Art director *Daren Ellis*

let them eat drugs: the streets vs the monarchy

INTERVIEWS JONATHAN PEARSON
PHOTOGRAPHY FREDERIKE HELWIG

COSIMO BORNIK, STUDENT

Do you feel like the monarchy represents you? I think they're more important for the older generation. **Who is your favourite royal?** Prince Charles, because he's a bit of a joke. He's really entertaining to watch because he's just such a dick. **How British do you feel?** Quite British. But for me, my identity is more about being a Londoner. **What's more important – getting rid of the monarchy or the police chilling out about drugs?** The police chilling out attitude towards drugs, without a doubt. Heroin and cannabis should be legalised. I agree with that policeman who said that all drugs should be legalised. It would solve so much

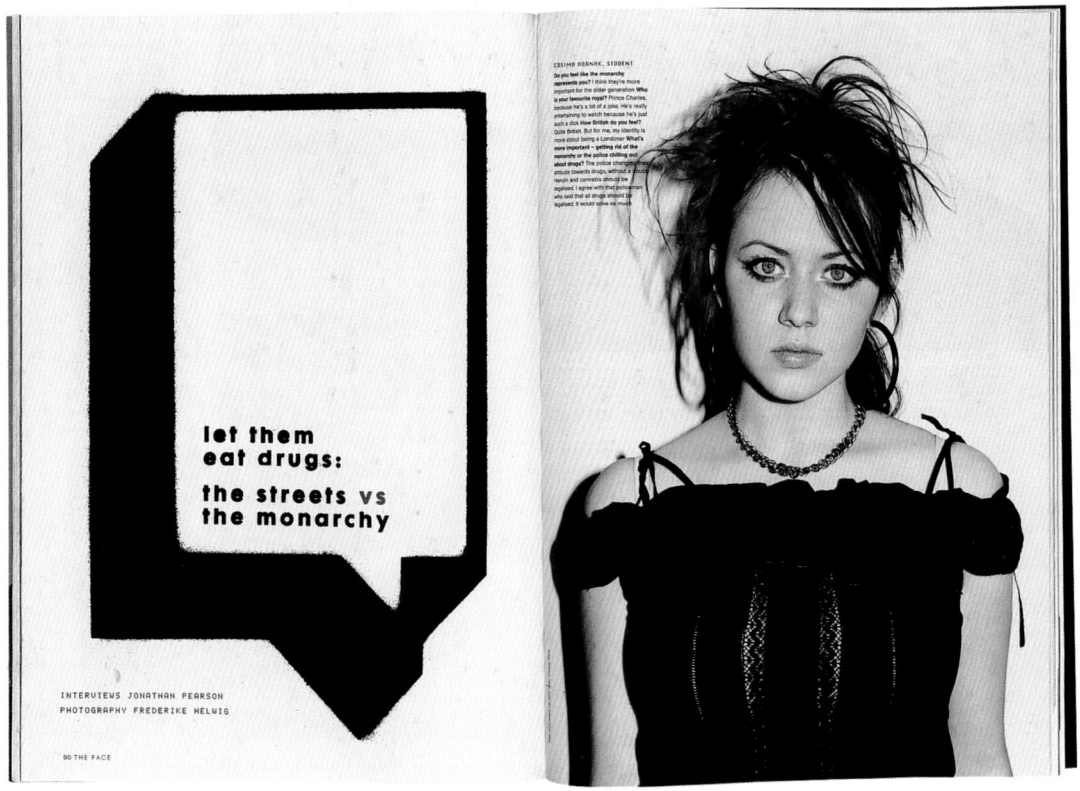

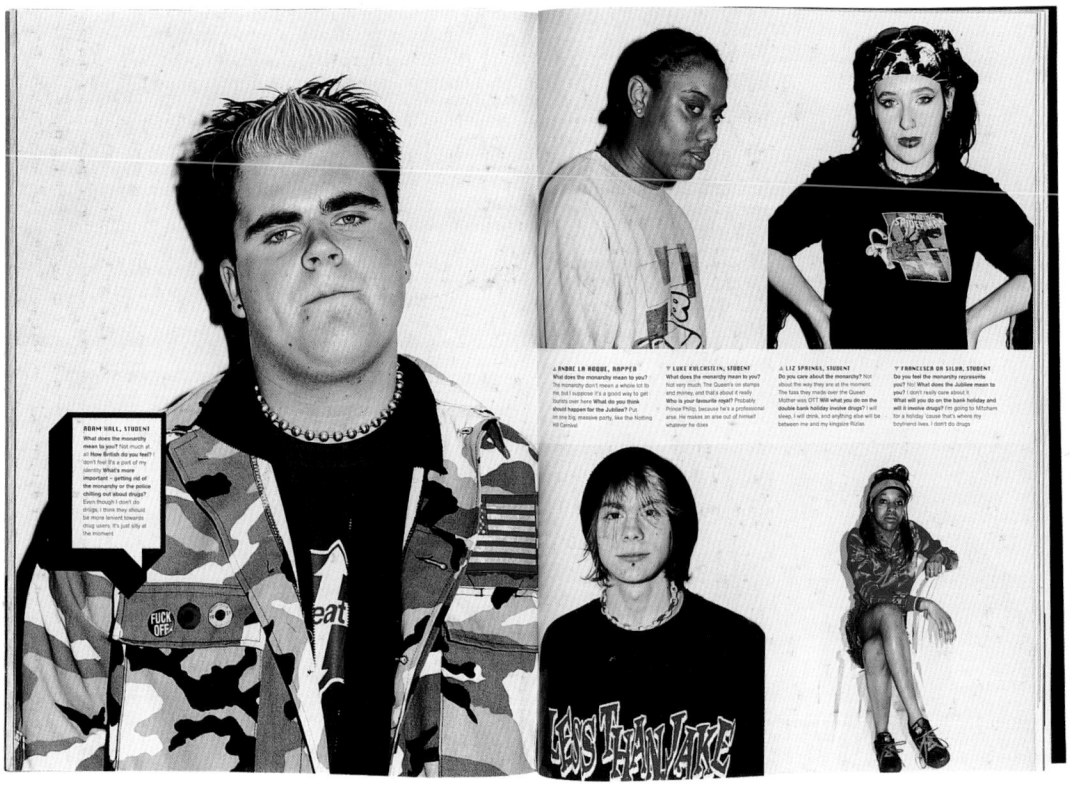

ADAM HALL, STUDENT

What does the monarchy mean to you? Not much at all. **How British do you feel?** I don't feel it's a part of my identity. **What's more important – getting rid of the monarchy or the police chilling out about drugs?** Even though I don't do drugs, I think they should be more lenient towards drug users. It's just silly at the moment.

▲ ANDRE LA ROQUE, RAPPER

What does the monarchy mean to you? The monarchy don't mean a whole lot to me, but I suppose it's a good way to get tourists over here. **What do you think should happen for the Jubilee?** Put on the big, massive party, like the Notting Hill Carnival.

▼ LUKE KULCHESKIN, STUDENT

What does the monarchy mean to you? Not very much. The Queen's on stamps and money, and that's about it really. **Who is your favourite royal?** Probably Prince Philip, because he's a professional arse. He makes an arse out of himself whatever he does.

▲ LIZ SPRINGS, STUDENT

Do you care about the monarchy? Not about the way they are at the moment. The fuss they made over the Queen Mother was OTT. **With what you do on the double bank holiday involve drugs?** I will sleep, I will drink, and anything else will be between me and my kingsize Ritalin.

▼ FRANCESCA DE SILVA, STUDENT

Do you feel the monarchy represents you? No! **What does the Jubilee mean to you?** I don't really care about it. **What will you do on the bank holiday and will it involve drugs?** I'm going to Mitcham for a holiday (cause that's where my boyfriend lives. I don't do drugs.

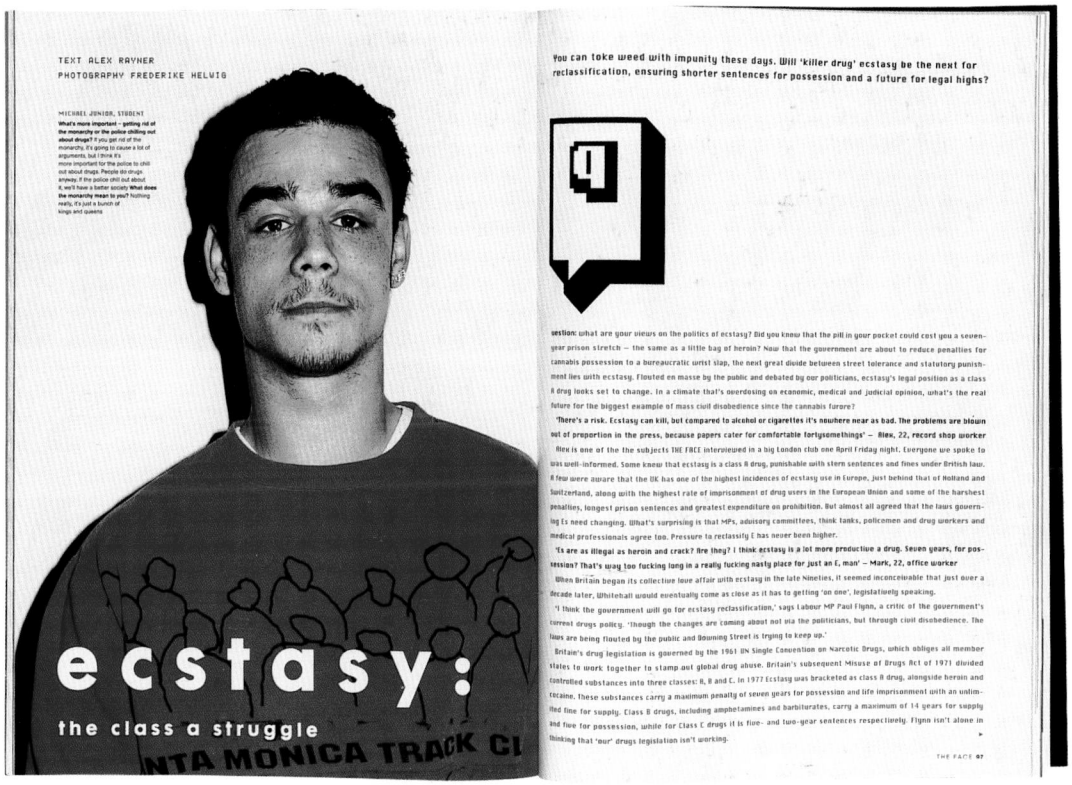

TEXT ALEX RAYNER
PHOTOGRAPHY FREDERIKE HELWIG

MICHAEL JUNIOR, STUDENT
What's more important – getting rid of the monarchy or the police chilling out about drugs? If you get rid of the monarchy, it's going to cause a lot of arguments, but I think it's more important for the police to chill out about drugs. People do drugs anyway. If the police chill out about it, we'll have a better society **What does the monarchy mean to you?** Nothing really, it's just a bunch of kings and queens

ecstasy: the class a struggle

You can toke weed with impunity these days. Will 'killer drug' ecstasy be the next for reclassification, ensuring shorter sentences for possession and a future for legal highs?

Question: what are your views on the politics of ecstasy? Did you know that the pill in your pocket could cost you a seven-year prison stretch – the same as a little bag of heroin? Now that the government are about to reduce penalties for cannabis possession to a bureaucratic wrist slap, the next great divide between street tolerance and statutory punishment lies with ecstasy. Flouted en masse by the public and debated by our politicians, ecstasy's legal position as a class A drug looks set to change. In a climate that's overdosing on economic, medical and judicial opinion, what's the real future for the biggest example of mass civil disobedience since the cannabis furore?

'There's a risk. Ecstasy can kill, but compared to alcohol or cigarettes it's nowhere near as bad. The problems are blown out of proportion in the press, because papers cater for comfortable fortysomethings' – Alex, 22, record shop worker

Alex is one of the the subjects THE FACE interviewed in a big London club one April Friday night. Everyone we spoke to was well-informed. Some knew that ecstasy is a class A drug, punishable with stern sentences and fines under British law. A few were aware that the UK has one of the highest incidences of ecstasy use in Europe, just behind that of Holland and Switzerland, along with the highest rate of imprisonment of drug users in the European Union and some of the harshest penalties, longest prison sentences and greatest expenditure on prohibition. But almost all agreed that the laws governing Es need changing. What's surprising is that MPs, advisory committees, think tanks, policemen and drug workers and medical professionals agree too. Pressure to reclassify E has never been higher.

'Es are as illegal as heroin and crack? Are they? I think ecstasy is a lot more productive a drug. Seven years, for possession? That's way too fucking long in a really fucking nasty place for just an E, man' – Mark, 22, office worker

When Britain began its collective love affair with ecstasy in the late Nineties, it seemed inconceivable that just over a decade later, Whitehall would eventually come as close as it has to getting 'on one', legislatively speaking.

'I think the government will go for ecstasy reclassification,' says Labour MP Paul Flynn, a critic of the government's current drugs policy, 'though the changes are coming about not via the politicians, but through civil disobedience. The laws are being flouted by the public and Downing Street is trying to keep up.'

Britain's drug legislation is governed by the 1961 UN Single Convention on Narcotic Drugs, which obliges all member states to work together to stamp out global drug abuse. Britain's subsequent Misuse of Drugs Act of 1971 divided controlled substances into three classes: A, B and C. In 1977 Ecstasy was bracketed as class A drug, alongside heroin and cocaine. These substances carry a maximum penalty of seven years for possession and life imprisonment with an unlimited fine for supply. Class B drugs, including amphetamines and barbiturates, carry a maximum of 14 years for supply and five for possession, while for Class C drugs it is five- and two-year sentences respectively. Flynn isn't alone in thinking that 'our' drugs legislation isn't working. ►

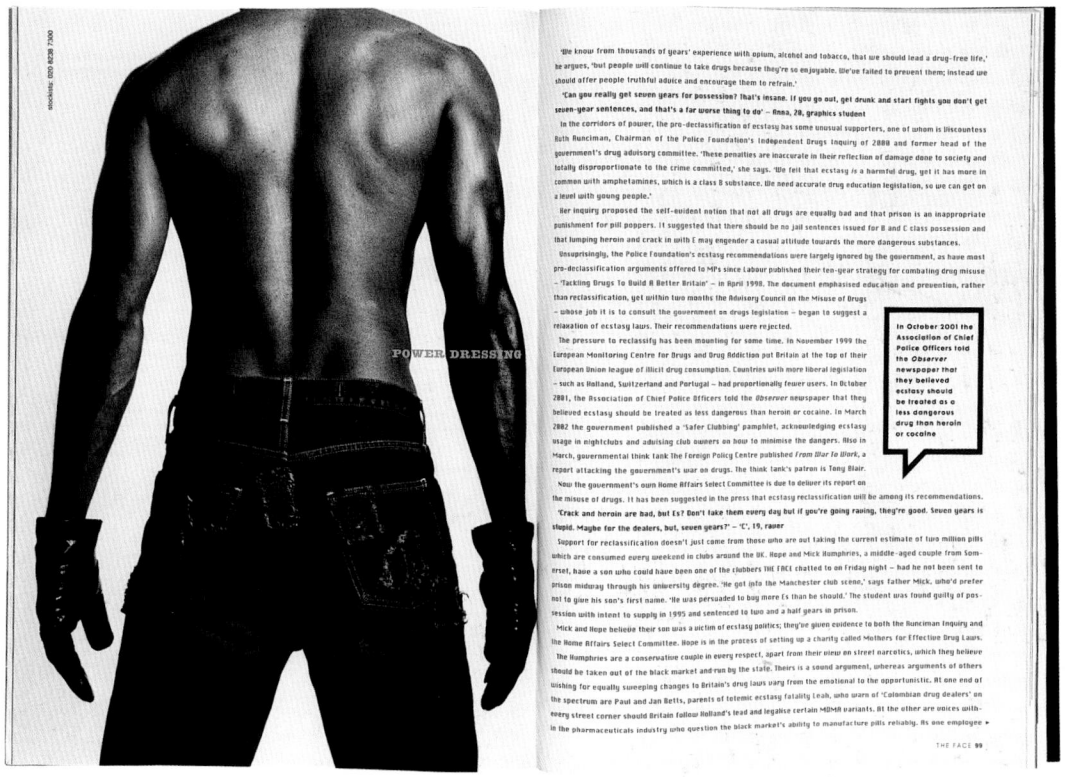

stockists: 020 8228 7300

POWER DRESSING

'We know from thousands of years' experience with opium, alcohol and tobacco, that we should lead a drug-free life,' he argues, 'but people will continue to take drugs because they're so enjoyable. We've failed to prevent them; instead we should offer people truthful advice and encourage them to refrain.'

'Can you really get seven years for possession? That's insane. If you go out, get drunk and start fights you don't get seven-year sentences, and that's a far worse thing to do' – Anna, 28, graphics student

In the corridors of power, the pro-declassification of ecstasy has some unusual supporters, one of whom is Viscountess Ruth Runciman, Chairman of the Police Foundation's Independent Drugs Inquiry of 2000 and former head of the government's drug advisory committee. 'These penalties are inaccurate in their reflection of damage done to society and totally disproportionate to the crime committed,' she says. 'We felt that ecstasy *is* a harmful drug, yet it has more in common with amphetamines, which is a class B substance. We need accurate drug education legislation, so we can get on a level with young people.'

Her inquiry proposed the self-evident notion that not all drugs are equally bad and that prison is an inappropriate punishment for pill poppers. It suggested that there should be no jail sentences issued for B and C class possession and that lumping heroin and crack in with E may engender a casual attitude towards the more dangerous substances.

Unsurprisingly, the Police Foundation's ecstasy recommendations were largely ignored by the government, as have most pro-declassification arguments offered to MPs since Labour published their ten-year strategy for combating drug misuse – 'Tackling Drugs To Build A Better Britain' – in April 1998. The document emphasised education and prevention, rather than reclassification, yet within two months the Advisory Council on the Misuse of Drugs – whose job it is to consult the government on drugs legislation – began to suggest a relaxation of ecstasy laws. Their recommendations were rejected.

In October 2001 the Association of Chief Police Officers told the *Observer* newspaper that they believed ecstasy should be treated as a less dangerous drug than heroin or cocaine

The pressure to reclassify has been mounting for some time. In November 1999 the European Monitoring Centre for Drugs and Drug Addiction put Britain at the top of their European Union league of illicit drug consumption. Countries with more liberal legislation – such as Holland, Switzerland and Portugal – had proportionally fewer users. In October 2001, the Association of Chief Police Officers told the *Observer* newspaper that they believed ecstasy should be treated as less dangerous than heroin or cocaine. In March 2002 the government published a 'Safer Clubbing' pamphlet, acknowledging ecstasy usage in nightclubs and advising club owners on how to minimise the dangers. Also in March, governmental think tank the Foreign Policy Centre published *From War To Work*, a report attacking the government's war on drugs. The think tank's patron is Tony Blair.

Now the government's own Home Affairs Select Committee is due to deliver its report on the misuse of drugs. It has been suggested in the press that ecstasy reclassification will be among its recommendations.

'Crack and heroin are bad, but Es? Don't take them every day but if you're going raving, they're good. Seven years is stupid. Maybe for the dealers, but, seven years?' – 'C', 19, raver

Support for reclassification doesn't just come from those who are out taking the current estimate of two million pills which are consumed every weekend in clubs around the UK. Hope and Mick Humphries, a middle-aged couple from Somerset, have a son who could have been one of the clubbers THE FACE chatted to on Friday night – had he not been sent to prison midway through his university degree. 'He got into the Manchester club scene,' says father Mick, who'd prefer not to give his son's first name. 'He was persuaded to buy more Es than he should.' The student was found guilty of possession with intent to supply in 1995 and sentenced to two and a half years in prison.

Mick and Hope believe their son was a victim of ecstasy politics; they've given evidence to both the Runciman Inquiry and the Home Affairs Select Committee. Hope is in the process of setting up a charity called Mothers for Effective Drug Laws.

The Humphries are a conservative couple in every respect, apart from their view on street narcotics, which they believe should be taken out of the black market and run by the state. Theirs is a sound argument, whereas arguments of others wishing for equally sweeping changes to Britain's drug laws vary from the emotional to the opportunistic. At one end of the spectrum are Paul and Jan Betts, parents of totemic ecstasy fatality Leah, who warn of 'Colombian drug dealers' on every street corner should Britain follow Holland's lead and legalise certain MDMA variants. At the other are voices within the pharmaceuticals industry who question the black market's ability to manufacture pills reliably. As one employee ►

The Face *(UK, Volume 3, Issue 65, June 2002) 222 x 297mm/8 3/4 x 11 3/4 inches*
The stylized speech bubble is used here to both symbolize the subject of and link the pages of a voxpop feature. Each time the speech bubble appears it has a different function: first it holds the headline, then a voxpop answer, then a drop capital at the start of the text, and finally, a pull-quote from the text.
Art director *Craig Tilford*

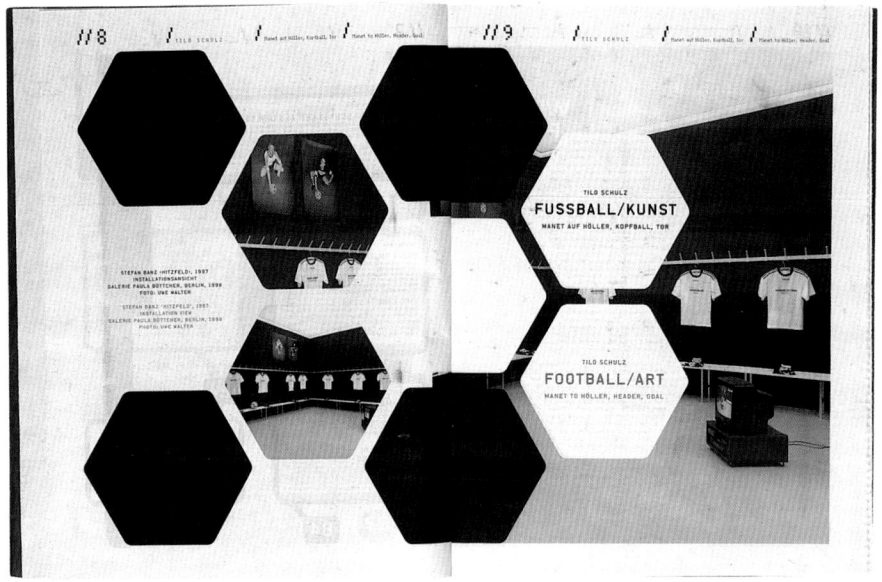

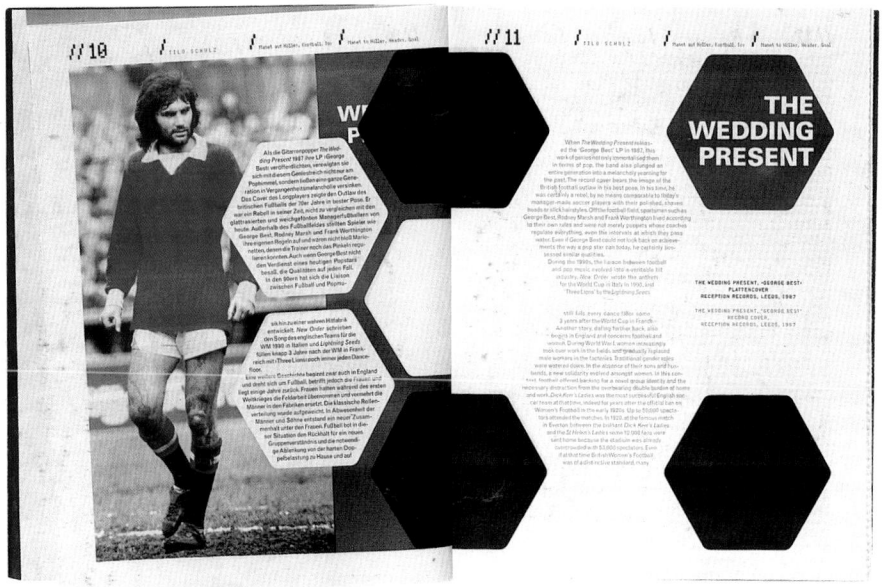

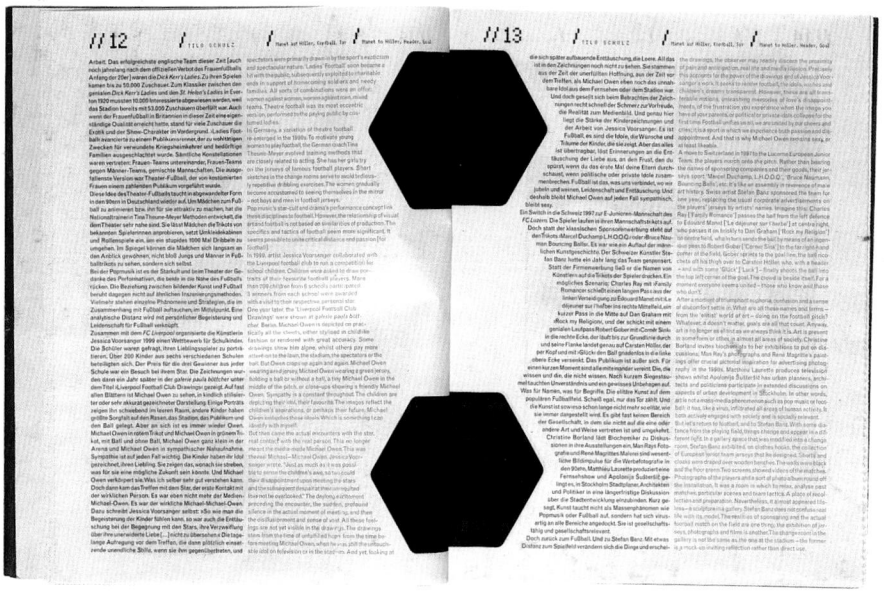

Spector Cut+Paste *(Germany, Issue 1, 2001)*
235 x 297mm/9 1/4 x 11 3/4 inches
A series of spreads are held together by a strong graphic device based on a football theme. Spread by spread, the number of pictures decreases as the volume of words increases, gently drawing the reader into the article.
Designer *Marcus Dressen*

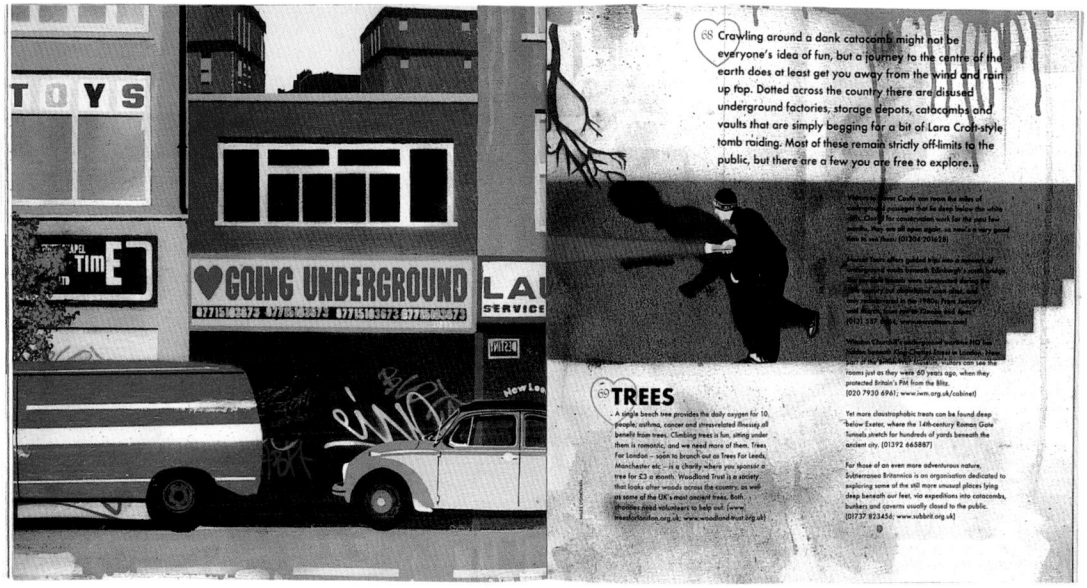

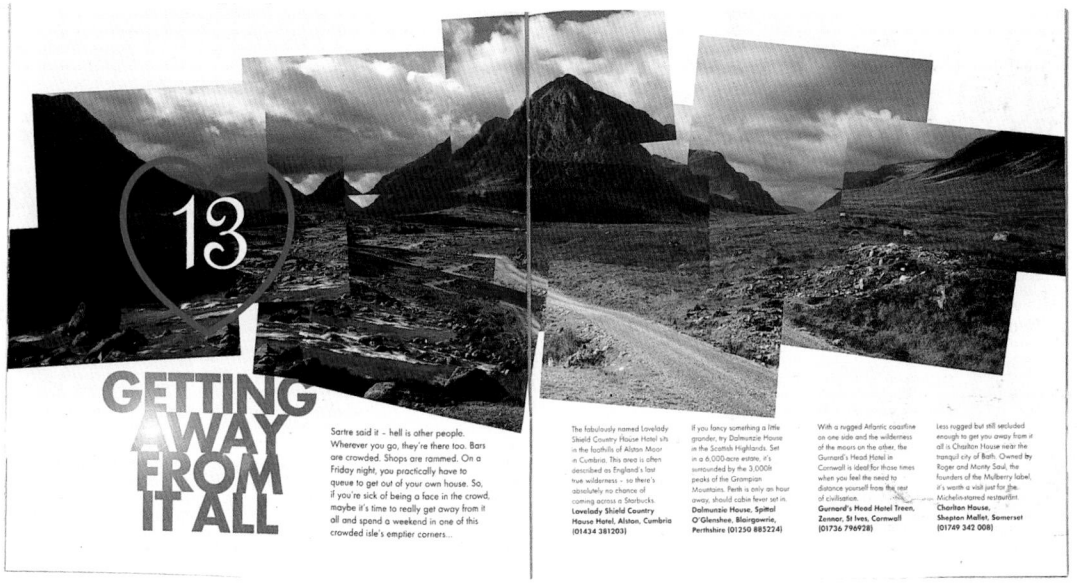

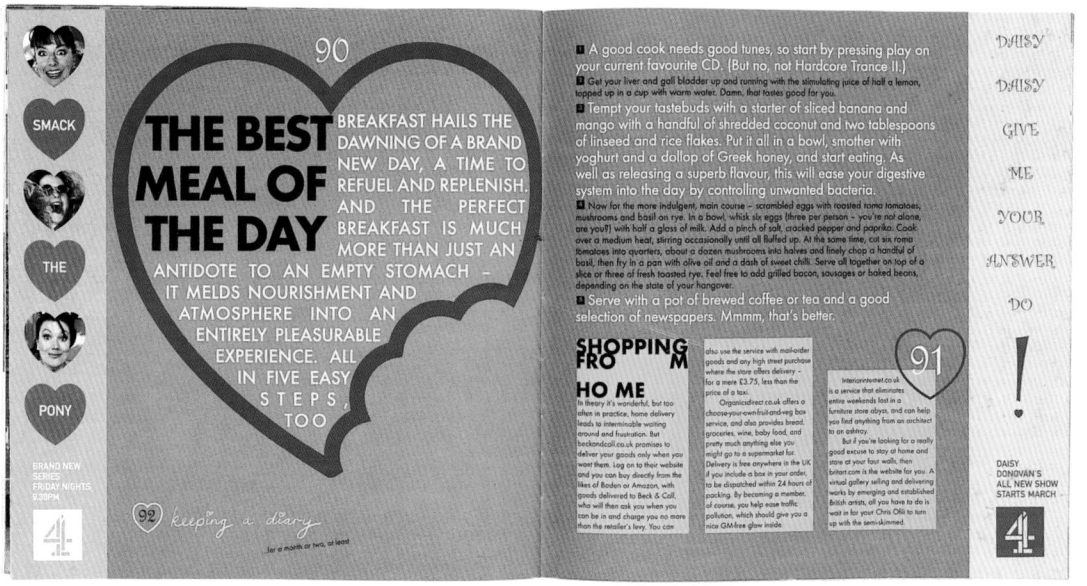

The Good Book *(UK, Issue 1, Spring 2002) 195 x 195mm/7 3/4 x 7 3/4 inches*
This promotional magazine for the new television season for Channel 4 listed '103 Reasons to Love Life'. This numbered editorial structure meant every page had a different subject matter. As a result the design of every entry reacts to its content making a very varied set of pages. The pace is relentless but somehow the randomness of the pages holds together well.
Design *4 Creative*

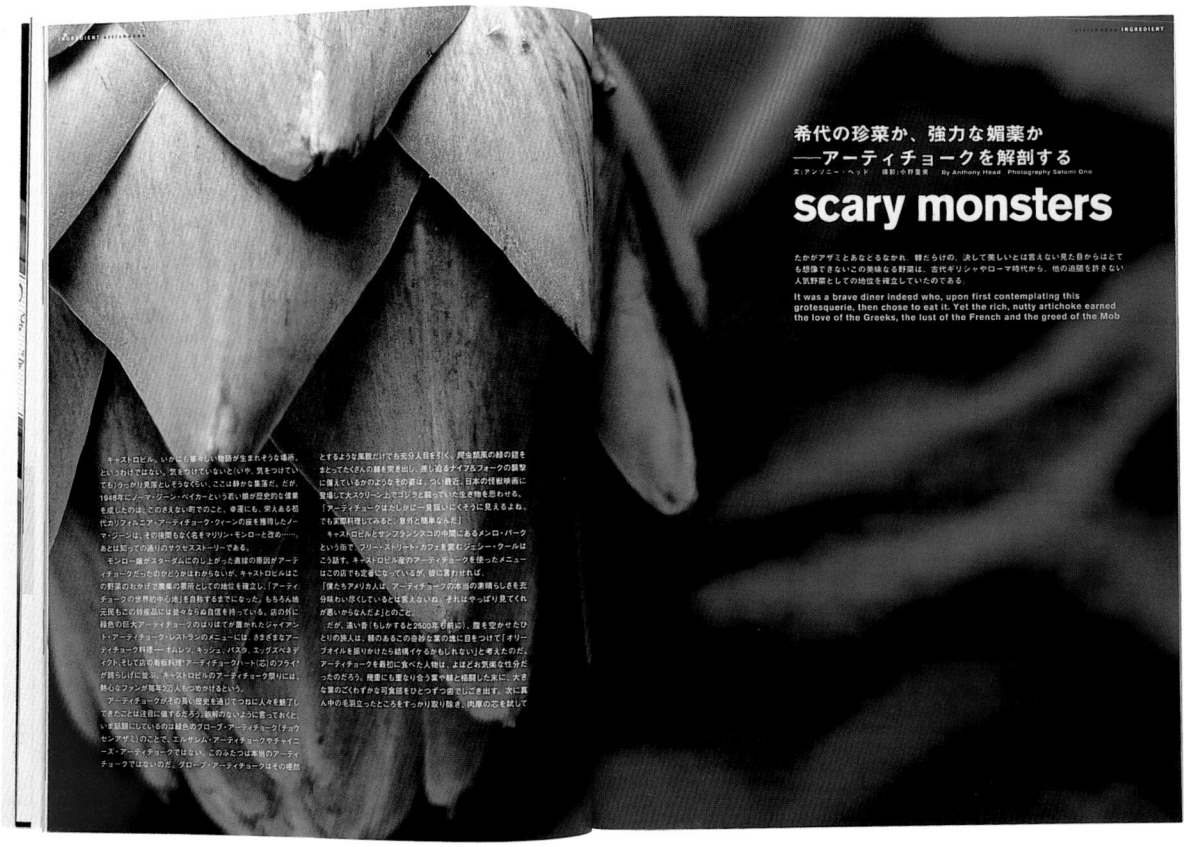

INGREDIENT

希代の珍菜か、強力な媚薬か
——アーティチョークを解剖する

文:アンソニー・ヘッド　撮影:小野聖果　By Anthony Head　Photography Satomi Ono

scary monsters

たかがアザミとあなどるなかれ。棘だらけの、決して美しいとは言えない見た目からはとても想像できないこの異端な野菜は、古代ギリシャやローマ時代から、他の追随を許さない人気野菜としての地位を確立していたのである。

It was a brave diner indeed who, upon first contemplating this grotesquerie, then chose to eat it. Yet the rich, nutty artichoke earned the love of the Greeks, the lust of the French and the greed of the Mob

キャストロビル。いかにも軽々しい物語が生まれそうな場所、というわけではない。気をつけていないと(いや、気をつけていても)うっかり見落としそうなくらい、ここは静かな集落だ。だが、1948年にノーマ・ジーン・ベイカーという若い娘が歴史的な爆撃を成したのは、この小さな町でのこと。幸運にも、栄えある初代ガリフォルニア・アーティチョーク・クィーンの座を獲得したノーマ・ジーンは、その後間もなく名をマリリン・モンローと改め——、あとは知っての通りのサクセスストーリーである。

モンローが一躍ポスターガールになり上がった直接の原因がアーティチョークだったのかどうかはわからないが、キャストロビルはこの野菜のもかげで無風の要所としての地位を確立し、「アーティチョークの世界的中心地」を自称するまでになった。もちろん地元民もこの特産品には並々ならぬ自信を持っている。店の外に緑色の巨大アーティチョークのぼりはためかれたジャイアント・アーティチョーク・レストランのメニューには、さまざまなアーティチョーク料理——オムレツ、キッシュ、パスタ、エッグスベネディクト、そして店の看板料理:アーティチョーク・ハート(芯)のフライが詰められて、盛況。キャストロビルのアーティチョーク祭りには、熱心なファンが毎年2万人もつめかけるという。

アーティチョークがその長い歴史を通じてつねに人々を魅了してきたことは注目に値するだろう。説明のないように言っておくと、いま話題にしているのは緑色のグローブ・アーティチョーク(チョウセンアザミ)のことで、エルサレム・アーティチョークやチャイニーズ・アーティチョークではない。このみたつは本当のアーティチョークではないのだ。グローブ・アーティチョークはその堂々たるような風貌だけでも充分人目を引く。昆虫類風の緑の鎧をまとってたくさんの棘を突き出し、厚い盾とナイフ&フォークの顔撃に備えているかのようなその姿は、つい最近、日本の怪獣映画に登場して大スクリーンでゴジラと闘っていた生き物を思わせる。「アーティチョークはたしかに一見弱いにくそうに見えるよね。でも変装料理してみると、意外と味身のある肉」

キャストロビルとセサフランシスコの中間にあるメンロ・パークという街で、フリーマストリート・カフェを営むジェシー・クールはこう話す。キャストロビル産のアーティチョークを使ったメニューはこの店でも定番になっているが、彼に言わせれば、

「僕たちアメリカ人は、アーティチョークの本当の素晴らしさを充分味わい尽くしているとは言えないね。それはやっぱり見てくれが悪いからなんだよ」とのこと。

だが、遠い昔(もしかすると2500年ほど前)、腹を空かせたひとりの旅人は、棘のあるこの奇妙な菜の芯に目をつけて「オリーブオイルを振りかけたら結構イけるかもしれない」と考えたのだ。アーティチョークを最初に食べた人物は、よほどお気楽な性分だったのだろう。雨風にも耐え合う葉や棘と格闘した末に、大きな葉のごくわずかな可食部をひとつずつ剥がしにありつき出す。次に真ん中の平坦なところをすっかり取り除き、肉厚の芯を試して

Eat, Issue 8, January/February 2002

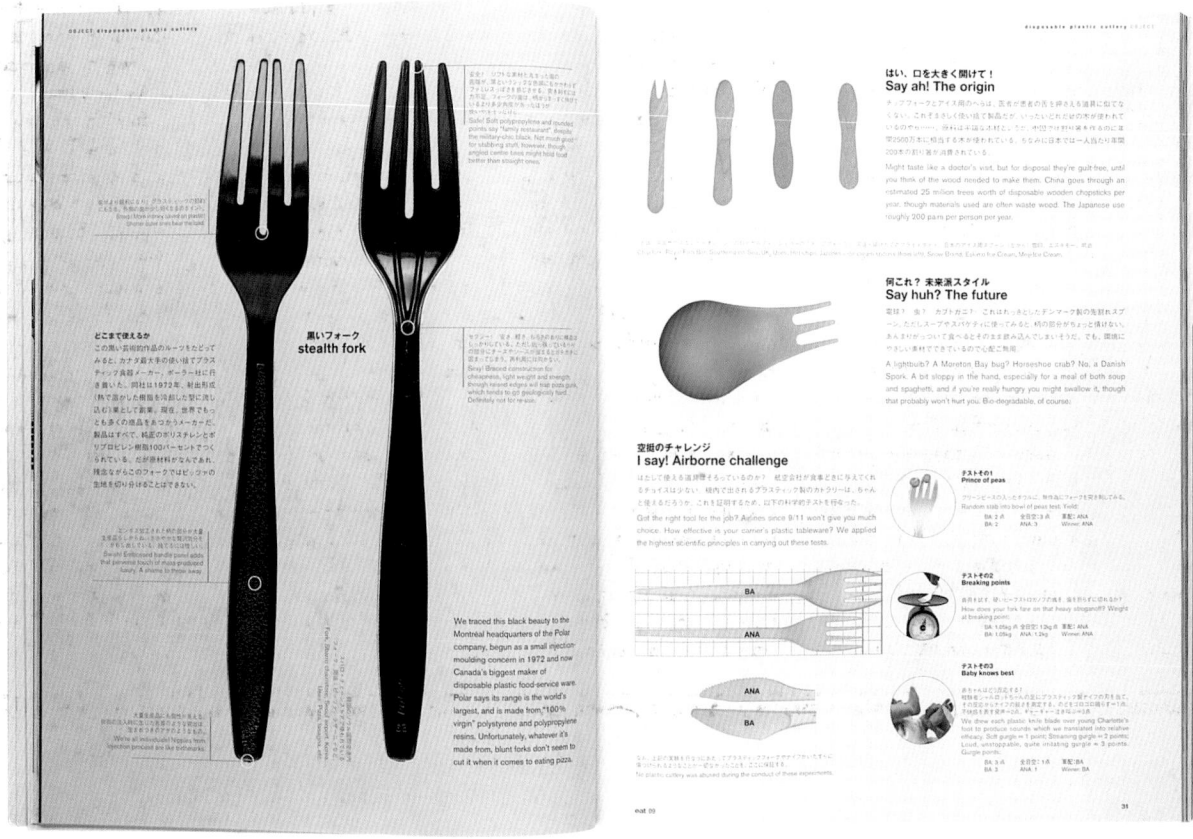

OBJECT disposable plastic cutlery

黒いフォーク
stealth fork

どこまで使えるか
この黒い芸術的作品のルーツをたどってみると、カナダ森林大手の使い捨てプラスチック食器メーカー、ポーラー社に行き着いた。同社は1972年、射出形成(熱で溶かした樹脂を冷却した型に流し込む)業として創業。現在、世界でもっとも多くの商品をあつかうメーカーだ。製品はすべて、純正のポリスチレンとポリプロピレン樹脂100パーセントでつくられている。だが原材料がなんであれ、残念ながらこのフォークではピッツァの生地を切り分けることはできない。

We traced this black beauty to the Montréal headquarters of the Polar company, begun as a small injection moulding concern in 1972 and now Canada's biggest maker of disposable plastic food-service ware. Polar says its range is the world's largest, and is made from "100% virgin" polystyrene and polypropylene resins. Unfortunately, whatever it's made from, blunt forks don't seem to cut it when it comes to eating pizza.

diagnosable plastic cutlery OBJECT

はい、口を大きく開けて！
Say ah! The origin

チップフォークとアイス用のヘラは、医者が患者の舌を押さえる道具に似てなくもない。これぞまさしく使い捨て製品だが、いったいどれだけの木が使われているのやら……。原料は本来は木材だと、でも、中型ひとつ分の材料を作るのには年2500万本に相当する木が使われている。ちなみに日本では一人当たり年間200本の割り箸が消費されている。

Might taste like a doctor's wait, but for disposal they're guilt-free, until you think of the wood needed to make them. China goes through an estimated 25 million trees worth of disposable wooden chopsticks per year, though materials used are often waste wood. The Japanese use roughly 200 pairs per person per year.

何これ？ 未来派スタイル
Say huh? The future

電球？ 虫？ カブトガニ？ これはれっきとしたデンマーク製の洗練されたスプーン。ただしスープやスパゲッティに使ってみると、柄の部分がちょっと頼りない。あんまりがっついて食べるとそのまま鉄の込入でしまいそうだ。でも、環境にやさしい素材でできているので心配ご無用。

A lightbulb? A Moreton Bay bug? Horseshoe crab? No, a Danish Spork. A bit sloppy in the hand, especially for a meal of both soup and spaghetti, and if you're really hungry you might swallow it, though that probably won't hurt you. Bio-degradable, of course.

空組のチャレンジ
I say! Airborne challenge

はたして使える道具なのか？ 航空会社が食事とともに与えてくれるチップスはひどい。結局ではおもちゃ。プラスチック製のカトラリーは、ちゃんと使えるだろうか。これを証明するため、以下のハイテクなテストを行なった。

Got the right tool for the job? Airlines since 9/11 won't give you much choice. How effective is your corner's plastic tableware? We applied the highest scientific principles in carrying out these tests.

BA
ANA

ANA
BA

テストその1
Prince of peas

グリンピースの入ったボウルに、無作為にフォークを突き刺してみる。
Random stab into bowl of peas test. Yield:

BA: 2点　全日空: 3点　軍配: ANA
BA: 2　ANA: 3　Winner: ANA

テストその2
Breaking points

自作ミートボール、硬いピーナッツのカンブリ、重さ何キロに耐えるか？
How does your fork fare on that heavy stroganoff? Weight at breaking point:

BA: 1.05kg 点　全日空: 1.2kg 点　軍配: ANA
BA: 1.05kg　ANA: 1.2kg　Winner: ANA

テストその3
Baby knows best

赤ちゃんはどこ刺激する！
特別者ーシャルロットちゃんの足にプラスチックナイフの刃を当て、その反応からナイフの鋭さを測定する。たとえばロロロ鋭すぎ＝1点、ちょっと鋭すぎ＝2点、ギューギューどうにか＝3点。
We drew each plastic knife blade over young Charlotte's foot to produce sounds, which we translated into relative efficacy. Soft gurgle = 1 point; Smearing gurgle = 2 points; Loud, unstoppable, quite irritating gurgle = 3 points. Gurgle points:

BA: 3点　全日空: 1点　軍配: BA
BA: 3　ANA: 1　Winner: BA

eat 09

31

Eat, Issue 9, March/April 2002

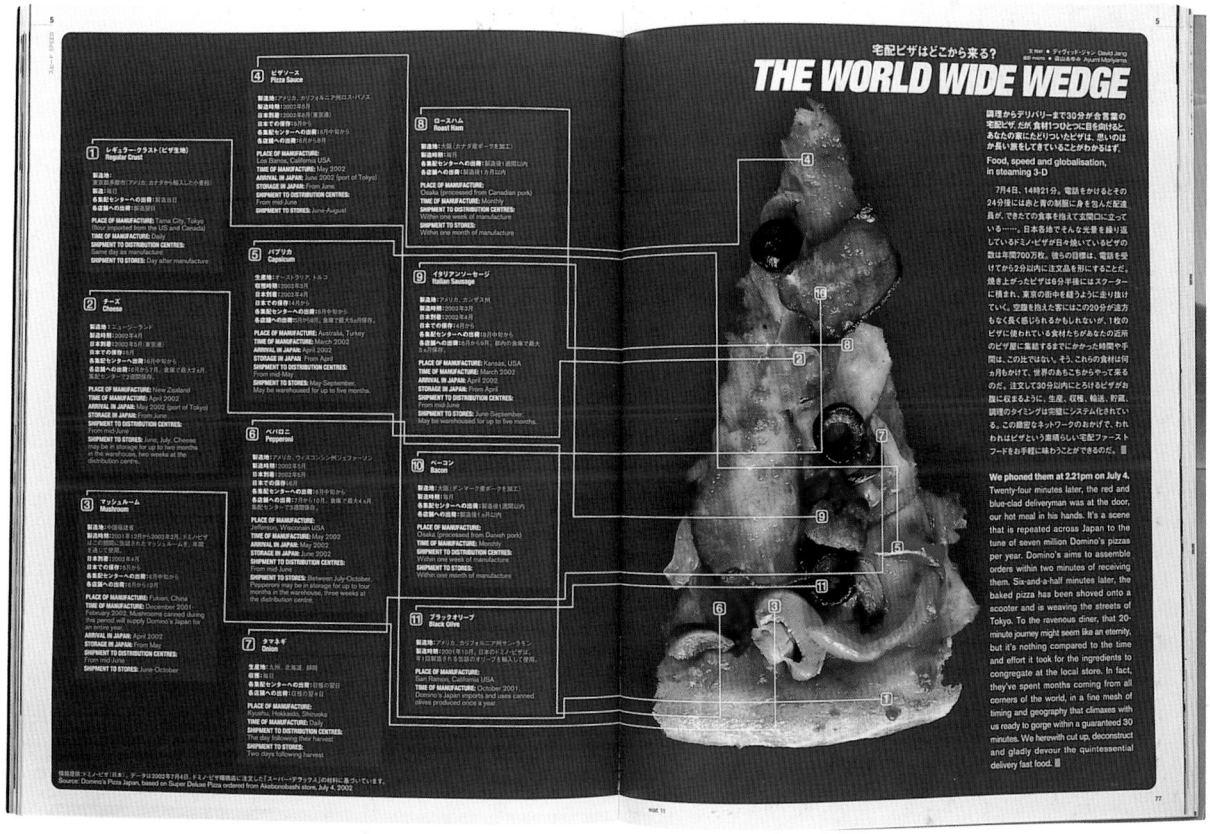

宅配ピザはどこから来る？

THE WORLD WIDE WEDGE

Food, speed and globalisation, in steaming 3-D

Eat, Issue 11, September 2002, 230 x 296mm/9 x 11 3/4 inches

How large is the Japanese publishing industry?
The total number of magazines bought in 2000 was 4,620 million, of which 2,960 million were monthlies. A lot of these sales were Manga comics, which can sell over 3 million per issue.

Is the industry based on newsstand sales or subscriptions?
99% newsstand. There are a few subscription based magazines and you can subscribe to others, but most people don't. You can't legally discount a magazine from the cover price, so there are no special discounts.

Are Japanese editions of western titles regarded as successful in their own right or are the original western magazines seen as 'cooler'?
The Japanese editions of western magazines that have been most successful are those that have adapted their content to the Japanese market. Many have not worked very well – *Vogue* has had numerous relaunches and the present incarnation has had, I think, three editors in two years.

Sports Graphic Number is one of the most successful sports magazines here and was originally the Japanese version of *Sports Illustrated*. *Elle* has probably been the most successful of the fashion magazines, but has lost some of its image recently by trying to make up for falling revenue with a spin-off range of branded items ranging from slippers to even toilet seat covers!

Original foreign magazines don't really compete with the above. Some western magazines are bought for flicking through, as a lifestyle accessory – most big bookshops in Tokyo and other major cities will have a foreign magazine section – but total sales are not large. *Fortune* is one of the biggest sellers with 4–5,000 copies. *Wallpaper** is always quoted, but about 1,000 per issue are actually sold here.

What are the main differences between Japanese and western magazines?
The big difference is the way Japanese magazines read from what we regard as the back through to the front. This is a must if you want to use vertical text, because it has to be read from right to left. If a story is restricted to a single spread then there is no problem, but if the story runs across multiple spreads then the page direction becomes important. Most magazines are therefore read right to left, using vertical text for the body plus horizontal for captions, notes and sidebars. You can run Japanese horizontally and then it runs left to right, but the traditional way is easier for Japanese readers. There are exceptions, primarily in design-related magazines that want to try something different, such as *Axis*, *Idea* and *Composite*.

Japanese people are far less confused by western titles than we are by theirs; they have been brought up with English, it's everywhere you look here in Tokyo. Western magazines are familiar things, whereas in the west you are unlikely to see a Japanese magazine unless you really want one.

Design-wise there's not much difference after that. Many westerners think that the average Japanese magazine looks very messy – this is partly to do with what you're used to, but I think for a lot of the cheaper information-based magazines content is far more important than design and it shows. On the other hand there are some beautifully designed magazines, so I guess that's much the same as anywhere.

One significant difference is the way magazines are put together. There is an editor-in-chief that runs the show, but there is another tier of editors that are allocated a section of the magazine to put together each issue. Often these editors are freelance and sometimes sections are farmed out to separate editorial companies. In

Interview

Steve Martin
Creative director
Eat magazine

LIBRARY & RESOURCES AREA EPSOM CAMPUS
THE SURREY INSTITUTE OF ART & DESIGN

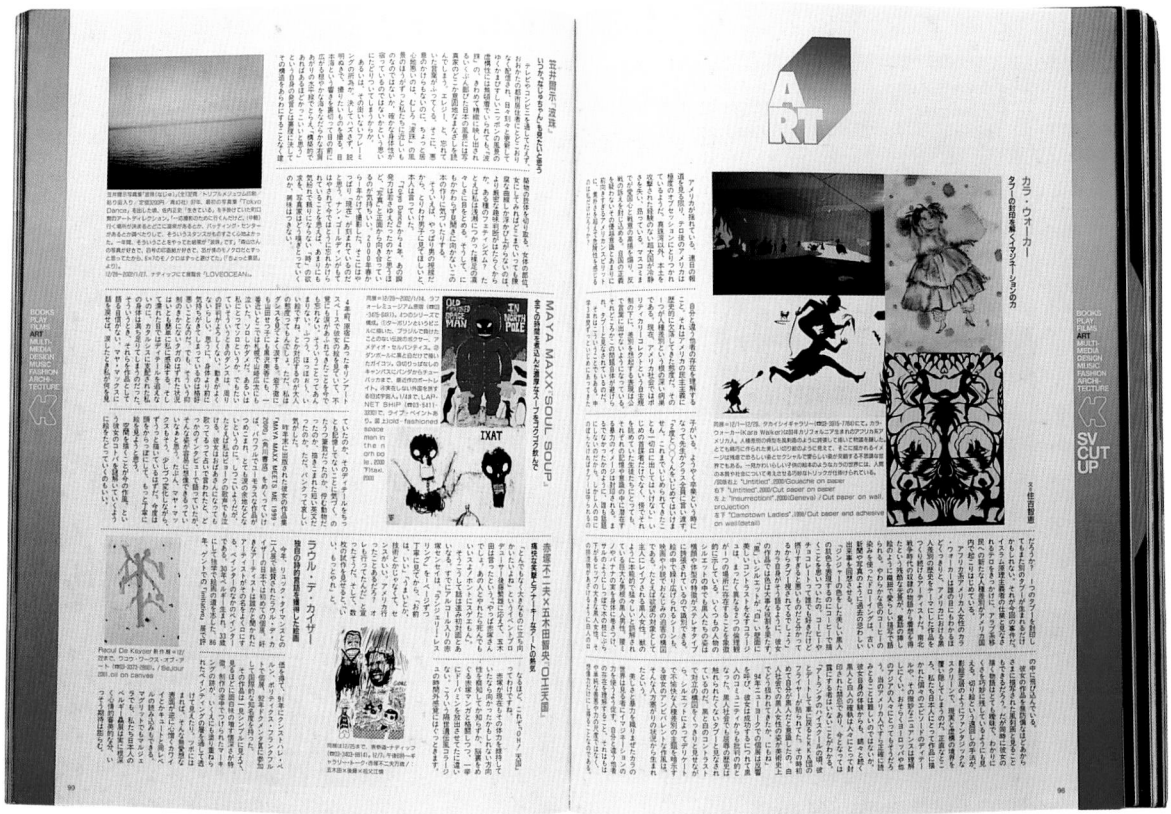

Studio Voice, January 2002, 226 x 300mm/8 7/8 x 11 7/8 inches

both cases the editor is expected to come up with idea, the layout, to book a photographer and have all content ready for production. This is why some magazines seem to change personality as you flick through.

This editorial dominance follows through to the top; it's the editors you hear about. One exception to this is a designer called Yasushi Fujimoto. In keeping with the system I mentioned above, he has his own company (Cap) and so works independently of the magazines he designs for. He and his team have art directed *Studio Voice*, *Taiyo*, *Ryuko-Tsushin*, *Marie Claire Japan*, *Ritz*, *Dune* and *GQ Japan*.

What do these differences mean for *Eat*?

The text in *Eat* is printed in both English and Japanese – half the editorial and design team are Japanese, half are English – but we follow the western model of production. Everything is done in-house with our dedicated team. But we can't just write in one language and translate to the other. There are the obvious cultural differences. When we ran a detailed story about Jewish culture and food it had absolutely no context in the Japanese world view so we couldn't include a Japanese translation - we just didn't have space to explain what is common knowledge to the westerner.

But there's also the different expectations from readers to take into account. Japanese readers don't like too many new facts in their writing, as it is considered offensive, while westerners expect to learn lots as they read. So while the English version of an article might be packed with information, the Japanese may be more vague and descriptive.

The exception to this is product information. Japanese lifestyle magazines work on the basis of 'If you want to be X, then you need to have this, wear that...' and there then follows 20 pages of product photos, much of which has been put together with the manufacturers. And you get the same formula for every target audience. In this way, the product is rarely criticized and thus the good relationships between the magazines and their clients are maintained.

Do companies pay for editorial space?

Absolutely. That is probably where most of the non-circulation income comes from. Companies are far more interested in paid editorial than straight advertising. It's a bit like 20-40% of the magazine being an advertorial, but without the little line at the top of the page to that effect. This is why there is less conventional advertising. It's changing a little, but we have had a major struggle trying to avoid tie-up at *Eat*.

After two years of publishing *Eat* I feel we've probably chosen the most difficult way to do everything. Being independent and doing the whole thing ourselves – content, production, sales (trying to do it with straight advertising instead of selling editorial) and distribution, we are doing the complete opposite of what is acceptable here. Just breaking even is a success for us and we rely on other projects to pay the bills. But I think there is a change taking place and we are starting to become more accepted, so we'll keep at it.

We are also constantly challenging our own staffs' assumptions about magazines. The Japanese team question the English and how we lay it out and vice versa. This makes us think differently.

Which are the other ground-breaking titles?

There are a lot of interesting magazines that come and go. But to have a major impact here you have to be mass market and that brings its own limitations. *Brutus* is probably the most ground breaking - it is a bi-monthly men's magazine that when it first launched was different for being a young lifestyle magazine.

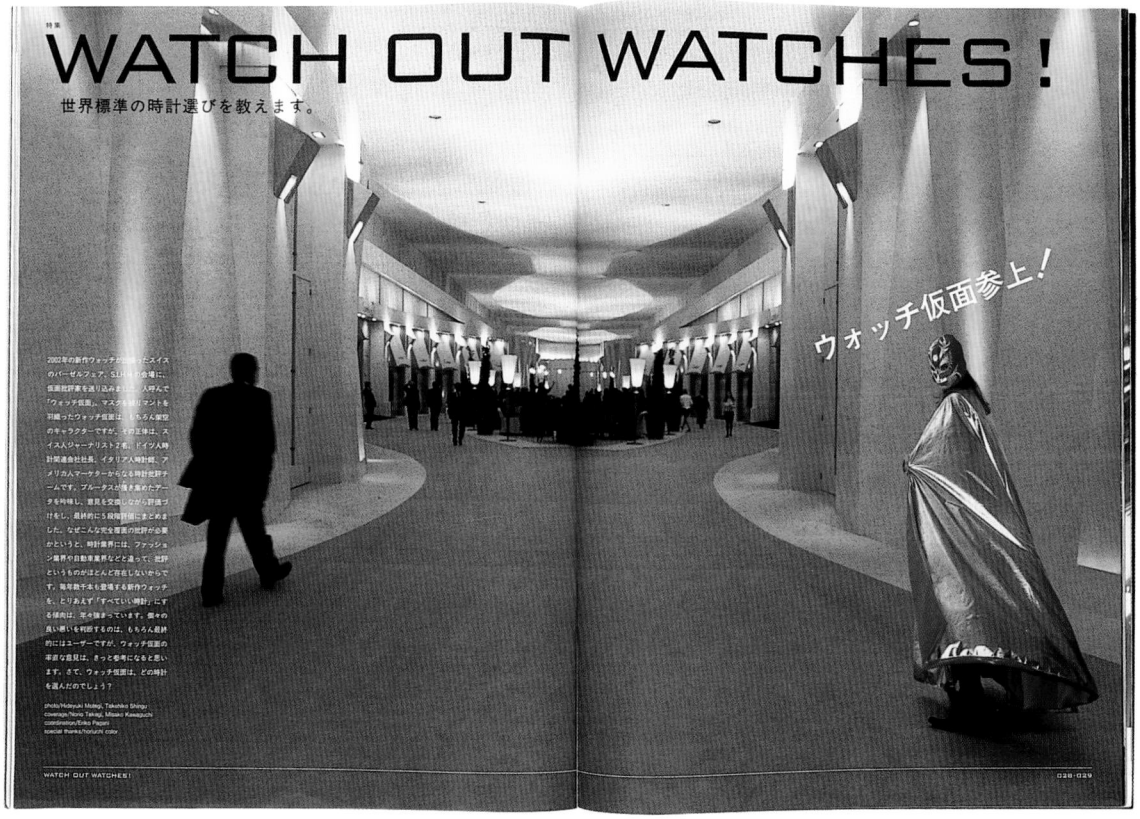

特集

WATCH OUT WATCHES!

世界標準の時計選びを教えます。

ウォッチ仮面参上!

2002年の新作ウォッチが出揃ったスイスのバーゼルフェア、S.I.H.H.の会場に、仮面批評家を送り込みました。人呼んで「ウォッチ仮面」。マスクを被りマントを羽織ったウォッチ仮面は、もちろん覆面のキャラクターですが、その正体は、スイス人ジャーナリスト2名、ドイツ人時計関連会社社長、イタリア人時計師、アメリカ人マーケターからなる時計批評チームです。ブルータスが集め集めたデータを吟味し、意見を交換しながら評価づけをし、最終的に5段階評価にまとめました。なぜこんな完全覆面の批評が必要かというと、時計業界には、ファッション業界や自動車業界などと違って、批評というものがほとんど存在しないからです。毎年数千本も登場する新作ウォッチを、とりあえず「すべていい時計」にする傾向は、充分揃っています。傾ヤの良い悪いを判断するのは、もちろん最終的にはユーザーですが、ウォッチ仮面の率直な意見は、きっと参考になると思います。さて、ウォッチ仮面は、どの時計を選んだのでしょう?

photo/Hideyuki Motegi, Takehiko Shingu
coverage/Nirvis Takagi, Misaki Kawaguchi
coordination/Eriko Pagani
special thanks/horiuchi color

Brutus, June 2002, 210 x 285mm/8 1/4 x 11 1/4 inches

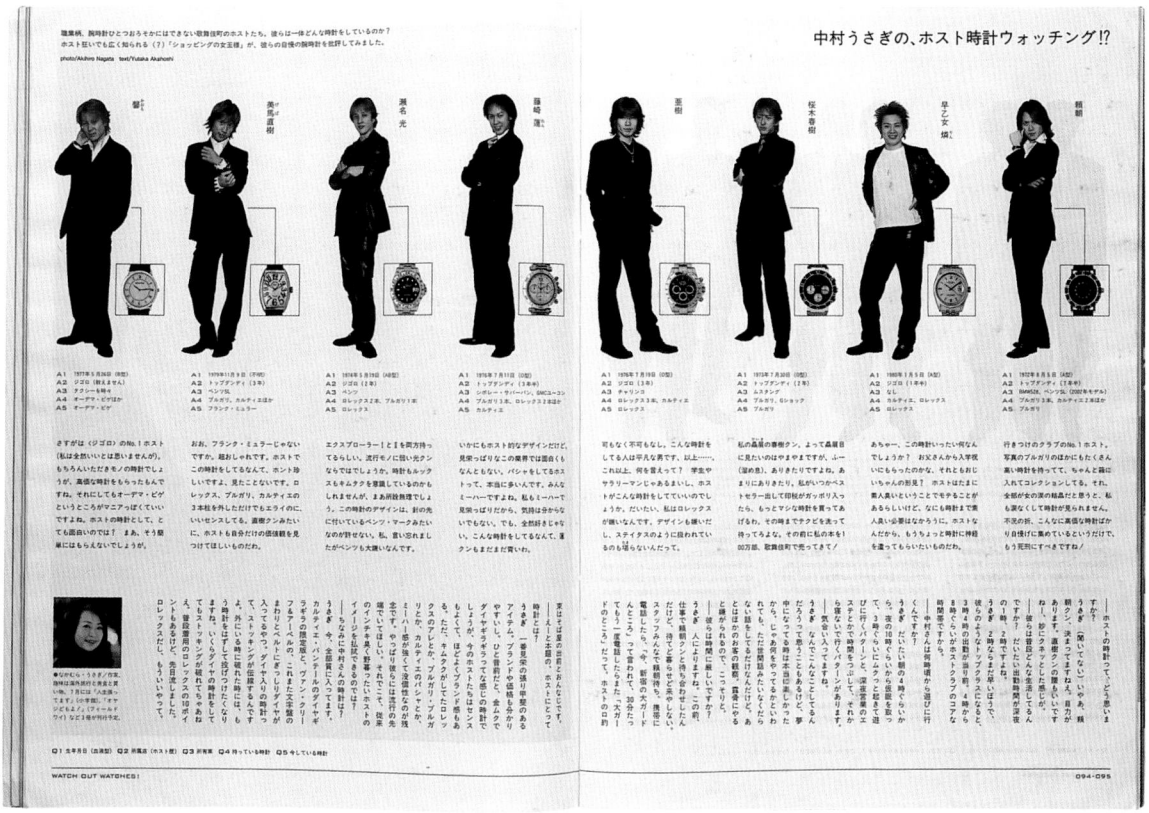

職業柄、腕時計ひとつおろそかにはできない歌舞伎町のホストたち。彼らは一体どんな時計をしているのか?
ホスト狂いでも広く知られる(?)「ショッピングの女王様」が、彼らの自慢の腕時計を批評してみました。

photo/Akihiro Nagata text/Yutaka Akahoshi

中村うさぎの、ホスト時計ウォッチング!?

御堂

A1 1973年5月26日(B型)
A2 ジゴロ(教えません)
A3 タグ・ホイヤー
A4 オーデマ・ピゲほか
A5 オーデマ・ピゲ

さすがは《ジゴロ》の№1ホスト(私は全然いいとは思いませんが)。もちろんいただきモノの時計でしょうが、高級な時計をもちったんですね。それにしてもオーデマ・ピゲというところがマニアっぽくていいですよね。ホストの時計として、とても面白いのでは? まあ、そう簡単にはもらえないでしょうが。

美馬(みまば)直樹

A1 1979年11月3日(アリ)
A2 ジゴロ(3年)
A3 ベンツSL
A4 ブルガリ、カルティエほか
A5 フランク・ミュラー

お、フランク・ミュラーじゃないですか。超おしゃれです。ホストでこの時計をしてるなんて、ホント珍しいですよ。見たことないです。ロレックス、ブルガリ、カルティエの3本組を外しただけでもエライのに、いいセンスしてる。唐傘クンみたいに、ホストも自分だけの個性観を見つけてほしいものだね。

黒名 光

A1 1976年1月29日(AB型)
A2 ジゴロ(2年)
A3 ベンツ
A4 ロレックス2本、ブルガリ1本
A5 ロレックス

エクスプローラーⅠとⅡを同方持ってるらしい、武行モノに拉い光クンならではでしょうか。時計もルックスもキムタクを意識してるのかもしれませんが、まあ所詮物真でしょう。この時計のデザインは、前の先に付いているベンツ・マークみたいなのが許せない。私、言い忘れましたがベンツを大嫌いなんです。いかにもホスト的なデザインだけど、見栄っぱりなこの業界では国会くらなんともないし、パシャをしてるホストって、本当に多いんです。みんなトーハーってずよね。私もトーハーって見栄っぱりだから、気持は分かるけどね。でも、全然好きじゃない。こんな時計をしてるなんて、浦クンもまだまだ青いわ。

藤崎 蓮(ふじさき)

A1 1976年7月19日(O型)
A2 トップランディ(3年半)
A3 シボレー・サバーバン、BMCスーコン
A4 ブルガリ3本、ロレックス2本ほか
A5 カルティエ

亜樹

A1 1976年7月19日(O型)
A2 ジゴロ(3年)
A3 チャリリコ
A4 ロレックス3本、カルティエ
A5 ロレックス

桜木春樹

A1 1975年7月30日(O型)
A2 トップランディ(2年)
A3 ムスタング
A4 ブルガリ、Gショック
A5 ブルガリ

私の高級の象徴クン。よって高級目に見たいのはやまやまですが、ふーん(溜め息)。ありきたりですよね。あまりにありきたり。私がいつかベストセラー品して印税がガッポリ入ったら、もっとマシな時計を買ってあげるわ。その時までケチビを凍って待ってろよな。その前に私のボキを100万部、歌舞伎町で売ってきて!

早乙女 焔(さおとめ)

A1 1980年1月5日(A型)
A2 ジゴロ(1年半)
A3 なし
A4 カルティエ、ロレックス
A5 ロレックス

あちゃー、この時計いったい何なんでしょうか? おじさんから入学祝いにもらったのかな。それとも初いちゃんの形見? ホストはたとえ素人臭いにせよこんなものを…。あるらしいけど、なにも時計まで素人臭い必要はなからうに。ホストなんだから、もうちょっと時計に神経を遣ってもらいたいものだね。

朝朝

A1 1972年8月5日(AB型)
A2 トップランディ(3年半)
A3 BMW525i、ベンツSL(2002年モデル)
A4 ブルガリ3本、カルティエ2本ほか
A5 ブルガリ

行きつけのクラブの№1ホスト。写真のブルガリのほかにもたくさん美い時計を持ってて、ちゃんと箱に入れてコレクションしてる。それ、全部がその店の給料だと思うと、私も涙なくして時計が見られませんね。不況の折、こんなに高価な時計ばかり自慢げに集めているというだけで、もう死刑にすべきですね!

●なかむら・うさぎ/作家。毎時は海外旅行と美食と買い物。1月には「人生第一…」(小学館)、「オヤジになると…」(フィールドワイド)などを発売予定。

Q1 生年月日(血液型) Q2 所属店(ホスト歴) Q3 所有車 Q4 持っている時計 Q5 今している時計

Brutus, June 2002

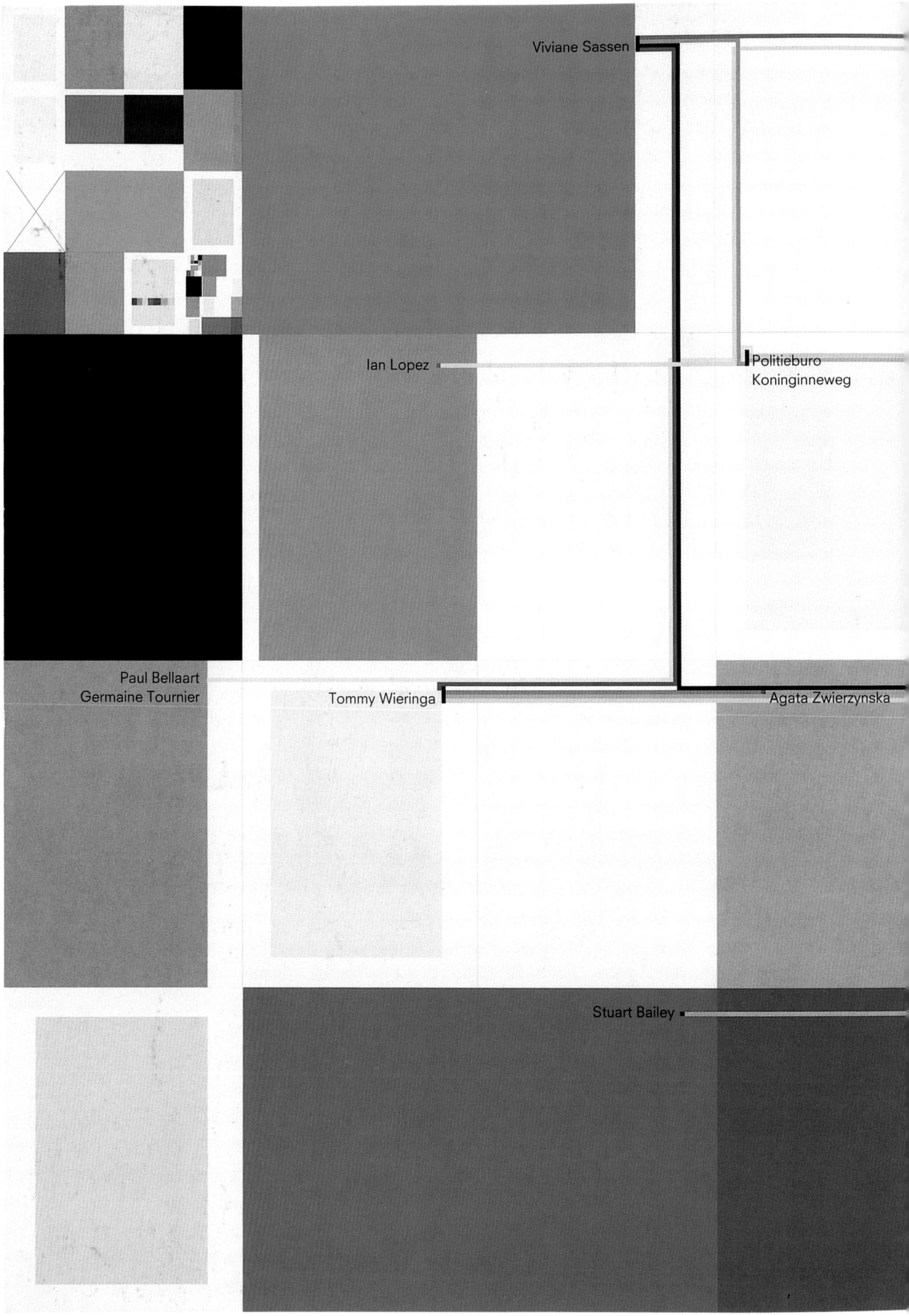
Viviane Sassen
Ian Lopez
Politieburo
Koninginneweg
Paul Bellaart
Germaine Tournier
Tommy Wieringa
Agata Zwierzynska
Stuart Bailey

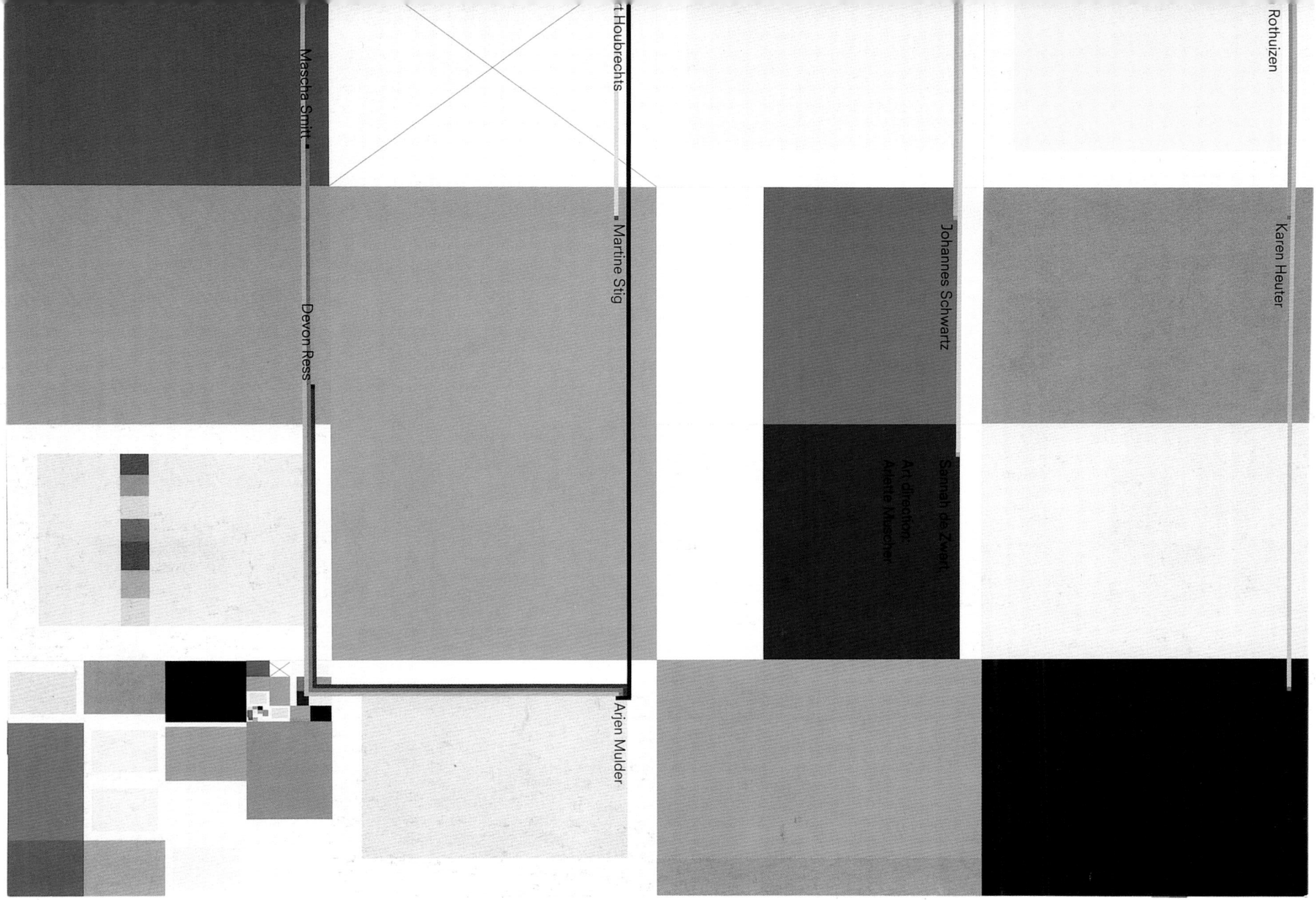

Sec *(The Netherlands, Issue 6) 165 x 220mm/6 ½ x 8 ¾ inches*
This magazine sets up art projects and publishes the results as magazines. In this example, one photograph was interpreted through text by four different writers, each of which were then in turn interpreted by three different artists. The project was published with the back and front covers (THIS SPREAD) acting as a diagramatic guide to the project and the way it is layed out in the magazine. Each block of colour represents a page, the top left hand corner being the front cover. This is followed by the original picture that started the process. Four colour lines lead out from this picture and direct the reader to the pages with the four written texts and from each of them three lines spread out to the artists' interpretations. The coloured lines appear on the pages themselves (OVERLEAF).
Design *OK, T/F*

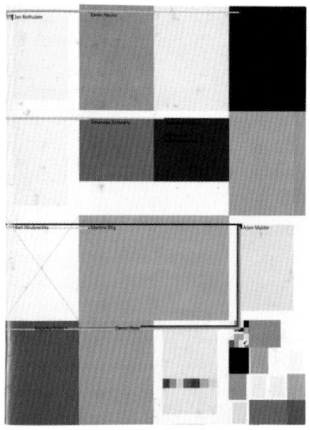

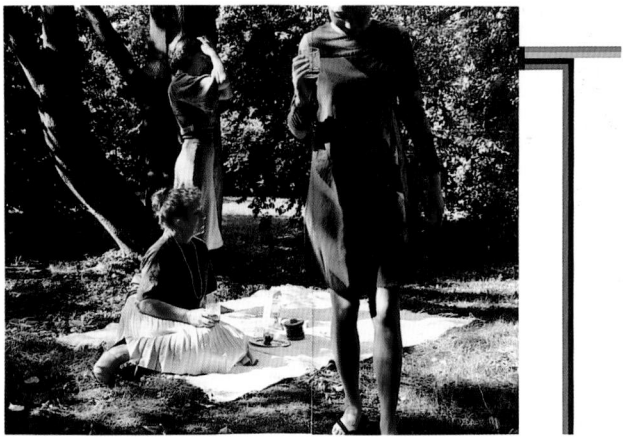

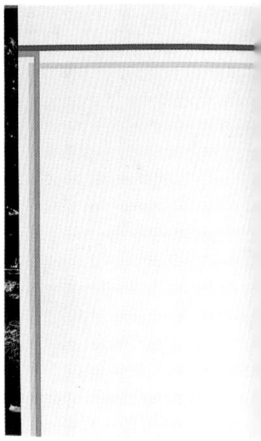

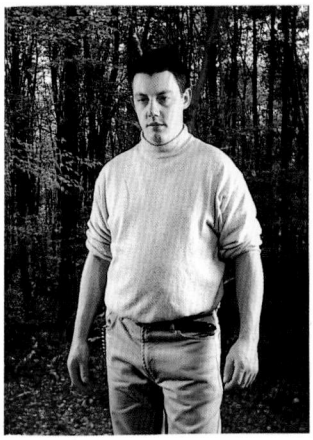

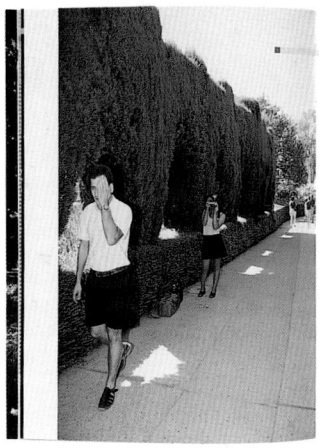

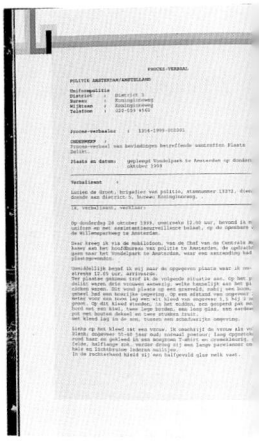

POLITIE AMSTERDAM/AMSTELLAND

Gefingerpolitie
Plaatsen : Plaatsen 3
Kamer : Koningsplein
Wijkteam : Koningsplein
Telefoon : 020-559 9555

Zaaknr-verbaalnr : 1314-1999-003001

ONDERWERP :
Inzage-verzoek van bewaakingen betreffende aanrandsten Plaats Delict

Plaats en datum: gelegenheid Vondelpark te Amsterdam op donderdag 28 oktober 1999

Verbalisant :

Luister de dienst, brigadier van politie, stamnummer 13272, dienstbonde aan District 3, Kamer Koningsplein.

Ik, verbalisant, verklaar:

Op donderdag 28 oktober 1999, omstreeks 12.00 uur, bevond ik mij, uniform en met assistentiemotorfiets belast, op de opmaat van de Willemsparkweg te Amsterdam.

Daar kreeg ik via de mobiltoon, van de Chef van de Centrale Meldkamer aan het hoofdbureau van politie te Amsterdam, de opdracht om naar het Vondelpark te Amsterdam, waar een aanranding had plaatsgevonden.

Onmiddellijk begaf ik mij naar de opgegeven plaats waar ik omstreeks 12.05 uur, arriveerde.

Ter plaatse bleek dat er sprake van de volgende situatie was. Op een gelid waren drie vrouwen aanwezig, welke hapsnapjs aan het genieten waren. Ook werd plaats op een zonneveld, zodat een kondom, welke aan de zijkant van de vrouw lag, kon worden gefotografeerd. Ook werd een kous (zg sok) lichtblauw, met zwarte ( ) strepen, op dit kleed gevonden; in het midden, een opgerold pakje van een kondom, welke aan de zijkant van de vrouw lag, een exemplaar van hetzelfde dekzel en een stukken lmoiet, welke aan de zijkant van het kleed lag in de zon, tussen een schaduwrijke omgeving.

Links op het kleed was een vrouw, de verdachte (de vrouw die op kleed, dichtbij de kous lag) van ongeveer 1.70 meter lang, zwarte haar en gekleed in een zwarten T-shirt en zwemshorts, zwarte halfhoge sok, zwarte dring ( ) een lange paarlemoer ketting en zwarte zonnebril op haar hoofd.
In de (schatbaard kleed (?) een halfgerold glaz melk vast.

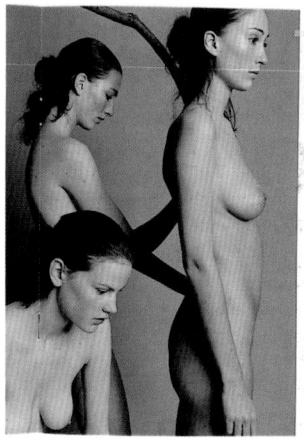

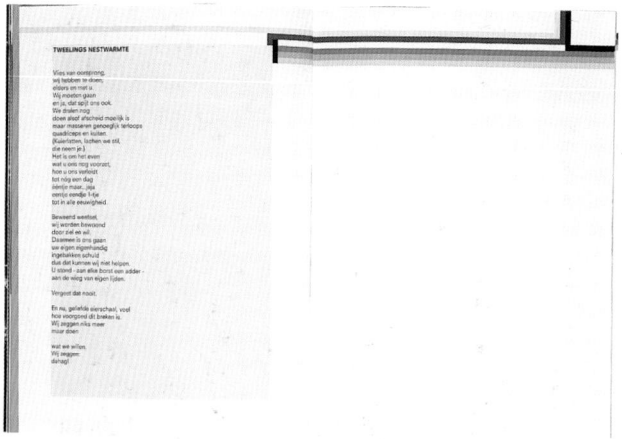

TWEELINGS NESTWARMTE

Vlies van oorsprong,
wij hebben te doen;
elders en niet u
Wij moeten gaan
en ja, dat spijt ons ook.
We draken nog
doen alsof afscheid mogelijk is
maar masseren gemoedijk tentoons
quadriceps en kuiten.
(Kuiletatten, lotten we ook,
die neem je.)
Het is om het even
wat u ons nog vertraat,
hoe u ons verleist
tot nog een dag
(dém)e maar, jaja
eenzie oondjo 1-6e
tot in alle eeuwigheid

Bewend weetlust,
wij worden liewsond
door zie en uit.
Daarmee is ons gaan
we eigen eigenhandig
ingebakken schuld
dus dat kunnen wij niet helpen.
U stond - aan elke bonst een adder -
aan de weg van eigen tuiten

Vergoed dat nooit.

En nu, geliefde aierschaal, voel
hoe voorgoed dit breken is.
Wij zeggen niks meer
maar steen

wat we willen,
Wij zeggen
dankgij

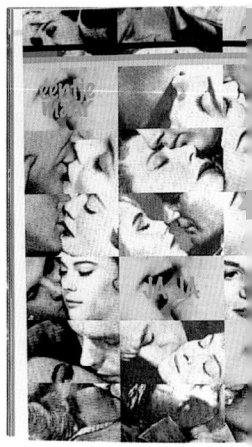

pinhoog gaat achter de aisiende vrouw in de lichtgroene jak en één stek naar links afbuigt tot in de linker bovenhoek van de foto. Dat maakt opnieuw een sterk, geconstrueerde indruk. Tussen boom en struik is een lichtere, grijsgroene vlek te zien; een grasveldje op de achtergrond, een open plek in het bos. De foto is niet artiest, maar ook niet onsteldijk boeiend.
Het ensemble ernsuit stel warmte uit door d dat geligt/wite zoekt. Tegelijk is zo aadscklijk gecoopd geen zienige informatie over de dde personages in het beeld op te nemen of in zo min mogelijk ata individuen en zoveel mogelijk ata topografische structuurelementen te gebruiken, dat het beeld niet echt uitnodigt om er long en aandachtig naar te kijken. Rechts aasst de mchter verticale vrouw (dat meisje) is een fanne gele vlek in het gras te zien, tussen de schaduwen van bomen. Deze vlek trijkt tnj langere bestudering (noodzakelijk omdat het mijn opdracht is de foto te beschrijven) het nuttpunt in het beeld te zijn. Ik gebod dat ik ook de zittende oudere vrouw eigenlijk geen persoonlijkheid vind hebben. En nu ik dit zeg, denk ik: alle drie de personages en dat o zo nauwkeurig gekozen witte tafelkleed in het gras, en ook die precies geplaatste stabbele boom en die frisse aanksperfecte stoeltjsjjjjj, daar tegenover, ze kennen me gecoten worden - laat het allemaal genust maar fotografische elementen zijn en niet meer dan dat. Ik kijk toch bij voorkeur naar die gele vlek rechtsonder. Daar gebeurt tenminste iets. O, maar ik merk nu dat de ouder vrouw naar de vlek zit te kijken, wat mijn kijenter begint te storen.
Nee, nu de foto een aantal dagen op mijn schrijftafel te hebben laten staan, op een meter van mijn stoel, begin ik te denken dat hij het beste uitkomt op een duizdinge afstand van de beschouwer dat je alleen dat warme groen en wit ziet, en niet wordt gehinderd door de afgebeelde personages en wat dis proberen voor te stellen (of uitstralkelijk juist niet willen zijn. Een mooie lichtgroene vlek aan de muur, als je er soms bij in de buurt komt ze je dat het nog wat voorstelt ook, maar de voorstelling is niet nodig voor het plezier dat de foto teweegbrengt. Laat het maar een vlek zijn, met die verticaal rechts (met donkere en lichtgroene banen) en die lichtgroene verticaal links en al die witte vlekkenghed daarmeen. Een klodder licht, zo komt hij het beste uit.

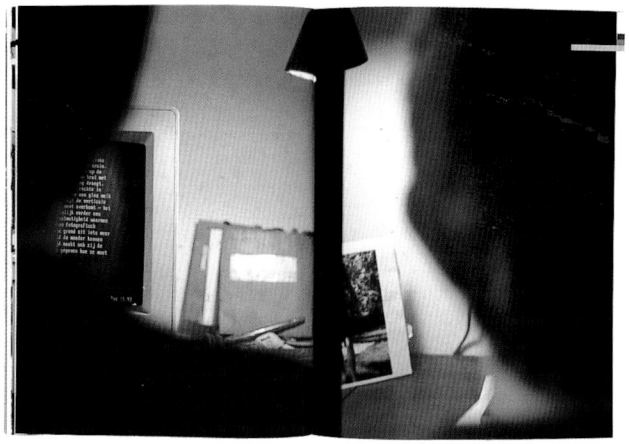

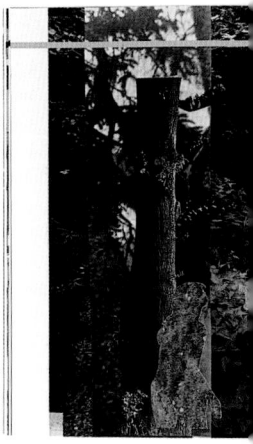

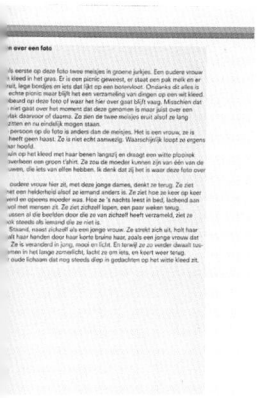

n over een foto

ls eerste op deze foto twee meisjes in groene jurkjes. Een oudere vrouw
n kleed in het gras. Er is een picnic geweed, er staat een pak melk en er
nut, lege bordjes en iets dat lijkt op een bonenhoed. Ondanks dit alles is
echte picnic maar blijft het een vertaalslag van dingen op een wit kleed.
ibeurd op deze foto of waar het hier over gaat blijft vaag. Misschien dat
niet gaat over het moment dat deze genomen is maar juist over een
dak dearnoor of daarna. Ze zien de twee meisjes eruit alsof ze lang
zitten en nu eindelijk mogen staan.
personen op de foto is anders dan de meisjes. Het is een vrouw, ze is
heeft geen haast. Ze is niet echt aanwezig. Waarschijnlijk loopt ze ergens
ar heeft.
uim op het kleed met haar benen langzijn en draagt een witte pipoinek
overheen een groen t'shirt. Ze zou de moeder kunnen zijn van één van de
uwen, die iets van alles hebben. Ik denk dat zij het is waar deze foto over

oudere vrouw Ner zit, met deze jonge dames, denkt ze terug. Ze ziet
het een heldenhaiid alsof ze iemand anders is. Ze ziet hoe ze keer op keer
end en opeens meender was. Hoe lie ze nachts keek in bed, lachend aan
vol met mensen zit. Ze ziet zichzelf lopen, een paar weken terug.
uisen of die beelden door die ze van zichzelf heeft verzameld, ziet ze
ok steeds als iemand die ze niet is.
fbaand, niaat zichzelf als een jonge vrouw. Ze strekt zich uit, holt haar
alt haar handen door haar korte bruine haar, zoals een jonge vrouw dat
Ze is veranderd in jung, maat en fiziit. En tarwijl ze zo verder dawalt tus-
omen in het lange zomerlicht, lacht ze om iets, en koert weer terug.
oude fotoiam dat nog steeds diep in gedachten op het witte kleed zit.

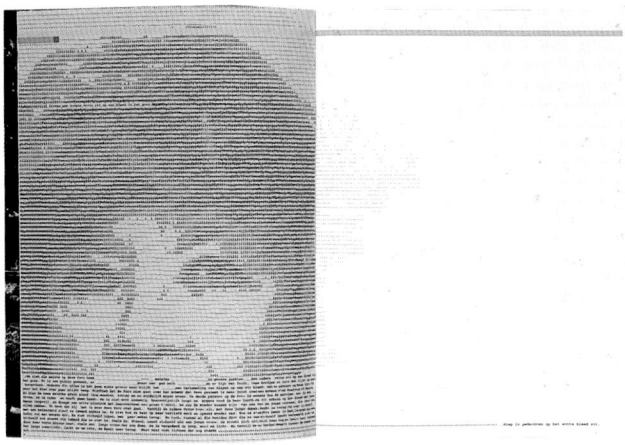

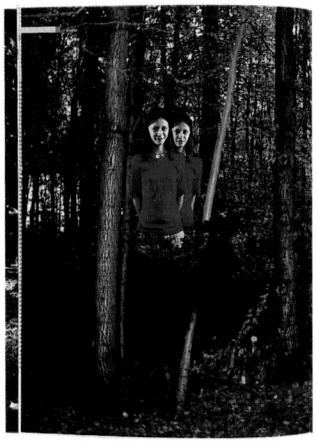

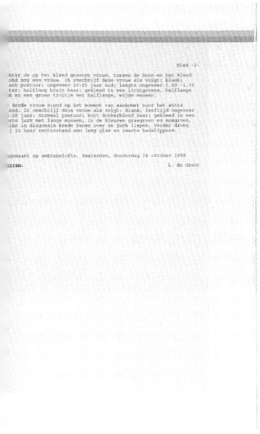

Blad -2-

ezer op het kleed geraken vrouw, tussen de bonen en het kleed
ond nog een vrouw. Ik overkijk(t) deze vrouw als volgt: blank;
aan puitiet; ingeweer 17-25 jaar oud; langzo ingeweer 1.50 -1.70
442; halflang kriin haar; gekleed in een lichtgroene, halflange
& en een groen t'shirtje met halflange, witte mouwen

Grote vrouw zicnd op het wieeed van zaakmet zuur het witte
ezer op het kleed. Ik overkijk(t) deze vrouw als volgt: blank;
- 25 jaar. Normal pantoiit; kort donkerbiiod haar; gekleed in een
rte jurk met lange mouwen, in de kleuren groengrein en mosgroen,
ldat de dirgenie heeft lange zwarte jurk lopen, zwarte dreep
; in haar kwiiiebaand een zeep glas en zwarte boekjiggoe.

ngemaakt op ooktobeldfie, Amsterdam, donderdag 28 oktober 1999
ZEIEN-

L. de Groot

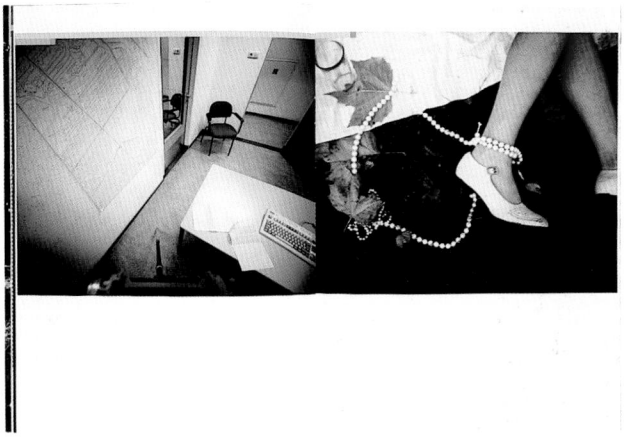

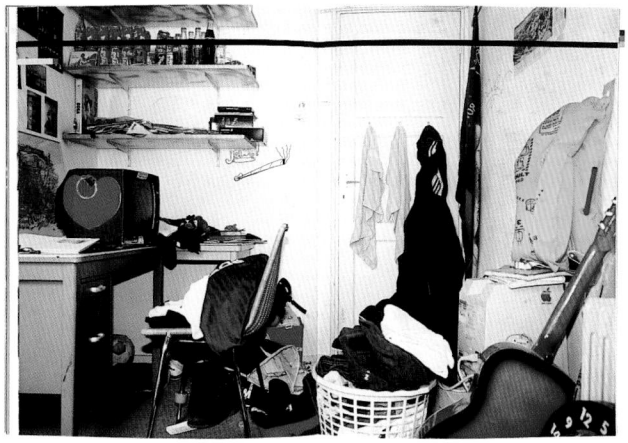

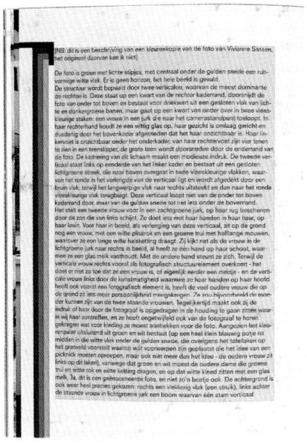

PS: dit is een beschrijving van een kleurenkopie van de foto van Vivianne Sassen, met uitgeknipt dommen kan ik niet)

De foto is groen met lichte vlekjes, met centraal onder de gulden sneede een natuurvoige witte vlak. Er is geen horizon, het hele beeld is gevuld.
De structuur wordt bepaald door twee verticalen, waarvan de meest dominante zo rechtop is. Deze staat op een zwart van de rechter kadermand, doorsnijdt de foto van onder tot boven en bestaat voor driekwart uit een gesloten vlak van lichte en donkergroene banen, maar gaat op een kwart van onder over in twee vlieskleurige stakers: een vrouw in een jurk die naar het camerastandpunt toekoopt. In haar rechterhand houdt ze een witbig glas op, haar gezicht is omlaag gericht en studerig door het bovenkloiiie afgeschaden dat het haar ondichtbaar is. Haar linkervoet is crackbbaar onder het onderkadar, van haar rechtervoet zijn vier tenen te zien in een teenslipper, de grote teen wordt doorsneden door de onderrand van de foto. De kidneing van dit lichaam maakt een modieuze indruk. De tweede verticaal staat iiiks op ondeiiste van het hiiker zoder en bestaat uit een gesloten lichtgroene streek, die naar boven overgaat in twee vlieskleiiige vlakken, waarvan het rende is het verlengde van de verticaal ligt en wordt afgedekt door een bruin vlak, terwijl het langwerpige vlak naar rechts uitsteekt en dan naar het ronde vlieskleiiige vlak reiaglaagt. Deze verticaal loopt niet van de onder tot boven kadermand door, maar van de gulden sneede tot niet iets onder de bovenrand.
Het stuit een zwarte vrouw voor in een zachtgroene jurk, op haar rug bestelvoren door de zon die van links schijnt. Ze doet iets met haar handen in haar haar, op haar kiiin. Voor haar in beeld, als verlenging van deze verticaal, zit op de grond nog een vrouw, met een witte pipoinek en een groene trui met halflange mouwen, waarover ze een lange witte haiskerting draagt. Zij kijkt net alle de vrouw in de lichtgroene jurk naar rechts in beeld, al heeft ze den hand op haar schoot, waarmee ze een glas melk vasthoudt. Met de andere hand snoert ze zich. Terwijl de verticale vrouw rechts vooraf de fotografiii

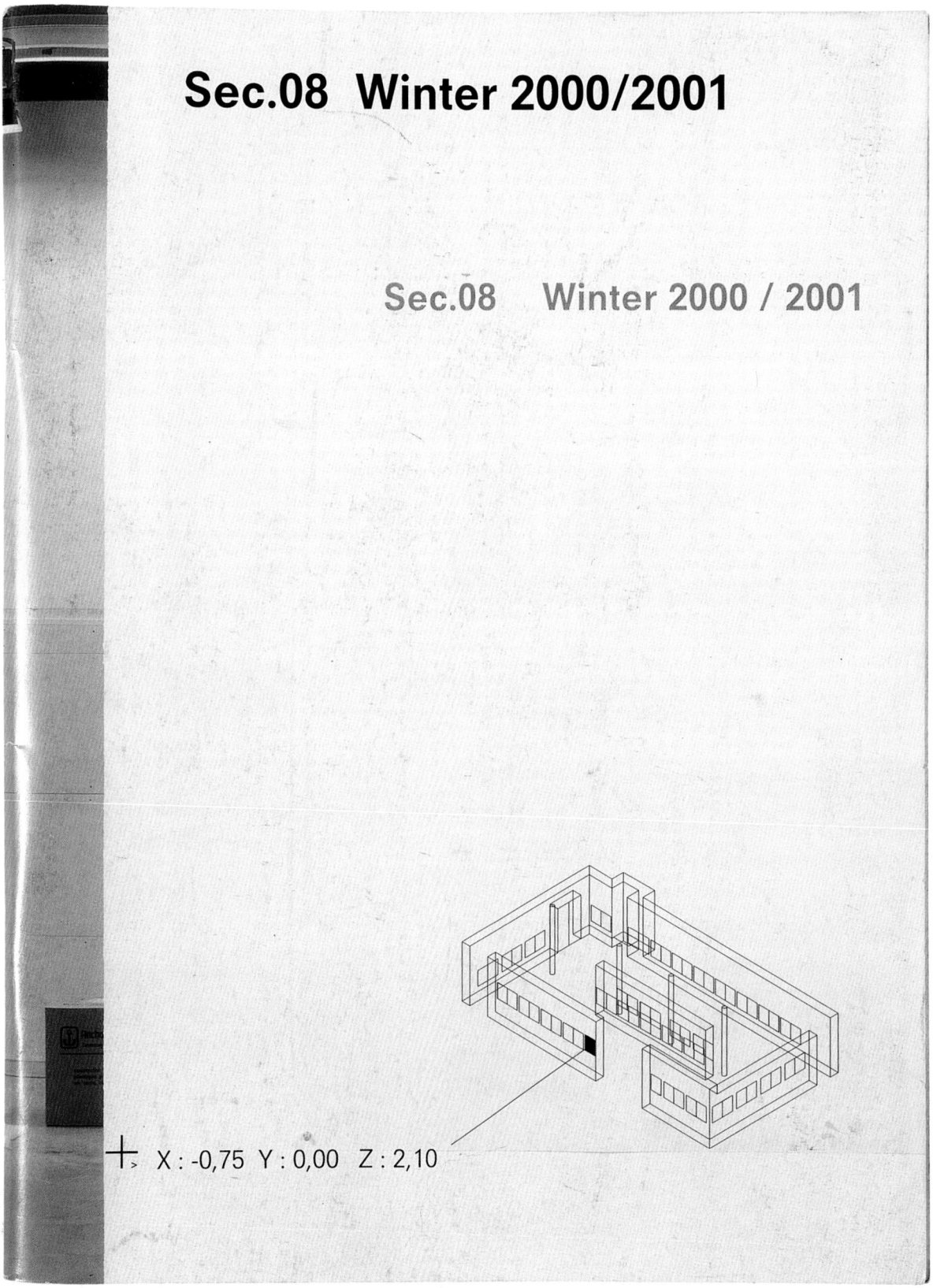

Sec *(The Netherlands, Issue 8, Winter 2000/01) 165 x 220mm/6 1/2 x 8 3/4 inches*
The magazine as art gallery: this issue is based on an art exhibition. The content of the issue was displayed in a gallery where guests were invited to view the work. This event was photographed. The magazine consists of these photographs of people viewing the art, the pages running in the order in which the works were hung. The artists' names are identified through map references to their works' position in the gallery (each page has a diagram of the gallery showing where the work was hung).
Design *Yolanda Huntelaar, Roosje Klap and Richard Niessen*

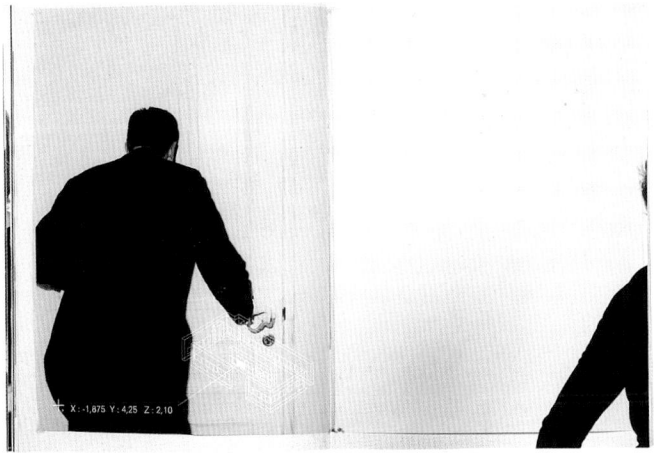
X : -1,875 Y : 4,25 Z : 2,10

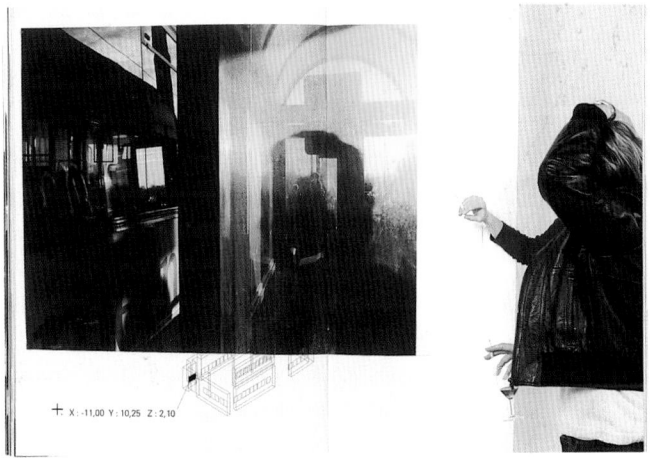
X : -11,00 Y : 10,25 Z : 2,10

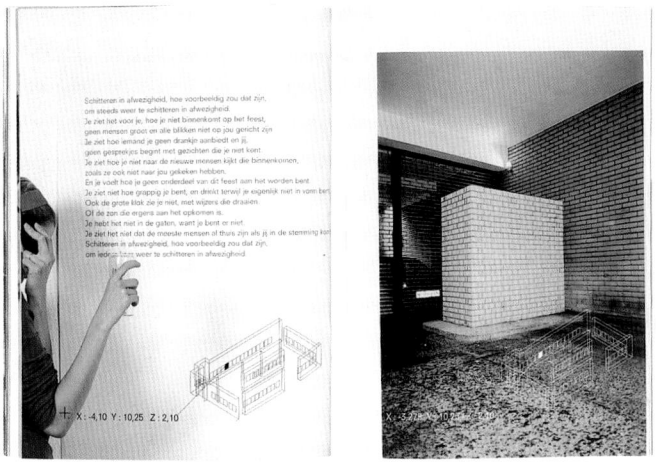
Schitteren in afwezigheid, hoe voorbeeldig zou dat zijn,
om steeds weer te schitteren in afwezigheid.
Je ziet niet voor je, hoe je niet binnenkomt op het feest,
geen mensen groet en alle blikken niet op jou gericht zijn
Je ziet hoe iemand je geen drankje aanbiedt en jij,
geen gesprekjes begint met gedichten die je niet kent.
Je ziet hoe je niet naar de nieuwe mensen kijkt die binnenkomen,
zoals ze ook niet naar jou gekeken hebben.
En je voelt hoe je geen onderdeel van dit feest aan het worden bent
Je ziet niet hoe grappig je bent, en denkt terwijl je eigenlijk niet in vorm bent
Ook de grote klok zie je niet, met wijzers die draaien.
Of de zon die ergens aan het opkomen is.
Je hebt het niet in de gaten, want je bent er niet.
Je ziet het niet dat de meeste mensen al thuis zijn als jij in de stemming kom
Schitteren in afwezigheid, hoe voorbeeldig zou dat zijn,
om iedereen weer te schitteren in afwezigheid.
X : -4,10 Y : 10,25 Z : 2,10

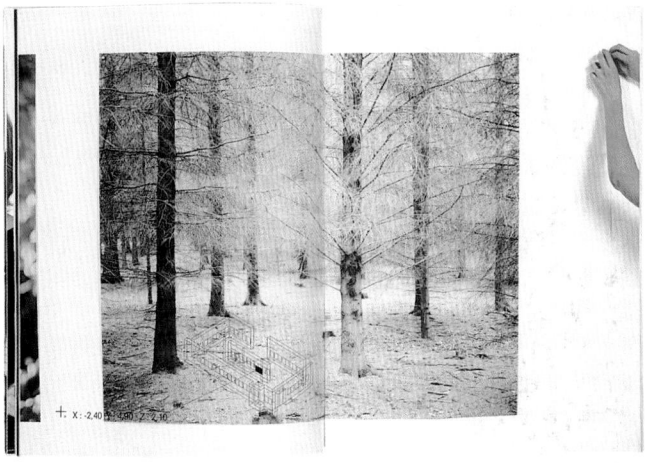
X : -2,40

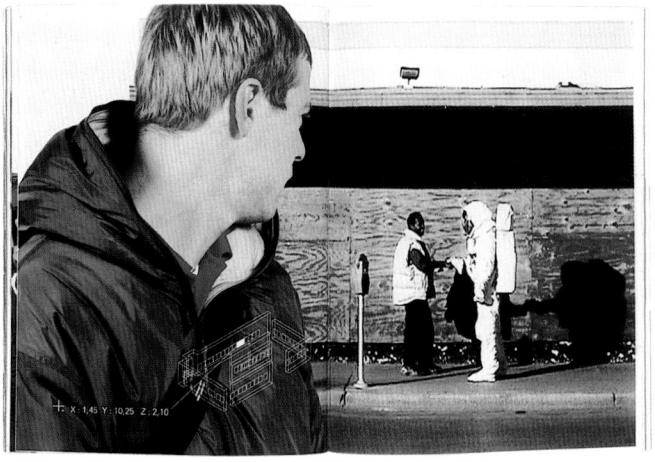
X : 1,45 Y : 10,25 Z : 2,10

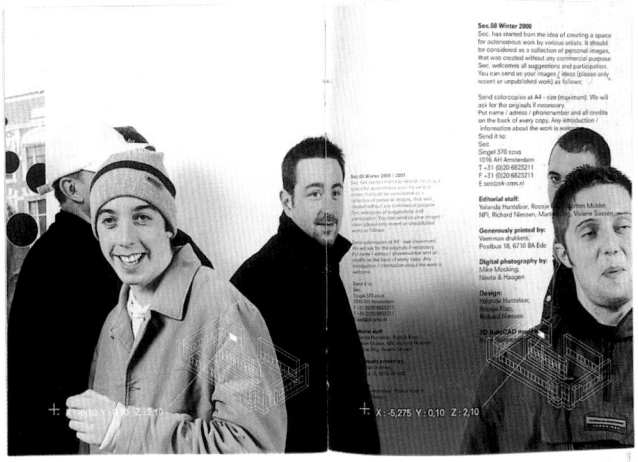
Sec.58 Winter 2000
Sec. has started from the idea of creating a space for autonomous work by various artists. It should be considered as a collection of personal images, that was created without any commercial purpose. Sec. welcomes all suggestions and participation. You can send us your images (discs (please only recent or unpublished work) as follows:
Send colorcopies at A4 - size (maximum). We will ask for the originals if necessary.
Put name / adress / phonenumber and all credits on the back of every copy. Any introduction / information about the work is welcome.
Send it to:
Sec.
Singel 370 ezwa
1016 AH Amsterdam
T +31 (0)20 6625211
F +31 (0)20 6625211
E sec@ok-oms.nl
Editorial staff:
Yolanda Huntelaar, Roozie
NPI, Richard Niessen, Martin
Generously printed by:
Veenman drukkerij,
Postbus 18, 6710 BA Ede
Digital photography by:
Mike Mocking,
Nauta & Haugen
Design:
Yolande Huntelaar,
Roozie Kooi,
Richard Niessen
3D AutoCAD images:
Sec.00 Winter 2000 / 2001
X : -5,275 Y : 0,10 Z : 2,10

TOP **Brainheart** *(Sweden, Issue 5, January 2002) 210 x 297mm/8 1/4 x 11 3/4 inches*
This magazine, covering Sweden's wireless technology industry, eschews the brash hi-tech styling generally associated with such magazines. Instead, it uses a nostalgic mix of small headlines, serif fonts and decorative borders to present its cutting-edge content.
Art director *Peter Assarsson*

BOTTOM **Oyster** *(Australia, Issue 39, April/May 2002) 240 x 330mm/9 1/2 x 13 inches*
Adaptations of traditional decorative flourishes are used in this fashion title to bring character to the simple layouts.
Art director *Tim McIntyre*

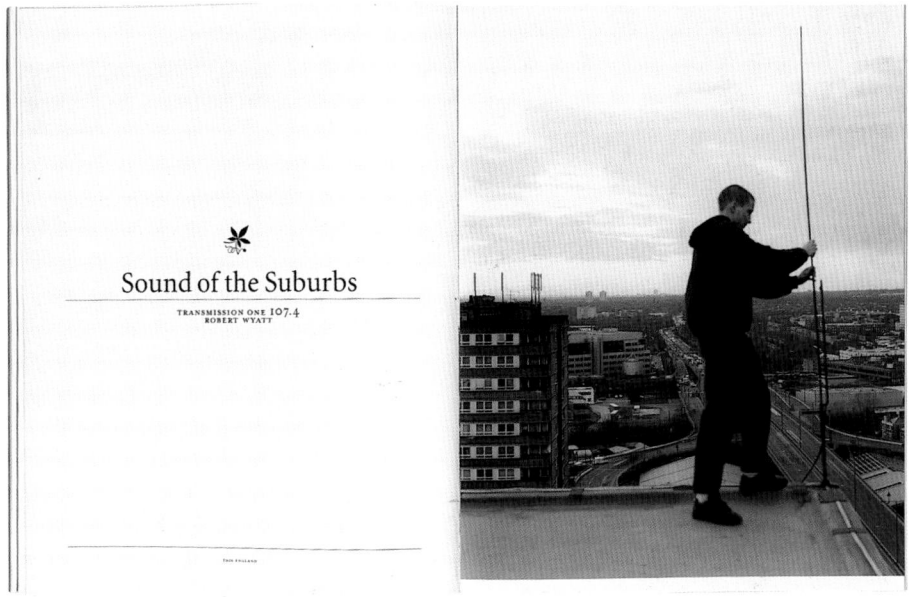

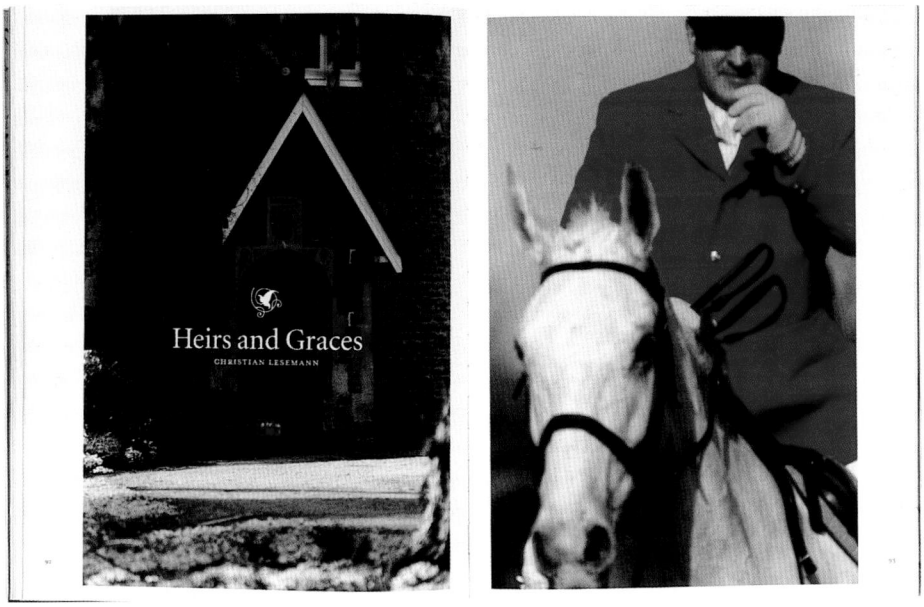

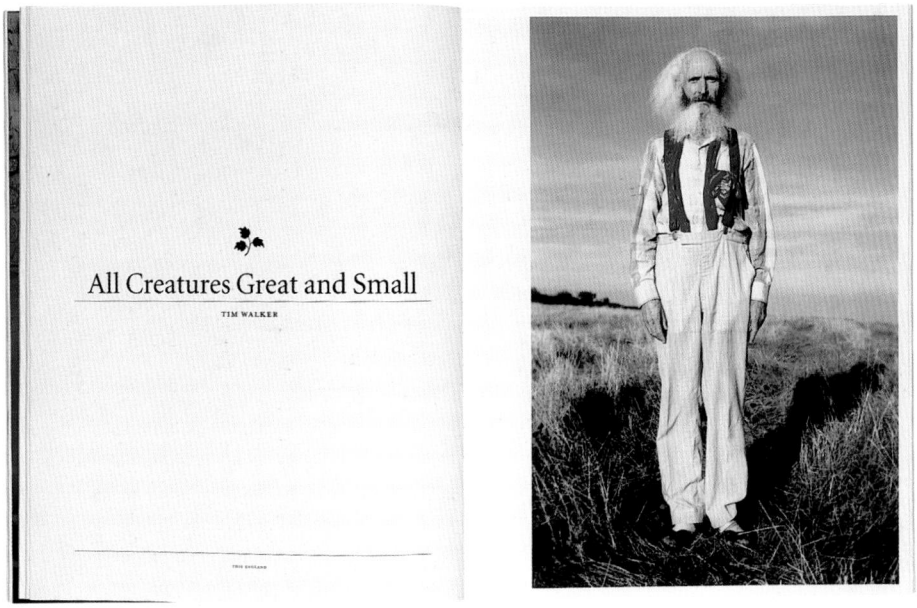

Big *(USA, Issue 34, 2001) 235 x 297mm/9 1/4 x 11 3/4 inches*
Each issue of this fashion/style magazine is themed, the whole look and feel being created each time by a different team of editors and designers. This issue about modern England used traditional book-style typography and decorative flourishes to emphasize its Englishness.
Art director *Daren Ellis*

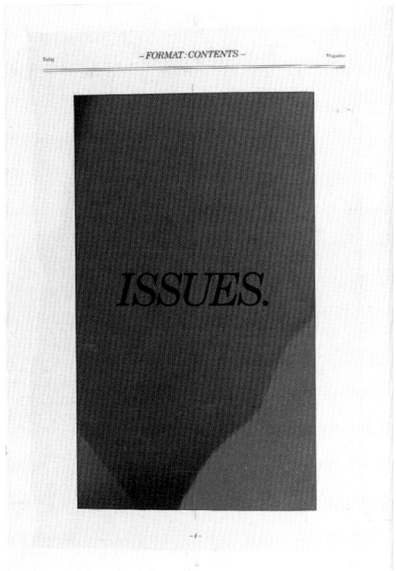

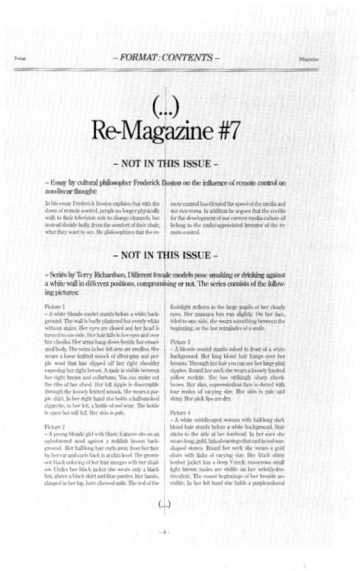

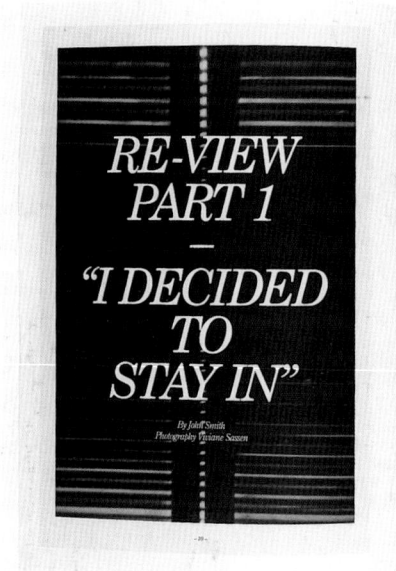

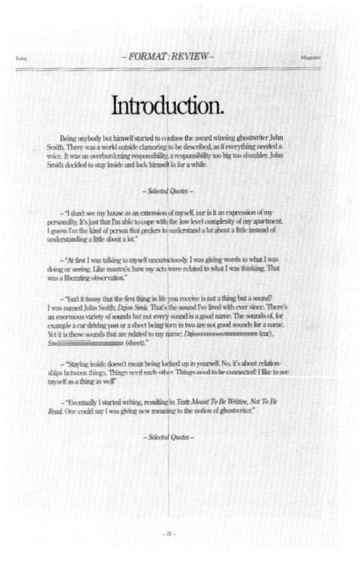
Today
– FORMAT: REVIEW –
Magazine
Introduction.
Being anybody but himself started to confuse the award winning ghostwriter John Smith. There was a world outside clamoring to be described, as if everything needed a voice. It was an overburdening responsibility, a responsibility too big too shoulder. John Smith decided to stay inside and lock himself in for a while.
– Selected Quotes –
– "I don't see my house as an extension of myself, nor is it an expression of my personality. It's just that I'm able to cope with the low level complexity of my apartment. I guess I'm the kind of person that prefers to understand a lot about a little instead of understanding a little about a lot."
– "At first I was talking to myself unconsciously. I was giving words to what I was doing or seeing. Like mantra's; how my acts were related to what I was thinking. That was a liberating observation."
– "Isn't it funny that the first thing in life you receive is not a thing but a sound? I was named John Smith; *Djjjon Smiii*. That's the sound I've lived with ever since. There's an enormous variety of sounds but not every sound is a good name. The sounds of, for example a car driving past or a door being torn in two are not good sounds for a name. Yet it is these sounds that are related to my name: *Djjjoooooooooommmmmmm* (car), *Smiii

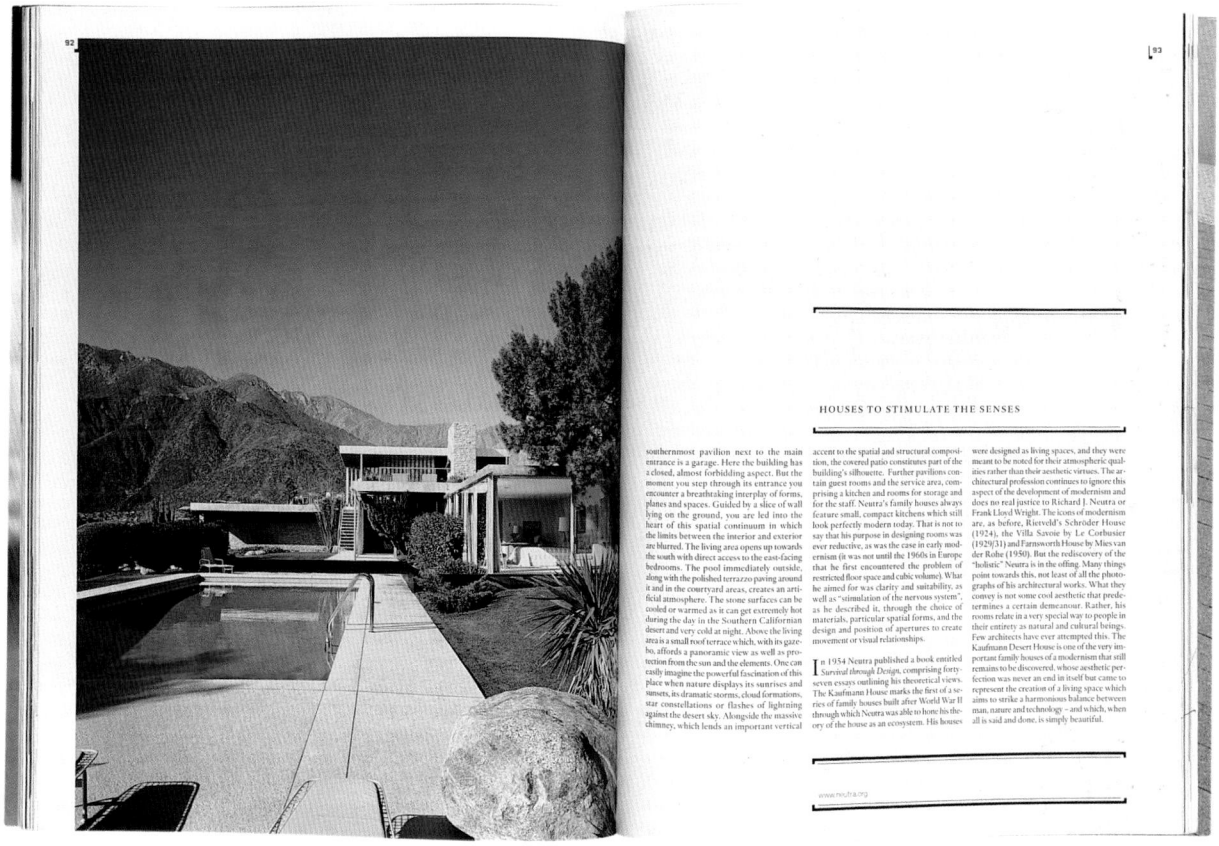

HOUSES TO STIMULATE THE SENSES

southernmost pavilion next to the main entrance is a garage. Here the building has a closed, almost forbidding aspect. But the moment you step through its entrance you encounter a breathtaking interplay of forms, planes and spaces. Guided by a slice of wall lying on the ground, you are led into the heart of this spatial continuum in which the limits between the interior and exterior are blurred. The living area opens up towards the south with direct access to the east-facing bedrooms. The pool immediately outside, along with the polished terrazzo paving around it and in the courtyard areas, creates an artificial atmosphere. The stone surfaces can be cooled or warmed as it can get extremely hot during the day in the Southern Californian desert and very cold at night. Above the living area is a small roof terrace which, with its gazebo, affords a panoramic view as well as protection from the sun and the elements. One can easily imagine the powerful fascination of this place when nature displays its sunrises and sunsets, its dramatic storms, cloud formations, star constellations or flashes of lightning against the desert sky. Alongside the massive chimney, which lends an important vertical accent to the spatial and structural composition, the covered patio constitutes part of the building's silhouette. Further pavilions contain guest rooms and the service area, comprising a kitchen and rooms for storage and for the staff. Neutra's family houses always feature small, compact kitchens which still look perfectly modern today. That is not to say that his purpose in designing rooms was ever reductive, as was the case in early modernism (it was not until the 1960s in Europe that he first encountered the problem of restricted floor space and cubic volume). What he aimed for was clarity and suitability, as well as "stimulation of the nervous system", as he described it, through the choice of materials, particular spatial forms, and the design and position of apertures to create movement or visual relationships.

In 1934 Neutra published a book entitled *Survival through Design*, comprising forty-seven essays outlining his theoretical views. The Kaufmann House marks the first of a series of family houses built after World War II through which Neutra was able to hone his theory of the house as an ecosystem. His houses were designed as living spaces, and they were meant to be noted for their atmospheric qualities rather than their aesthetic virtues. The architectural profession continues to ignore this aspect of the development of modernism and does no real justice to Richard J. Neutra or Frank Lloyd Wright. The icons of modernism are, as before, Rietveld's Schröder House (1924), the Villa Savoie by Le Corbusier (1929/31) and Farnsworth House by Mies van der Rohe (1950). But the rediscovery of the "holistic" Neutra is in the offing. Many things point towards this, not least of all the photographs of his architectural works. What they convey is not some cool aesthetic that predetermines a certain demeanour. Rather, his rooms relate in a very special way to people in their entirety as natural and cultural beings. Few architects have ever attempted this. The Kaufmann Desert House is one of the very important family houses of a modernism that still remains to be discovered, whose aesthetic perfection was never an end in itself but came to represent the creation of a living space which aims to strike a harmonious balance between man, nature and technology – and which, when all is said and done, is simply beautiful.

www.neutra.org

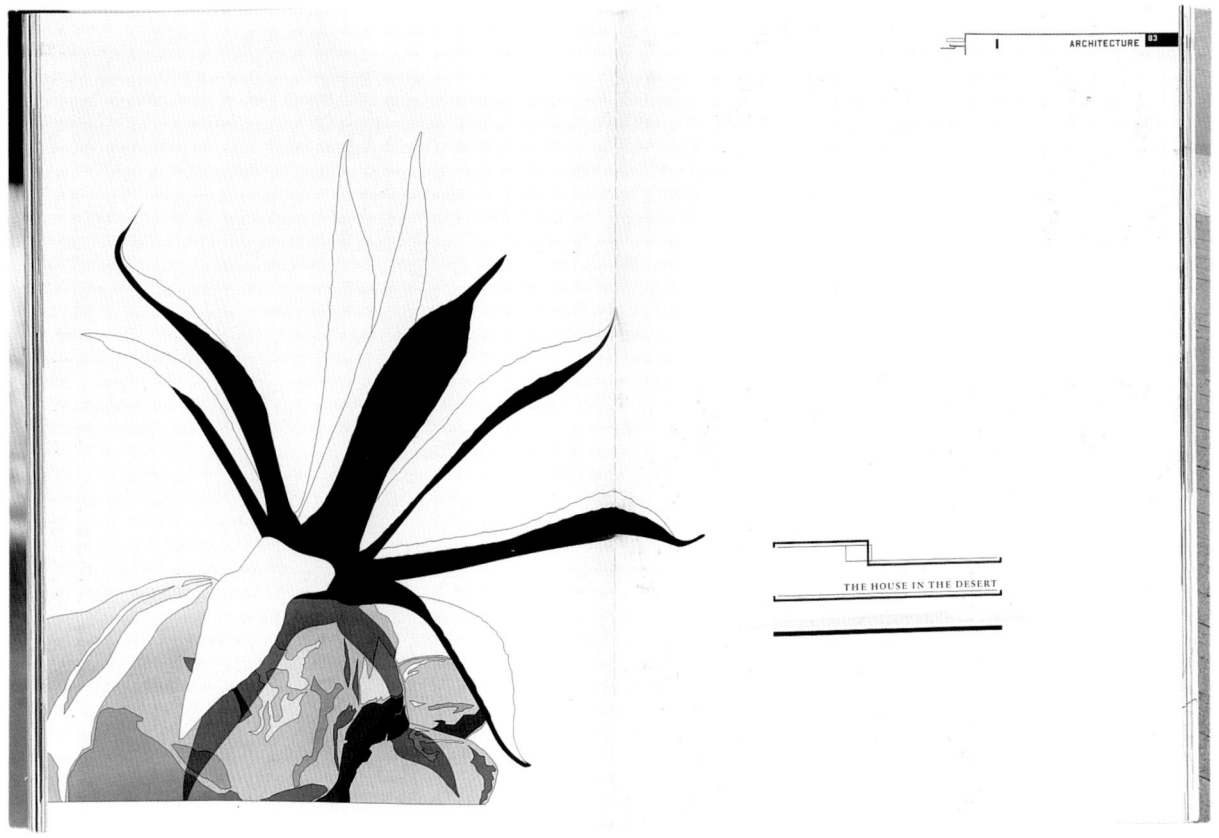

THE HOUSE IN THE DESERT

Premium *(Germany, Issue 2, 2001) 230 x 300mm/9 x 11 7/8 inches*
Using 'The Culture of Luxury' to promote Ford's Premier Automative Group brands, the design of this magazine is intensely detailed. Quiet typography is mixed with distorted elements of tramline rules to produce a simultaneous modern–traditional impression.
Art director *Paul Neulinger*

WORDS LUCY CAVENDISH
PHOTOGRAPHS WOLFGANG LUDES
ART DIRECTION KIRSTEN WILLEY
MAKE-UP SONIA KASHUK @ THE WALL GROUP
HAIR SATORU @ ORIBE SALON

CHRISTY TURLINGTON

WHEN PEOPLE FIRST MEET ME, THEY ALWAYS ASSUME I'LL BE STUPID OR BORING.

christy turlington

WHY DO THEY THINK THAT?

lucy cavendish

OH, BECAUSE ALL MODELS ARE DUMB. DIDN'T YOU KNOW THAT?

lucy

NOT REALLY.

christy

IT'S HARD TO GET TAKEN SERIOUSLY. I MEAN WHAT COULD BE MORE RIDICULOUS THAN A FORMER MODEL WHO NOW LIVES HER LIFE ON AYURVEDIC PRINCIPLES AND HAS STARTED UP A SKINCARE BUSINESS?

IT HAS TO BE SAID that Christy Turlington isn't ridiculous or stupid or boring. She may be slightly long-winded at times – her devotion to Ayurveda is almost fanatical – but her knowledge is admirable. I meet her early on a Friday evening at her hotel suite in London. She opens the door. For a minute I am not sure if the person standing in front of me is Christy Turlington or whether the other tall, preposterously slim person standing next to her is Christy Turlington.

That, in itself, is quite off-putting. How can I not recognise one of the most photographed women of the Nineties? The face of Calvin Klein and Maybelline? It's a model thing. The whole point is that their looks can be endlessly →

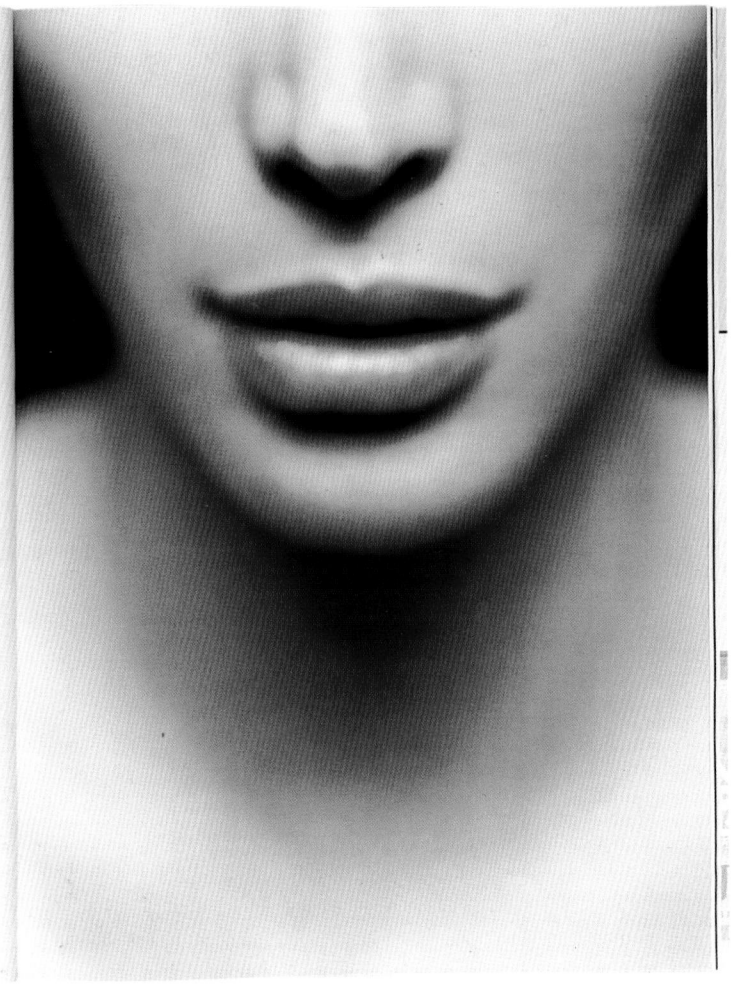

Bare *(UK, Issue 3, January/February 2001) 230 x 300mm/9 x 11 7/8 inches*
Soft photography and a gentle approach to type and colour give this magazine a distinctly different feel to other titles in the women's market.
Art director *Kirsten Willey*

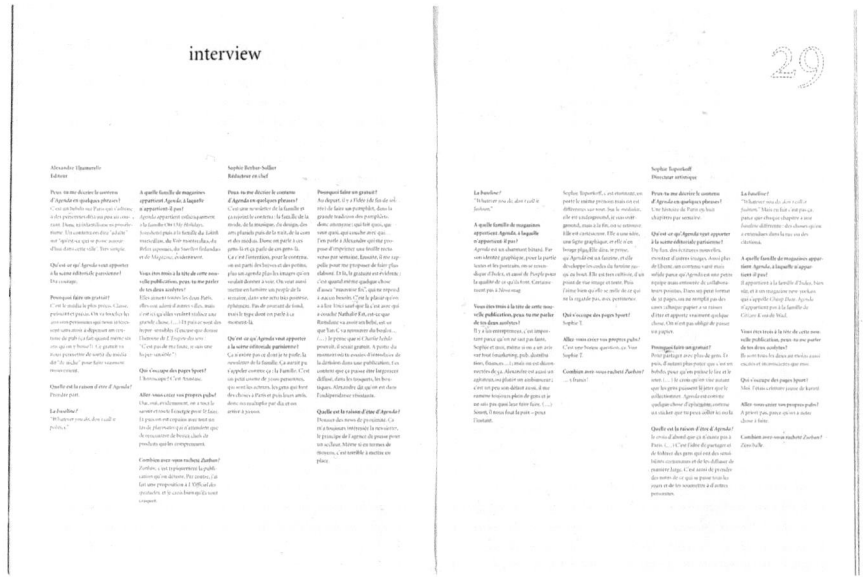

interview

29

Alexandre Ilgunnerly
Editeur

Sophie Berbier-Sollier
Rédacteur en chef

Sophie Toporkoff
Directeur artistique

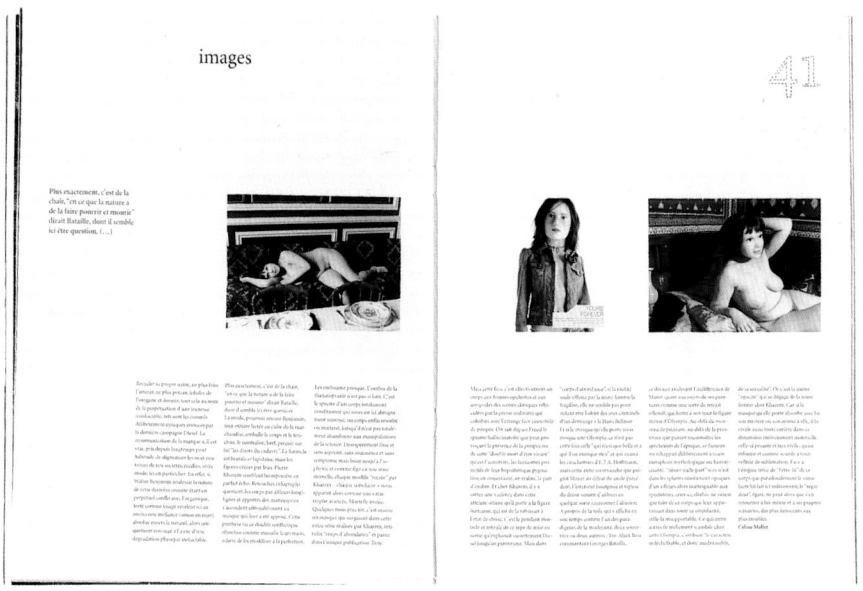

images

41

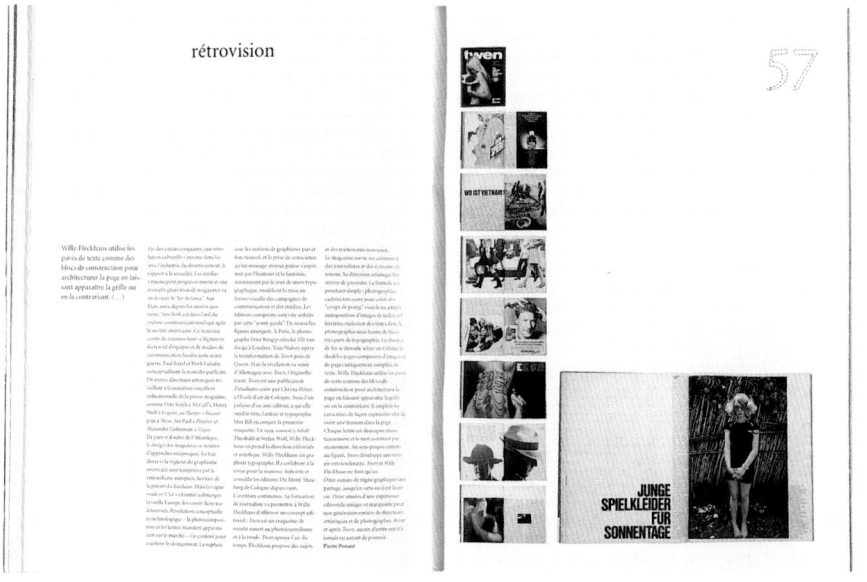

rétrovision

57

Magazine *(France, Issue 13, February/March 2002)*
200 x 260mm/7 7/8 x 10 1/4 inches
This magazine about magazines has an extremely simple yet sophisticated design that lets the content – sample pages from other magazines – stand out.
Art director *Rachel/H5*

The New Art Museum in Århus provides an improved setting for the museum's collection of Vilhelm Lundstrøm – one of the most influential Danish painters in the first decades of the 20th century. By Kim Flyvbjerg

Feeling Blue

At the time of his death in 1950, Vilhelm Lundstrom had become one of the most influential Danish painters of his time. For 35 years his art had been considered provoking and had been admired and despised, and diagnosed as downright insane by representatives of the medical profession. Today his works can be found in every major Danish art museum, and when the occasional Lundstrom painting is sold, the prices they fetch are ever increasing.

Vilhelm Lundstrom was born on Amager. He was a weak, tubercular boy who kept to himself. His father forced him to take on an apprenticeship as a decorator, but when he was 20 the young Vilhelm was accepted at the Royal Academy of Art in Copenhagen where he astonished everybody by drawing a model in a pure cubist style.

From then on he was an artist with capital A, and he took part actively in the vibrant artistic environment in Copenhagen. During World War I the Danish capital was often referred to as 'the waiting room for Paris' since many Norwegian and Swedish painters, sculptors, writers and musicians were living in the city. They discussed and exchanged ideas with Danish artists and enjoyed not having shortage of food or drink.

The relative wealth, owing to Denmark's neutrality policy, meant that much of modern French art could be seen in Copenhagen. The Scandinavian artists got a taste of what was to come when the war ended and it became possible once again to move freely through Europe. The Danish National Gallery had a large exhibition of French art in 1914, and the merchant Christian Tetzen-Lund purchased great modernist works and was pleased to put them on display. Among other he acquired two late cubist works by Picasso, which are said to have had a significant influence on Lundstrom.

Vilhelm Lundstrom exhibited a number of clearly cubist inspired compositions in 1917 at the Artists' Autumn Exhibition. He mixed slag in his colours and used collage elements in his naturalist paintings. Today this might seem quite innocent, but at the time the technique caused offence:

"When a person ventures to paste old newspaper clippings, dirty chemise lace and tin foil scraps on his dirty oil smeared canvas, then one can go no further in achieving the highest personal freedom to offend and ridicule the noble audience," the art critic of the newspaper Politiken wrote.

Then Vilhelm Lundstrom was just 20 years old and had not yet developed the calm nature and self-confidence which later would leave him indifferent to criticism. In a letter to a friend living in the USA, Knud Merrild, he wrote about his experiences:

"I dare not show up at the exhibition on Sundays for fear of being apprehended and murdered. It is not amusing, I had not expected so much consternation, the press has not merely been satirical, but mean."

The following year Lundstrom went all the way and exhibited three abstract compositions made from old wooden crates. These were deemed even more provocative, but to make matters worse, the exhibition coincided with the publication of a rather bizarre theory on modern art by an otherwise well-reputed professor. Bacteriologist Carl Julius Salomonsen believed that modern art was simply caused by a contagious mentaj illness, during which the artists entered a state of sick, hysterical excitement >

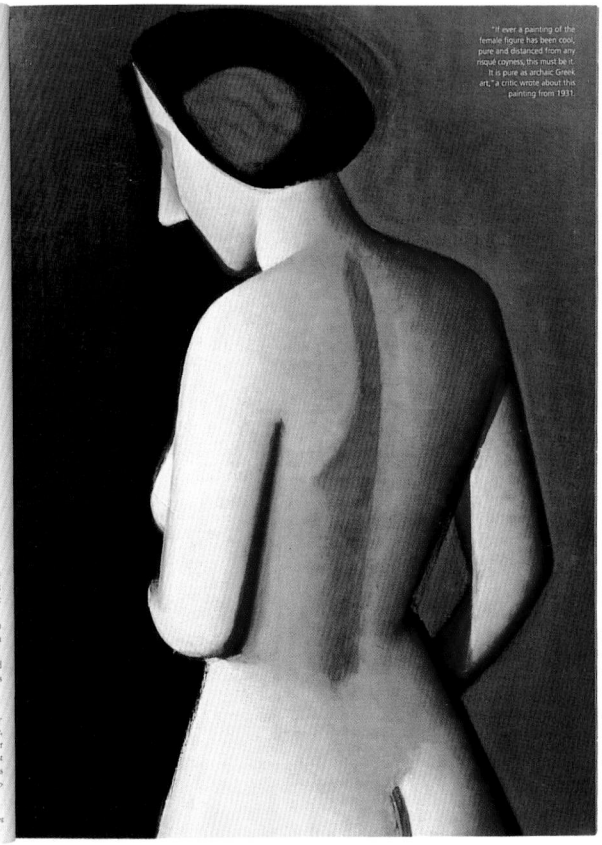

"If ever a painting of the female figure has been cool, pure and distanced from any risqué coyness, this must be it. It is pure as archaic Greek art," a critic wrote about this painting from 1931.

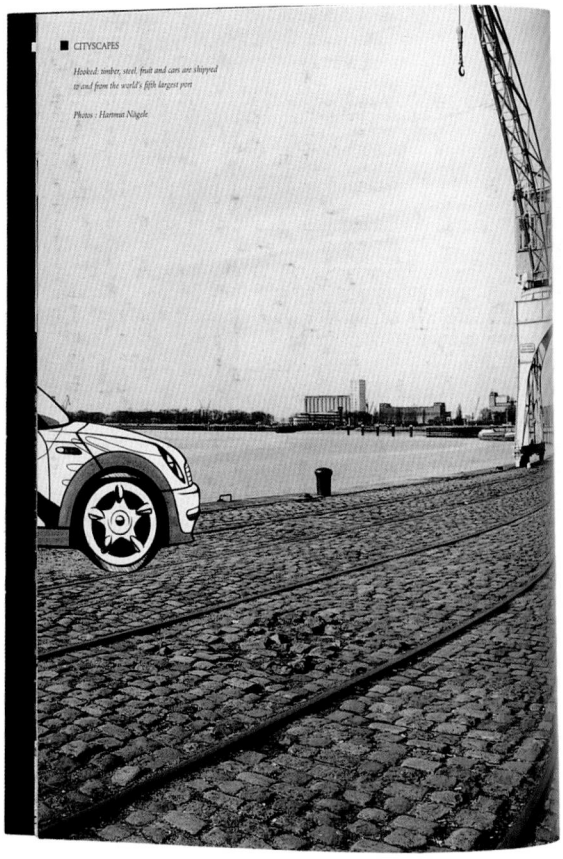

■ CITYSCAPES

Hooked: timber, steel, fruit and cars are shipped to and from the world's fifth largest port

Photos : Hartman Nägele

■ INTRO

THE BEST KEPT SECRET

The age of secrecy is over. Secrets have had their day, like the Secret Seven and, more recently, the secret services. The need for secrecy has gone into sharp decline. Nothing remains undisclosed and little is hidden from the public eye. We are living in the information age. We know everything, have seen and experienced so much. Been there, done that. What next?...

So what do you know about Antwerp?

Oh, Antwerp. That's in Flanders, isn't it? Don't they speak Flemish there? But wait a minute, is it in Belgium or Holland? Antwerp, Anvers. Very old city, with a great past. How did we get onto Antwerp of all places? And what's its population?

Antwerp, city of secrets.

Welcome to the first issue of MINIInternational, a brand-new magazine for a brand-new car. The car is the MINI, a unique car, an icon that bridges nations, classes, generations and cultures with an elemental lightness and an effortless smile. The MINI is built in Oxford by the BMW Group. The first issue of the magazine is dedicated to Antwerp, a city in Flanders beloved of trendsetters and businesspeople from Paris to Sydney because for several years it has been generating some of the most thrilling fashion designers around and, for a population of around 650,000, has a fantastically high proportion of creatives and artists. Or to put it another way, when fashion editors from New York's Madison Avenue or Tokyo's Shibuya district learn how to spell and pronounce such Flemish names as Ann Demeulemeester or Walter Van Beirendonck, to mention but two, there's got to be something behind it.

And that, reader, is more or less what you will discover in this magazine. It's not your run-of-the-mill customer car magazine, it's much more than that. MINIInternational is a magazine with an international spirit. It values style and creativity. Each issue of MINI International will focus on an exciting city. Cities are the habitat of an urban, cosmopolitan generation, the arena in which modern life is played out.

Yet the notion that cities have to be big to be exciting and inspiring seems all-too antiquated these days. It's partly down to our increasingly mobile society, the media, and modern-day communication channels such as the Internet. Metropolises have their clichés too, and though the provinces still exist as a geographical phenomenon, as a mindset they're well up in the league of endangered species – which happens to be good news for a change.

In the 21st century there's nothing secretive about secrets. Secrets are what you don't yet know. Prepare for some surprises as we unveil the well-kept secrets of the old, new city of Antwerp. And prepare to be surprised by a car that is all-too-often underrated. Enjoy unwrapping the secrets of Antwerp with MINIInternational, the urban magazine, and with MINI, the car designed for an urban generation.

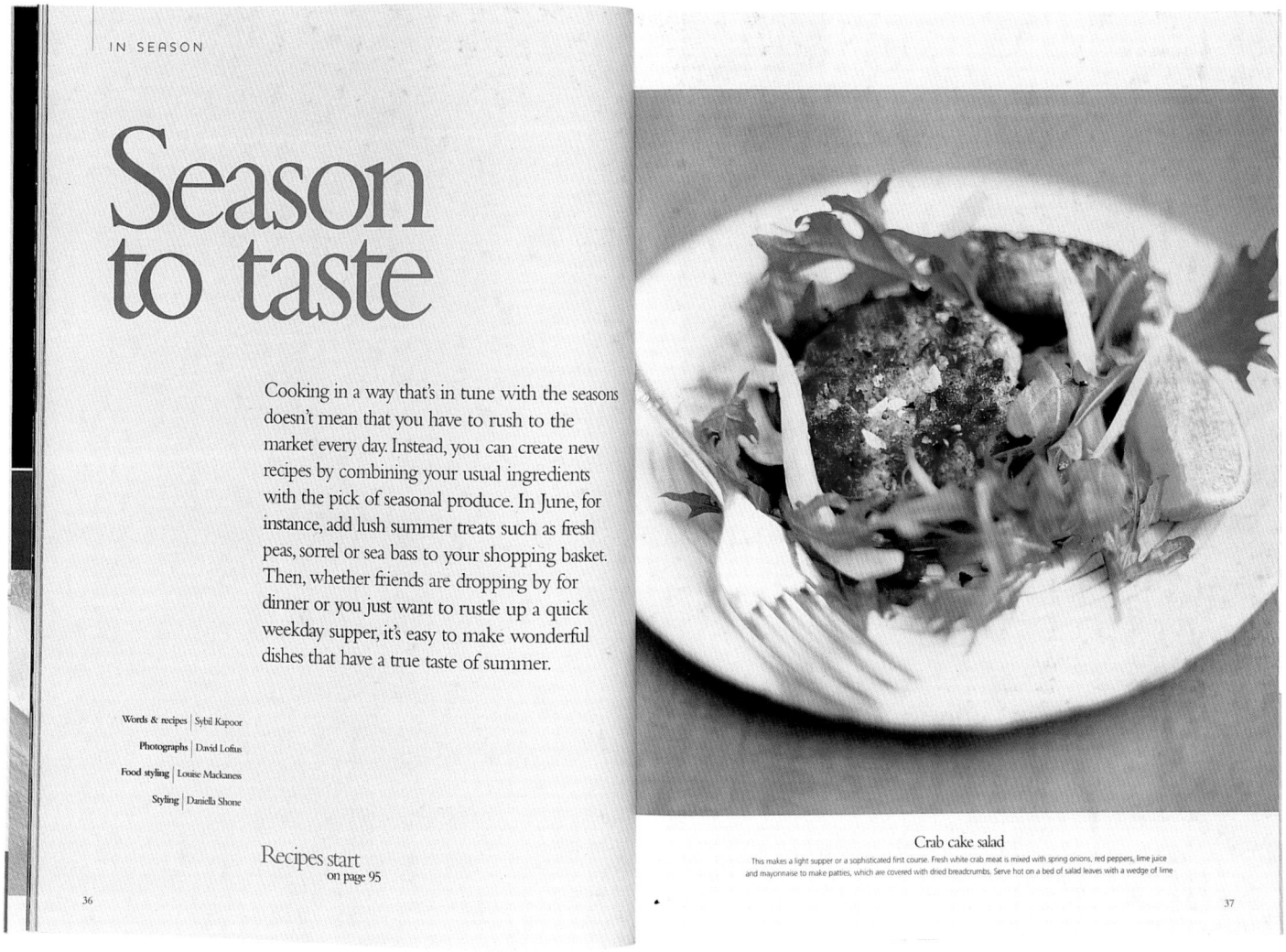

IN SEASON

Season to taste

Cooking in a way that's in tune with the seasons doesn't mean that you have to rush to the market every day. Instead, you can create new recipes by combining your usual ingredients with the pick of seasonal produce. In June, for instance, add lush summer treats such as fresh peas, sorrel or sea bass to your shopping basket. Then, whether friends are dropping by for dinner or you just want to rustle up a quick weekday supper, it's easy to make wonderful dishes that have a true taste of summer.

Words & recipes | Sybil Kapoor
Photographs | David Loftus
Food styling | Louise Mackaness
Styling | Daniella Shone

Recipes start on page 95

36

Crab cake salad

This makes a light supper or a sophisticated first course. Fresh white crab meat is mixed with spring onions, red peppers, lime juice and mayonnaise to make patties, which are covered with dried breadcrumbs. Serve hot on a bed of salad leaves with a wedge of lime

37

OPPOSITE **Copenhagen Living** *(Denmark, Issue 4, Winter/Spring 2000/01)*
204 x 275mm/8 x 10 7/8 inches
Creative director *Andres Peter Mejer*
Mini International *(Germany, Issue 1, 2001)*
207 x 265mm/8 1/8 x 10 1/2 inches
Art director *Mike Meiré*
These examples show design stripped down to basics for different purposes. *Copenhagen Living* (TOP) uses modernist principles – the headline ranging right to balance the standfirst to its left and the line length of the text carefully kept to a legible length – to express its Scandinavian origin. *Mini International* (BOTTOM) uses a similarly spare design but knowingly breaks such rules, relying on its relationship with the photography and illustration throughout to lift it above the mundane.

THIS PAGE **Waitrose Food Illustrated** *(UK, June 2002)*
220 x 300mm/8 3/4 x 11 7/8 inches
A simple, clean design similar in approach to *Copenhagen Living* but where the addition of colour and tight kerning and a spatial relationship with the accompanying photograph make it more reader-friendly.
Art director *Brian Saffer*

IndomabileAnjelica

Una grande figlia d'arte scopre la regia: *Agnes Browne*, ambientato nell'amata Irlanda della sua infanzia, è il felice debutto della Huston, attrice da Oscar, sulle orme di papà John

di Silvia Bizio
Foto di Helmut Newton

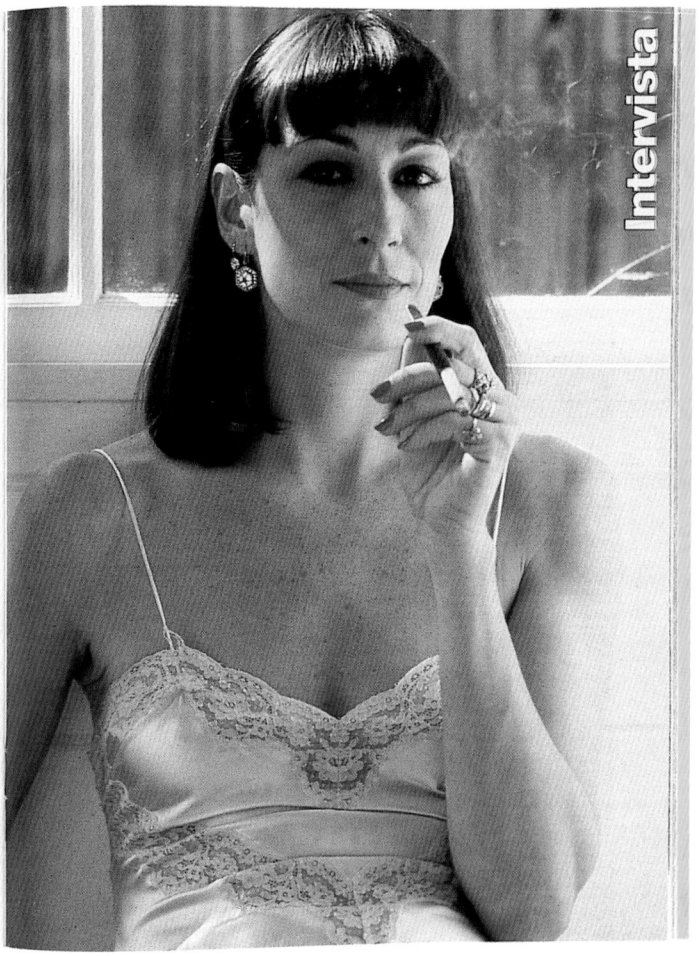

D *(La Repubblica delle Donne)* *(Italy, 29 July 1999)*
210 x 276mm/8 1/4 x 10 7/8 inches
High production values and good quality paper enable this weekly newspaper supplement to use white space, typography and spare design with the confidence of a monthly magazine.
Art director *Joel Berg*

ENTREVISTA
[02]

Es uno de los pocos modistas de alta costura que marcaron la pauta fuera y dentro de España. Desde la familia Franco hasta la reina Sofía, ha vestido al poder femenino de este país durante más de medio siglo. Ahora, con casi 80 años, sigue con la aguja en la mano para crear ropa de hombre.

Manuel Pertegaz

Sesentaañoscreandomoda

Por **Arcadi Espada.** Fotografía de **Carles Ribas**

La anécdota germinal de la vida de Manuel Pertegaz (Olba, Teruel, 1922) tiene lugar en una sastrería del paseo de Gràcia de Barcelona, donde el aprendiz cose con 20 años. Una de las oficialas le enseña un corte de abrigo y le comenta que no sabe a quién dárselo.

–Ya te lo haré yo, mujer.

–¿Tú, Manolo?

Se lo dio. Siempre hay un ángel neorrealista en los milagros. A los pocos días, la mujer entró con su abrigo en la sastrería. La dueña no daba crédito.

–¿Pero de dónde has sacado ese abrigo, Conchi?

–Manolo...

A partir de ahí empezó una vida de ›

12 EPS

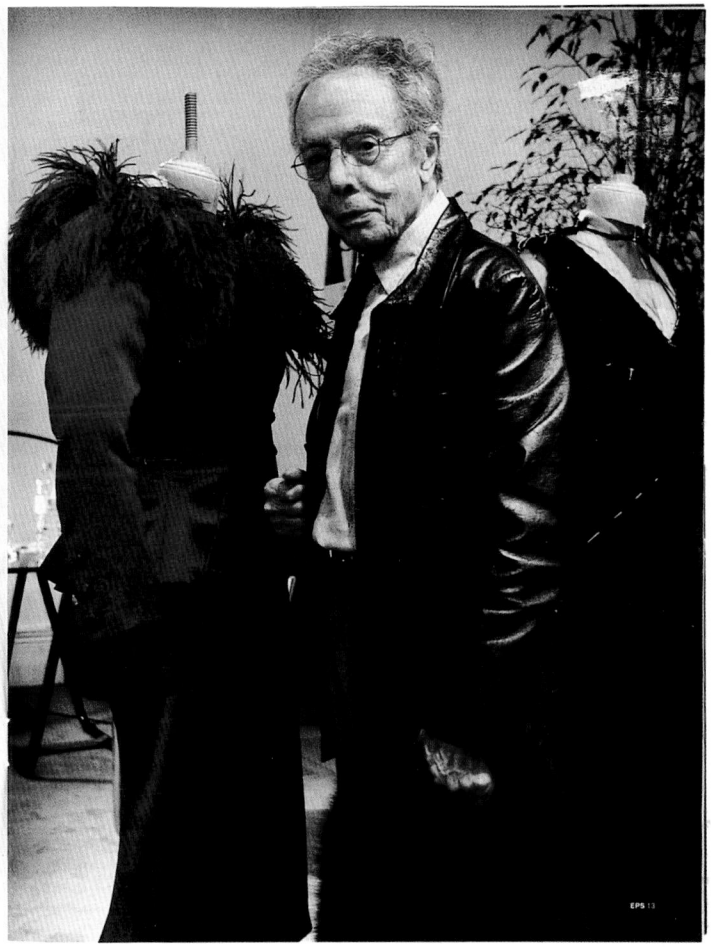

EPS 13

EP[S] ***(El País)*** *(Spain, 10 March 2002)*
212 x 272mm/8 3/8 x 10 3/4 inches
A simple set of elements – two typefaces and three colours – are used to create a clean, modern design that retains a newspaper's journalistic seriousness while not denying its 'magazine-ness'.
Art director *David Garcia*

Arena Homme Plus *(UK, Issue 17, Spring/Summer 2002)*
230 x 300mm/9 x 11 7/8 inches
A rare 80-page run of black-and-white fashion stories here is broken up by small headlines at the start of each separate story. Impact is added to these start pages through the use of random fragments of the headlines blown up out of all proportion on the page.
Art directors *Joseph Logan and Tim McIntyre*

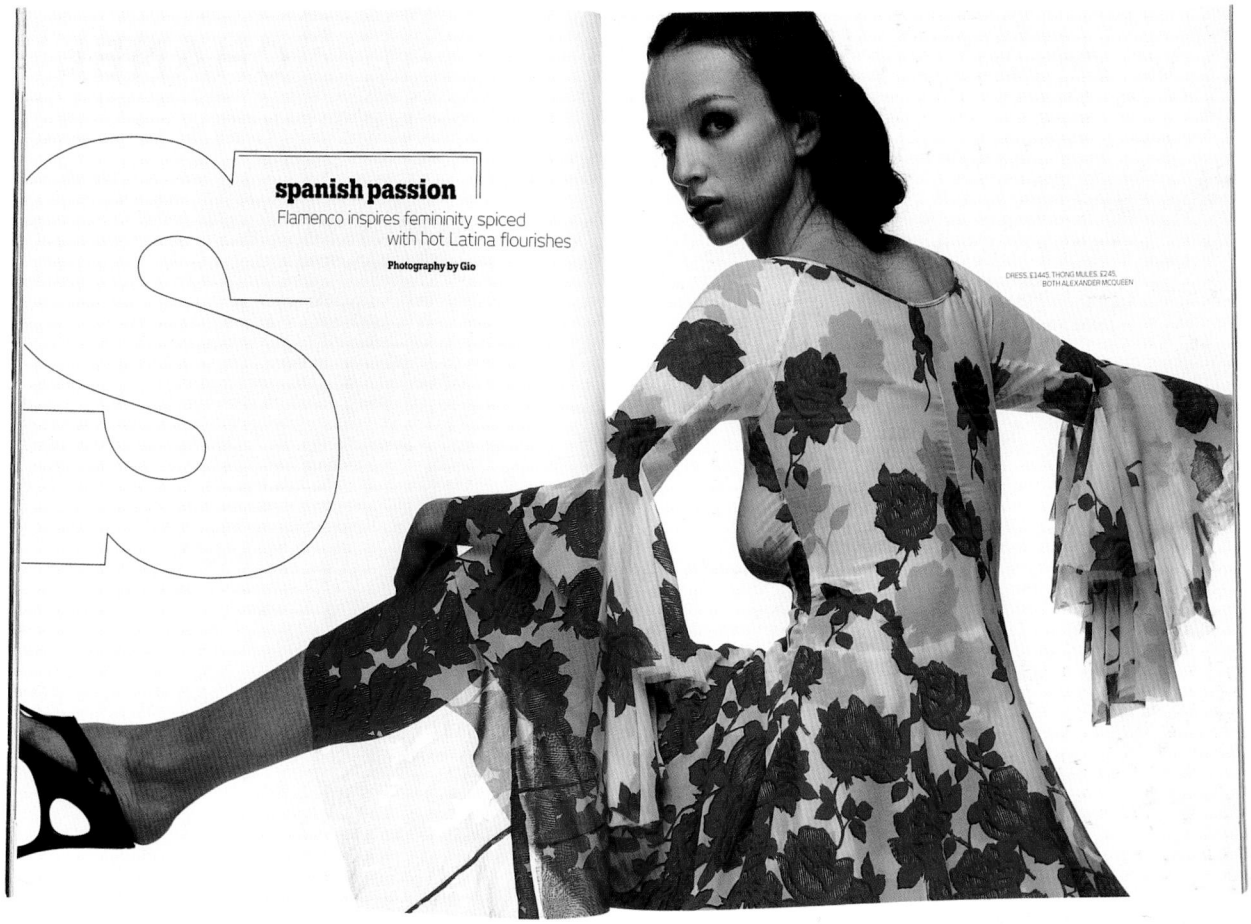

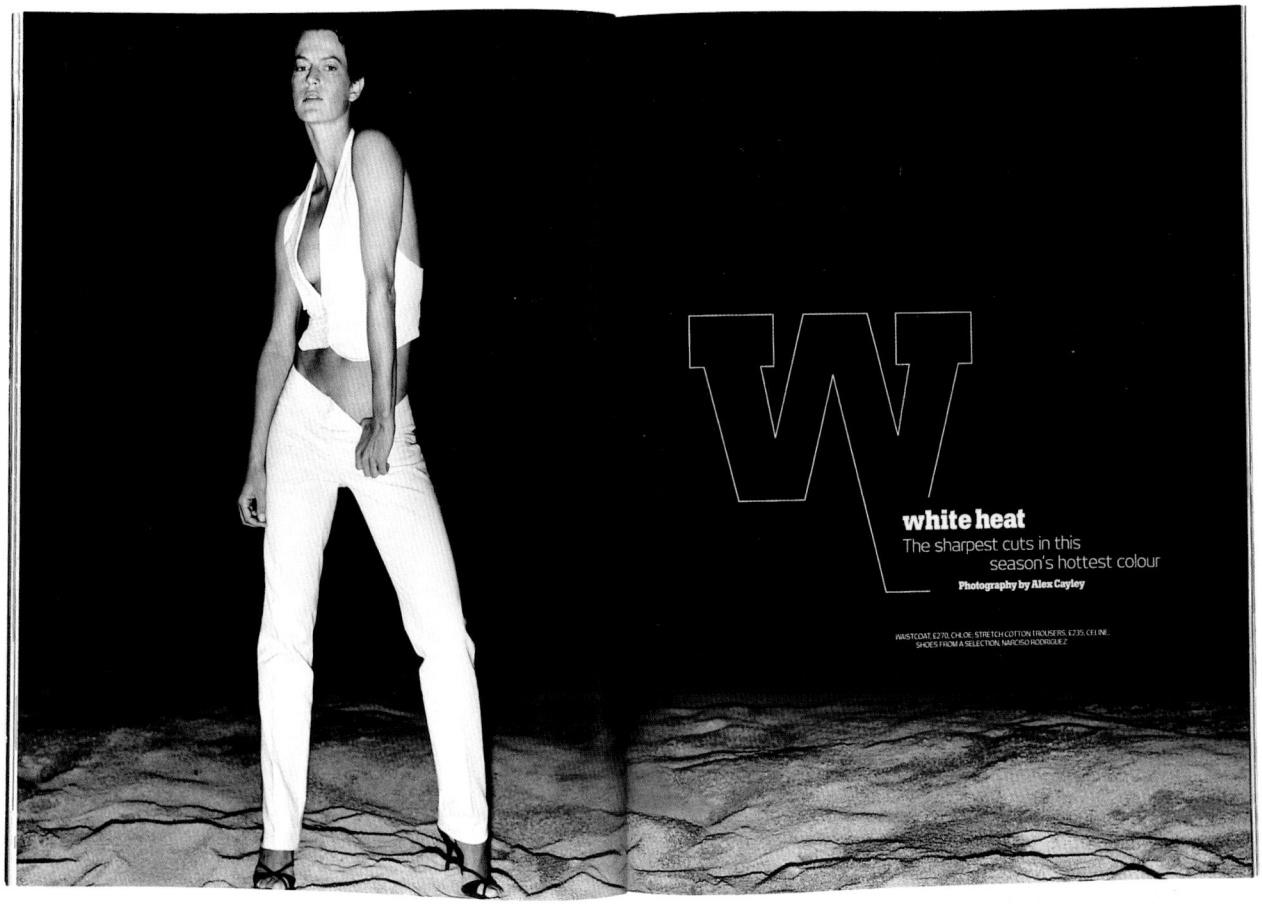

Harvey Nichols Magazine *(UK, Issue 27, Spring 2002)*
220 x 285mm/8 3/4 x 11 1/4 inches
Drama is added to the opening pages of these fashion stories by using an enlarged, outlined version of the first letter of the headline.
Art director *Sam Walton*

THIS PAGE **Label** *(Italy, Issue 2, Summer 2001)*
190 x 300mm/7 ½ x 11 7/8 inches
The problem of presenting text in two languages simultaneously is overcome by running Italian on a black background and English on white. The grey boxes add shape and dynamism to the spread.
Art director *Roberto Maria Clemente*

OPPOSITE, TOP **Neo2** *(Spain, Issue 17, May/June 2001)*
215 x 275mm/8 ½ x 10 7/8 inches
The randomly shaped text columns and overblown pull-quotes lend an air of chaos to this piece about the probability of catastrophy.
Art directors *Ipsum Planet*

OPPOSITE, BOTTOM **Another Magazine** *(UK, Issue 2, Summer 2002)*
250 x 320mm/9 7/8 x 12 3/4 inches
Here, the relationship between the text columns and the inset pictures varies to avoid the usual gutters of white space between the two.
Creative director *Alex Wiederin*

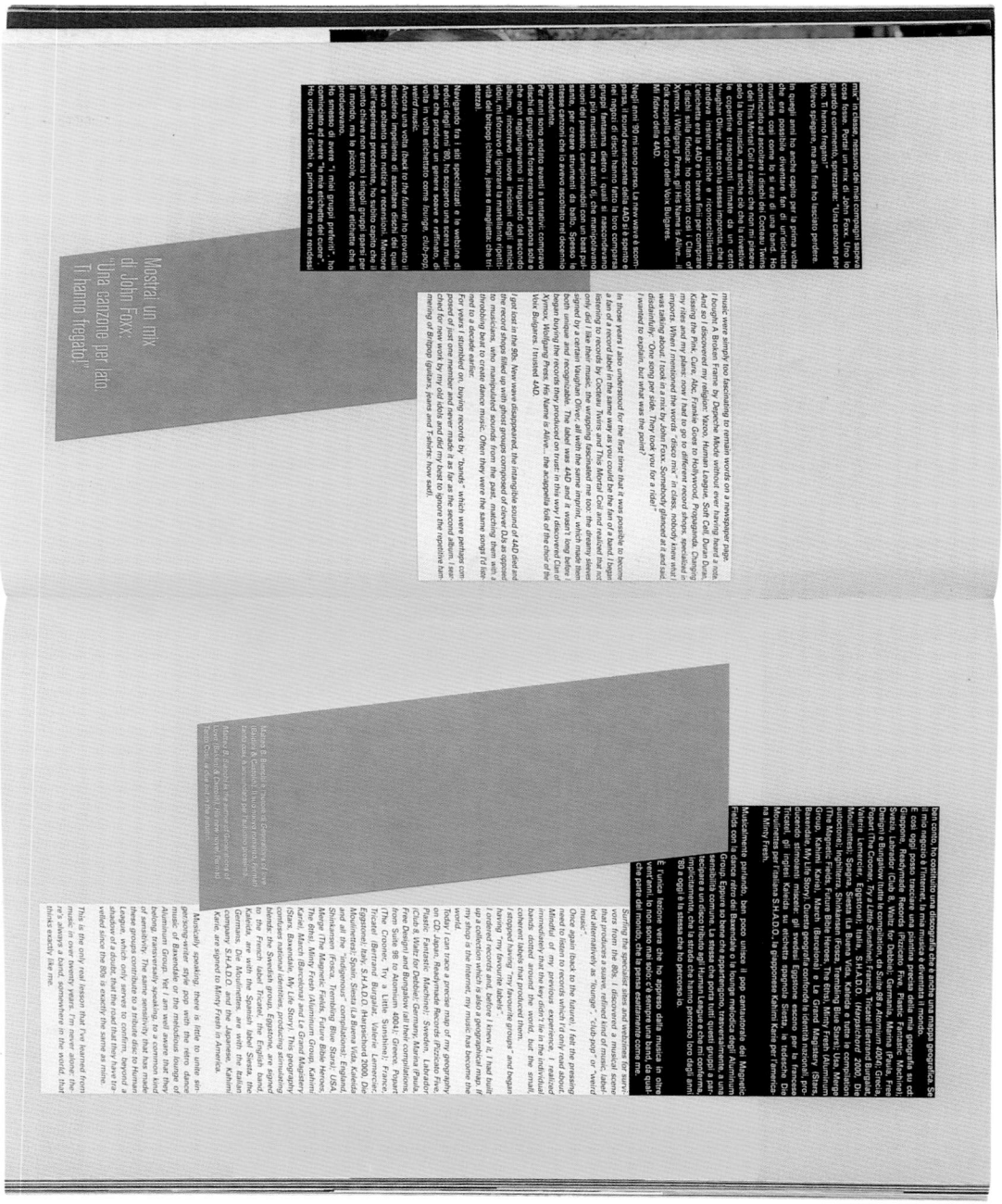

texto_<depravados@eresmas.net>

APOCALIPSIS

01. que sí, ya falta poco//. El apocalipsis se ha convertido últimamente en un lugar demasiado concurrido. Ya casi parece un parque de atracciones con sus trenes del terror, sus payasos locos y los niños con sus videojuegos. "¿Has visto lo del apocalipsis? ¡Sí, ¡cómo mola!".

Cuando preparaba este E-diktó, inspirado por los últimos informes sobre vacas locas y los terremotos de la India y El Salvador, dudaba ya de la consistencia de este manoseado apocalipsis. Sonaba demasiado a película de serie b. Hasta que leí lo de las novatadas en la Casa Blanca. Es tradición, por lo visto, que el poder derrotado deje la gran mansión echa unos zorros, como cuando en el último día de curso marcabas tu nombre en el pupitre. Los de Clinton se habían excedido en la broma, según los chicos de Bush. Imaginando ese patio de colegio aberrado volvieron con fuerza renovada mis antiguos temores apocalípticos. También vi de otra manera el vilipendiado recuento electoral yanqui. No creo que se trate de una chapuza del sistema, sino al contrario, el sistema funcionó tan bien que detectó la chapuza de la democracia de fin de siglo. (En Europa todavía no se hila tan fino, aquí los recuentos son arcaicamente concluyentes). Y es que llegados a este punto de la función, ¿a quién le importa quién gane? Algorin o Jorgito, ambos dejarán su nombre en el pupitre al final de curso.

De repente, toda paranoia catastrofista recobra validez: el mundo lo domina una panda de bromistas infantiloides con las mismas inquietudes y valores que el mocoso de tu sobrino. Con el reloj del Apocalipsis puesto a punto otra vez, visité los clásicos sitios conspiranoicos y comprobé que el asunto está que arde. La mayoría han dejado de lado las fantasías extraterrestres y las fabulaciones sobre JFK. Ahora se refieren a artículos del ABC News, a investigaciones científicas y a premios Nobel. Las claves con las que juegan los nuevos apocalípticos son absolutamente reales. Los profetas iluminados ya no tienen voz ni voto. Hoy son los científicos quienes nos hablan del fin del mundo.

Para empezar, hablemos del teorema matemático del cosmólogo Brandon Carter, base fundamental y aterradora de cualquier pensamiento apocalíptico. Basándose en las más elocuentes leyes de la probabilidad, dice Carter que si el mundo se acabase en los próximos 50-100 años, a nosotros nos habría tocado vivir en el tiempo de máxima densidad planetaria, concretamente en el tiempo en el que vivió un 10% de toda la humanidad. Si, por el contrario, la humanidad perdurase durante miles de años más, multiplicando progresivamente su población, nuestro lugar en el tiempo pertenecería a un ridículo y poco probable 0,1% o 0,01% del conjunto total de los humanos. Es decir, que por simple probabilidad, es mucho más factible que formemos parte de ese 10% que de ese 0,01% de los humanos, con lo cual ya debe quedar poco para el fin de la especie. El teorema, llamado El Argumento del Juicio Final, irrita a científicos de todo el mundo por el simple hecho de que matemáticamente es irrebatible y filosóficamente antinatural.

El teorema de Carter no especifica cómo será ese final, pero indudablemente, acelera cualquier amenaza apocalíptica. Todo lo que sigue a continuación sale de la boca y la pluma de científicos y periodistas informados. No se habla en ningún momento de teorías paranoides, sino de realidades presentes y de consecuencias lógicas. La ficción la dejamos para otro capítulo, esto va en serio.

02. catástrofes (geo-terror)//. Ya hemos hablado en otros E-diktós de cómo la teoría de Gaia de James Lovelock se puede volver fácilmente en contra de los postulados ecologistas de nueva izquierda. Sí, como dice Lovelock, el planeta es capaz de reajustar el ecosistema en su propio beneficio, sería muy lógico que empezase por eliminar parte o toda la raza humana, su peor enemiga. Gaia tiene a su disposición todo un arsenal geológico (y biológico como veremos más adelante) para ganar esa batalla sin dificultad. Salinización de los océanos, terremotos, maremotos, aumento de la temperatura global, e incluso, si entendemos Gaia como ente cosmológico, asteroides desviados. Si la Tierra se enfrenta al hombre, ¿en qué lugar quedan los ecologistas? Habría que inventar un nuevo crimen para ellos: traición a la especie.

En 1976, un terremoto se llevó por delante a unas 750.000 personas en Tangshan, China. 900.000 personas murieron en 1887 a causa de la inundación del río Huang He, también en China. Y más de 1 millón de vidas se extinguieron el 13 de noviembre de 1970 en el Delta del Ganges en Bangladesh. El efecto de El Niño superaba también el millón de pérdidas humanas durante los últimos años 90. Muchos meteorólogos y astrólogos pronostican que entramos en una era de grandes catástrofes naturales o "clima violento" como denominan con cierto pudor. No hace falta más que ver los informativos.

Pero quizá una de las mayores amenazas que se discuten es la del impacto de asteroides. Según John Leslie, es más fácil morir a causa del impacto de un asteroide que ganar la lotería. Se ha estimado la probabilidad de morir así como de 1 entre 20.000. Ya se están gastando millones de dólares en la búsqueda de asteroides cercanos a la órbita terrestre, pero el trabajo es lento y extenso. Dentro de 25 años se podrán haber detectado cerca del 90% de todos los objetos de diámetro superior a 1 km. Hasta entonces habrá que esperar. El astrónomo de la Universidad de Cambridge P.C.W. Davies ha calculado que en el año 2126, el cometa Swift-Tuttle (un trillón de toneladas de hielo a 65 km/seg.) cruzará la órbita terrestre a una distancia de solo 2 semanas de nosotros. Uno de los mayores problemas con los asteroides es que, en ocasiones, su ruta se desvía inesperadamente. Otro problema grave es que, a juicio de algunos observadores, las medidas que la NASA dispone para evitar una colisión son mucho más peligrosas que la colisión misma.

03. guerra (ciber-terror)//. Ahora que las armas nucleares están al alcance de cualquier chiflado, ya no tiene sentido pelearse por ellas ni por su distribución. Sólo nos queda confiar en eso de la buena voluntad del ser humano. Los temores bélicos modernos son más cibernéticos. La ciberguerra está ya en marcha y si da más miedo que ninguna es porque es más barata y accesible que cualquier otra en la historia bélica. Para muestra, el famoso Efecto 2000, que ya no se sostiene ni como chiste, pero en su día tuvo en vilo a más de uno. Y es que la tecnología nos ha conducido a un punto de indefensión tan ridículo como el de depender de los dígitos de un reloj. Si el Efecto 2000 no provocó ningún desastre no fue porque supieran detectarlo a tiempo, sino porque no era tal peligro, claro que esto no supo determinarlo nadie hasta que no hubo pasado de largo.

Cada día se producen millones de errores en los sistemas informáticos de todo el mundo. Errores que pasan completamente inadvertidos porque a simple vista no causan daños. No son

LA IMPOSIBILIDAD DE DETECTAR SEÑALES PROCEDENTES DE CIVILIZACIONES EXTRATERRESTRES PUEDE DEBERSE A QUE TODAS ELLAS SE AUTO-DESTRUYEN POCO DESPUÉS DE DESARROLLAR CIERTAS TECNOLOGÍAS AVANZADAS. (John Leslie, profesor emérito de Filosofía de la Universidad de Guelph).

CUALQUIER TERRORISTA PODRÁ DISEÑAR UN VIRUS DE RÁPIDA PROPAGACIÓN CON UN ÍNDICE DE MORTALIDAD DEL 100%. LA NANOTECNOLOGÍA LE PERMITIRÁ CONSTRUIR UN SISTEMA DE DISPERSIÓN PARA QUE EL VIRUS SE EXTIENDA POR TODO EL PLANETA EN POCO TIEMPO. (Will Ware, Foresight Institute).

PHOTOGRAPHY **OLIVER HELBIG**
TEXT **AMANDA GRISCOM**

buck the system

From the San Francisco airport, it's a seven hour drive, due north, to the homestead of Richard and Karen Perez. From the vineyards through the cattle farms and into the snow-capped Sierras,

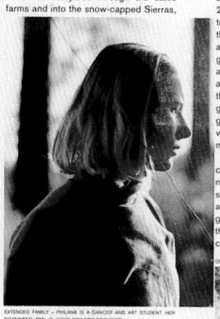

EXTENDED FAMILY – PHILANA IS A DANCER AND ART STUDENT. HER BOYFRIEND, BEN, IS *HOME POWER*'S DESIGNER

nature supplies the entertainment. As you head down the far side of Mt Shasta, the highway becomes a road that ribbons through the foothills along the Oregon border. If you know where you're going, the road becomes a trail.

The last outpost of man is a lean-to liquor store with a gas-pump and a donut stand. Beyond here, you will find mastodon bones and Indian burial sites and the occasional software programmer gone AWOL, but not much else. As you head into the hills, the sign nailed to the Ponderosa trunk warns: "California Energy Grid Ends Here."

Living "off the grid" means out of range of the power company. No one really knows how many off-gridders there are in the US. The usual estimate is 200,000 "homeowners", which doesn't tell you much. The Amish are off grid – they shun electricity (and other modern amenities). There are fringe groups off grid – they shun the state. And there are many others who, for one reason or another, choose to rely on themselves for their basic needs. Not only do they generate their own electricity, but they grow their own food, pump their own water, burn their own garbage and maintain their own roads.

The only thing that can be said for certain about off-gridders is that their number is rising. Sales of small-scale solar generators – the kinds for homes and small farms and businesses – are growing at 30 per cent a year. It is one of those cases of an industry and its market converging: the technology gets cheaper,

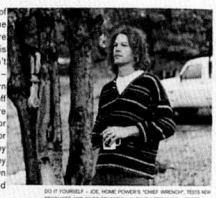

DO IT YOURSELF – JOE, HOME POWER'S "CHIEF WRENCH", TESTS NEW PRODUCTS AND GIVES READERS HANDS-ON TECHNICAL ADVICE

more efficient and easier to use, while the users discover they can afford, install, operate and maintain it for themselves. Richard and Karen Perez have played a big part in that. If going off grid is a grassroots movement, their magazine, *Home Power*, is the fertiliser.

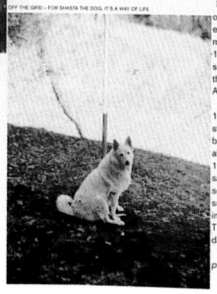

OFF THE GRID – FOR SHASTA THE DOG, IT'S A WAY OF LIFE

The modern photovoltaic cell, a wafer of silicon that converts sunlight to electricity, noiselessly and without fuel or moving parts, was born unexpectedly in 1953, the accidental brainchild of scientists at Bell, a corporate lab then at the heart of what is sometimes called the American military industrial complex.

The Cold War was freezing in the mid 1950s, the space race was on the starting line, and the photovoltaic cell, a break-through without a purpose, was about to find its calling. On March 17, 1958, the US Navy launched its first satellite into orbit. The Vanguard IV – solar panels encircling its tiny frame, sunshine powering its radio – would stay in touch with Earth for years to come. The age of telecommunications had dawned, with a little help from the sun.

When Richard Perez heard about the *photovoltaic effect* in his high school ›

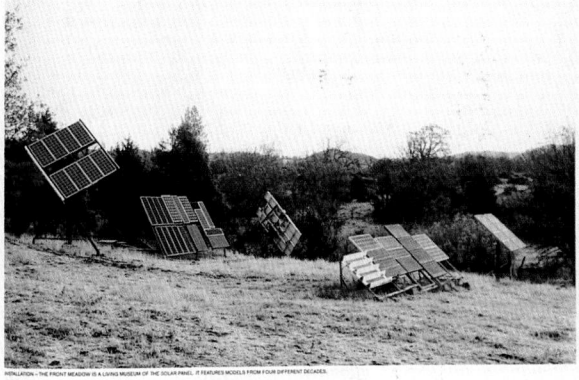

MEMLAKION – THE FRONT MEADOW IS A LIVING MUSEUM OF THE SOLAR PANEL. IT FEATURES MODELS FROM FOUR DIFFERENT DECADES.

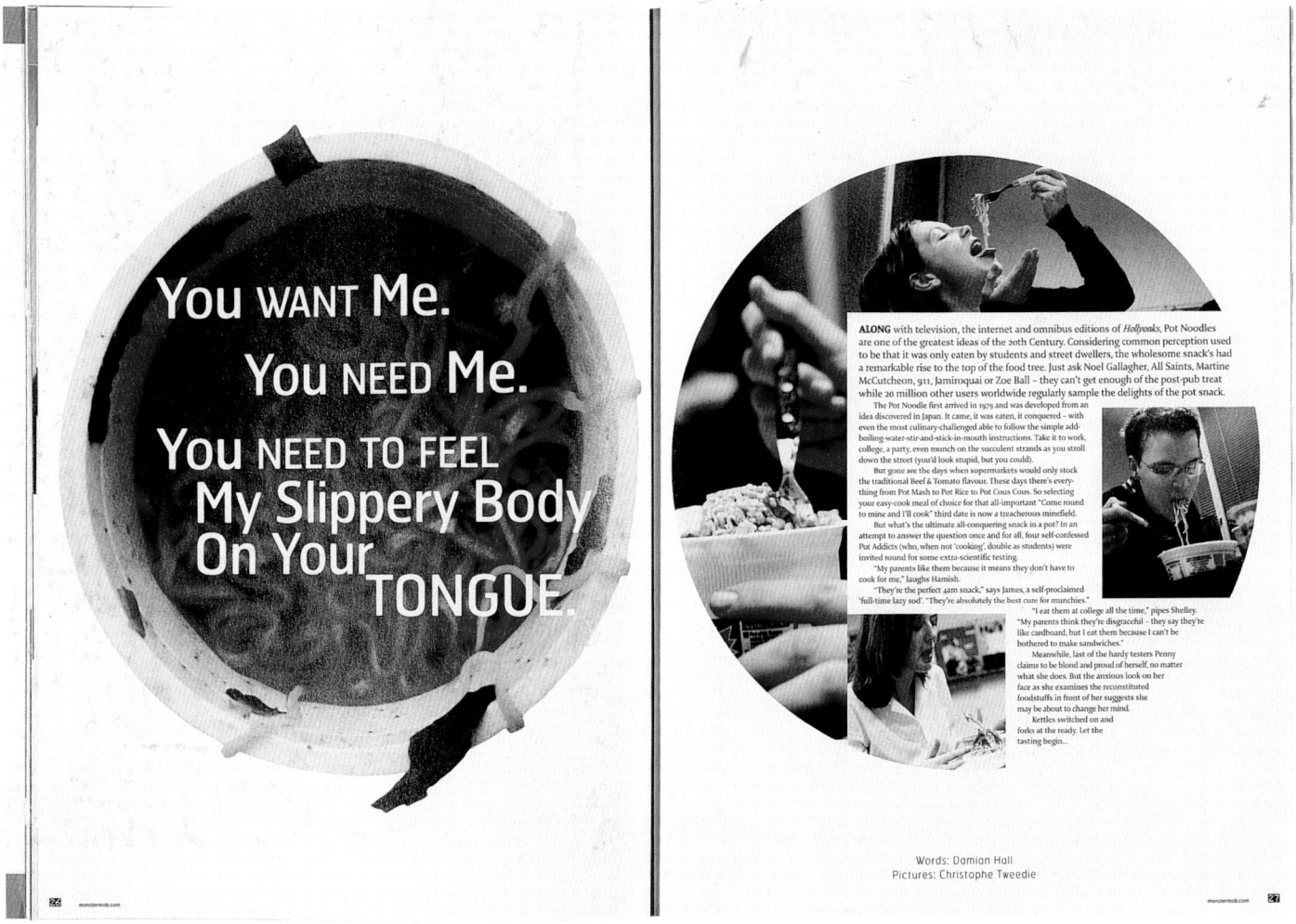

You WANT Me.
You NEED Me.
You NEED TO FEEL
My Slippery Body
On Your TONGUE.

ALONG with television, the internet and omnibus editions of *Hollyoaks*, Pot Noodles are one of the greatest ideas of the 20th Century. Considering common perception used to be that it was only eaten by students and street dwellers, the wholesome snack's had a remarkable rise to the top of the food tree. Just ask Noel Gallagher, All Saints, Martine McCutcheon, 911, Jamiroquai or Zoe Ball – they can't get enough of the post-pub treat while 20 million other users worldwide regularly sample the delights of the pot snack.

The Pot Noodle first arrived in 1979 and was developed from an idea discovered in Japan. It came, it was eaten, it conquered – with even the most culinary-challenged able to follow the simple add-boiling-water-stir-and-stick-in-mouth instructions. Take it to work, college, a party, even munch on the succulent strands as you stroll down the street (you'd look stupid, but you could).

But gone are the days when supermarkets would only stock the traditional Beef & Tomato flavour. These days there's everything from Pot Mash to Pot Rice to Pot Cous Cous. So selecting your easy-cook meal of choice for that all-important "Come round to mine and I'll cook" third date is now a treacherous minefield.

But what's the ultimate all-conquering snack in a pot? In an attempt to answer the question once and for all, four self-confessed Pot Addicts (who, when not 'cooking', double as students) were invited round for some extra-scientific testing.

"My parents like them because it means they don't have to cook for me," laughs Hamish.

"They're the perfect 4am snack," says James, a self-proclaimed 'full-time lazy sod'. "They're absolutely the best cure for munchies."

"I eat them at college all the time," pipes Shelley. "My parents think they're disgraceful – they say they're like cardboard, but I eat them because I can't be bothered to make sandwiches."

Meanwhile, last of the hardy testers Penny claims to be blond and proud of herself, no matter what she does. But the anxious look on her face as she examines the reconstituted foodstuffs in front of her suggests she may be about to change her mind.

Kettles switched on and forks at the ready. Let the tasting begin...

Words: Damian Hall
Pictures: Christophe Tweedie

monstermob.com 26

monstermob.com 27

Mob *(UK, Issue 1, Summer 2001) 220 x 297mm/8 3/4 x 11 3/4 inches*
Deliberately styled to look slightly messy and unkempt to reflect the subject matter and the target audience (teenage users of Monstermob mobile phone ringtones), the type and image combine to become more than the sum of their parts in this feature about pot noodles.
Group art editor *Martin Tullett*

I'd Like To Buy The World a Shelf-Stable Children's Lactic Drink

Coca-Cola confronts a global marketplace that has lost its thirst for bubbly brown sugar water.

Kazuki Yamane, Makoto Sato and I hop out of our chauffeured car at the corner of a busy Tokyo intersection. The two men are wearing suits, and I follow them into the bustle, distracted by teeming madness all around me. Some sort of shrieking dance squad is handing out free cosmetics samples. Multiple massive TV screens beam loops of commercials down to the street. The pedestrian flow is a blocks-thick surge of teenagers tapping at their cellphones.

This neighborhood, Shibuya, is the frenzied, wired heart of nearly all Japanese teenage culture. It is also an important consumer lab for the Coca-Cola Company. Yamane and Sato — both middle-aged Coke execs — have taken me here to view the newest Coke innovation. They're sure it's another triumph of Coca-Cola marketing genius, and angling fast through the crowds now, dicing up flocks of schoolgirls, I can tell this main attraction is drawing near. The excitement builds on Sato's face. Our steps begin to slow. And then, at last, beside the entrance to a busy shopping boutique, I come face to face with the gleaming future of soft

By Seth Stevenson

Photographs by Thomas Hannich

38

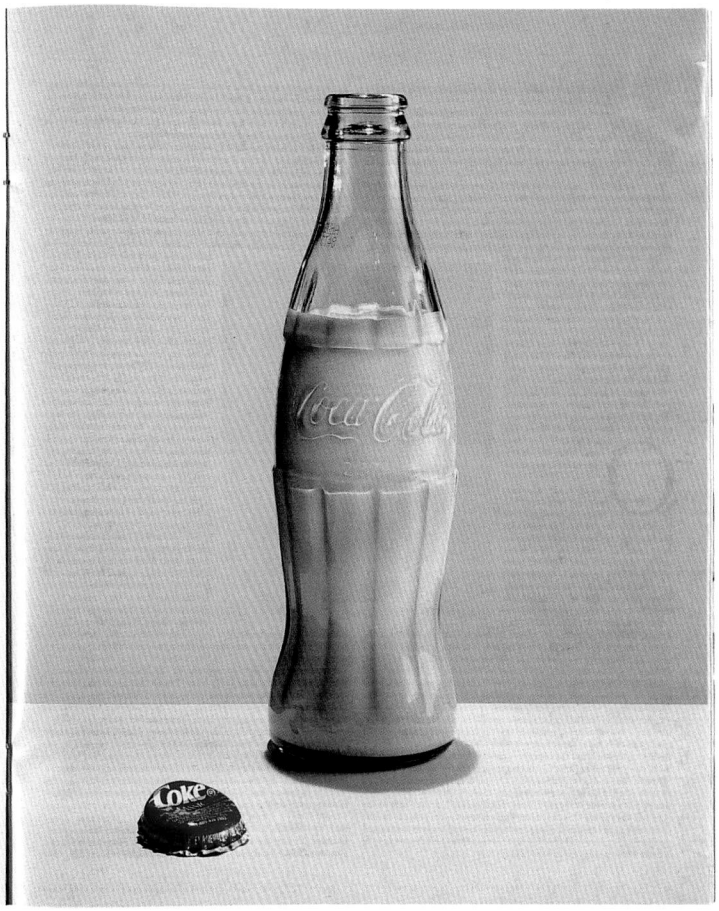

New York Times Magazine *(USA, Issue 1, 10 March 2002)*
240 x 297mm/9 ½ x 11 ¾ inches
A feature about what Coca-Cola is planning for the future of its drinks brands is illustrated through a combination of text and image. The photograph reflects the headline ('I'd like to build the world a shelf-stable children's lactic drink') and the shape of the text echoes the photograph.
Art director *Janet Froelich*

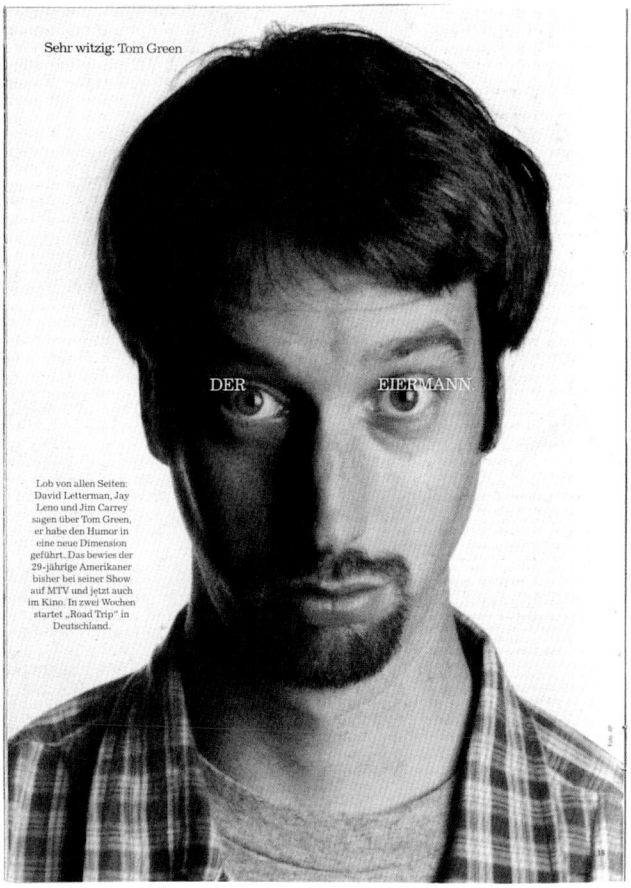

Sehr witzig: Tom Green

DER EIERMANN.

Lob von allen Seiten: David Letterman, Jay Leno und Jim Carrey sagen über Tom Green, er habe den Humor in eine neue Dimension geführt. Das bewies der 29-jährige Amerikaner bisher bei seiner Show auf MTV und jetzt auch im Kino. In zwei Wochen startet „Road Trip" in Deutschland.

Foto: dpa

Das langweilige Gesicht ist Tom Greens Stärke. Bei seinen Opfern schafft es Vertrauen und bei seinen Zuschauern dieses leichte Gefühl der Abneigung, das ein Komiker braucht, um die Leute zum Lachen zu bringen. Wenn Tom Green singt, sieht er aus wie ein braver Pfadfinderanführer. Sein berühmtestes Lied geht so: „Hey, Kids, fühlt eure Hoden, damit ihr keinen Krebs bekommt. Fasst euch an die Eier, dann kriegt ihr keinen Krebs! Und ihr sterbt auch nicht! Ich weiß es, denn ich hatte Krebs in den Eiern, und ich bemerkte es beim Onanieren! Zum Glück tue ich das oft!" Dann der Refrain: „Warum fasst ihr euch an die Eier? Weil wir keinen Krebs wollen. Warum? Weil wir uns gerne an die Eier fassen." Den Song hat er neulich vor 10 000 Schülern vorgetragen. Alle haben mitgesungen.

In den USA ist Tom Green ein Superstar, seitdem er in seiner MTV-Show aus Bildern der eigenen Hodenoperation ein „Nut-Cancer-Special" gemacht hat. Die Programmchefs von MTV waren sich nicht ganz sicher, ob es eine gute Idee sei, in der „Tom Green Show" Scherze über ein solches Thema zu machen, doch Tom überzeugte sie: „Gott sagte zu mir: Heilige Scheiße, Tom, ich schenke deinen Geschlechtsteilen eine heilbare Form von Krebs. Und dir die Lizenz, darüber im Fernsehen Witze zu machen." Die besten Szenen der Operation wurden gezeigt, das vom Krebs angefressene Testikel im Reagenzglas, die weinenden Eltern, Diskussionen mit den Ärzten – die Show war Tom Greens Durchbruch: David Letterman, Jay Leno, Conan O'Brian, Jim Carrey, die Farrelli-Brüder, also alle, die sich mit Witzen auskennen, gratulierten: Green habe den Humor in eine neue Dimension geführt und von allen Fesseln des guten Geschmacks befreit. Bei der Oscar-Party klopfte ihm George Clooney auf die Schulter: „Junge, das mit deinen Eiern war das Lustigste, was ich jemals gesehen habe." Green sagt: „Ich bin für die Leute jetzt nicht mehr der durchgeknallte Typ von MTV. Ich bin jetzt der Typ, der nur noch ein Ei hat."

Greens Humor funktioniert eigentlich ganz einfach: Er konfrontiert Menschen mit absurden Situationen, taucht mit der Kamera auf und macht ein Gesicht, als wäre alles in bester Ordnung. Dabei ist er immer höflich, sachlich, heimtückisch. Wenn er einem Kind ein Autogramm gibt, fragt er, wie der Name buchstabiert wird: S-T-E-V-E-N. Green schreibt dann: „Für Stephen". Und lächelt freundlich.

Als er bei einem Baseballspiel in der amerikanischen Provinz den Stadionsprecher spielte, redete er so lange Unsinn, bis er von den aufgebrachten Hinterwäldlern verprügelt wurde. Als Polizist verkleidet führte er einmal eine Kuh in einen Supermarkt und brachte Kunden dazu, an ihren Eutern zu nuckeln. Und Monica Lewinksy schleppte er nach Ottawa, um ihren Eltern mit ihr einen Überraschungsbesuch abzustatten. Tom Greens Eltern stehen häufig im Zentrum seiner Aktionen. Möglicherweise ist das die späte Rache dafür, dass Herr Green, ein Offizier, den kleinen Tom früher jeden Morgen um 7.30 Uhr aus dem Bett holte, indem er ihm die Decke wegzog. In seiner ersten eigenen Show beim kanadischen Fernsehsender CNBC malte Tom Green jedenfalls sein Elternhaus in der Nacht psychedelisch an. Und filmte dann die Reaktionen am nächsten Morgen. Seitdem sind Tom Greens Eltern seine Lieblingsopfer: Mal überraschte er sie mitten in der Nacht mit einem Kameateam und zwang sie, ein Bon-Jovi-Video zu schauen. Mal stellte er seinen Eltern eine Skulptur, welche die beiden in einer eindeutigen Sexposition zeigte, in den Garten: die Greens schalteten ihren Anwalt ein, verhinderten zunächst die Ausstrahlung, und beruhigten sich erst wieder, als Tom ihnen Tickets für die Oprah-Winfrey-Show besorgte.

Wie viele andere Komiker auch, ist Tom Green zu seinem Beruf gekommen, weil er sich als Kind nur mit Witzen bemerkbar machen konnte. Der entscheidende Moment kam in der 6. Klasse beim Schulwettbewerb im freien Vortrag. Tom hatte in den vorangegangenen Jahren knapp gegen seinen Widersacher Darryl Page verloren. Diesmal referierte Tom über Comedy-Theorie. Matter Page meldete sich mit Zwischenfragen, weil sie spürte, ihr Sohn könne verlieren: „Du sagtest, Witze seien ein gutes Mittel, um sich aus schwierigen Situationen zu befreien. Aber du hast kein Beispiel gegeben." Tom konterte mit einem lahmen Gag über Zeugnisse, den er in irgendeinem Witzbuch gelesen hatte. Ein schlechter Witz, aber aus seinem Mund lustig. Tom erinnert sich: „Das war die beeindruckendste Erfahrung meines Lebens. Alle lachten. Die Lehrer, die Eltern, die Schüler und auch Lesley Dewsnap. Später durfte ich sie sogar küssen."

Später, mit 13, war Tom ein hervorragender Skateboarder. Und als er einmal mit seinen Kumpels Phil Giroux und Glenn Humpnik auf den Brettern durch die Straßen von Ottawa jagte, kam ihm die Idee, die seinen Humor so einmalig macht. „Als Skateboarder hatten wir damals nur Ärger, und wir entschlossen uns, die schlechten Dinge gut zu finden. Wir nannten das ‚flippen'. Ein gebrochener Fuß war für uns das Schönste auf der Welt. So hatten wir immer viel zu lachen."

Als der Arzt ihm mitteilte, dass er Krebs habe, heulte Green, wie er sagt, tagelang, bekam Todesangst und Depressionen. Er wollte aufgeben. Seiner Freundin Drew Barrymore und seinem alten Kumpel Glenn Humpnik hat er es zu verdanken, dass er aus der größten Krise seinen größten Erfolg machte. Humpnik erinnerte ihn an die Skateboard-Zeit, als sie Katastrophen in Späße verwandelten. „Das machen wir jetzt auch!", forderte Humpnik. Und da der Plan aufging, hat der Mann mit einem Ei nun die freie Auswahl: Filme, Shows oder Plattenverträge. Er hat sich entschieden, nicht zu viel zu arbeiten: „Ich will mehr Zeit mit Drew verbringen." Dennoch wird wohl noch in diesem Jahr eine Platte von ihm erscheinen. Und Greens Kino-Komödie „Road Trip", für die er auch das Buch schrieb, kommt Ende August in Deutschland in die Kinos. Ein Teil des Eintrittsgeldes geht an die „Tom-Green-Eierkrebs-Stiftung". **Lars Jensen**

7 August 2000

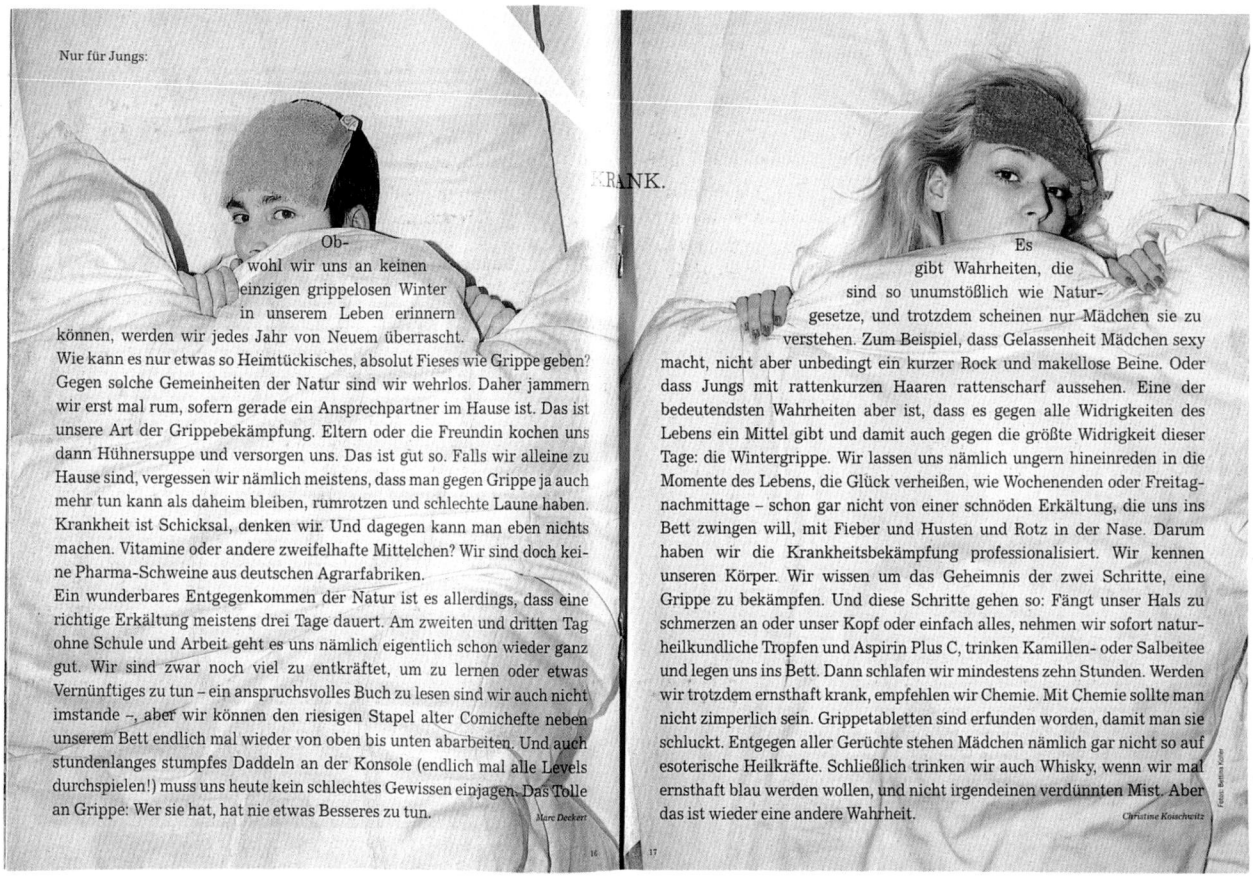

Nur für Jungs:

KRANK.

Obwohl wir uns an keinen einzigen grippelosen Winter in unserem Leben erinnern können, werden wir jedes Jahr von Neuem überrascht. Wie kann es nur etwas so Heimtückisches, absolut Fieses wie Grippe geben? Gegen solche Gemeinheiten der Natur sind wir wehrlos. Daher jammern wir erst mal rum, sofern gerade ein Ansprechpartner im Hause ist. Das ist unsere Art der Grippebekämpfung. Eltern oder die Freundin kochen uns dann Hühnersuppe und versorgen uns. Das ist gut so. Falls wir alleine zu Hause sind, vergessen wir nämlich meistens, dass man gegen Grippe ja auch mehr tun kann als daheim bleiben, rumrotzen und schlechte Laune haben. Krankheit ist Schicksal, denken wir. Und dagegen kann man eben nichts machen. Vitamine oder andere zweifelhafte Mittelchen? Wir sind doch keine Pharma-Schweine aus deutschen Agrarfabriken.

Ein wunderbares Entgegenkommen der Natur ist es allerdings, dass eine richtige Erkältung meistens drei Tage dauert. Am zweiten und dritten Tag ohne Schule und Arbeit geht es uns nämlich eigentlich schon wieder ganz gut. Wir sind zwar noch viel zu entkräftet, um zu lernen oder etwas Vernünftiges zu tun – ein anspruchsvolles Buch zu lesen sind wir auch nicht imstande –, aber wir können den riesigen Stapel alter Comichefte neben unserem Bett endlich mal wieder von oben bis unten abarbeiten. Und auch stundenlanges stumpfes Daddeln an der Konsole (endlich mal alle Levels durchspielen!) muss uns heute kein schlechtes Gewissen einjagen. Das Tolle an Grippe: Wer sie hat, hat nie etwas Besseres zu tun. *Marc Deckert*

Es gibt Wahrheiten, die sind so unumstößlich wie Naturgesetze, und trotzdem scheinen nur Mädchen sie zu verstehen. Zum Beispiel, dass Gelassenheit Mädchen sexy macht, nicht aber unbedingt ein kurzer Rock und makellose Beine. Oder dass Jungs mit rattenkurzen Haaren rattenscharf aussehen. Eine der bedeutendsten Wahrheiten aber ist, dass es gegen alle Widrigkeiten des Lebens ein Mittel gibt und damit auch gegen die größte Widrigkeit dieser Tage: die Wintergrippe. Wir lassen uns nämlich ungern hineinreden in die Momente des Lebens, die Glück verheißen, wie Wochenenden oder Freitagnachmittage – schon gar nicht von einer schnöden Erkältung, die uns ins Bett zwingen will, mit Fieber und Husten und Rotz in der Nase. Darum haben wir die Krankheitsbekämpfung professionalisiert. Wir kennen unseren Körper. Wir wissen um das Geheimnis der zwei Schritte, eine Grippe zu bekämpfen. Und diese Schritte gehen so: Fängt unser Hals zu schmerzen an oder unser Kopf oder einfach alles, nehmen wir sofort naturheilkundliche Tropfen und Aspirin Plus C, trinken Kamillen- oder Salbeitee und legen uns ins Bett. Dann schlafen wir mindestens zehn Stunden. Werden wir trotzdem ernsthaft krank, empfehlen wir Chemie. Mit Chemie sollte man nicht zimperlich sein. Grippetabletten sind erfunden worden, damit man sie schluckt. Entgegen aller Gerüchte stehen Mädchen nämlich gar nicht so auf esoterische Heilkräfte. Schließlich trinken wir auch Whisky, wenn wir mal ernsthaft blau werden wollen, und nicht irgendeinen verdünnten Mist. Aber das ist wieder eine andere Wahrheit. *Christine Kosschwitz*

Fotos: Bettina Kistler

22 January 2001

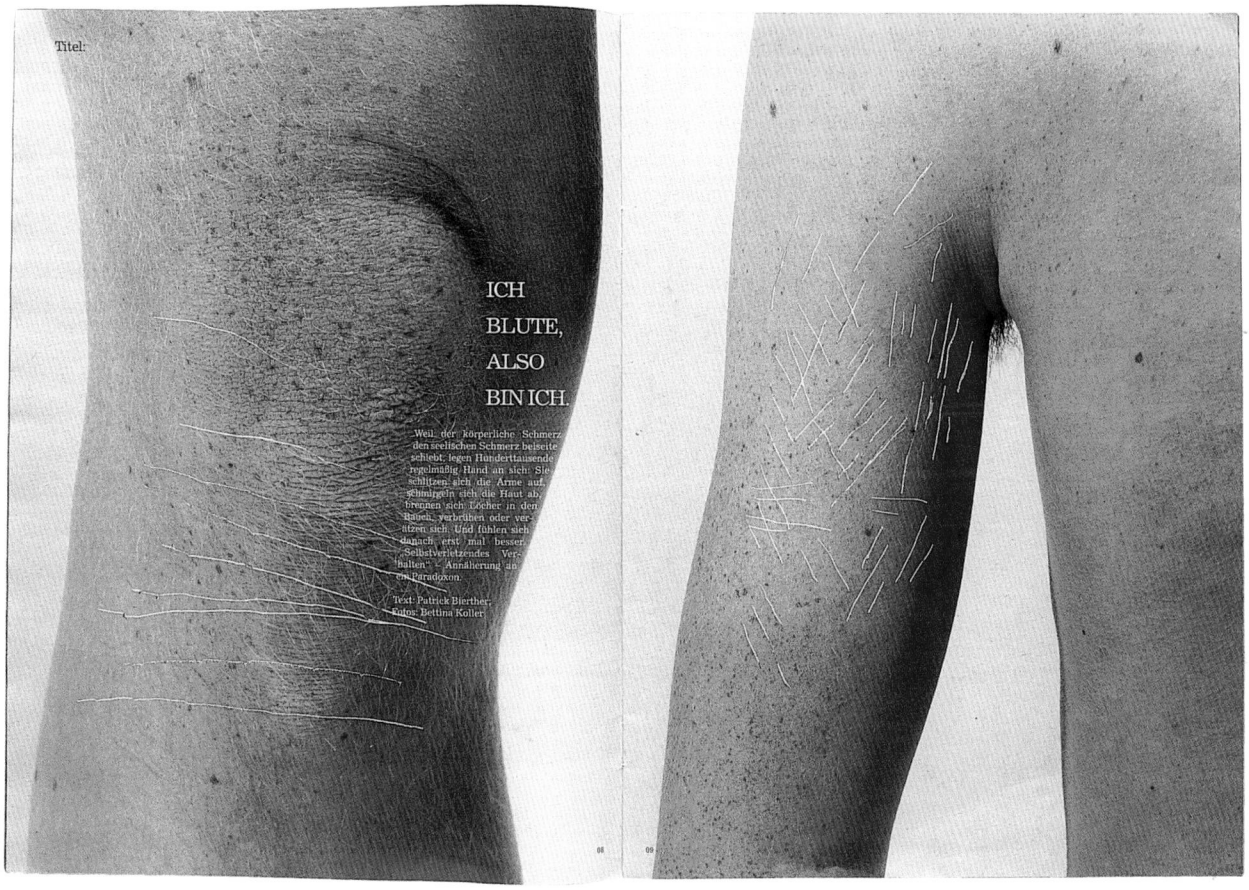

4 September 2000, 214 x 282mm/8 ½ x 11 ⅛ inches

Who published *Jetzt*?
Jetzt, which means 'Now', was published every Monday with the newspaper, *Süddeutsche Zeitung*. It was an attempt to attract younger readers to buy the newspaper – teenagers and people in their twenties. *Süddeutsche Zeitung* is a very traditional-looking newspaper, one of the biggest in Germany. I art directed the magazine for three years, from 1999 until its closure in July 2002.

How did the design of *Jetzt* relate to the rest of the newspaper?
We used the same type of newsprint paper and the same column sizes and typeface, called Excelsior. But we had our own grid and were able to play around a lot more with the design.

How big was the design team?
There were just two of us, myself and Sandra Eichler.

What was the content about?
The content was just about normal young people; their problems, music, apartments, love and politics... all the things that concern them. We covered serious subjects, like when we ran a story about a Jewish girl and a Palestinian girl, both of whom grew up in Germany. They were friends but returned to their homeland and were unable to mix. We also had lighter stories, for example a story we set up where we gave DM50 to people and asked them to use the money to get all the way to London through exchanges. We followed these people as they bought a football, swapped it with someone else for a lamp, and more, until they arrived in London. And we ran an issue about how movies can influence your sex life!

How did your designs respond to that content?
The design was inspired by the content without trying to show what is mentioned in the text. The design had the aim of inspiring the imagination of the reader and helping the text to express what can't be written.

We tried to awaken the creativity of the reader, for example, by using text to make illustrations so that the reader was able to make his own picture. We also ran a story about 15-year olds who injure themselves with knives and needles. To illustrate this we photographed close-up shots of skin and then wounded the pictures with knives. By doing this the reader didn't see actual wounds but saw the pain.

You must have worked very closely with the editor and the writers.
We did. The editor, Timm Klotzeck, was a good friend and professional partner.

We would be involved right from the beginning, planning the stories, thinking about how to make the ideas look good. We had a say in what went into the magazine – photographers would come to us with ideas and we would match them with writers to go out and work on those ideas.

***Jetzt* was very design-led and you seemed to have a lot of freedom to design what you**

Interview
Mirko Borsche
Art director
Jetzt magazine

LIBRARY & RESOURCES AREA EPSOM CAMPUS
THE SURREY INSTITUTE OF ART & DESIGN

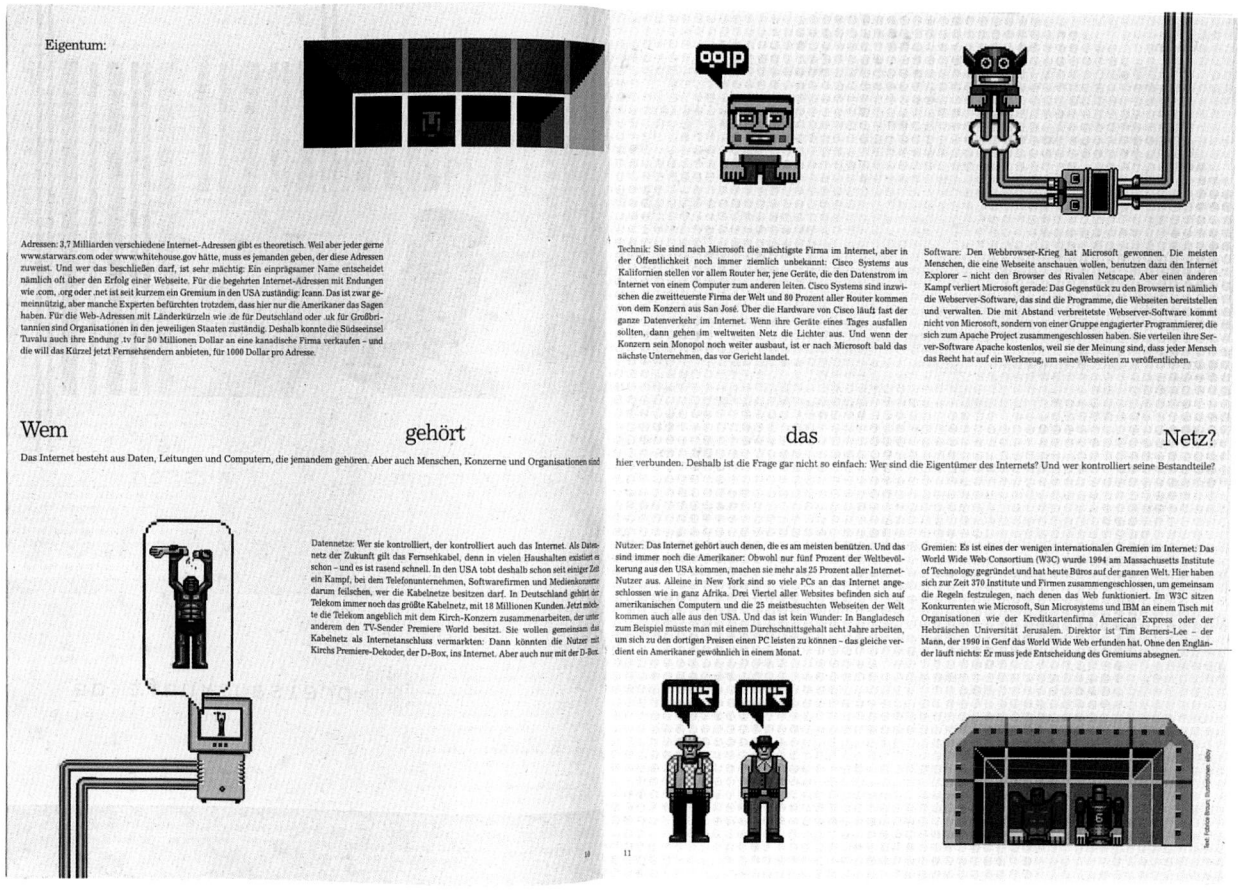

Eigentum:

Adressen: 3,7 Milliarden verschiedene Internet-Adressen gibt es theoretisch. Weil aber jeder gerne www.starwars.com oder www.whitehouse.gov hätte, muss es jemanden geben, der diese Adressen zuweist. Und wer das beschließen darf, ist sehr mächtig: Ein einprägsamer Name entscheidet nämlich oft über den Erfolg einer Webseite. Für die begehrten Internet-Adressen mit Endungen wie .com, .org oder .net ist seit kurzem ein Gremium in den USA zuständig: Icann. Das ist zwar gemeinnützig, aber manche Experten befürchten trotzdem, dass hier nur die Amerikaner das Sagen haben. Für die Web-Adressen mit Länderkürzeln wie .de für Deutschland oder .uk für Großbritannien sind Organisationen in den jeweiligen Staaten zuständig. Deshalb konnte die Südseeinsel Tuvalu auch ihre Endung .tv für 50 Millionen Dollar an eine kanadische Firma verkaufen – und die will das Kürzel jetzt Fernsehsendern anbieten, für 1000 Dollar pro Adresse.

Wem gehört das Netz?

Das Internet besteht aus Daten, Leitungen und Computern, die jemandem gehören. Aber auch Menschen, Konzerne und Organisationen sind hier verbunden. Deshalb ist die Frage gar nicht so einfach: Wer sind die Eigentümer des Internets? Und wer kontrolliert seine Bestandteile?

Datennetze: Wer sie kontrolliert, der kontrolliert auch das Internet. Als Datennetz der Zukunft gilt das Fernsehkabel, denn in vielen Haushalten existiert es schon – und es ist rasend schnell. In den USA tobt deshalb schon seit einiger Zeit ein Kampf, bei dem Telefonunternehmen, Softwarefirmen und Medienkonzerne darum feilschen, wer die Kabelnetze besitzen darf. In Deutschland gehört der Telekom immer noch das größte Kabelnetz, mit 18 Millionen Kunden. Jetzt möchte die Telekom angeblich mit dem Kirch-Konzern zusammenarbeiten, der unter anderem den TV-Sender Premiere World besitzt. Sie wollen gemeinsam das Kabelnetz als Internetanschluss vermarkten: Dann könnten die Nutzer mit Kirchs Premiere-Dekoder, der D-Box, ins Internet. Aber auch nur mit der D-Box.

Technik: Sie sind nach Microsoft die mächtigste Firma im Internet, aber in der Öffentlichkeit noch immer ziemlich unbekannt: Cisco Systems aus Kalifornien stellen vor allem Router her, jene Geräte, die den Datenstrom im Internet von einem Computer zum anderen leiten. Cisco Systems sind inzwischen die zweitteuerste Firma der Welt und 80 Prozent aller Router kommen von dem Konzern aus San José. Über die Hardware von Cisco läuft fast der ganze Datenverkehr im Internet. Wenn ihre Geräte eines Tages ausfallen sollten, dann gehen im weltweiten Netz die Lichter aus. Und wenn der Konzern sein Monopol noch weiter ausbaut, ist er nach Microsoft bald das nächste Unternehmen, das vor Gericht landet.

Software: Den Webbrowser-Krieg hat Microsoft gewonnen. Die meisten Menschen, die eine Webseite ansehaun wollen, benutzen dazu den Internet Explorer – nicht den Browser des Rivalen Netscape. Aber einen anderen Kampf verliert Microsoft gerade: Das Gegenstück zu den Browsern ist nämlich die Webserver-Software, das sind die Programme, die Webseiten bereitstellen und verwalten. Die mit Abstand verbreitetste Webserver-Software kommt nicht von Microsoft, sondern von einer Gruppe engagierter Programmierer, die sich zum Apache Project zusammengeschlossen haben. Sie verteilen ihre Server-Software Apache kostenlos, weil sie der Meinung sind, dass jeder Mensch das Recht hat auf ein Werkzeug, um seine Webseiten zu veröffentlichen.

Nutzer: Das Internet gehört auch denen, die es am meisten benützen. Und das sind immer noch die Amerikaner: Obwohl nur fünf Prozent der Weltbevölkerung aus den USA kommen, machen sie mehr als 25 Prozent aller Internet-Nutzer aus. Alleine in New York sind so viele PCs an das Internet angeschlossen wie in ganz Afrika. Drei Viertel aller Websites befinden sich auf amerikanischen Computern und die 25 meistbesuchten Webseiten der Welt kommen auch alle aus den USA. Und das ist kein Wunder: In Bangladesch zum Beispiel müsste man mit einem Durchschnittsgehalt acht Jahre arbeiten, um sich zu den dortigen Preisen einen PC leisten zu können – das gleiche verdient ein Amerikaner gewöhnlich in einem Monat.

Gremien: Es ist eines der wenigen internationalen Gremien im Internet: Das World Wide Web Consortium (W3C) wurde 1994 am Massachusetts Institute of Technology gegründet und hat heute Büros auf der ganzen Welt. Hier haben sich zur Zeit 370 Institute und Firmen zusammengeschlossen, um gemeinsam die Regeln festzulegen, nach denen das Web funktioniert. Im W3C sitzen Konkurrenten wie Microsoft, Sun Microsystems und IBM an einem Tisch mit Organisationen wie der Kreditkartenfirma American Express oder der Hebräischen Universität Jerusalem. Direktor ist Tim Berners-Lee – der Mann, der 1990 in Genf das World Wide Web erfunden hat. Ohne den Engländer läuft nichts: Er muss jede Entscheidung des Gremiums absegnen.

Text: Fabian Bruns; Illustrationen: eBoy

10

11

20 March 2000

wanted. What was your philosophy about the design?
I didn't have a lot of freedom as it was a newspaper magazine and not a design magazine. The whole look developed because we had very little money for commissioning. Sandra and I are both from painting rather than design-led backgrounds so we would do the illustrations and save what budget we had left for commissioning photography.

I developed a typographic style of illustration that used the look of the main newspaper in a different way. My philosophy was to use that to give the magazine a special look. The words are very important to me but I try to make them more interesting for the reader. I think no-one needs to see a blond girl walking down the street if the text says so but you can show the atmosphere of what the author wants to say.

For example, we put together a special issue about drugs in which we looked at the subject from many people's viewpoints – the users, the parents, the police – and the designs for each article were just about expressing feelings such as happiness, envy or feeling unconscious. Every article had a different word and picture to start it. In this way, we were able to create the atmosphere of the subject.

How did that philosophy and the design develop during your time on the magazine?
It developed weekly. It's very hard to be creative every week, but once you start working your design starts to grow every day.

Were there designs you did that were turned down by the editor?
Of course. I did a lot of typographic designs I couldn't use. I want to make a book with them. There were also a lot of free interpretations that the editor didn't want to use.

Do you regard the project as successful?
It was successful when we closed the magazine! Young intellectual Germans loved it. The newspaper had built a base of young readers – there were about 60,000 more young readers than the other German newspapers had. There was a small riot to get their *Jetzt* back! Hundreds of people blocked the main entrance to the office. They wrote thousands of letters – national newspapers, magazines and television stations covered the story. So it was successful in that sense. The problem was the drop in advertising that all newspapers suffered during 2002. It meant the newspaper had to cut back on all 'extra' projects, so *Jetzt* was cancelled.

What projects are you working on now?
I'm doing illustrations for other magazines, including the main 'grown-up' *Süddeutsche Zeitung* magazine, but also for web magazines Tiger (www.tigermagazine.org) and thisisamagazine.com, and for record labels.

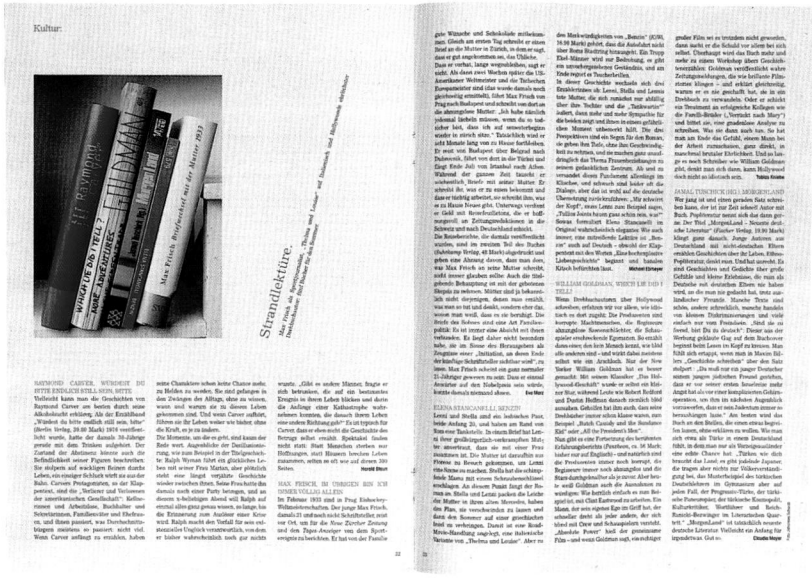

Kultur:

Strandlektüre.

Max Frisch, Reisegepäck auf der Mauer, 1933

RAYMOND CARVER, WÜRDEST DU BITTE ENDLICH STILL SEIN, SETTE

Vielleicht kann man die Geschichten von Raymond Carver am besten durch seine Alkoholsucht erklären. Als der Erzählband „Würdest du bitte endlich still sein, bitte" (Berlin Verlag, 24.00 Mark) 1976 veröffentlicht wurde, hatte der damals 38-Jährige gerade mit dem Trinken aufgehört. Der Zustand der Abstinenz könnte auch die Befindlichkeit seiner Figuren beschreiben. Sie stolpern auf wackligen Beinen durchs Leben, ein einziger Schluck wirft sie aus der Bahn. Carvers Protagonisten, so der Klappentext, sind die „Berliner und Weissenseer der amerikanischen Gesellschaft": Kellerinnen und Arbeitslose, Buchhalter und Sekretärinnen, Familienväter und Ehefrauen, und ihnen passiert, was Durchschnittsbürgern meistens so passiert: nicht viel. Wenn Carver anfängt zu erzählen, haben seine Charaktere schon keine Chance mehr, zu Helden zu werden. Sie sind gefangen in den Zwängen der Alltags. Manchmal wann und warum sie zu diesen Leben geworden sind. Und wenn Carver aufhört, führen sie ihr Leben weiter wie bisher ohne die Kraft, es zu ändern.

Die Momente, um die es geht, sind kaum der Rede wert. Augenblicke der Desillusionierung, wie zum Beispiel in der Titelgeschichte: Ralph Wyman fährt ein glückliches Leben mit seiner Frau Marion, aber plötzlich steht eine längst vergessene Geschichte wieder zwischen ihnen. Seine Frau hatte damals nach einer Party betrogen, und an diesem 4-Schalotten Abend will Ralph auf einmal alles ganz genau wissen, so lange, bis die Erinnerung zum Auslöser einer Krise wird. Ralph macht den Vorfall für sein entsetzliches Unglück verantwortlich, von dem er bisher wahrscheinlich noch gar nicht wusste. „Gibt es andere Männer, fragte er sich betrunken, die auf ein bestimmtes Ereignis in ihrem Leben blicken und darin die Anfänge einer Katastrophe wahrnehmen konnten, die danach ihrem Leben eine andere Richtung gab?" Es ist typisch für Carver, dass er eben nicht die Geschichte des Betrugs selbst erzählt. Spektakel finden nicht statt. Statt Menschen stehen nur Bruchstücke, nicht Binnen bewohnen Leben zusammen, selten es oft wie auf diesen 300 Seiten.

Harald Braun

MAX FRISCH, IN UMRIGEN BIN ICH IMMER VÖLLIG ALLEIN

Im Februar 1933 sind in Prag Einbeziehungs-Weltmeisterschaften. Der junge Max Frisch, damals 21 und noch nicht Schriftsteller, reist vor Ort, um für die *Neue Zürcher Zeitung* und den *Tages-Anzeiger* von dem Sportereignis zu berichten. Er hat von der Familie gute Wünsche und Schokolade mitbekommen. Gleich am ersten Tag erkennt er einen Jungen an der Mutter in Tränen, in dem er sagt, dass er gut angekommen sei, das Übliche. Dass er verhaut, lange weggeschickt, sagt er nicht. Als dieses zwei Wochen später die US-Amerikaner Weltmeister und die Tschechen Europameister sind (das wurde damals noch gleichzeitig ermittelt), fährt Max Frisch von Prag nach Budapest und schreibt von dort an die ahnungslose Mutter: „Ich habe nämlich jedenfall Heimweh, wenn du so traurig bist, dass ich auf neuerbergeben sonder in ernst. Sie." Tatsächlich wird er acht Monate lang von zu Hause fortbleiben. Er reist von Budapest über Belgrad nach Palestina, fährt von dort an die Türkei und fängt Ende Juli von Istanbul nach Athen. Während der ganzen Zeit tauscht er wöchentlich Briefe mit seiner Mutter. Er schreibt ihr, was er zu essen bekommt und dass er tüchtig arbeitet, er schreibt ihm, was er zu Hause Neues gibt. Unterwegs verdient er Geld mit Reisereflexionen, die er hoffnungsvoll an Zeitungsredaktionen in der Schweiz und nach Deutschland schickt. Die Reisebeiträge, die damals veröffentlicht wurden, sind im zweiten Teil des Buches (*Sabotage* Verlag, 48 Mark) abgedruckt und geben eine Ahnung davon, dass man dem, was Max Frisch an seiner Mutter schreibt, nicht immer glauben sollte. Auch die tiefgehende Behauptung ist mit der gebotenen Skepsis zu nehmen. Mütter sind ja bekanntlich nicht dazugemacht, dass man ernsthaft was zu tut und denkt, sondern eher dazu, wenn man weg, dass es ein bewährt. Die Briefe des Sohnes sind eine fast *Facsimile*-publik. Es ist immer eine Absicht mit ihnen verbunden. Es liegt daher nicht besonders nahe, sie im Sinne des Herausgebers als Zeugnisse einer „Initiation, an deren Ende der künftige Schriftsteller sichtbar wird", zu lesen. Max Frisch scheint ein ganz normaler 21-Jähriger gewesen zu sein: Dass er einmal Architekt auf den Nidelpanza sein würde, konnte damals niemand ahnen.

Eva Mayer

ELENA STANCANELLI SENZIN

Lenzi und Stella sind aus Berlin. Anfang 20, und haben am Rand von Rom eine Tankstelle. In einem Brief hat Lenzi ihrer großmutterlich-verkauzenhaften Mutter anvertraut, dass sie mit einer Frau zusammen ist. Die Mutter ist daraufhin aus Florenz zu Besuch gekommen, um Lenzi ein Stück zu machen. Stella hat die schnippische Mama mit einem Schwanenhalsinsel eingeladen. An diesem Punkt fängt der Roman an. Stella und Lenzi packen die Leiche der Mutter in ihren alten Mercedes, haben den Plan, sie verscheuchen zu lassen und dann den Sommer auf einer griechischen Insel zu verbringen. Damit ist eine Road-Movie-Handlung angelegt, eine italienische Variante von „Thelma und Louise". Aber es den Minkwindigkeiten von „Bonnie" (DM, 34.90 Mark) gibt, dass die Autobahn nicht über Roma Nuntiata hinausgeht. Ein Trupp Ehel-Minner wird zur Bedrohung, es gibt ein unvorhergesehenes Geständnis, und am Ende regiert es Tuscherbrüten.

In dieser Geschichte wechseln sich drei Erzählstimmen ab: Lenzi, Stella und Lenzis tote Mutter, die sich zunächst nur abfällig über ihre Tochter und die „Tuttlesarin" äußert, dann mehr und mehr Sympathie für die beiden zeigt und ihnen in seinen gräßlichen Moment unbewirkt hilft. Die drei Perspektiven sind ein Segen für den Roman, er gibt ihm Tiefe, ohne ihm Geschwindigkeit zu nehmen, und sie machen ganz unaufdringlich das Thema Frauenbeziehungen zu seinem gedanklichen Zentrum. Als seid zu versuchen dieses Pandemonie allerdings im Klischee, und schwach sind leider oft die Dialoge, aber das ist wohl auf die deutsche Übersetzung zurückzuführen. „Mir schwirrt der Kopf", meint Lenzi zum Beispiel einer, „Tullius Jeanis haben ganz schön was, was." Serena formuliert Elena Stancanelli im Original wahrscheinlich eleganter. Wie auch immer, eine mitreißende Lektüre ist „Senzin" auch auf Deutsch – obwohl der Klappentext mit den Worten „Eine hochergötzende Liebesgeschichte" beginnt und besonders Kitsch befürchten lässt.

Michael Stringer

WILLIAM GOLDMAN, WHICH LIE DID I TELL?

Wenn Drehbuchautoren über Hollywood schreiben, erfahren wir vor allem, wie idiotisch es dort zugeht. Die Produzenten sind korrupte Machtmenschen, die Regisseure abzugeben Konsonanzkünstler, die Schauspieler emotionelle Egomanen. Es entsteht dann einer, den kein Mensch kennt, wie klid alle anderen sind – und wirkt dabei meistens selbst wie ein Arschloch. Nur der New Yorker William Goldman hat es besser gemacht. Mit seinem Klassiker „Das Hollywood-Geschäft" wurde er selbst ein Mitstar Star, während Leute wie Robert Redford und Dustin Hoffman damals niemich bild annahen. Gehörlos hat ihn auch, dass seine Drehbücher immer schon klasse waren, zum Beispiel „Butch Cassidy und die Sundance Kid" oder „All the President's Men".

Man gibt es eine Fortsetzung des berühmten Erfahrungsberichts (Paradoxon, ca. 36 Mark) und zur Englisch- und natürlich auch der Produzenten immer noch korrupt, die Regisseure immer noch abzugeben und die Stars dumthypnotisiert als je immer. Aber heute weiß Goldman auch die Autoskonen zu würdigen: Wie bestlich einfach es man Beispiel ist, mit Clint Eastwood zu arbeiten. Ein Mann, der sein eigenes Ego im Griff hat, der schnellar denkt als jeder andere, der sich hinter mit Dame und Schauspielern verstellt. „Absolute Power" hieß der gemeinsame Film – und wenn Goldman sagt, ein solcher grauer Film sei es trotzdem nicht geworden, dann merkt er die Schuld vor allem bei sich selbst. Überhaupt wird das Buch mehr und mehr zu einem Workshop über Geschichtenerzählen: Goldman veröffentlicht wahre Zeitungsmeldungen, die wie brillante Filmstoffe klingen – und erklärt gleichzeitig, warum er es nie geschafft hat, die in ein Drehbuch zu verwandeln. Oder er schickt ein Treatment an erfolgreiche Kollegen wie die Fanelli-Brüder („Vertraut nach Mary") und bittet sie, eine gnadenlose Analyse zu erstellen. Was sie dann auch tun. So hat man am Ende das Gefühl, einem Mann bei der Arbeit zuzuschauen, ganz direkt, in manchmal brutaler Ehrlichkeit. Und so lange es noch Schreiber wie William Goldman gibt, denkt man sich dann, kann Hollywood doch nicht so idiotisch sein.

Tobias Kramer

JAMAL TUSCHICK (HG.) MORGENLAND

Wer ganz ist und eiten geraden Satz schreiben kann, der ist ist Zeit schreiben. Autor mit Buch. *Pupfiteratur* nennt sich das dann gerne. Der Titel „MorgenLand – Neueste deutsche Literatur" (Fischer Verlag, 19.90 Mark) klingt ganz danach. *Junge Autoren* aus Deutschland mit nicht-deutschen Eltern erzählen Geschichten über die Leben, Ethos-Pupfiteratur denkt man. Tatsächl ausredet. Es sind Geschichten und Gedichte ihrer große Gefühle und kleine Erlebnisse, die man als Deutsche mit deutschen Eltern nie haben wird, so die man nie gedacht hat, trotz ausländischer Freunde. Manche Texte sind schön, andere schrecklich, manche handeln von kleinen Diskriminierungen und viele einfach nur vom Fremdsein. „Sind die so fremd, bist Du in deiner Haut" ist der Werbung geklaute Gag auf dem Buchcover begleitet beim Lesen im Kopf zu kreisen. Man hält sich ertappt, wenn man in Maxim Biller's „Geschichte schreiben" über den Satz stolpert: „Da stoß ich zum jungen Deutschen sitzen junges jüdischen Freund gerieben, dass er vor seiner ersten Intuitivne neue Angst hat als vor einer komplizierten Gelände-operation, um ihn im schoben Augenblick vorzuwerfen, dass er sein Judentum immer so berauschigen kann." Am besten wird das Buch an den Stellen, die einen etwas begreifen lassen, ohne erklären zu wollen. Wie man sich etwa als Türke in einem Deutschland fühlt, in dem man nur als Versicgsausländer oder eine Chance hat. „Türken wir dich brauchst dir Land, es gibt jakkinde Japaner, die tragen aber nichts nur Volkscrstandsgang bei, das Mutterbeispiel des türkischen Deutschlehrers im Gymnasium aber und jedem Fall, der Pregnanz-Werke, der türkische Patenonjunge; der türkische Kunstapfel, Kulturtrittbrett, Wortlitzer und Reich-Ranicki-Bewunger im Literarischen Quartett." „MorgenLand" ist natürlich neueste deutsche Literatur Vielleicht ein Anfang für impudentes. Gut so.

Claudia Meyer

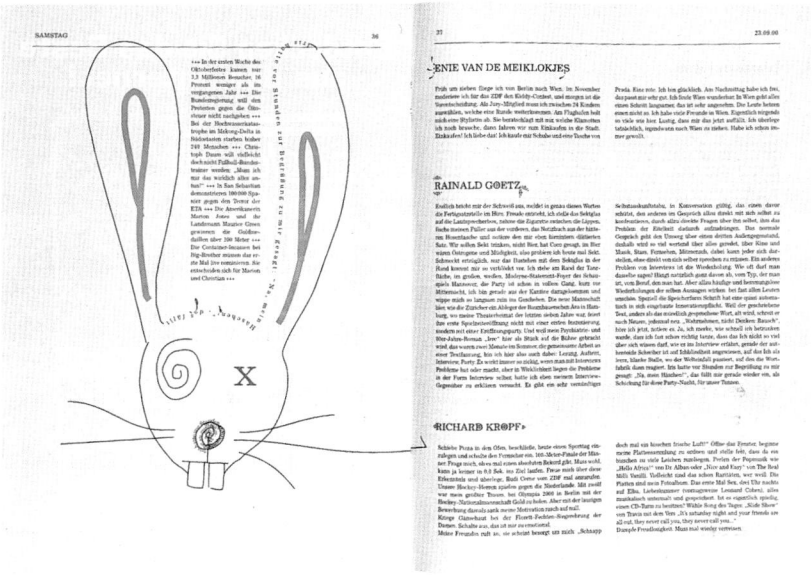

SAMSTAG 36

+++ In der ersten Woche des Oktoberfestes kamen nur 3,3 Millionen Besucher, 16 Prozent weniger als im vergangenen Jahr +++ Die Bundesregierung will den Protesten gegen die Ökosteuer nicht nachgeben +++ Bei der Hochwasserkatastrophe im Mekong-Delta in Südostasien starben bisher 248 Menschen +++ Christoph Daum will vielleicht doch nicht Fußball-Bundestrainer werden. „Man ist nur das wirklich aber ganz" +++ In San Sebastian demonstrieren 100.000 Spanier gegen den Terror der ETA +++ Die Amerikanerin Marion Jones und der Landsmann Maurice Green gewinnen die Goldmedaillen über 100 Meter +++ Die Container-Insassen bei Big-Brother müssen das erste Mal live nominieren. Sie entscheiden sich für Marion und Christian +++

Strandkorb zu Strandkorb zu Strandkorb zu Strandkorb

X

Hermann, der Fall

27 23.09.00

GENIE VAN DE MEIKLOKJES

Früh um sieben Uhr bin ich von Berlin nach Wien. Im November moderiere ich für den Kinder-Contest, und morgen ist die Vorentscheidung. Als Jury-Mitglied muss ich zwischen 24 Kindern auswählen, welche eine Runde weiterkommen. Am Flughafen holt mich eine Stylistin ab. Sie beratschlagt mit mir welche Klamotten ich noch brauche, dann fahren wir zum Einkaufen in die Stadt. Einkaufen! Ich liebe das! Ich kaufe mir Schuhe und eine Tasche von Prada. Eine tolle. Ich bin glücklich. Am Nachmittag habe ich frei, das passt mir sehr gut. Ich liebe Wien wunderbar. In Wien geht alles einen Schritt langsamer. Das ist sehr angenehm. Die Leute hetzen einem nicht an. Ich habe viele Freunde in Wien. Eigentlich nirgends so viele wie hier. Leider kann ich dass nur alles jetzt nicht. Ich überlege tatsächlich, irgendwann nach Wien zu ziehen. Habe ich schon immer gewollt.

RAINALD GOETZ

Endlich bricht mir der Schweiß aus, weil er in genau diesem Warten die Fortsetzung seiner in Hirn-Female entwickelt, ich stelle das Sektglas auf die Lautsprecherbox, nehme die Zigarette zwischen die Lippen, fische meinen Pulier aus der vorderen, das Notizbuch aus der hinteren Hosentasche und notiere den ersten eine kommenden dilettieren Satz. Wir sollen Sekt trinken, nicht Bier, hat Cuno gesagt, an Ihrer wissen Outsogeter und Mitlegbeit, also problem ich heute mal Sekt. Schmecht erträglich, nur das Hantieren mit dem Sektglas in der Hand kommt mir so vertrickt vor. Ich stehe am Rand der Tanzfläche, im grellen, weißen, Moderne-Statement-Foyer der Schauspiel-Mateneer, der Party ist schon in vollen Gang, kein von Mitternacht, ich bin gerade aus der Kantine dazugekommen und wippe nicht so langsam rein im Geschehen. Die neue Mannschaft hier wie die Zuschauer-ein Ableger des Hamburgerschen Ensemble, wo meine Theaterkontakt die letzten sieben Jahre war. Heute ihre erste Spielzeiteröffnung nicht mit einer ersten Inszenierung, sondern mit einer Ersffnungsparty. Und weil neue Psychiatrie- und 50er-Jahre-Roman „Jew" hier als Stück auf die Bühne gebracht wird das wenn zwei Monate im Sommer die gemeinsame Arbeit an einer Textfassung, bin ich hier also auch dabei: Leipzig. Außerdem, interessiert Party. Es wird immer so zickig, wenn man mit Interessen Problems hat oder macht, aber in Wirklichkeit liegen die Probleme in der Form Interview selbst, hatte ich eben meinem Interview-Gegenüber zu erklären versucht. Es gibt ein sehr vernünftiges Schutzmechanismus, in Konversation gültig, das einen davor schützt, den anderen im Gespräch allzu direkt mit sich selbst zu konfrontieren, durch allzu direkte Fragen über ihn selbst, ihn das Problem der Eitelkeit dadurch anfassbringen. Das normale Gegenteil gibt ein Umweg über etwas dritten Anderungsmaterial, dadurch wird es viel wertvoll über alles gesagt, über Kino und Musik, Stars, Fernsehen, Mitmenschen, dabei kann jeder sich durchsetzen, ohne direkt von sich selbst sprechen zu müssen. Ein anderes Problem von Interviews ist die Wiederholung. Wie oft darf man dasselbe sagen? Hängt natürlich ganz davon ab, vom Typ, der man ist, vom Beruf, den man hat. Aber allzu häufige und bestimmtpüber Wiederholungen der selben Aussagen werben bei fast allen Leuten unendlich. Spezial die Sprechverbaren Sicherlich hat eine quasi automatisch in sich eingeladene Immersionspflicht. Weil der geschriebene Text, anders als das mündlich gesprochene Wort, ist wird, scheint er nach Neuem, jedenfalls neu. „Wahrnehmen, nicht Denken Bauch", hies ich jetzt, schien es, ich, mich, wie schnell ich herausfinden wurde, dass ich fast schon richtig tatze, dass das Ich nicht so viel über sich wissen darf, wie es im Interview erfährt, gerade der anhemmende Schreiber ist auf Schädelbohrt angewiesen, auf den ich ich leben, klarke Sadie, wo der Wahrnehmt passiert, auf den die Wortfabrik dann reagiert. Ich hatte vor Stunden zur Begrüßung zu mir gesagt: „Ja, wem Hinthorn", das fällt mir gerade wieder ein, als Schützung für diese Party-Nacht, für unser Tanzen.

RICHARD KRÖPF

Schlecht Pizza in den Oten, beschämde, heute einen Sportlag eingeräugen und schnäle den Fernseher ein. 100-Meter-Finale der Männer. Frage noch, ob es mal einen absoluten Rekord gibt. Muss wohl. Kann ja keiner in 9.5 Sek. ins Ziel laufen. Pwar mich über diese Effekmäla und überlege, Bodi Cotne vom ZDF mal anzugeben. Unsere Hockey-Mannen spielen gegen die Niederlande. Mir zwölf war mein größter Traum bei Olympia 2000 in Berlin mit der Hockey-Nationalmannschaft Gold zu holen. Aber mit der jungen Bewerbung damals aank meine Motivation rasch auf null. Kringe Gänsehaut bei der Fleerst Fechten-Ragnebung der Damen. Schade aus, das ist nur zu emotional. Meine Freundin ruft an, sie scheint besorgt um mich. „Schnapp doch mal ein bisschen frische Luft!" Offne das Fenster begimne meine Platzenumzählung zu ordnen und stelle fest, dass da ein bunchen an viele Leichen, nunlegen. Freien der Popmusik wie „Hello Africa!" von Di Albao oder „Nice and Easy" von The Real Milli Vanilli. Vielleicht sind das schon Raritäten, weil weil. Die Platten sind neun Fotoalbum. Das erste Mal Sex, dies Die nachts auf Elbe. Liebeszimmer tonnagemeine Leonard Cohen; alles musikalisch unternaut und gesprochen! Ist es eigentlich sinnig, einen CD-Turm zu bauttten? Wähle Song des Tages „Kiele Show" von Travis mit dem Vers „Ich ertrinke nicht und your friends are all out, they never call you, they never call you..."

Dunyale Freudlosigkeit. Muss mal wieder vertreten.

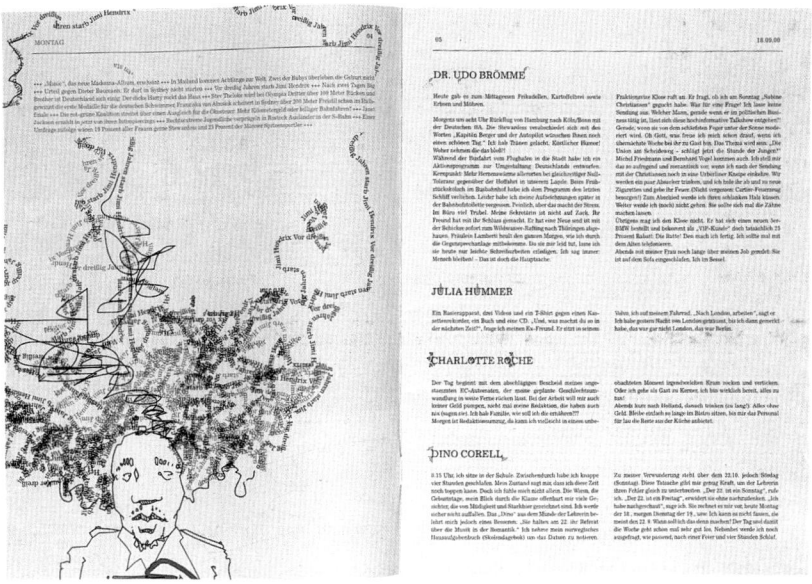

MONTAG 04

+++ „Mania", das neue Madonna-Album, erscheint +++ In Malmö kommen Artikrgen zur Welt. Zwei der Babys überlebten die Geburt nicht +++ Urwal gegen Dieter Bohlmann. Er darf in Berlin nicht starten +++ Vor dreißig Jahren stark Jürgi Hendrix +++ Nach zwei Tagen Big +++ Urwal gegen Dieter Bohlmann. Er darf in Berlin nicht starten +++ Der Olympia-Dritte über 100 Meter Rücken aus Brasilien ist Deutschland sich einig: Der dicke Harry rockt das Haus +++ Ihre Tochter wird bei Olympia Dritte über 200 Meter Freistil schon im Halbgewinnt die erste Medaille für die deutschen Schwimmer Franziska von Almsick schaffen? In Sydney über 200 Meter Freistil schon im Halbfinale +++ Das mit-grüne Kneiftuch steckt über einen Angebot für die Oktoberer Mehr Klimaanlagen für eine kühlere Bundestrabrik? +++ Jesse Jackson erzählt in seiner neuen Show von seinen Jugendjahren +++ Bundeskanzler Gerhard Schröder in der Schulbank Umfrage zufolge wissen 13 Prozent aller Frauen gerne Steve ahnen und 21 Prozent der Männer Spitzensportler +++

05 18.09.00

DR. UDO BRÖMME

Heute gab es zum Mittagessen Frikadellen, Kartoffelbrei sowie Erbsen und Möhren.

Morgens um acht Uhr Rückflug von Hamburg nach Köln/Bonn mit der Deutschen Bk. Die Stewardess verabschiedet sich mit den Worten „Kapitän Berger und der Autopilot wünschen Ihnen noch einen schönen Tag." Ich lieb Thüner geladet. Kürtlicher Bürner! Weber nehmen die das hinlo!

Während der Bundesrat vom Flughafen in die Stadt habe ich ein Aktienprogramm zur Umgestaltung Deutschlands entworfen. Kernpunkt: Mehr Hermenneutik allerorten bei gleichzeitiger Sub-Toleranz gegenüber der Hoffahrt in unserem Lande. Beim Frühstückstisch im Bundesrat habe ich dem Programm den letzten Schliff verliehen. Leider habe ich meine Aufzeichnungen später in der Bundesratsbroschüre vergessen. Freitich, aber das macht der Nieser. Im Büro wird Trubel. Meine Sekretärin ist nicht auf Zack. Ihr Freund hat von der Schlaue gemacht. Er hat eine Neue und ist mit der Beliebten sofort zum Wildenauer-Sattlag nach Thüringen abgehauen. Prinzlein Lambert brüllt den ganzen Morgen, wie ich durch die Gegensprechanlage mitbekomme. Da ist nur Geld tut, lasse ich heute nur leichte Sicherheitsfragen erlaubigen. Ich sag immer: Mensch bleiben! – Das ist doch die Hauptsache.

JULIA HÜMMER

Ein Rasierapparat, drei Videos und ein T-Shirt gegen einen Kassettenrekorder, ein Buch und eine CD. „Und, was macht du so in der nächsten Zeit?", frage ich meinen Ex-Freund. Er sitzt in seinem Fahrtenschreiber, ich bin auf meinem Fahrrad. „Nach London, arbeiten", sagt er. Ich habe gestern Nacht von London geträumt, bis ich dann gemerkt habe, das war gar nicht London, das war Berlin.

CHARLOTTE ROCHE

Der Tag beginnt mit dem abschlappen Bonbeid meines ungestammten EC-Automaten, der meine geplante Geschlechtsumwandlung zu weiss Farne vorkam lässt. Bei der Arbeit will mir auch immer Geld pumpen, nicht mal meine Reisäkten, die haben auch nie Geld. Ich hab Familie, wie soll ich da arbeiten?!! Morgen ist Redaktionssamstag, da kann ich vielleicht in einem unbeobachteten Moment ungewohnten Raum rocken und verticken. Oder ich gehe ein Gast zu Kiemer, ich bin wirklich bereit, alles zu tun!

Abends kam nach Holland, danach trinken (zu lang?). Alles ohne Geld. Hiebe einfach so lange im Hinter sitzen, bis mir das Personal für lau die Reste aus der Küche anbietet.

DINO CORELLI

8.15 Uhr. Ich sitze in der Schule. Zwischendurch habe ich kroppe vier Stunden geschlafen. Mein Zustand sagt mir, dass ich diese Zeit noch kaputt kann. Doch ich fühle mich nicht allein. Die Wiesn, die Geburtstage, mein Blick durch die Klasse offenbart mir viele Gesichter, die von Müdigkeit und Sturkheit gezeichnet sind. Ich wurde sicher nicht auffallen. Das „Drive" aus dem Munde der Lehrerin heisst auch jedoch einen Bessernen. „Sie halten um 22 die Referat über die Musik in der Romantik." Ich nehme mein nutzergnädes Hausaufgabenbuch (Hektoniadagebuch) um das Datum zu notieren. Zu meiner Verwunderung steht über dem 23.10. jedoch Sitzung (Sonntag). Diese Tatsache gibt mir gutzig Kraft, um der Lehrerin ihren Fehler gleich zu unterbreiten. „Der 22. ist ein Sonntag", rufe ich. „Der 23. ist ein Freitag", ernährt sie ohne nachzudenken. „Ich habe nachgerechnet", sage ich. Sie nehmet er mir von heute Montag der 18., morgen Dienstag der 19., usw. Ich kann so nicht lassen, die meint den 22. 8 Wann soll ich das denn machen? Der Tag und damit die Woche geht schon viel mehr gut los. Nebenbei werde ich noch angeduzt, wir pauken, nach einer Fever und vier Stunden Schlaf.

Q: WHAT IS PROFESSIONALISM? A:

04 Pauline v. Mourik Broekman, London
05 Harmony Korine, New York
06 Tricia Jones, London
07 Hans-Peter Jochum, Berlin
10 Smiley Baldwin, Berlin
12 Ines Kaag, Berlin
14 Milk, London
14 Gary Wolf, San Francisco
16 Matthew Fuller, London
17 Niklas Maak, Munich
18 Mina Hagedorn, Berlin
18 Gob Squad, London/Berlin
19 David Hudson, Berlin
20 Wendy&Jim, Vienna
21 Moritz von Uslar, Munich
24 David Lindeman, Hamburg/Berlin
26 Jesko Fezer, Berlin
34 Kate Merkle, Berlin
36 Prof. Claudius Lazzeroni, Berlin
38 Hedi Slimane, Paris
40 Kira Buhnse, Düsseldorf
42 Vogt+Weizenegger, Berlin
43 Bobby Roth, Berlin
44 Oliver Vogt, Berlin
45 Daniel Josefsohn, Berlin
45 Terry Jones, London
46 Chicks on Speed feat. Walter Schönauer, Berlin

Issue 1, Winter 2000/01

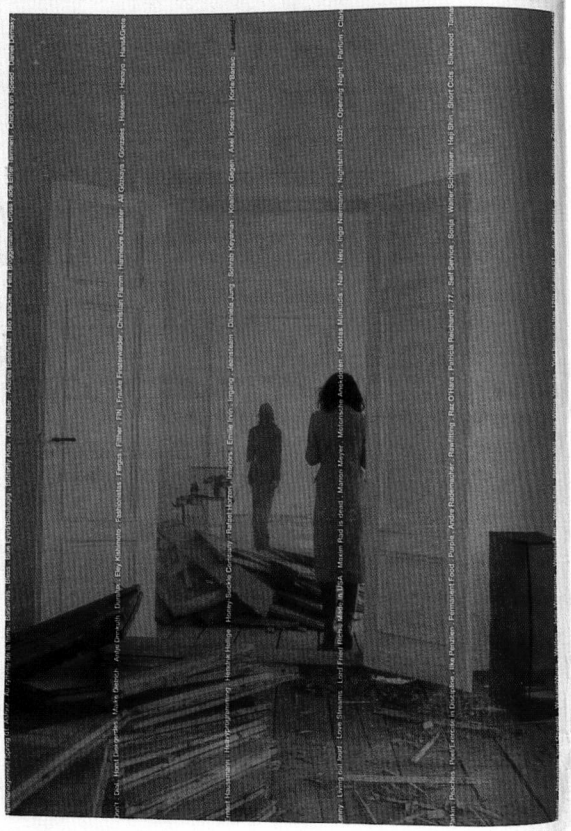

Interview: Sandra von Mayer-Myrtenhain, Jörg Koch **Photography:** Elisha Smith-Leverock

7

BERLIN DESTROYERS

WE POSED FIVE QUESTIONS TO BERLINERS WHO ARE BUSY DESTROYING THE IMAGE OF NEW BERLIN TRUE DESTROYERS. THEY PROVIDE A KALEIDOSCOPIC VIEW ON BERLIN BEYOND THE HYPE BY TALKING ABOUT THEIR JOBS.

Issue 2, Summer 2001

CHICKS ON SPEED VS. LE TIGRE

22 **Chicks on Speed** artists, Berlin

How do you feel LTIB on Chicks on Speed Records?
[illegible] feels [illegible] cooked up [illegible] outta [illegible] and a thousand [illegible] yellow and white birdies flew out crying out bass drums and beautiful screams.

We want to make a video. Can we do it with you [illegible]?
JD: [illegible] to see you [illegible] for [illegible] who [illegible] gathered some [illegible] own video component of our live performance. But perhaps we can work together when we come to Berlin in the spring.

I'd love to know how you do your choreography? Do you practice? Is it a group effort or is one of you specially into dance moves?
JD: I feel like [illegible] the first time [illegible] practice [illegible] at I [illegible] sneaks and [illegible] beats, "Ladies let's get to [illegible]" and [illegible] history, [illegible] a few [illegible] of hip hop [illegible] class and [illegible] undergroun[illegible] dance [illegible] "dykes can dance" which [illegible] international [illegible] big league [illegible] moves and we got what we got with a little help from our star choreographer, Jennifer Allen. And yes we practice but from the looks of our videos, not as much as we should.

We would love to do a concert together, Le tigre, Peaches and us, what do you think? Where could we do this?
Kathleen: We're [illegible] hope this spring, maybe we could do it in Paris? That would be fun.

Do you think it is necessary for women in business to collaborate with other women? Why? Should women understand how male business structures function?
Kathleen: As [illegible] simply [illegible] being the opposite of business men or by trying to [illegible] as much [illegible] them" as we can. We need new [illegible]! We have to [illegible] business' that put human needs, desires and [illegible] first, above [illegible] one's that are [illegible] and [illegible] values. [illegible] we will create models, see what works and what doesn't and [illegible] with alternatives to capitalism. Of course, we need each other to achieve this goal.

What do you think about the disappearance of older women in society?
Kathleen: I am thoroughly disgusted by the lack of respect shown to all women, but especially older ones. This can be seen not only in a mainstream that teaches us that once we are beyond the age typically associated with beauty and youth, we might as well just off ourselves, but also amongst young feminists who ignore or immediately degrade the work and lives of older ones. Sadly I have fallen for this ageist bullshit myself, and only recently (at age 32) have sought out mentors to learn from and share with. It is crucail that we make contact outside our generational borders, as we are so actively cut off from our own histories, even as we are still creating them.

Is it a problem for Europeans to fully understand the meanings of your texts, do you feel the issues apply in the European context?
Johanna: We love touring Europe. It's fascinating to see the difference in our audiences and their reception of our work. In the United States we are more clearly situated in a "post-riot grrrl" context, which is rooted in punk and indie rock aesthetics. Although we remain influenced by this scene (and the history of feminist punk music and writing), our interests in multi-media, art theory, and electronic music have lead us to make connections with other "scenes". This is why we are such fans of Chicks on Speed and Peaches! As outsiders, Europe seems to be more supportive of art and experimentation, and there seems to be less rigid barriers between genres of music. This really appeals to us a feminist artists who are making electronic music. As far as the intelligibility of our lyrics to a European audience, it's hard for us to judge! There is always the difficulty of language barriers. We have made an effort while touring in Germany and Japan to get "phone calls" on stage from friends (pre-recorded on minidisc) who can translate certain ideas. When performing for English-speakers we generally talk a lot about our songs and we don't want to lose that element of our show when we're not in the States or U.K.

How important is it to play instruments in the musical context of today 2001? (live and in the studio)
Kathleen: I hope there is a future without wanky guitar solos by men filling up the airwaves but I like how surf guitar and some older guitar stuff like Buddy Holly and Gene Vincent sounds.ie. I like guitar to sound like ice cream sundaes being eaten on the beach, not a steak covered with maggots. But that's just me. I don't think playing instruments is that important unless you don't have any content or ideas in your work in which case you are a craftsperson. That is actually what most rock music is about today, exploring the craft of guitar playing. We make conceptual art, we are trying to problemitaze the hi-art/low art division without sentimentalization or condescendsion. Sometimes playing instruments is fun and makes our music have more depth in a live setting which I like. The mini disc play back is like a flat image that we are painting on top off.

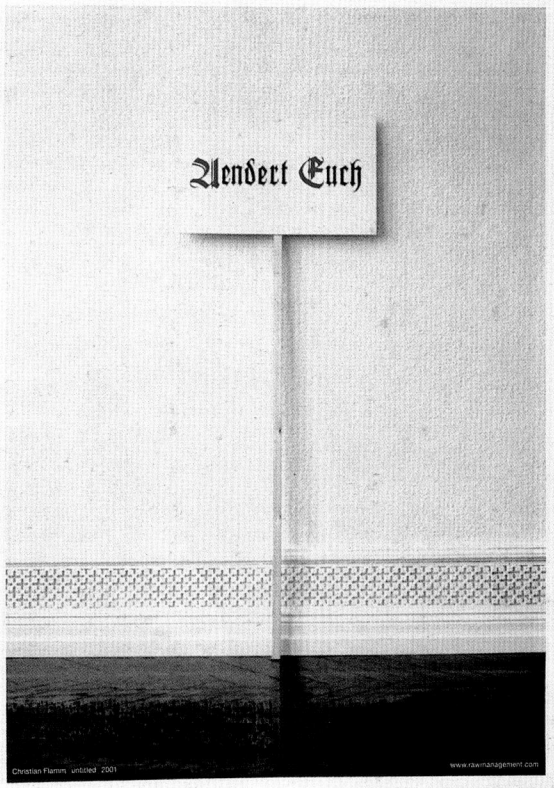

Issue 3, Winter 2001/02

032c *(Germany) 230 x 315mm/9 x 12 ½ inches*
Strong, direct typography in red and black on newsprint gives this independent magazine a very bold, direct identity, described by its editor as a 'punk fanzine designed by Dieter Rams'.
Art director *Vladimir Llovet Casademont*

on relevance and vanity

A look at thirty magazines, shifting paradigms, and the future of publishing.

V COMPOSITE ISSUE

NYLON FLAUNT COMMONS & SENSE

SPOON NEST TANK

Stu VERY EXIT RICHARDSON

INDEX SLEAZE NATION CRASH WISH THE

VANIDAD

BIG PLIST +81

WHATEVER

LOOP SURFACE

MADE IN USA STOCKHOLM NEW RE

Issue 14, Spring/Summer 2001

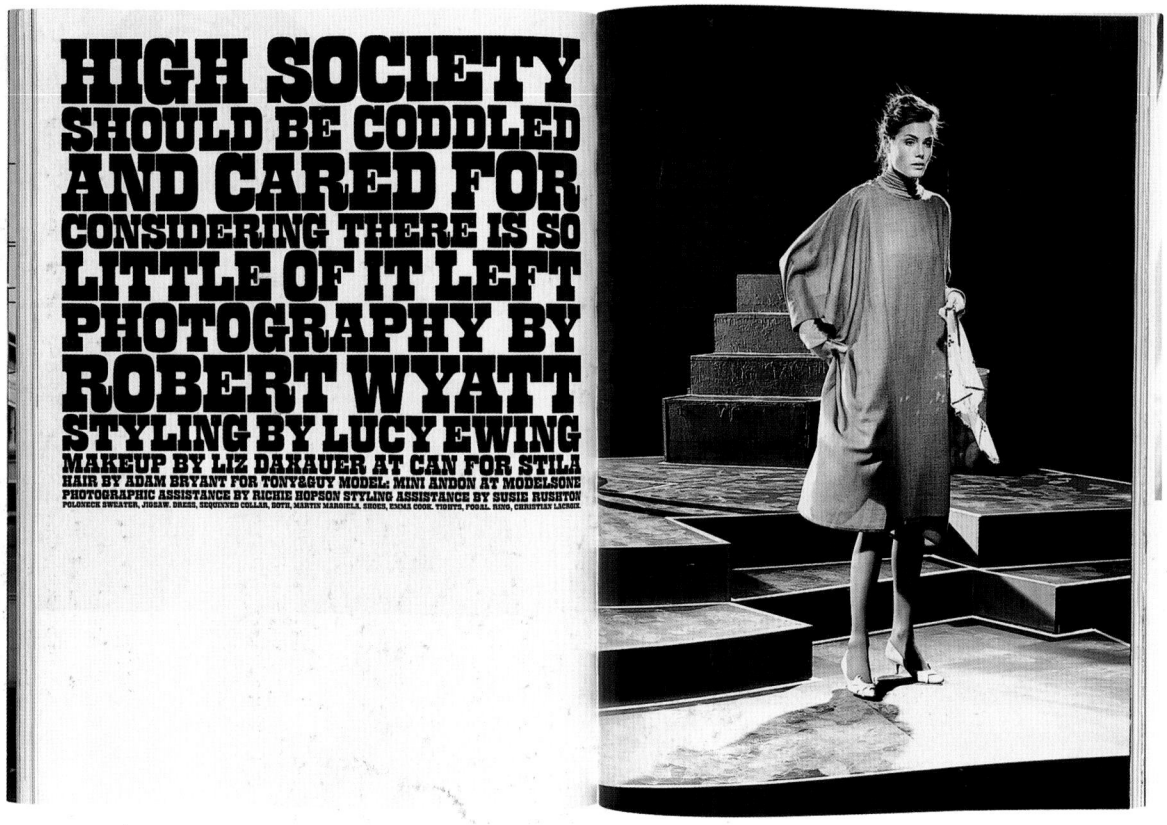

Issue 14, Spring/Summer 2001

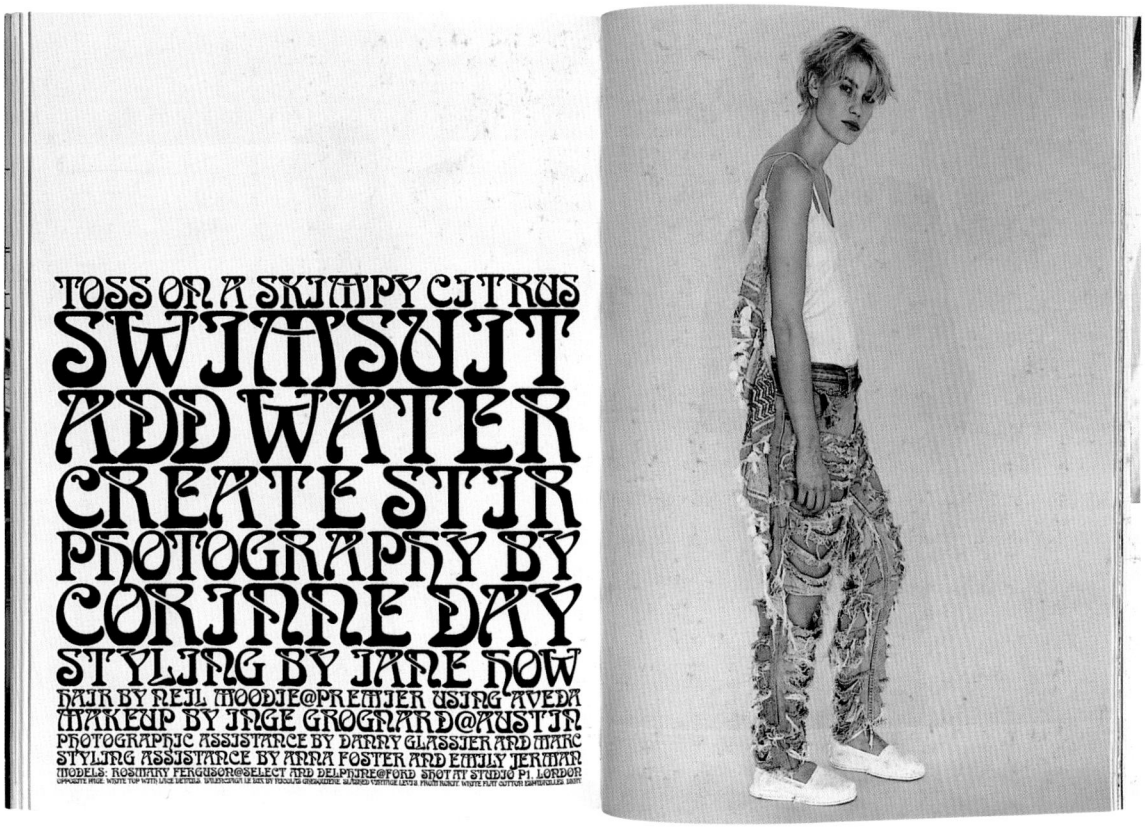

Issue 14, Spring/Summer 2001

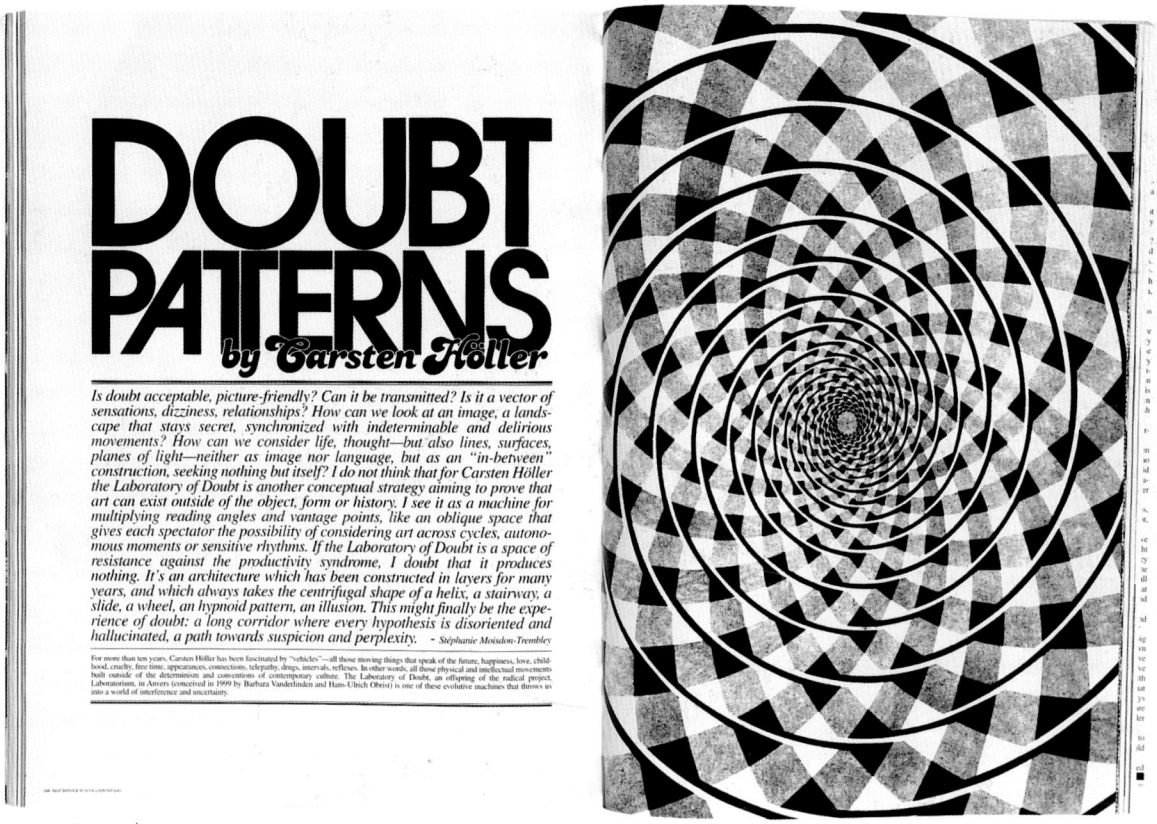

Issue 15, Autumn/Winter 2001

Self Service *(France) 220 x 297mm/8 3/4 x 11 3/4 inches*
Stark black-and-white typography has long been a trademark of this magazine, one of the earliest of the new breed of microzines. These spreads show recent moves toward use of decorative typefaces associated with 1970s rubdown lettering.
Art direction *Work in Progress*

THIS PAGE **Surface** *(USA, Issue 29,) 230 x 275mm/9 x 10 7/8 inches*
Exuberant use of colour, decorative typefaces and text overlaid on photographs gives this independent glossy interiors magazine an identity far removed from its cooler competitors.
Design *Exquisite Corporation*

OPPOSITE **Details** *(USA, Issue 1, October 2000) 230 x 275mm/9 x 10 7/8 inches*
The design of this opening page of the latest relaunch of this men's title has become a defining statement for the look of the magazine. The use of a gridded set of brief number-based stories is now a much-copied device.
Art director *Rockwell Harwood*

KNOW TELL

A random roundup of necessary numbers, nomenclature and newsbreaks.

THE CORPULENT Marlon Brando, on location in Canada shooting Frank Oz's *The Score*, reportedly arrived on the set every day undressed from the waist down. Sources say that Brando is trying to motivate the former Muppets puppeteer to film him from the shoulders up to hide his considerable waistline.

[SLANG]

"pack of Newports"—*adj.* hard, difficult. Origin: Skateboarders on the X-Games circuit. Usage: "That kickout was a pack of Newports, my man." (Ant.: "cooking fish sticks")

www.

www.airdisaster.com This obsessive catalog of air disaster lore, crash investigation updates and graphic photos is highlighted by a selection of actual cockpit voice recorders, or CVRs, which capture the final minutes of conversation between the pilots and the control tower. One disturbing example: The pilot of a Chicago-bound 737 is flirting with a female flight attendant, discussing her "mating habits." He says to his copilot, "If we crashed right now, this conversation is what our wives would have to remember us by." Just then, the stall alarm sounds; ten seconds later, the crews' screams are cut short by the plane's impact with the ground.

IN 1984, A HARD UP SEATTLE RECORDING STUDIO PAID THEIR PAST-DUE SODA BILL TO A PEPSI DELIVERYMAN. INSTEAD OF CASH, THE STUDIO MANAGER GAVE HIM THE ONLY EXISTING RECORDING OF A JIMI HENDRIX PERFORMANCE. THE PEPSI MAN RETURNED IT IN JULY.

THE LOS GATOS, California, Ferrari franchise now outsells any other in the world. Silicon Valley's IPO set gobble up about 225 cars a year, or about $40,000,000 worth. The most popular model is this year's $175,000 360 Modena (red, of course), by far the most expensive Ferrari on the market.

74%

of people experience "hugging, kissing and intimacy" after using an aftershave containing the designer pheromone Athena 10X. According to its advertisement Athena 10X was invented by the same University of Pennsylvania endocrinologist who codiscovered the human pheromone in 1986.

[THE CHEMICAL COMPOUND OF COCAINE] This drug has never really gone away, but it'll have a higher profile this fall, with the side-by-side release of *Blow* and *Traffic*, two coke-heavy action flicks.

3,000,000,000

It's

BEEN WIDELY REPORTED THAT CARY GRANT TOOK OVER 100 THERAPEUTIC ACID TRIPS IN THE '50s. BUT WORD RECENTLY CIRCULATED THAT THE *NORTH BY NORTHWEST* STAR, LIKE TIM LEARY, SOUGHT TOTAL CLARITY IN THE AFTER-LIFE: GRANT REPORTEDLY DROPPED A HIT OF HIGH-POWERED BLOTTER ON HIS DEATHBED.

Psychologists at the Money, Meaning & Choices Institute in Silicon Valley have diagnosed a malady peculiar to the nouveau riche: Sudden Wealth Syndrome. Tech millionaires and heirs to large fortunes are among its victims. Some symptoms of SWS: confusion, guilt, denial, paranoia, panic attacks and "ticker shock," which links the patient's mood to stock market fluctuations.

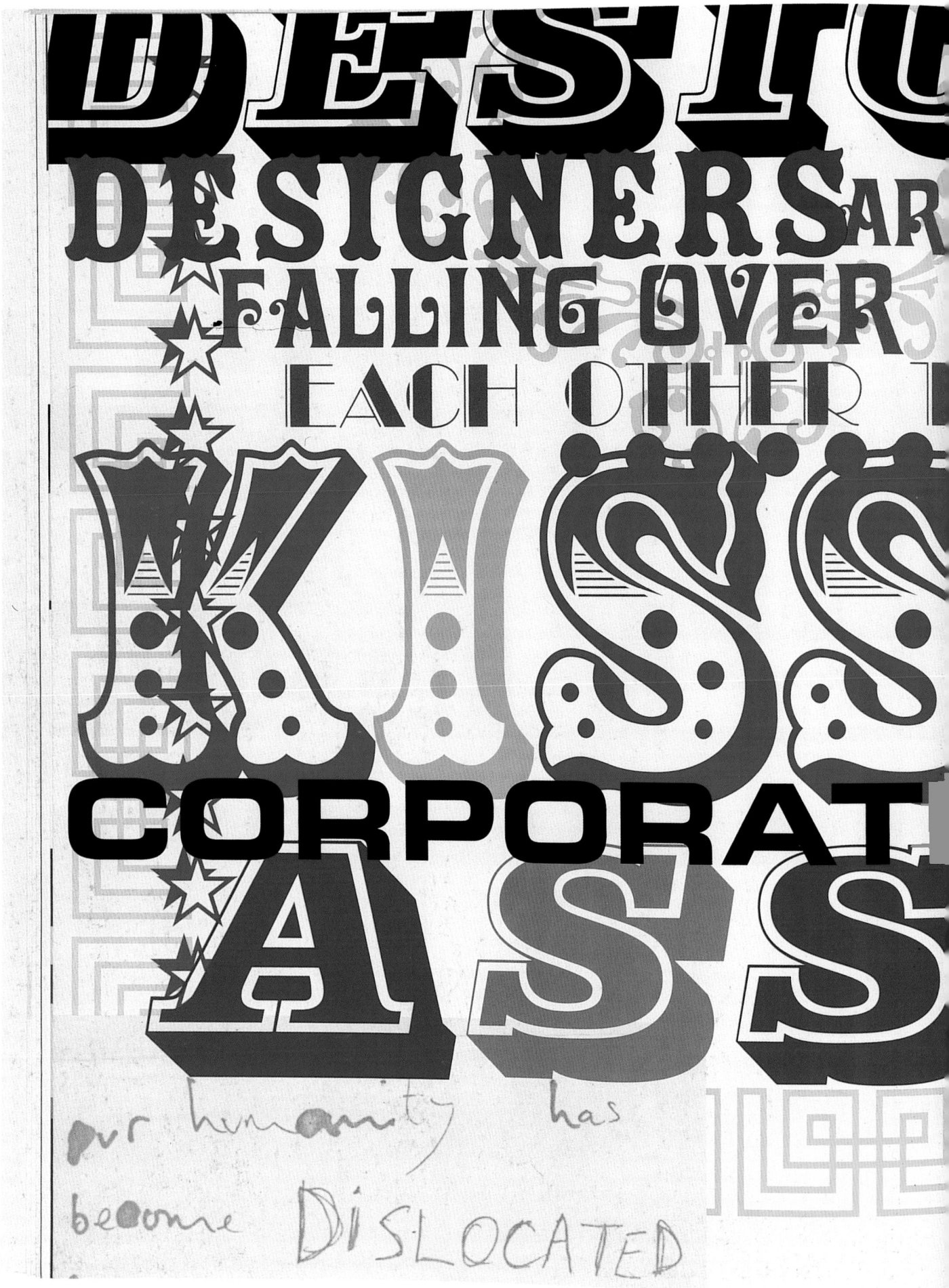
DESIG
DESIGNERS AR
FALLING OVER
EACH OTHER
KISS
CORPORAT
ASS
our humanity has
become DISLOCATED

Do you remember the time when your car didn't have a cupholder and a regular coffee was just that? You know - regular.

"I have tried to find other designers, but I can't find anyone with his humour, irony, irreverence, and wit. Philippe always pulls new rabbits out of a hat."

Ian Schrager

Design is now a fashion system.

You see it, don't you?

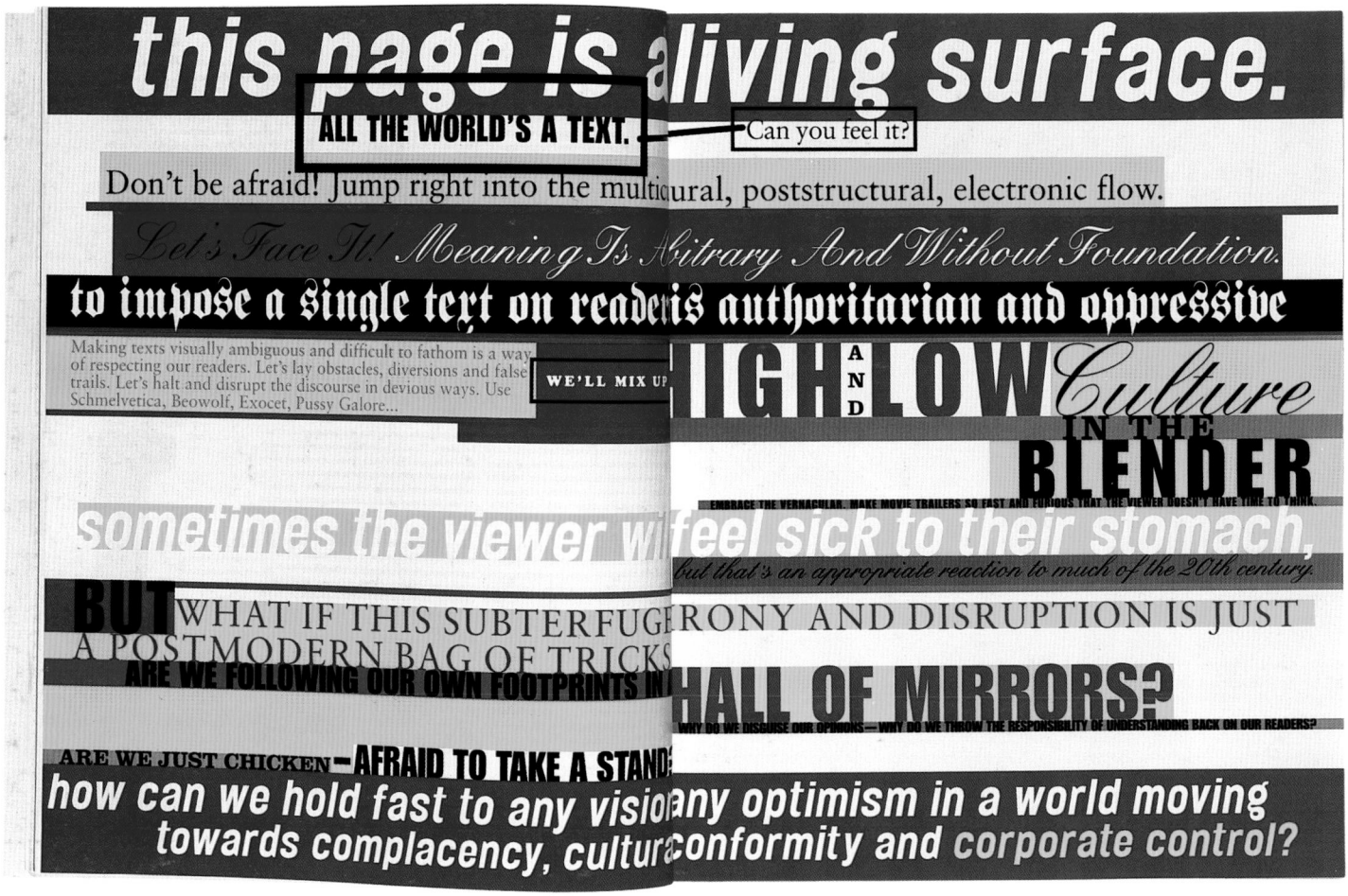

PREVIOUS PAGES, THIS PAGE & OPPOSITE **Adbusters** *(Canada, Issue 37, September/October 2001)*
230 x 274mm/9 x 10 7/8 inches
This issue offers a tour-de-force visual rant against the way design has become the servant of global capitalism. The colour pages reproduced here are self-explanatory in their tone. The first black-and-white spread criticizes the concept of the grid, describing it as a reductionist tool to replace spontaneity. Behind this description is an egg, the visual antithesis of the grid/square. The next spread features circles of typefaces spinning out from the centre, starting with Gutenberg's first printed words from 1455 and swirling out chronologically to reach the typefaces of the 20th century. Guest art director *Jonathan Barnbrook*

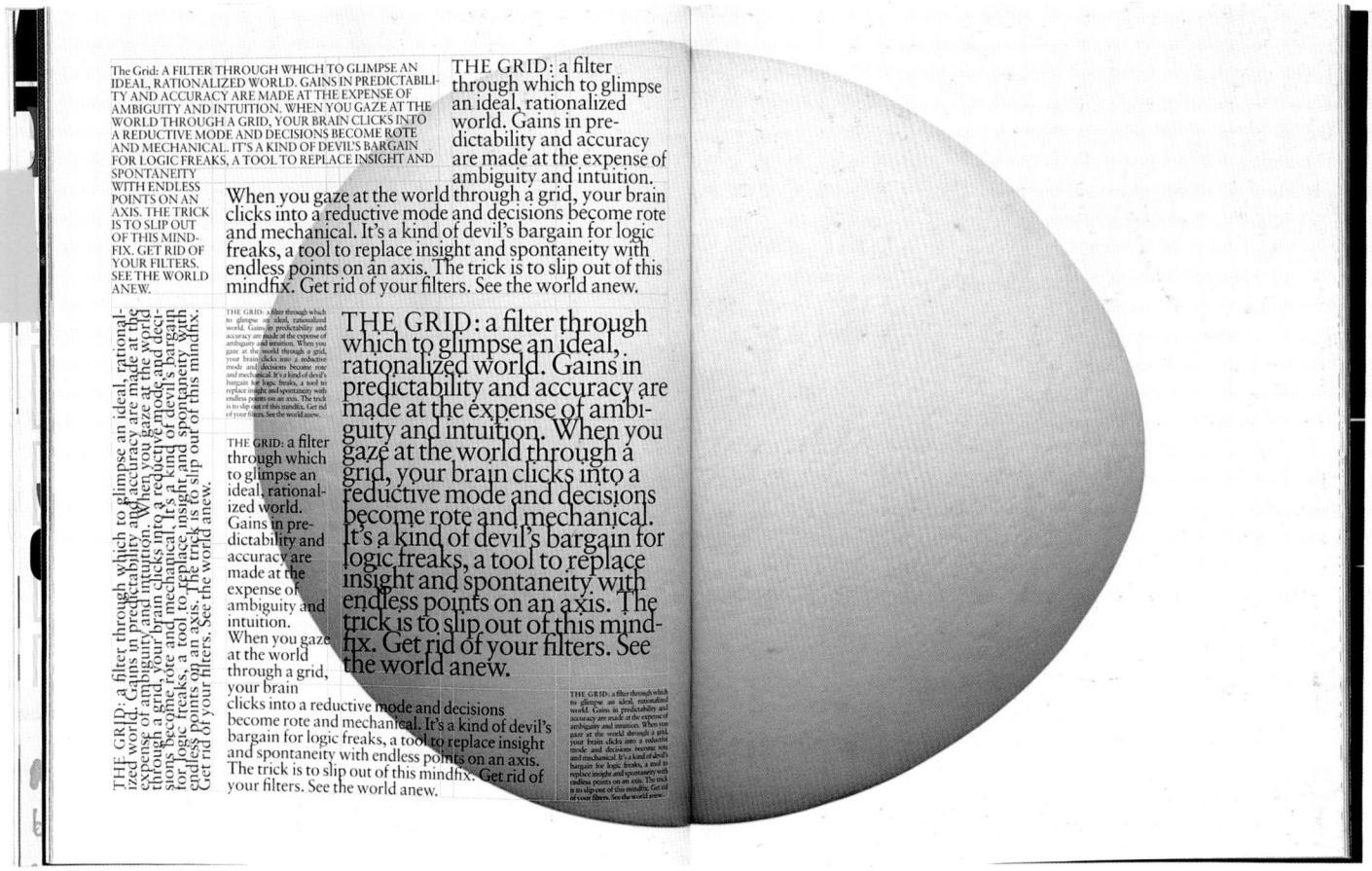

The Grid: A FILTER THROUGH WHICH TO GLIMPSE AN IDEAL, RATIONALIZED WORLD. GAINS IN PREDICTABILITY AND ACCURACY ARE MADE AT THE EXPENSE OF AMBIGUITY AND INTUITION. WHEN YOU GAZE AT THE WORLD THROUGH A GRID, YOUR BRAIN CLICKS INTO A REDUCTIVE MODE AND DECISIONS BECOME ROTE AND MECHANICAL. IT'S A KIND OF DEVIL'S BARGAIN FOR LOGIC FREAKS, A TOOL TO REPLACE INSIGHT AND SPONTANEITY WITH ENDLESS POINTS ON AN AXIS. THE TRICK IS TO SLIP OUT OF THIS MIND-FIX. GET RID OF YOUR FILTERS. SEE THE WORLD ANEW.

THE GRID: a filter through which to glimpse an ideal, rationalized world. Gains in predictability and accuracy are made at the expense of ambiguity and intuition. When you gaze at the world through a grid, your brain clicks into a reductive mode and decisions become rote and mechanical. It's a kind of devil's bargain for logic freaks, a tool to replace insight and spontaneity with endless points on an axis. The trick is to slip out of this mindfix. Get rid of your filters. See the world anew.

THE GRID: a filter through which to glimpse an ideal, rationalized world. Gains in predictability and accuracy are made at the expense of ambiguity and intuition. When you gaze at the world through a grid, your brain clicks into a reductive mode and decisions become rote and mechanical. It's a kind of devil's bargain for logic freaks, a tool to replace insight and spontaneity with endless points on an axis. The trick is to slip out of this mindfix. Get rid of your filters. See the world anew.

THE GRID: a filter through which to glimpse an ideal, rationalized world. Gains in predictability and accuracy are made at the expense of ambiguity and intuition. When you gaze at the world through a grid, your brain clicks into a reductive mode and decisions become rote and mechanical. It's a kind of devil's bargain for logic freaks, a tool to replace insight and spontaneity with endless points on an axis. The trick is to slip out of this mindfix. Get rid of your filters. See the world anew.

THE GRID: a filter through which to glimpse an ideal, rationalized world. Gains in predictability and accuracy are made at the expense of ambiguity and intuition. When you gaze at the world through a grid, your brain clicks into a reductive mode and decisions become rote and mechanical. It's a kind of devil's bargain for logic freaks, a tool to replace insight and spontaneity with endless points on an axis. The trick is to slip out of this mindfix. Get rid of your filters. See the world anew.

THE GRID: a filter through which to glimpse an ideal, rationalized world. Gains in predictability and accuracy are made at the expense of ambiguity and intuition. When you gaze at the world through a grid, your brain clicks into a reductive mode and decisions become rote and mechanical. It's a kind of devil's bargain for logic freaks, a tool to replace insight and spontaneity with endless points on an axis. The trick is to slip out of this mindfix. Get rid of your filters. See the world anew.

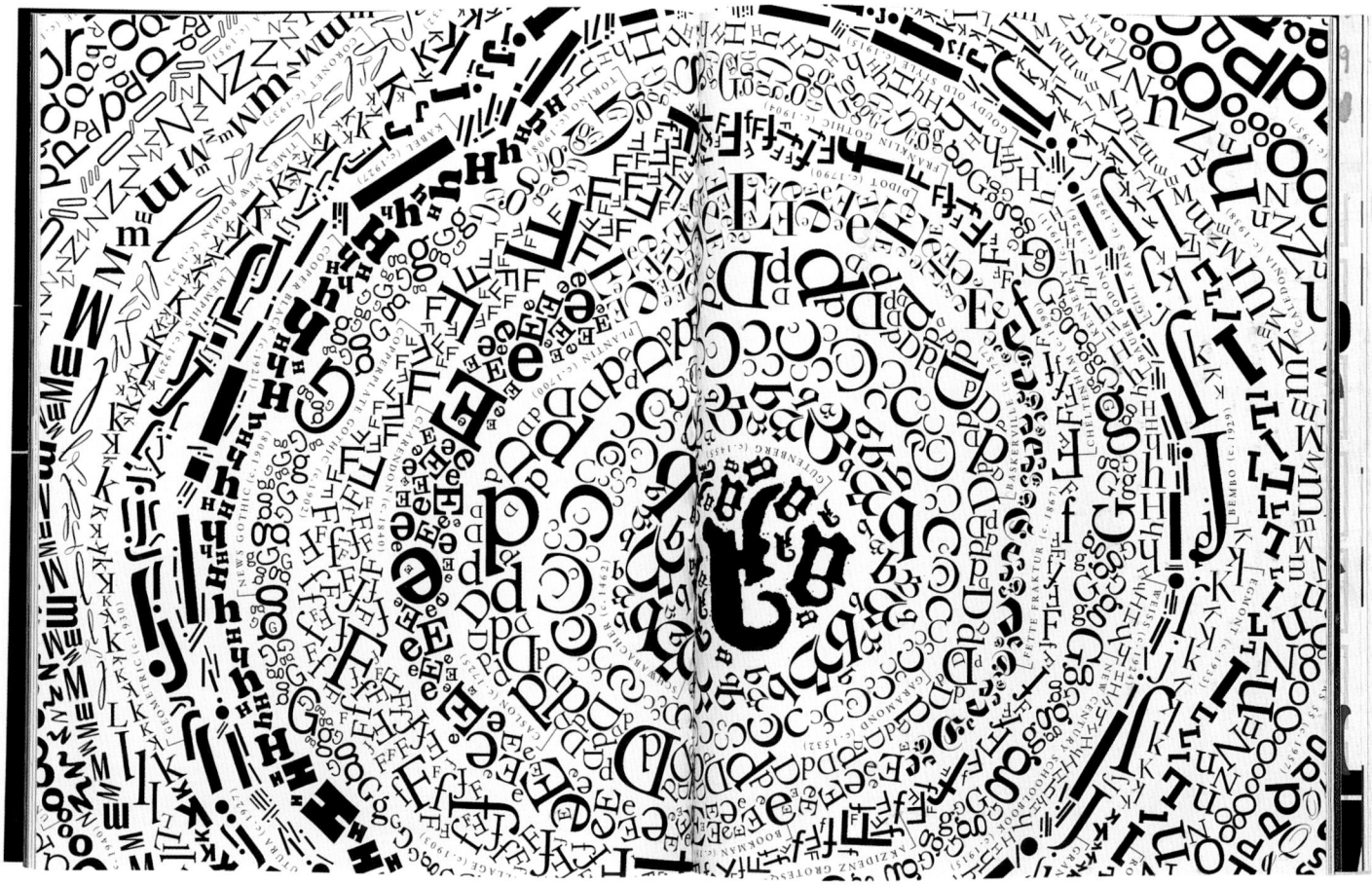

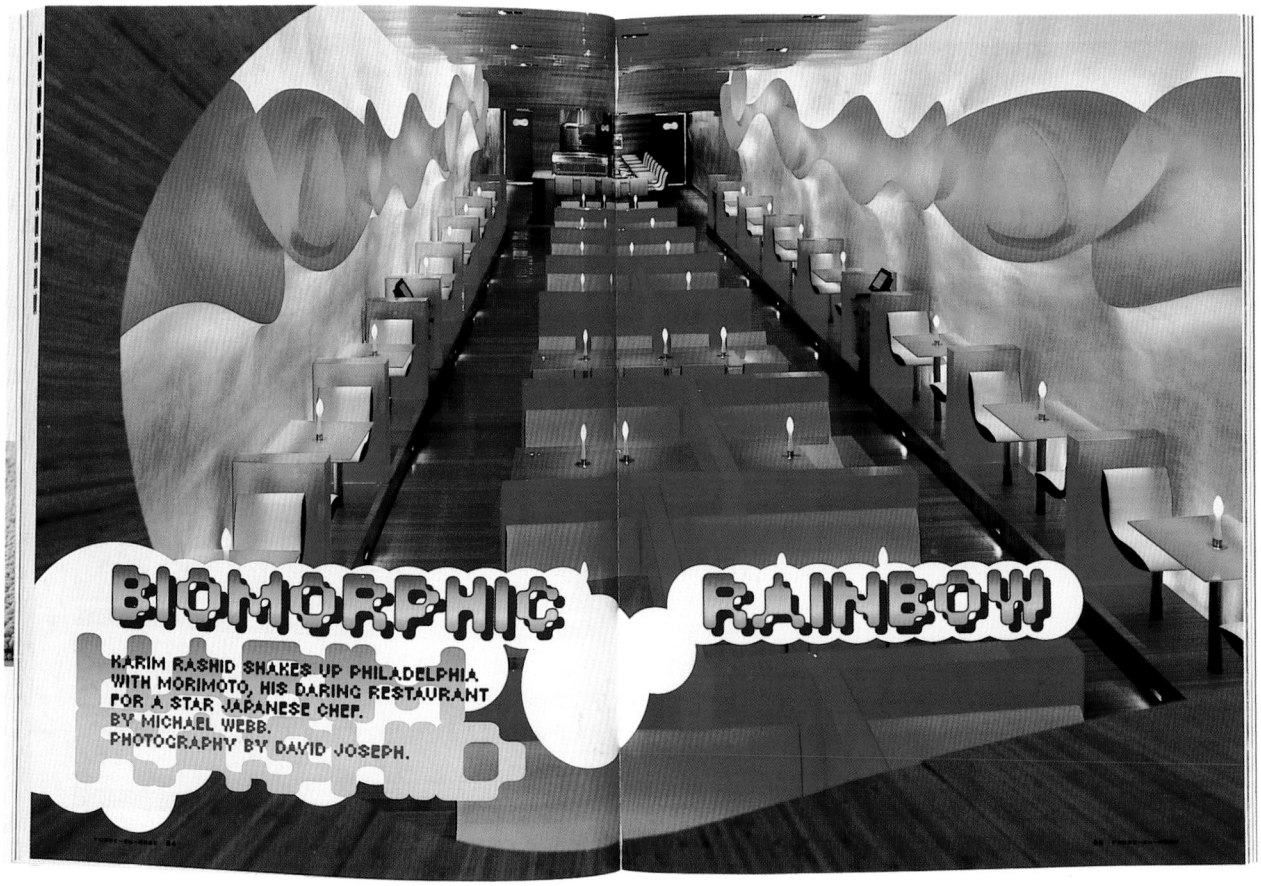

BIOMORPHIC RAINBOW

KARIM RASHID SHAKES UP PHILADELPHIA WITH MORIMOTO, HIS DARING RESTAURANT FOR A STAR JAPANESE CHEF.
BY MICHAEL WEBB.
PHOTOGRAPHY BY DAVID JOSEPH.

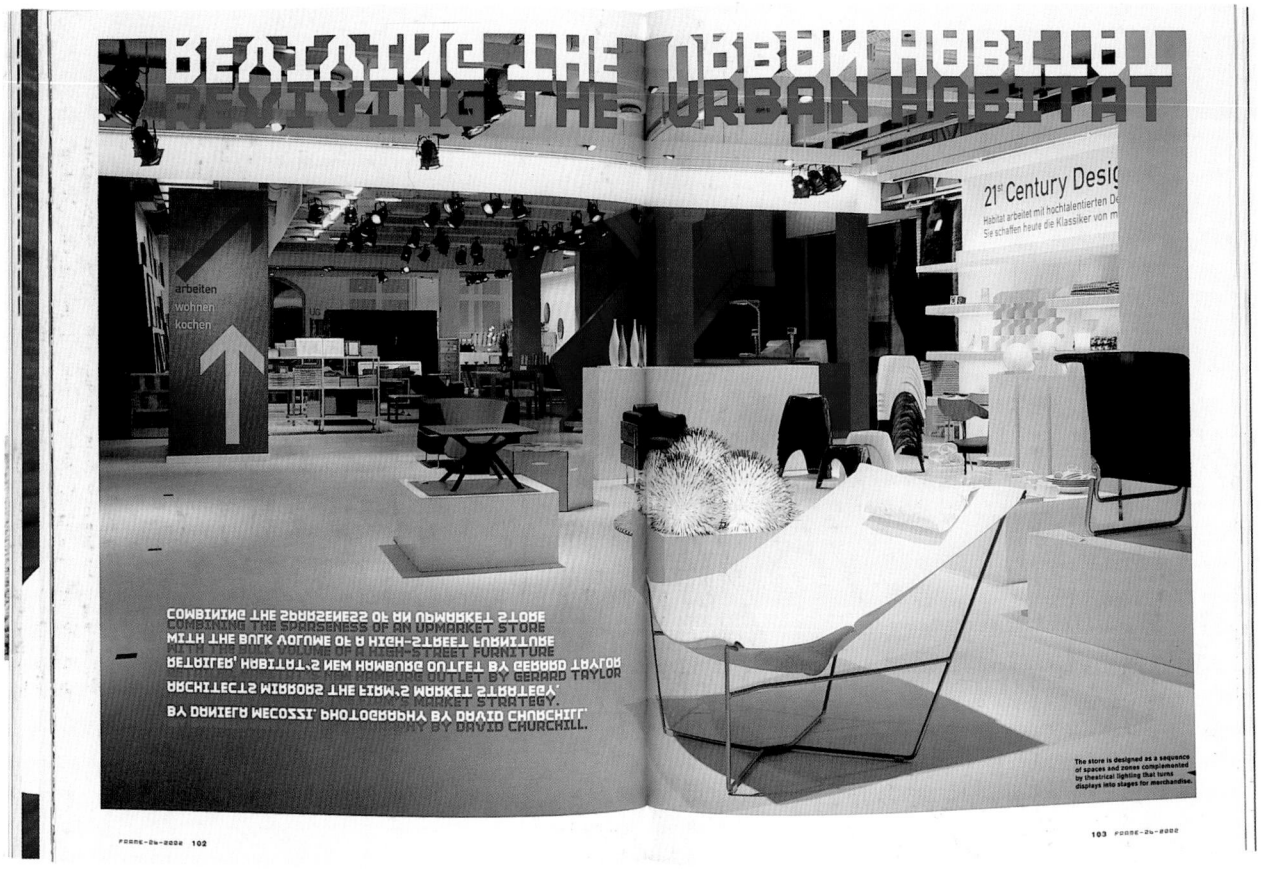

COMBINING THE SPARSENESS OF AN UPMARKET STORE WITH THE BULK VOLUME OF A HIGH-STREET FURNITURE OUTLET BY GERARD TAYLOR

ARCHITECTS MIRADOR THE FIRM'S MARKET STRATEGY.
BY DANIELA MECOZZI. PHOTOGRAPHY BY DAVID CHURCHILL.

The store is designed as a sequence of spaces and zones complemented by theatrical lighting that turns displays into stages for merchandise.

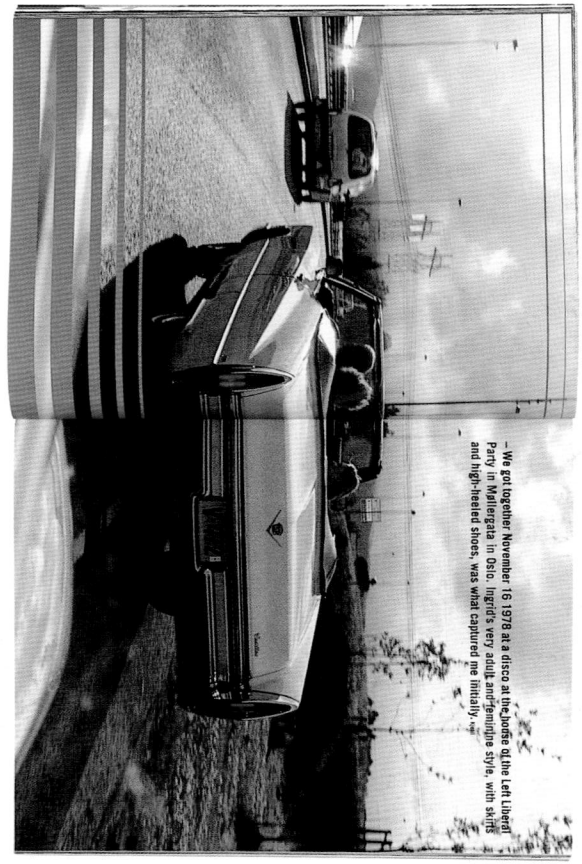

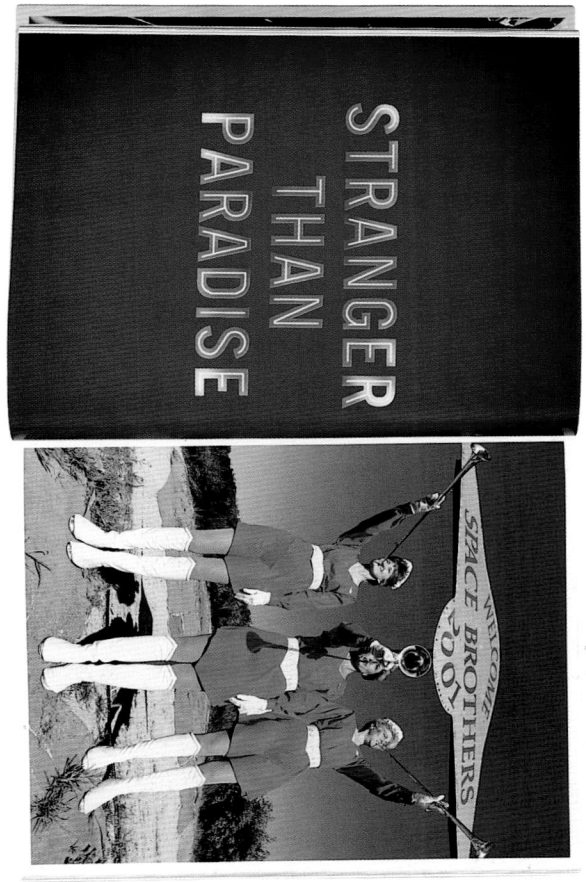

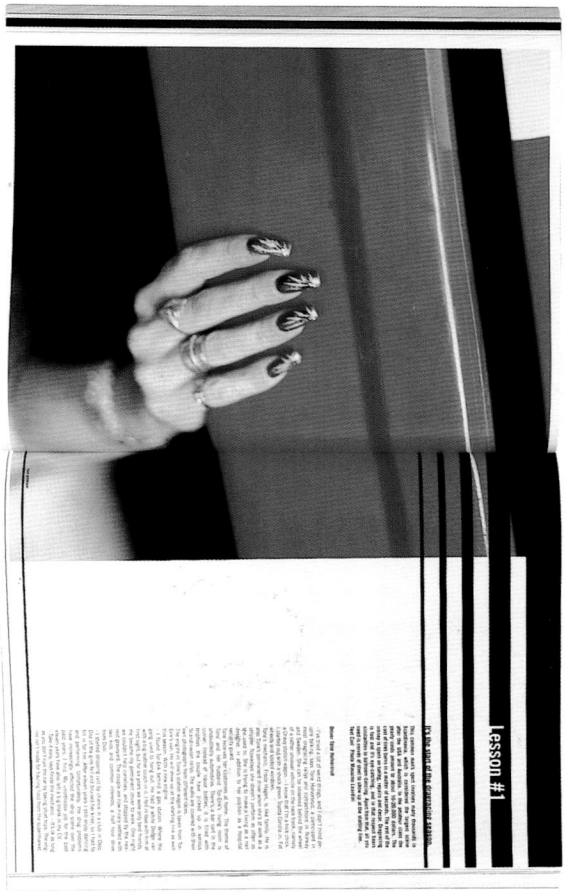

OPPOSITE **Frame** *(The Netherlands, Issue 26, May/June 2002) 230 x 297mm/9 x 11 3/4 inches*
This interior design magazine takes its design cues from its content on a page-by-page basis, so that every feature uses different fonts and styles. The result is the opposite of the clean, modernist design ideal and means the magazine can quickly adapt to and reflect on trends in interior and graphic design.
Art director *Roelof Mulder*

THIS PAGE **Carl's Cars** *(Sweden, Issue 2, 2002) 230 x 280mm/9 x 11 inches*
This independent magazine about car culture has a visual identity based primarily on its photography. Where graphics do feature, they take their cue from cars – the go-faster stripes and the vernacular of car logos.
Creative director *Stéphanie Dumont*

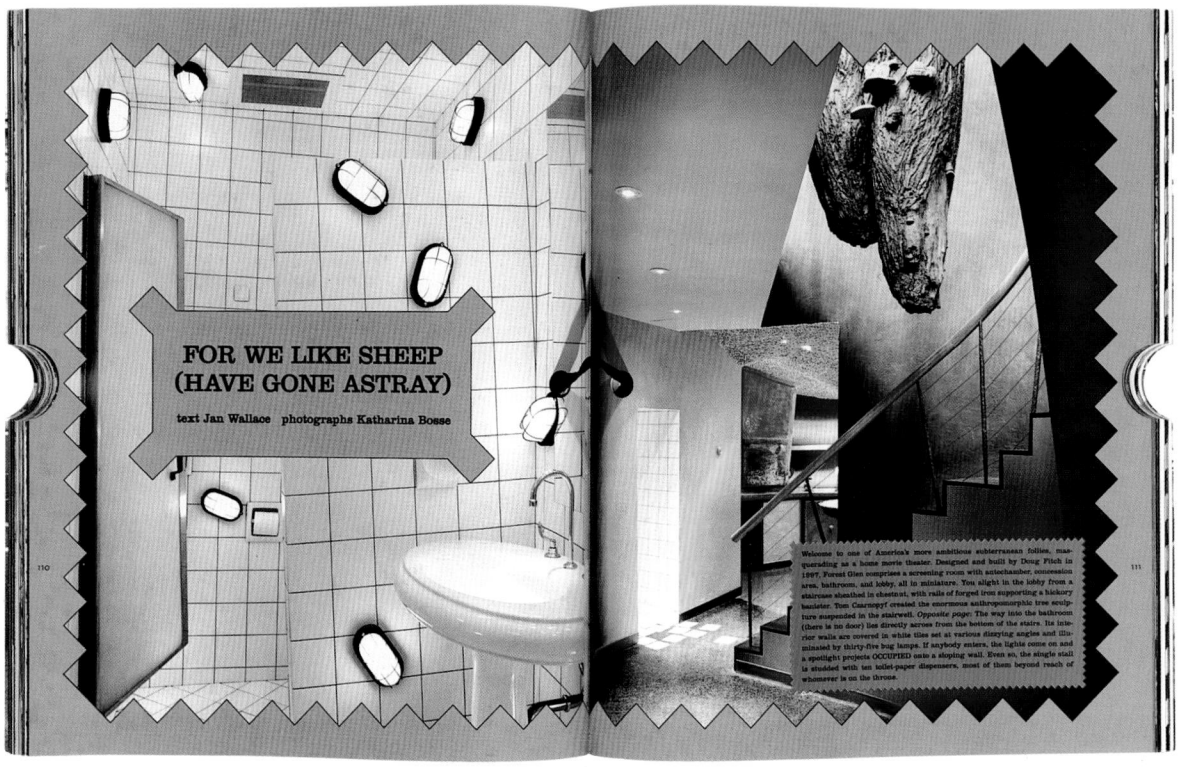

Welcome to one of America's more ambitious subterranean follies, masquerading as a home movie theater. Designed and built by Doug Fitch in 1997, Forest Glen comprises a screening room with antechamber, concession area, bathroom, and lobby, all in miniature. You alight in the lobby from a staircase sheathed in chestnut, with rails of forged iron supporting a hickory banister. Tom Czarnopyf created the enormous anthropomorphic tree sculpture suspended in the stairwell. *Opposite page:* The way into the bathroom (there is no door) lies directly across from the bottom of the stairs. Its interior walls are covered in white tiles set at various dizzying angles and illuminated by thirty-five bug lamps. If anybody enters, the lights come on and a spotlight projects OCCUPIED onto a sloping wall. Even so, the single stall is studded with ten toilet-paper dispensers, most of them beyond reach of whomever is on the throne.

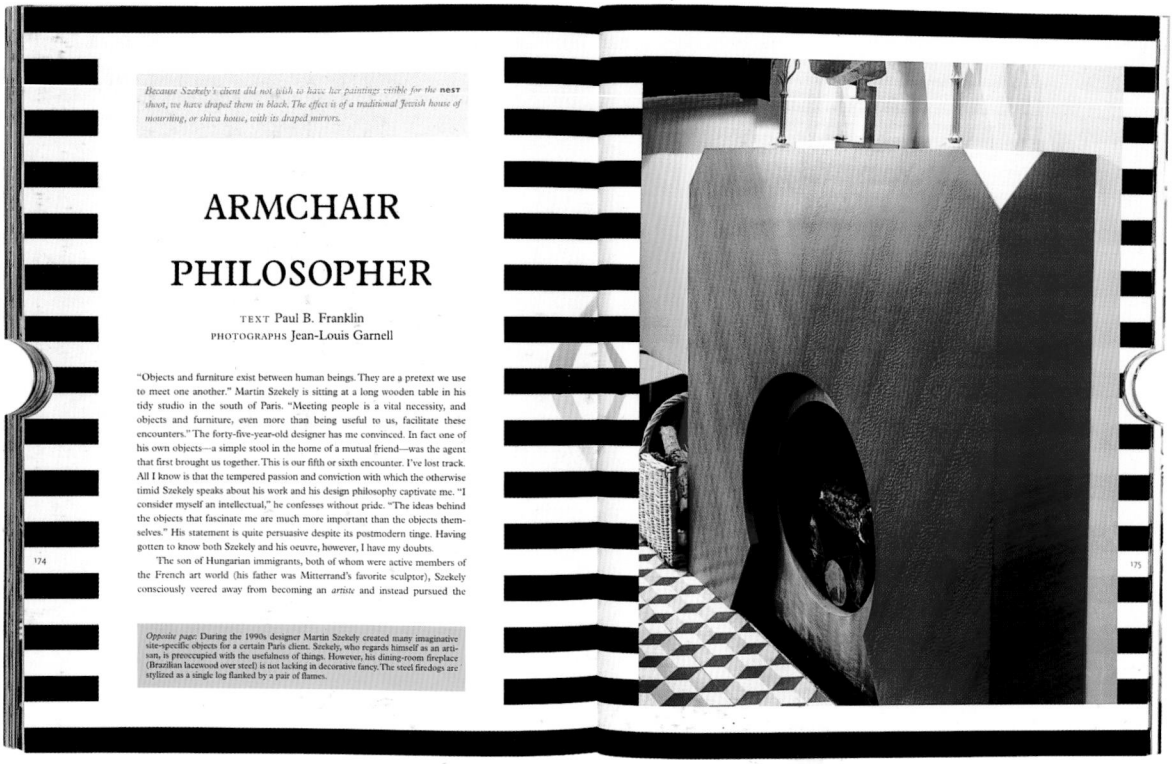

Because Szekely's client did not wish to have her paintings visible for the NEST *shoot, we have draped them in black. The effect is of a traditional Jewish house of mourning, or shiva house, with its draped mirrors.*

ARMCHAIR PHILOSOPHER

TEXT Paul B. Franklin
PHOTOGRAPHS Jean-Louis Garnell

"Objects and furniture exist between human beings. They are a pretext we use to meet one another." Martin Szekely is sitting at a long wooden table in his tidy studio in the south of Paris. "Meeting people is a vital necessity, and objects and furniture, even more than being useful to us, facilitate these encounters." The forty-five-year-old designer has me convinced. In fact one of his own objects—a simple stool in the home of a mutual friend—was the agent that first brought us together. This is our fifth or sixth encounter. I've lost track. All I know is that the tempered passion and conviction with which the otherwise timid Szekely speaks about his work and his design philosophy captivate me. "I consider myself an intellectual," he confesses without pride. "The ideas behind the objects that fascinate me are much more important than the objects themselves." His statement is quite persuasive despite its postmodern tinge. Having gotten to know both Szekely and his oeuvre, however, I have my doubts.

The son of Hungarian immigrants, both of whom were active members of the French art world (his father was Mitterrand's favorite sculptor), Szekely consciously veered away from becoming an *artiste* and instead pursued the

Opposite page: During the 1990s designer Martin Szekely created many imaginative site-specific objects for a certain Paris client. Szekely, who regards himself as an artisan, is preoccupied with the usefulness of things. However, his dining-room fireplace (Brazilian lacewood over steel) is not lacking in decorative fancy. The steel firedogs are stylized as a single log flanked by a pair of flames.

Nest *(USA, Issue 19, Summer 2001) 230 x 280mm/9 x 11 inches*
This interiors magazine has developed a brash, almost naïve, exuberance based on the nature of much of its content: the unreconstructed busy-ness of rich US interiors. Traditional wallpaper and tile patterns are a key influence.
Graphics director *Tom Beckham*

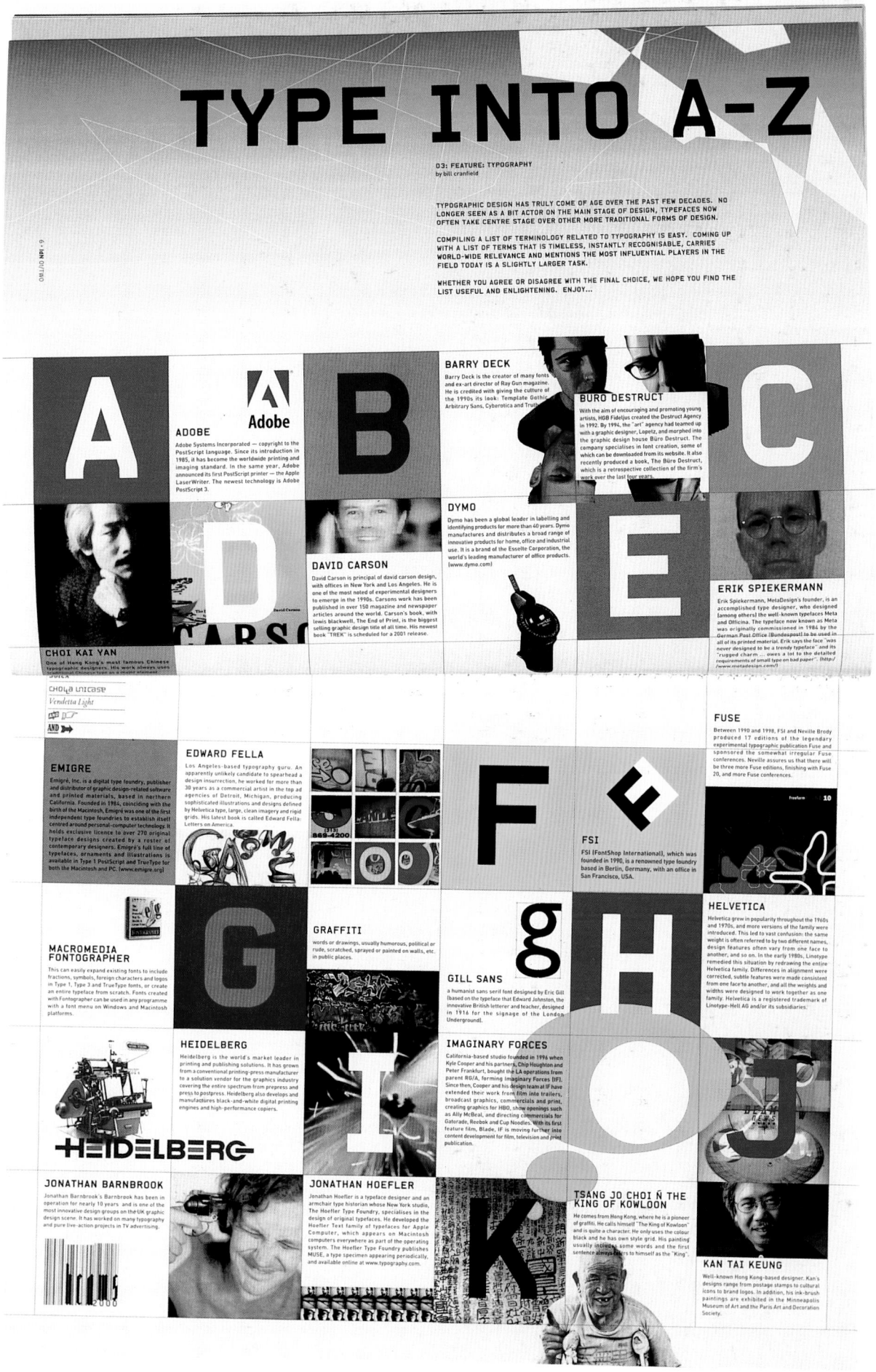

TYPE INTO A-Z

D3: FEATURE: TYPOGRAPHY
by bill cranfield

TYPOGRAPHIC DESIGN HAS TRULY COME OF AGE OVER THE PAST FEW DECADES. NO LONGER SEEN AS A BIT ACTOR ON THE MAIN STAGE OF DESIGN, TYPEFACES NOW OFTEN TAKE CENTRE STAGE OVER OTHER MORE TRADITIONAL FORMS OF DESIGN.

COMPILING A LIST OF TERMINOLOGY RELATED TO TYPOGRAPHY IS EASY. COMING UP WITH A LIST OF TERMS THAT IS TIMELESS, INSTANTLY RECOGNISABLE, CARRIES WORLD-WIDE RELEVANCE AND MENTIONS THE MOST INFLUENTIAL PLAYERS IN THE FIELD TODAY IS A SLIGHTLY LARGER TASK.

WHETHER YOU AGREE OR DISAGREE WITH THE FINAL CHOICE, WE HOPE YOU FIND THE LIST USEFUL AND ENLIGHTENING. ENJOY...

ONLINO NR - 9

A

ADOBE

Adobe Systems Incorporated — copyright to the PostScript language. Since its introduction in 1985, it has become the worldwide printing and imaging standard. In the same year, Adobe announced its first PostScript printer — the Apple LaserWriter. The newest technology is Adobe PostScript 3.

B

BARRY DECK

Barry Deck is the creator of many fonts and ex-art director of Ray Gun magazine. He is credited with giving the culture of the 1990s its look: Template Gothic, Arbitrary Sans, Cyberotica and Truth.

BÜRO DESTRUCT

With the aim of encouraging and promoting young artists, HGB Fideljus created the Destruct Agency in 1992. By 1994, the "art" agency had teamed up with a graphic designer, Lapetz, and morphed into the graphic design house Büro Destruct. The company specialises in font creation, some of which can be downloaded from its website. It also recently produced a book, The Büro Destruct, which is a retrospective collection of the firm's work over the last four years.

C

CHOI KAI YAN

One of Hong Kong's most famous Chinese typographic designers. His work always uses traditional Chinese type as a major element.

CHOI a UNICASE
Vendetta Light
AND

D

DAVID CARSON

David Carson is principal of david carson design, with offices in New York and Los Angeles. He is one of the most noted of experimental designers to emerge in the 1990s. Carsons work has been published in over 150 magazine and newspaper articles around the world. Carson's book, with lewis blackwell, The End of Print, is the biggest selling graphic design title of all time. His newest book "TREK" is scheduled for a 2001 release.

DYMO

Dymo has been a global leader in labelling and identifying products for more than 40 years. Dymo manufactures and distributes a broad range of innovative products for home, office and industrial use. It is a brand of the Esselte Corporation, the world's leading manufacturer of office products. (www.dymo.com)

E

ERIK SPIEKERMANN

Erik Spiekermann, MetaDesign's founder, is an accomplished type designer, who designed (among others) the well-known typefaces Meta and Officina. The typeface now known as Meta was originally commissioned in 1984 by the German Post Office (Bundespost) to be used in all of its printed material. Erik says the face "was never designed to be a trendy typeface" and its "rugged charm ... owes a lot to the detailed requirements of small type on bad paper". (http://www.metadesign.com/)

EMIGRE

Emigré, Inc. is a digital type foundry, publisher and distributor of graphic design-related software and printed materials, based in northern California. Founded in 1984, coinciding with the birth of the Macintosh, Emigré was one of the first independent type foundries to establish itself centred around personal-computer technology. It holds exclusive licence to over 270 original typeface designs created by a roster of contemporary designers. Emigré's full line of typefaces, ornaments and illustrations is available in Type 1 PostScript and TrueType for both the Macintosh and PC. (www.emigre.org)

EDWARD FELLA

Los Angeles-based typography guru. An apparently unlikely candidate to spearhead a design insurrection, he worked for more than 30 years as a commercial artist in the top ad agencies of Detroit, Michigan, producing sophisticated illustrations and designs defined by Helvetica type, large, clean imagery and rigid grids. His latest book is called Edward Fella: Letters on America.

F

FSI

FSI (FontShop International), which was founded in 1990, is a renowned type foundry based in Berlin, Germany, with an office in San Francisco, USA.

FUSE

Between 1990 and 1998, FSI and Neville Brody produced 17 editions of the legendary experimental typographic publication Fuse and sponsored the somewhat irregular Fuse conferences. Neville assures us that there will be three more Fuse editions, finishing with Fuse 20, and more Fuse conferences.

Freeform 10

G

MACROMEDIA FONTOGRAPHER

This can easily expand existing fonts to include fractions, symbols, foreign characters and logos in Type 1, Type 3 and TrueType fonts, or create an entire typeface from scratch. Fonts created with Fontographer can be used in any programme with a font menu on Windows and Macintosh platforms.

GRAFFITI

words or drawings, usually humorous, political or rude, scratched, sprayed or painted on walls, etc. in public places.

GILL SANS

a humanist sans serif font designed by Eric Gill (based on the typeface that Edward Johnston, the innovative British letterer and teacher, designed in 1916 for the signage of the London Underground).

H

HELVETICA

Helvetica grew in popularity throughout the 1960s and 1970s, and more versions of the family were introduced. This led to vast confusion: the same weight is often referred to by two different names, design features often vary from one face to another, and so on. In the early 1980s, Linotype remedied this situation by redrawing the entire Helvetica family. Differences in alignment were corrected, subtle features were made consistent from one face to another, and all the weights and widths were designed to work together as one family. Helvetica is a registered trademark of Linotype-Hell AG and/or its subsidiaries.

I

HEIDELBERG

Heidelberg is the world's market leader in printing and publishing solutions. It has grown from a conventional printing-press manufacturer to a solution vendor for the graphics industry covering the entire spectrum from prepress and press to postpress. Heidelberg also develops and manufactures black-and-white digital printing engines and high-performance copiers.

IMAGINARY FORCES

California-based studio founded in 1996 when Kyle Cooper and his partners, Chip Houghton and Peter Frankfurt, bought the LA operations from parent RG/A, forming Imaginary Forces (IF). Since then, Cooper and his design team at IF have extended their work from film into trailers, broadcast graphics, commercials and print, creating graphics for HBO, show openings such as Ally McBeal, and directing commercials for Gatorade, Reebok and Cup Noodles. With its first feature film, Blade, IF is moving further into content development for film, television and print publication.

J

JONATHAN BARNBROOK

Jonathan Barnbrook's Barnbrook has been in operation for nearly 10 years and is one of the most innovative design groups on the UK graphic design scene. It has worked on many typography and pure live-action projects in TV advertising.

JONATHAN HOEFLER

Jonathan Hoefler is a typeface designer and an armchair type historian whose New York studio, The Hoefler Type Foundry, specialises in the design of original typefaces. He developed the Hoefler Text family of typefaces for Apple Computer, which appears on Macintosh computers everywhere as part of the operating system. The Hoefler Type Foundry publishes MUSE, a type specimen appearing periodically, and available online at www.typography.com.

K

TSANG JO CHOI Ñ THE KING OF KOWLOON

He comes from Hong Kong, where he is a pioneer of graffiti. He calls himself "The King of Kowloon" and is quite a character. He only uses the colour black and he has own style grid. His painting usually includes some words and the first sentence always refers to himself as the "King".

KAN TAI KEUNG

Well-known Hong Kong-based designer. Kan's designs range from postage stamps to cultural icons to brand logos. In addition, his ink-brush paintings are exhibited in the Minneapolis Museum of Art and the Paris Art and Decoration Society.

IdN *(Hong Kong, Volume 8, Number 2, 2002) 235 x 297mm/9 1/4 x 11 3/4 inches*
This 'A–Z of Type' is typical of the way this digital design magazine turns its page designs at odd angles and overlays text and image, reflecting the area of design it covers.
Creative director *Victor Cheung*

BORN IN THE USA

Celebrated science-fiction author; chronicler of hacker wars and founder of Green design movement 'Viridian', **Bruce Sterling** is also bastard child to Texas' phenomenally powerful oil industry. In this capacity, he knows a thing or two about how America's big boys do business and, after nearly a decade, a fair bit about the leadership style of their very own President, George W. Bush. During a recent visit to Germany, only a couple of weeks prior to Bush withdrawing from the Kyoto agreement on Climate Change, **Ulrich Gutmair** and **Martin Conrads** quizzed Sterling on what positive political intervention might look like in the Brave New World of immanent eco-catastrophe.

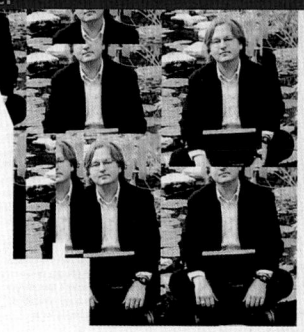

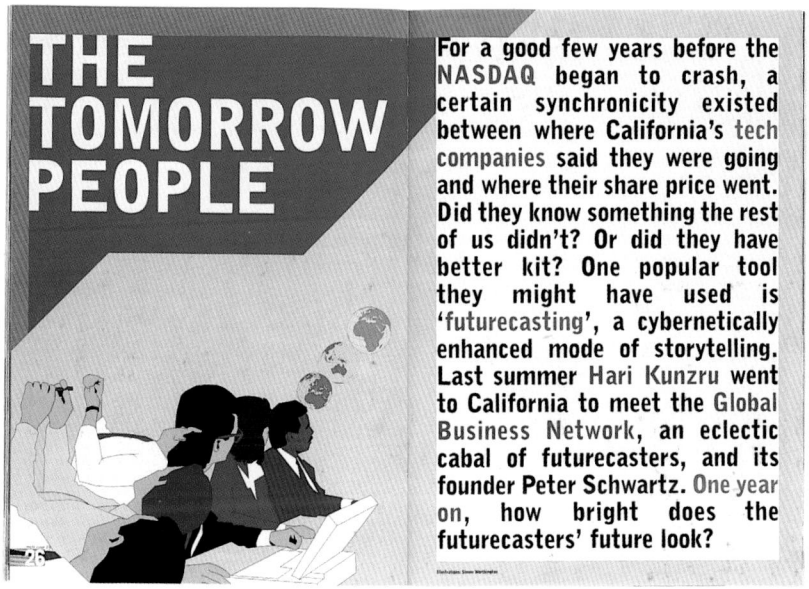

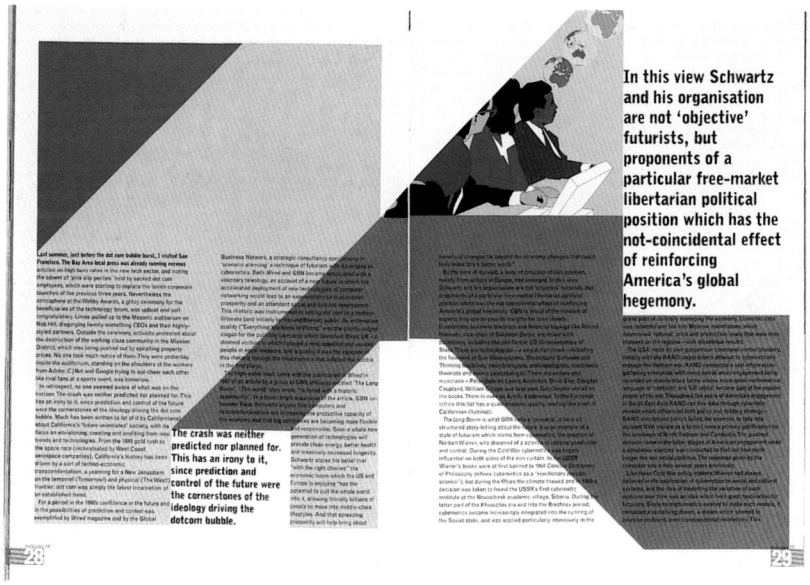

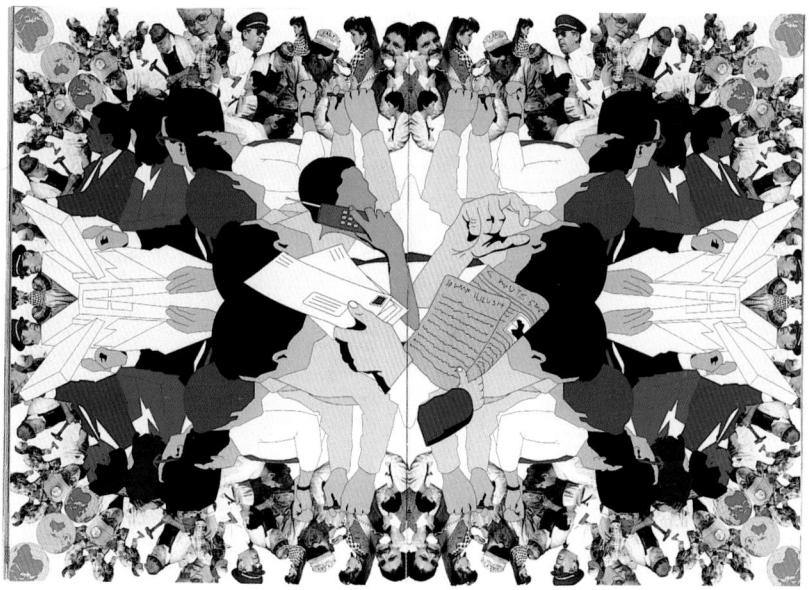

Mute *(UK, Issue 19, 2001) 200 x 275mm/7 7/8 x 10 7/8 inches*
Critical of the way technology is harnessed against people rather than to help them, this magazine has developed a graphic style that is bright and colourful yet has a distinctly unsettling quality to it that reflects the editorial content. Images are savagely cropped or run repeatedly; ghostly shapes are cut into pictures and areas of colour.
Designer *Damian Jacques*

Bigger than life itself

History

Designing heroes

43

Stereotypes

The imperial scam

Bravery and fear

Every era creates heroic imagery that conforms to its specific needs

Superman

Graphic façades

Myth

Recruitment

By Steven Heller

Heroic imagery has long adorned canvas and poster for reasons as varied as patriotism and paternalism, valour and ego. To be called a hero – or to be shown as such – is the highest of human distinctions, and heroism is a status to which everyone aspires, if only subconsciously. The true hero is born with, or acquires, real virtues, while the synthetic one is a composite of ideal attributes. In either case, the heroic image has considerable sway over public perception. Nevertheless, a hero is not always actually 'heroic' in appearance or stature, so designing heroes that conform to accepted models necessitates the creation of symbolic beings that are bigger and bolder than life.

In heroic art the diminutive Napoleon was depicted as taller; Hitler was shown as being physically stronger than nature had originally intended. The exaggerating, flattering lens is routinely used to elevate rulers and warriors as well as sports and media stars. Michael Deaver, Ronald Reagan's chief of staff and principal 'image maker', once explained that placing the then president in a heroic light relied, quite literally, on effective lighting to smooth out the gnarled parts and give an aura to his countenance.

Film-makers routinely create larger-than-life live-action characters whose heroic personae the public unquestioningly embrace simply because of a few special effects. But the grandest fictional heroes are not made of flesh

1. Klimaschin's poster for USSR Agricultural Exhibition, 1939, uses classical poses to represent the common farm labourer as a hero of the state. Lithograph.

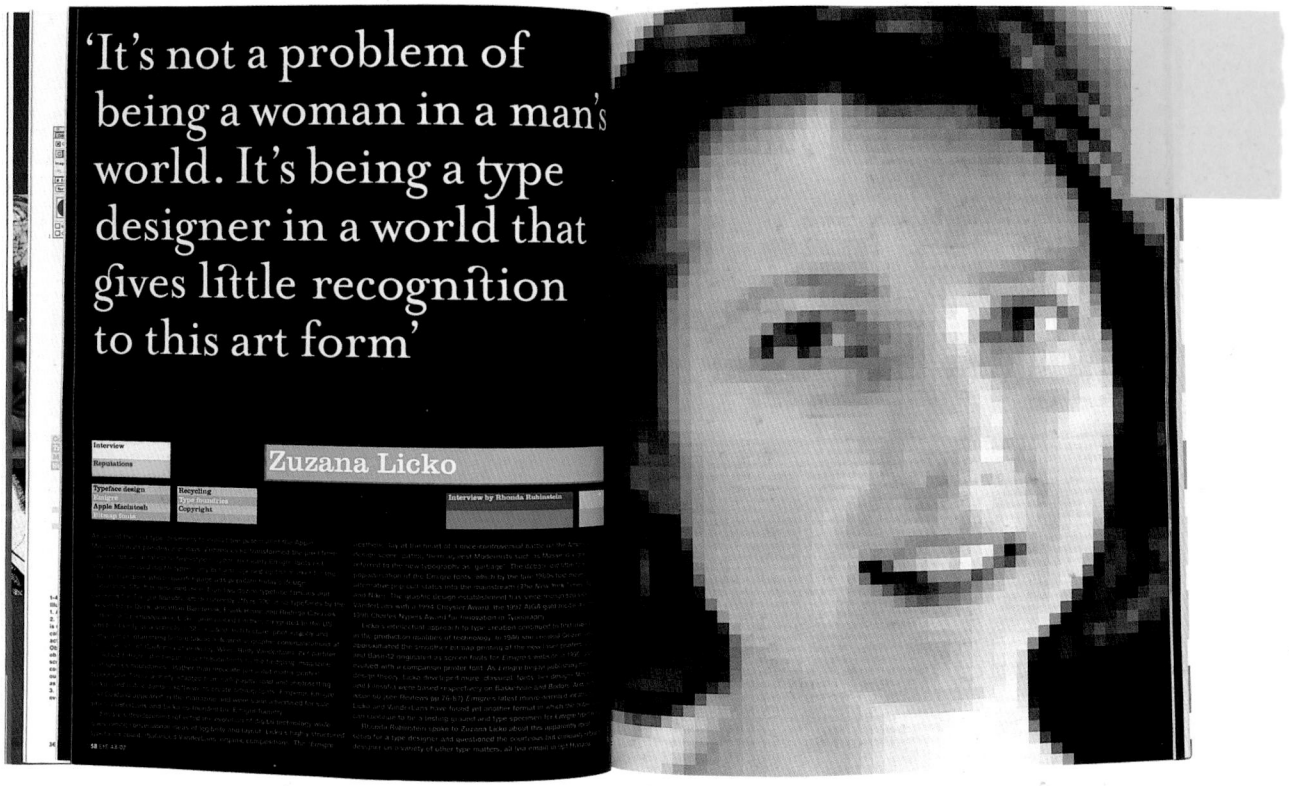

Issue 43, Spring 2002, 237 x 297mm/9 3/8 x 11 7/8 inches

***Eye* is a magazine about design. How difficult is it designing in that context?**
When designing a magazine about design the layout must not try to compete with the content it is presenting. Having said that, the magazine itself as an object is part of its subject so should therefore be worthy as an example of what it preaches – if it is not, perhaps the magazine loses some credibility. It's a fine balance.

We show works of graphic design and we provide text that tells our readers all about it. You might say that's enough, but talking to our readers it seems that they enjoy it more when visual examples and text are both intertwined in a pleasing or often dramatic way.

Of course, the reading of the original work changes, that's unavoidable as it is removed from its context after all. So whilst respect is paid to the nature of the original (scale for instance), this can only be done up to a point, since it might be more important to deliver opinion on how that work participates in a narrative of ideas instead. This may require comparison of several works on a page that, if presented according to exact relative scale, may produce a layout that is messy and which then disrupts the visual narrative flow.

The most important thing is showing the work as close to the real thing as possible and in a no-nonsense way. If there's a lot of material all the same size, I run it the same size.

Eye was a nice thing to be asked to do, a privilege, but very humbling – it's about other people's work.

What was the philosophy behind the recent redesign?
I wanted to increase the presence of *Eye*'s voice in proceedings and lessen the degree to which each layout responded specifically to its content, to lessen the degree to which I was interpreting ideas and styles in each article.

When I first started on *Eye*, I was interpreting everything, responding to each piece of content and it was getting too much – I began to feel my visual interpretation was making the experience of *Eye* dense and overwrought. I wanted a systematic, drier and low-key format which could be distinctive without being too cool. The design has to be straightforward to show the work well.

For a while the editor and I had been using themes (both explicit and secret ones) to focus ideas for each issue. The redesign had to suit the nature of these themes and I thought a design where a set format dominates over visual responses to specific articles would work well with them.

I also wanted to reduce the feeling of starting from zero as each issue loomed. Both the editor and myself wanted the magazine to be less all-consuming to allow us time for our other work, and the systematic nature of the redesign helps limit our options, stopping us spending two days designing an opening spread, for example.

Describe the redesign.
It's simpler, and doesn't attempt to draw attention to itself. We have a 12-column grid on which both text and images can be hung in a rich variety of ways. It's a very flexible structure. The design of *Eye* can't be full of rules, it has to be open to anything happening. The images we run are all different shapes and sizes and can often make for a messy layout.

I wanted the magazine to become more like a book, to reduce the amount of 'clever' headline writing and use the headlines just as information. At one stage a further idea was to completely lose the headlines, using the keywords and standfirsts alone to start the features. But the editor felt headlines were necessary from a journalistic standpoint.

You have relegated the visual importance of headlines?
In the main feature well, the opening spreads of each article

Interview
Nick Bell
Art director
***Eye* magazine**

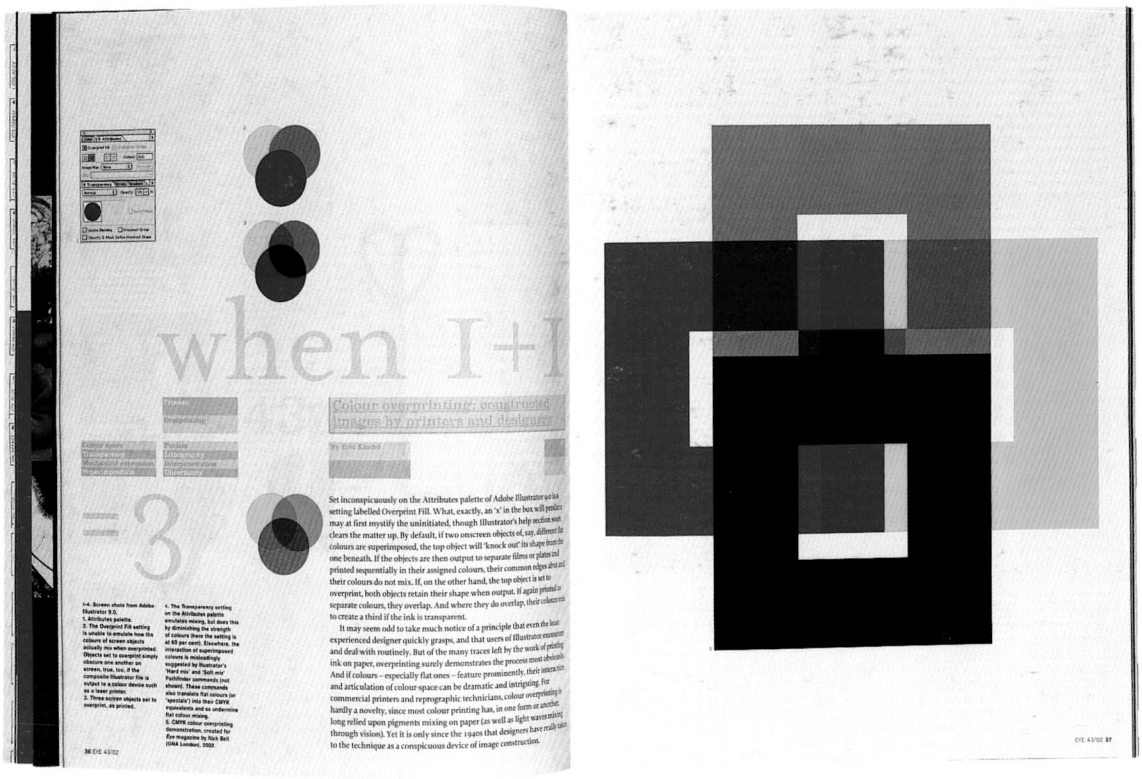

when I+I

Colour overprinting: constructed images by printers and designers

By Eric Kindel

Set inconspicuously on the Attributes palette of Adobe Illustrator 9.0 is a setting labelled Overprint Fill. What, exactly, an 'x' in the box will produce may at first mystify the uninitiated, though Illustrator's help section soon clears the matter up. By default, if two onscreen objects of, say, different flat colours are superimposed, the top object will 'knock out' its shape from the one beneath. If the objects are then output to separate films or plates and printed sequentially in their assigned colours, their common edges abut and their colours do not mix. If, on the other hand, the top object is set to overprint, both objects retain their shape when output. If again printed to separate colours, they overlap. And where they do overlap, their colours mix to create a third if the ink is transparent.

It may seem odd to take much notice of a principle that even the least experienced designer quickly grasps, and that users of Illustrator encounter and deal with routinely. But of the many traces left by the work of printing ink on paper, overprinting surely demonstrates the process most obviously. And if colours – especially flat ones – feature prominently, their interaction and articulation of colour space can be dramatic and intriguing. For commercial printers and reprographic technicians, colour overprinting is a hardly a novelty, since most colour printing has, in one form or another, long relied upon pigments mixing on paper (as well as light waves mixing through vision). Yet it is only since the 1940s that designers have really taken to the technique as a conspicuous device of image construction.

1–4. Screen shots from Adobe Illustrator 9.0.
1. Attributes palette.
2. The Overprint Fill setting is unable to emulate how the colours of screen objects actually mix when overprinted. Objects set to overprint simply obscure one another on screen, true, too, if the composite Illustrator file is output to a colour device such as a laser printer.
3. Three screen objects set to overprint, as printed.
4. The Transparency setting on the Attributes palette emulates mixing, but does this by diminishing the strength of colours (here the setting is at 60 per cent). Elsewhere, the interaction of superimposed colours is misleadingly suggested by Illustrator's 'Hard mix' and 'Soft mix' Pathfinder commands (not shown). These commands also translate flat colours (or 'specials') into their CMYK equivalents and so undermine flat colour mixing.
5. CMYK colour overprinting demonstration, created for *Eye* magazine by Nick Bell (UAA London), 2002.

38 EYE 43/02

EYE 43/02 37

Issue 43, Spring 2002

are now designed as a set to make each individual issue distinct from others. We change the headline font every issue and this was prompted by the same aim.

The standfirst and byline are now contained in colour boxes along with the addition of a keyword list that was to influence how the *Eye* website was to look – it was being redesigned at the same time as the magazine. Although more systematic, the colour of these boxes changes every issue and there is a selection of box layout variables to choose from. Every opening is very distinctive, and these colour boxes add more distinctiveness.

So the redesign means that the look of each issue is now a result of an overarching idea to represent the issue as a whole rather than a collection of interpretations specfic to each of the main articles.

What fonts have you used for the headlines so far?

For the relaunch issue we used Radio FM, designed by Magnus Rakeng who designed *Eye*'s new logo. Mrs Eaves was used in second issue because we had an interview with its designer, Susanna Licko.

Tabloid Compressed in issue three was used partly in response to the amount of content that issue contained about newspaper design, and partly to counter the criticism that we were over-academic .

How did the new logo come about?

We had already decided to use the Radio FM font for the redesign issue because it connected with ideas I had about the logo harking back to the early naïve days of corporate identity with logos like Ford, AEG and Pepsi. These seemed like precious,

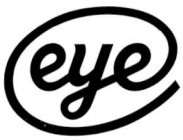

cherished badges that companies wore in a different way. I wanted a logo that looked unfashionably hand-drawn and crafted, one that showed the movements of the hand and the pride of the person that created it – all very much NOT now, it seemed to me. So with his Radio FM as a model, Magnus gave us just what we wanted and when we decided that it should appear in chocolate brown on the cover of the launch issue of the redesign it reminded me of the Cadbury's logo. It was warm, friendly and cosy and part of our attempt to stop designers thinking (incorrectly) that *Eye* is somehow an academic magazine. *Eye* is primarily visual; it features graphic design and we want the design of the magazine itself to communicate an enjoyment in the activity of graphic design itself.

What has the response been to the redesign?

On the whole the response has been very positive and encouraging. We tend not to hear from those that don't like it. But I did read on the 'Lines and Splines' website that they think there are too many typefaces being used. (We take pleasure in breaking this 'rule'). Some people hate it – one regular contributor thought the design seemed arbitrary and assumed that the use of colour was for some kind of complex colour-coding. He felt provoked to say that he didn't want to write for *Eye* anymore. He doesn't see it as the right environment for his writing which was a surprise since so many aspects of the layout have been simplified and made more flexible. But the most flattering comment was from another designer, who told us we were now doing things with *Eye* that you don't see tried out in other magazines.

The good thing is we elicited a response rather than silence. I would like to hear much more criticism from readers. Designers are much less passionate about what they like and don't like these days, it seems to me.

LIBRARY & RESOURCES AREA FARNHAM CAMPUS
THE SURREY INSTITUTE OF ART & DESIGN

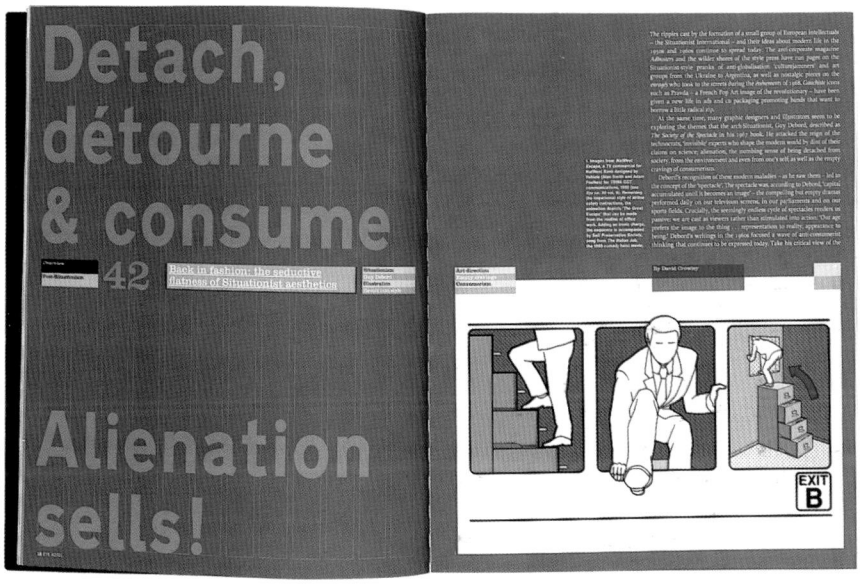

Issue 42, Winter 2001

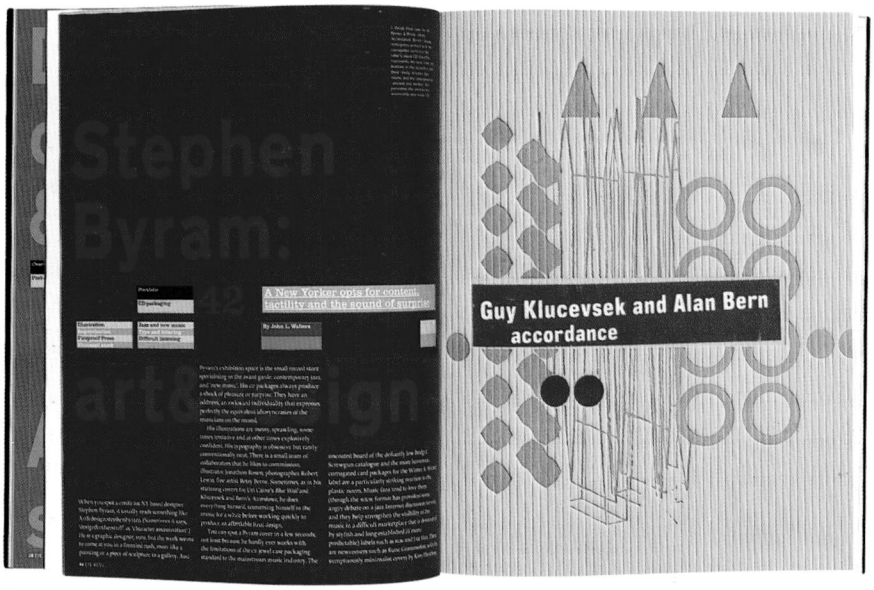

Issue 42, Winter 2001

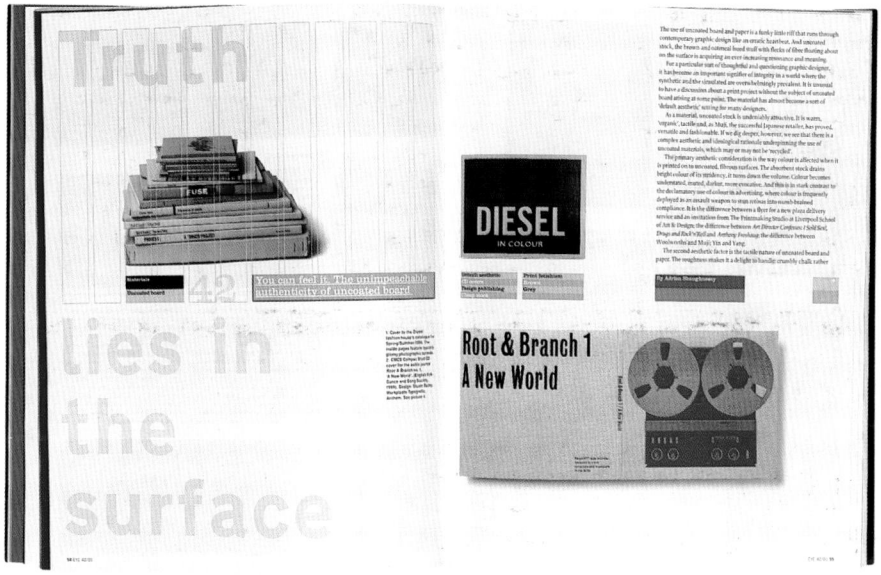

Issue 42, Winter 2001

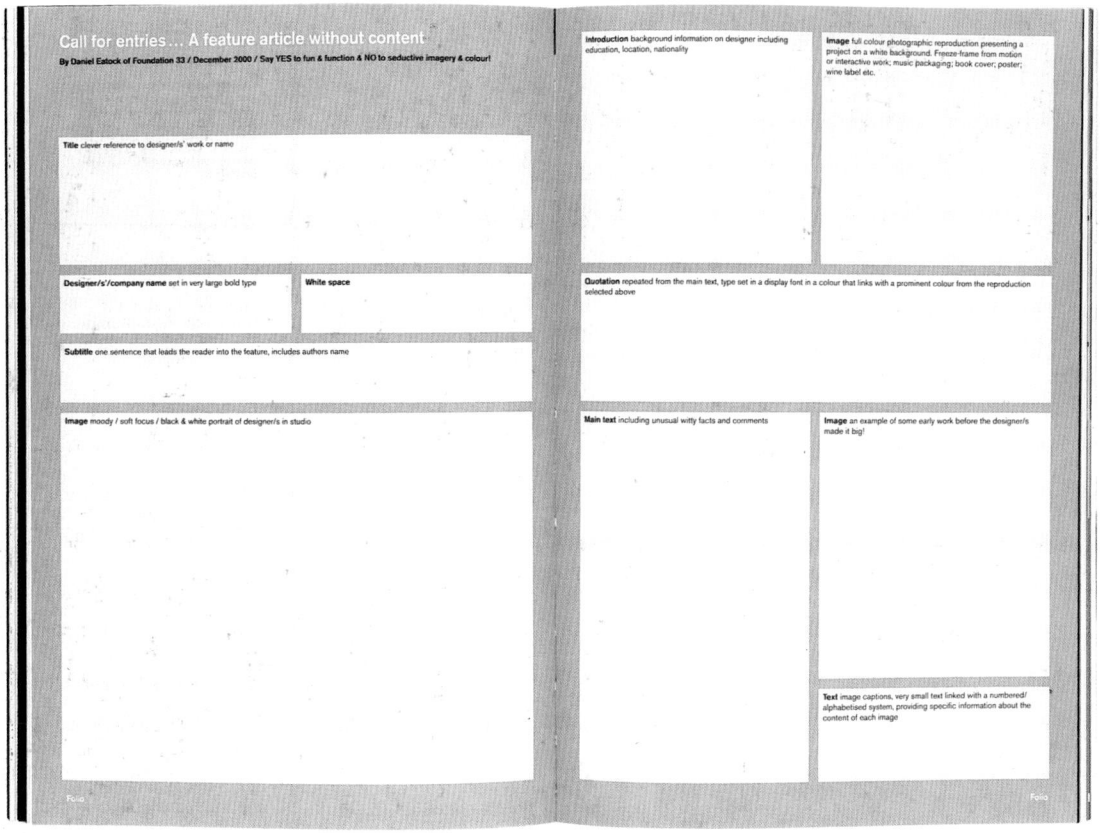

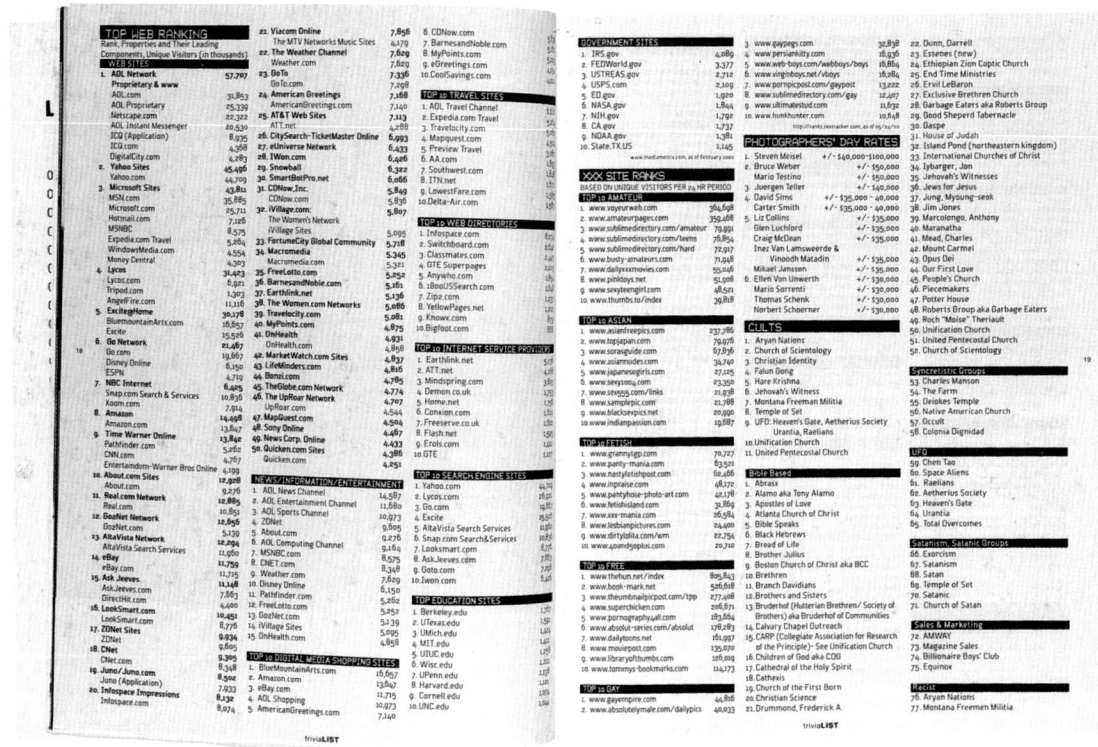

TOP WEB RANKING

Rank, Properties and Their Leading Components, Unique Visitors (in thousands)

WEB SITES

1.	AOL Network	57,797
	Proprietary & www	
	AOL.com	31,853
	AOL Proprietary	25,339
	Netscape.com	22,322
	AOL Instant Messenger	20,530
	ICQ (Application)	8,935
	ICQ.com	4,368
	DigitalCity.com	4,283
2.	Yahoo Sites	45,496
	Yahoo.com	44,719
3.	Microsoft Sites	43,811
	MSN.com	35,885
	Microsoft.com	25,711
	Hotmail.com	7,116
	MSNBC	8,575
	Expedia.com Travel	5,264
	WindowsMedia.com	4,554
	Money Central	4,303
4.	Lycos	31,423
	Lycos.com	6,921
	Tripod.com	1,323
	AngelFire.com	11,116
5.	Exciteg/Home	30,178
	BluemountainArts.com	16,657
	Excite	15,526
6.	Go Network	21,467
	Go.com	19,667
	Disney Online	6,150
	ESPN	4,719
7.	NBC Internet	8,425
	Snap.com Search & Services	10,836
	Xoom.com	7,914
8.	Amazon	14,498
	Amazon.com	13,847
9.	Time Warner Online	13,842
	Pathfinder.com	5,262
	CNN.com	4,767
	Entertaindom-Warner Bros Online	4,199
10.	About.com Sites	12,908
	About.com	9,276
11.	Real.com Network	12,885
	Real.com	10,893
12.	DozNet Network	12,696
	DozNet.com	5,139
13.	AltaVista Network	12,294
	AltaVista Search Services	11,960
14.	eBay	11,759
	eBay.com	11,715
15.	Ask Jeeves	11,348
	Ask.Jeeves.com	7,663
	DirectHit.com	4,400
16.	LookSmart.com	10,451
	LookSmart.com	8,776
17.	ZDNet Sites	9,934
	ZDNet	9,605
18.	CNet	9,305
	CNet.com	8,348
19.	Juno / Juno.com	8,902
	Juno (Application)	7,833
20.	Infospace Impressions	8,232
	Infospace.com	8,074
21.	Viacom Online	7,856
	The MTV Networks Music Sites	4,179
22.	The Weather Channel	7,829
	Weather.com	7,629
23.	GoTo	7,336
	GoTo.com	7,298
24.	American Greetings	7,168
	AmericanGreetings.com	7,140
25.	AT&T Web Sites	7,113
	ATT.net	4,288
26.	CitySearch-TicketMaster Online	6,993
27.	eUniverse Network	6,433
28.	IWon.com	6,426
29.	Snowball	6,322
30.	SmartBellPro.net	6,266
31.	CDNow, Inc.	5,849
	CDNow.com	5,836
32.	iVillage.com:	5,807
	The Women's Network	
	iVillage Sites	5,095
33.	FortuneCity Global Community	5,718
34.	Macromedia	5,345
	Macromedia.com	5,321
35.	FreeLotto.com	5,252
36.	BarnesandNoble.com	5,161
37.	Earthlink.net	5,136
38.	The Women.com Networks	5,086
39.	Travelocity.com	5,081
40.	MyPoints.com	4,875
41.	OnHealth	4,931
	OnHealth.com	4,898
42.	MarketWatch.com Sites	4,837
43.	LifeMinders.com	4,816
44.	Bonzi.com	4,785
45.	TheGlobe.com Network	4,774
46.	The UpRoar Network	4,747
	UpRoar.com	4,544
47.	MapQuest.com	4,504
48.	Sony Online	4,467
49.	News Corp. Online	4,433
50.	Quicken.com Sites	4,386
	Quicken.com	4,251

NEWS/INFORMATION/ENTERTAINMENT

1.	AOL News Channel	14,587
2.	AOL Entertainment Channel	11,680
3.	AOL Sports Channel	10,973
4.	ZDNet	9,605
5.	About.com	9,276
6.	AOL Computing Channel	9,164
7.	MSNBC.com	8,575
8.	CNET.com	8,348
9.	Weather.com	7,629
10.	Disney Online	6,150
11.	Pathfinder.com	5,262
12.	FreeLotto.com	5,252
13.	DozNet.com	5,139
14.	iVillage Sites	5,095
15.	OnHealth.com	4,898

TOP 10 DIGITAL MEDIA SHOPPING SITES

1.	BlueMountainArts.com	16,657
2.	Amazon.com	13,847
3.	eBay.com	11,715
4.	AOL Shopping	10,973
5.	AmericanGreetings.com	7,140
6.	CDNow.com	5,849
7.	BarnesandNoble.com	5,161
8.	MyPoints.com	4,875
9.	eGreetings.com	3,911
10.	CoolSavings.com	3,411

TOP 10 TRAVEL SITES

1.	AOL Travel Channel	8,115
2.	Expedia.com Travel	5,264
3.	Travelocity.com	5,081
4.	Mapquest.com	4,504
5.	Preview Travel	3,911
6.	AA.com	3,183
7.	Southwest.com	1,842
8.	ITN.net	1,671
9.	LowestFare.com	1,136
10.	Delta-Air.com	1,136

TOP 10 WEB DIRECTORIES

1.	Infospace.com	8,074
2.	Switchboard.com	2,634
3.	Classmates.com	2,416
4.	GTE Superpages	2,211
5.	Anywho.com	1,874
6.	1800USSearch.com	1,842
7.	Zipz.com	1,457
8.	YellowPages.net	1,211
9.	Knowx.com	891
10.	Bigfoot.com	888

TOP 10 INTERNET SERVICE PROVIDERS

1.	Earthlink.net	5,136
2.	ATT.net	4,288
3.	Mindspring.com	3,811
4.	Demon.co.uk	1,771
5.	Home.net	1,136
6.	Conxion.com	1,611
7.	Freeserve.co.uk	1,511
8.	Flash.net	1,511
9.	Etoh.com	1,211
10.	GTE	1,117

TOP 10 SEARCH ENGINE SITES

1.	Yahoo.com	44,719
2.	Lycos.com	26,921
3.	Go.com	19,667
4.	Excite	15,526
5.	AltaVista Search Services	11,960
6.	Snap.com Search&Services	10,836
7.	Looksmart.com	8,776
8.	Ask.Jeeves.com	7,663
9.	Goto.com	7,298
10.	Iwon.com	6,426

TOP 10 EDUCATION SITES

1.	Berkeley.edu	1,787
2.	UTexas.edu	1,551
3.	UMich.edu	1,401
4.	MIT.edu	1,401
5.	UIUC.edu	1,351
6.	Wisc.edu	1,211
7.	UPenn.edu	1,151
8.	Harvard.edu	1,121
9.	Cornell.edu	1,061
10.	UNC.edu	1,041

triviaLIST

GOVERNMENT SITES

1.	IRS.gov	4,089
2.	FEDWorld.gov	3,377
3.	USTREAS.gov	2,712
4.	USPS.com	2,109
5.	ED.gov	1,920
6.	NASA.gov	1,844
7.	NIH.gov	1,792
8.	CA.gov	1,737
9.	NOAA.gov	1,381
10.	State.TX.US	1,145

www.mediametrix.com, as of February 2000

XXX SITE RANKS

BASED ON UNIQUE VISITORS PER 24 HR PERIOD

TOP 10 AMATEUR

1.	www.voyeurweb.com	364,698
2.	www.amateurpages.com	259,468
3.	www.sublimedirectory.com/amateur	79,991
4.	www.sublimedirectory.com/teens	76,854
5.	www.sublimedirectory.com/hard	72,917
6.	www.busty-amateurs.com	71,948
7.	www.dailyxxxmovies.com	55,016
8.	www.pinkboys.net	51,508
9.	www.sexyteengirl.com	48,501
10.	www.thumbs.to/index	39,818

TOP 10 ASIAN

1.	www.asianfreepics.com	237,386
2.	www.topjapan.com	79,976
3.	www.sorasguide.com	67,836
4.	www.asianmodes.com	34,740
5.	www.japanesegirls.com	27,125
6.	www.sexy2004.com	23,350
7.	www.sex555.com/links	21,938
8.	www.samplepic.com	21,788
9.	www.blacksexpics.net	20,990
10.	www.indianpassion.com	19,687

TOP 10 FETISH

1.	www.grannytgp.com	70,727
2.	www.panty-mania.com	63,501
3.	www.hastylittlehost.com	62,466
4.	www.inpraise.com	48,172
5.	www.pantyhose-photo-art.com	42,178
6.	www.fetishisland.com	31,869
7.	www.xxx-mania.com	26,984
8.	www.lesbianpictures.com	24,400
9.	www.dirtylolita.com/wm	22,754
10.	www.4pandg4plus.com	20,710

TOP 10 FREE

1.	www.thehun.net/index	805,843
2.	www.hook-mark.net	526,618
3.	www.theumbrellapicpost.com/tpp	277,408
4.	www.superchicken.com	206,631
5.	www.pornography4all.com	183,664
6.	www.absolut-service.com/absolut	178,283
7.	www.dailytoons.net	161,997
8.	www.moviepost.com	135,670
9.	www.libraryofthumbs.com	126,019
10.	www.tommys-bookmarks.com	114,173

TOP 10 GAY

1.	www.gayempire.com	44,816
2.	www.absolutelymale.com/dailypics	40,833
3.	www.gaypegs.com	32,838
4.	www.persiankitty.com	18,936
5.	www.web-boys.com/webboys/boys	16,864
6.	www.virginboys.net/vboys	16,284
7.	www.pornpicpost.com/gaypost	13,222
8.	www.sublimedirectory.com/gay	12,467
9.	www.ultimatestud.com	11,832
10.	www.hunkhunter.com	10,648

http://ranks.sextracker.com, as of 09/19/00

PHOTOGRAPHERS' DAY RATES

1.	Steven Meisel	+/- $40,000-$100,000
2.	Bruce Weber	+/- $50,000
	Mario Testino	+/- $50,000
3.	Juergen Teller	+/- $40,000
4.	David Sims	+/- $35,000 - 40,000
	Carter Smith	+/- $35,000 - 40,000
5.	Liz Collins	+/- $35,000
	Glen Luchford	+/- $35,000
	Craig McDean	+/- $35,000
	Inez Van Lamsweerde & Vinoodh Matadin	+/- $35,000
	Mikael Jansson	+/- $35,000
6.	Ellen Von Unwerth	+/- $30,000
	Mario Sorrenti	+/- $30,000
	Thomas Schenk	+/- $30,000
	Norbert Schoerner	+/- $30,000

CULTS

1. Aryan Nations
2. Church of Scientology
3. Christian Identity
4. Falun Gong
5. Hare Krishna
6. Jehovah's Witness
7. Montana Freeman Militia
8. Temple of Set
9. UFO: Heaven's Gate, Aetherius Society Urantia, Raelians
10. Unification Church
11. United Pentecostal Church

Bible Based

1. Abrasx
2. Alamo aka Tony Alamo
3. Apostles of Love
4. Atlanta Church of Christ
5. Bible Speaks
6. Black Hebrews
7. Bread of Life
8. Brother Julius
9. Boston Church of Christ aka BCC
10. Brethren
11. Branch Davidians
12. Brothers and Sisters
13. Bruderhof (Hutterian Brethren/ Society of Brothers) aka Bruderhof of Communities
14. Calvary Chapel Outreach
15. CARP (Collegiate Association for Research of the Principle)- See Unification Church
16. Children of God aka COG
17. Cathedral of the Holy Spirit
18. Cathexis
19. Church of the First Born
20. Christian Science
21. Drummond, Frederick A.
22. Dunn, Darrell
23. Essenes (new)
24. Ethiopian Zion Coptic Church
25. End Time Ministries
26. Ervil LeBaron
27. Exclusive Brethren Church
28. Garbage Eaters aka Roberts Group
29. Good Sheperd Tabernacle
30. Gaspe
31. House of Judah
32. Island Pond (northeastern kingdom)
33. International Churches of Christ
34. Jybarger, Jan
35. Jehovah's Witnesses
36. Jews for Jesus
37. Jung, Myoung-seok
38. Jim Jones
39. Marcolongo, Anthony
40. Maranatha
41. Mead, Charles
42. Mount Carmel
43. Opus Dei
44. Our First Love
45. People's Church
46. Piecemakers
47. Potter House
48. Roberts Droup aka Garbage Eaters
49. Roch "Moise" Theriault
50. Unification Church
51. United Pentecostal Church
52. Church of Scientology

19

Syncretistic Groups

53. Charles Manson
54. The Farm
55. Oneiokes Temple
56. Native American Church
57. Occult
58. Colonia Dignidad

UFO

59. Chen Tao
60. Space Aliens
61. Raelians
62. Aetherius Society
63. Heaven's Gate
64. Urantia
65. Total Overcomes

Satanism, Satanic Groups

66. Exorcism
67. Satanism
68. Satan
69. Temple of Set
70. Satanic
71. Church of Satan

Sales & Marketing

72. AMWAY
73. Magazine Sales
74. Billionaire Boys' Club
75. Equinox

Racist

76. Aryan Nations
77. Montana Freemen Militia

triviaLIST

TOP **Dot Dot Dot** *(UK, Issue 2, 2001) 164 x 234mm/6 1/2 x 9 1/4 inches*
This independent design magazine uses a format typical of a design award entry form to take a dig at 'normal' design magazines. The form, titled 'Calls for entries… A feature article without content' has blank fields for the reader to fill in, including: 'Title – clever reference to designer/s' work or name' and 'Image – moody / soft focus / black & white portrait of designer/s in studio'.
Design *Jurgen Albrecht, Stuart Bailey, Peter Bilak and Tom Unverzagt*

BOTTOM **List** *(USA, Issue 1, 2000) 220 x 275mm/8 3/4 x 10 7/8 inches*
Taking the recent editorial obsession with listmaking to its extreme, this unique magazine consists solely of written and pictorial lists. Information includes the full guest list for the launch party of *Talk* magazine, details of the most expensive photographer's day rates, and reproduction of the polaroids taken during a casting session for a Macy Gray video.
Designers *Steven Baillie and Danae Grandison*

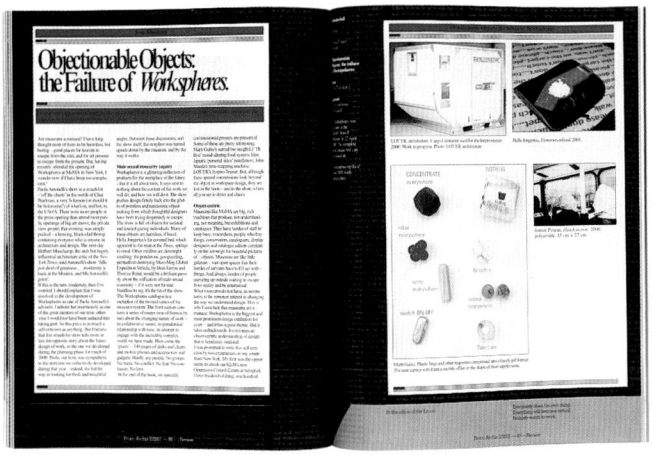

Issue 2, 2001

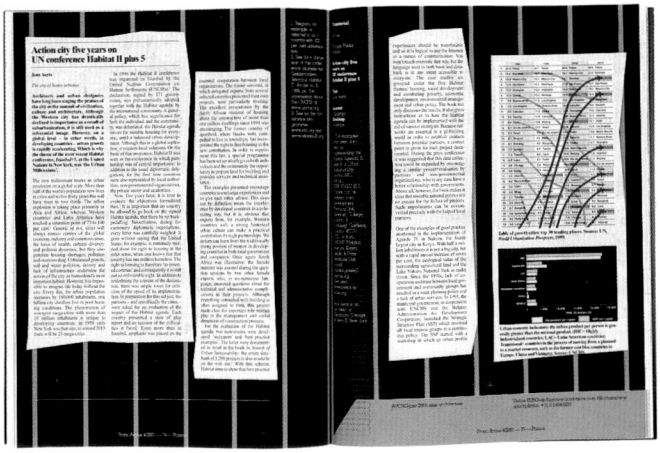

Issue 4, 2001

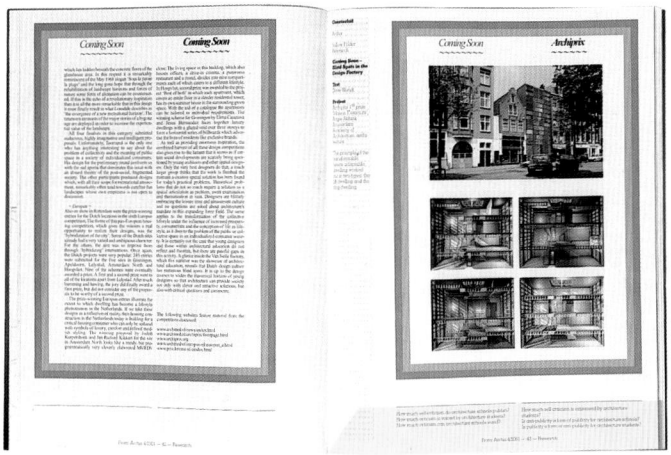

Issue 4, 2001

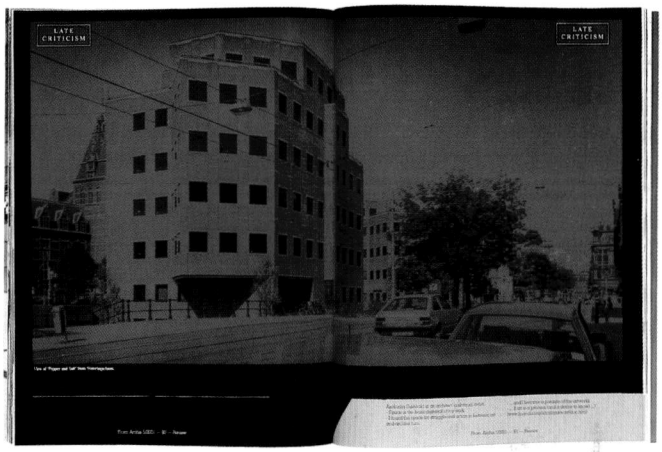

Issue 5, 2001

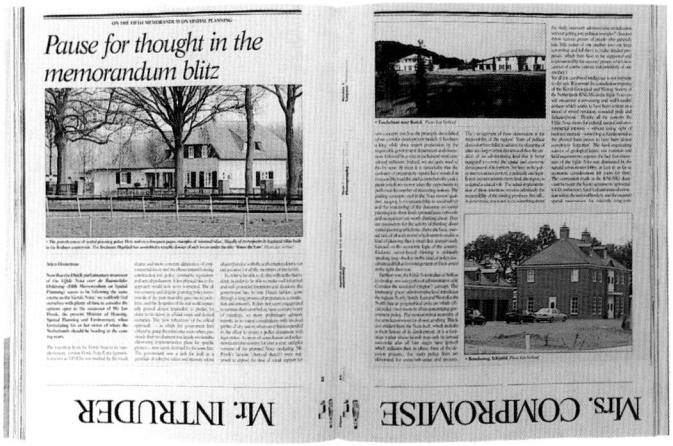

Issue 1, 2002

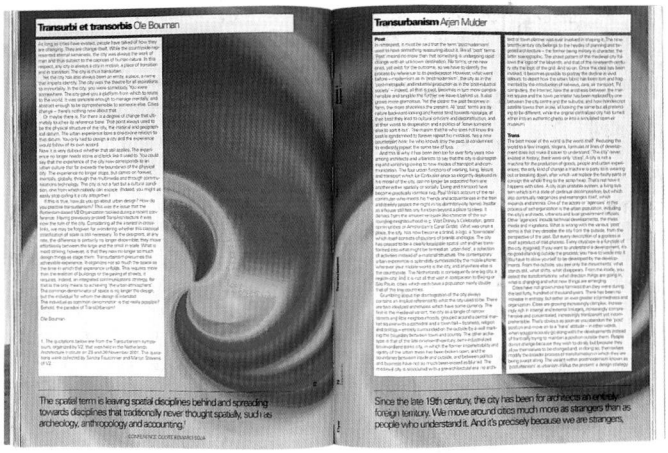

Issue 1, 2002

Archis *(The Netherlands)*
220 x 275mm/8 3/4 x 10 7/8 inches
This architecture magazine has become an experiment in editorial design. It is designed to be interactive – all the pages are perforated so they can be removed and re-ordered. The design itself involves complex layering, starting with the covers (SEE PAGE 62), taking advantage of the ease with which pages created on the computer can be copied and reproduced. Much of the content is presented as if taken from other publications, the layouts mimicking the designs of various newspapers, typed reports and trade magazines.
Designers *Maureen Mooren and Daniel van der Velden*

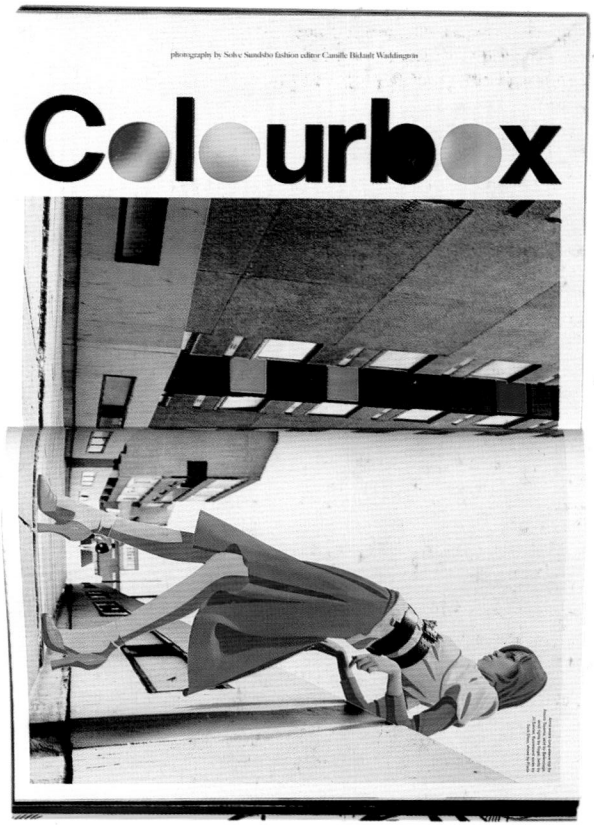

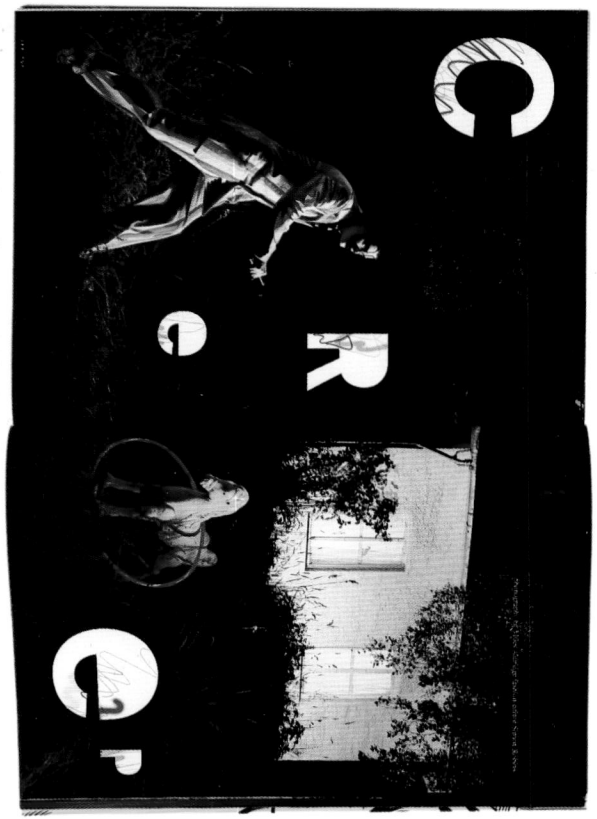

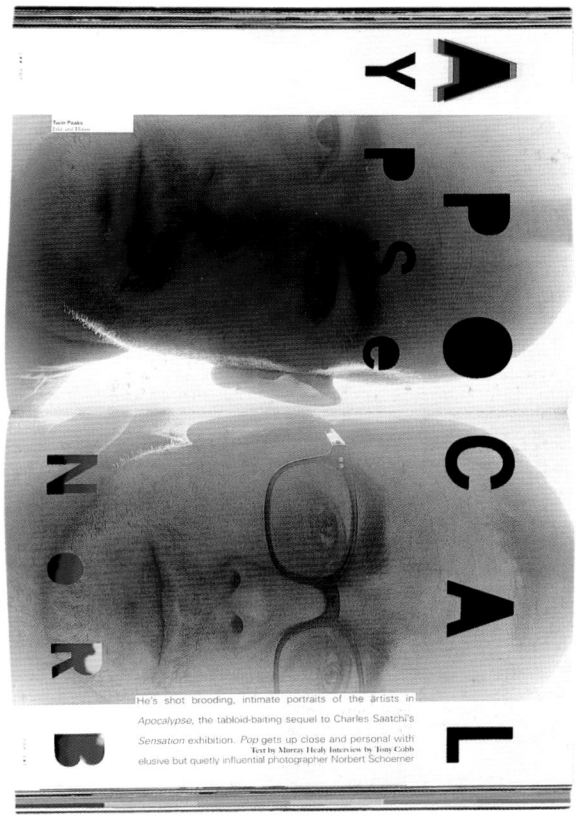

Pop *(UK, Issue 1, Autumn/Winter 2000/01) 230 x 300mm/9 x 11 7/8 inches*
Making use of the way type and image are reduced to a single set of digital information in the production process, the type has been retouched as much as the images; the irony being that the technology has been used to distress the type and image rather than clean it up.
Art directors *Lee Swillingham and Stuart Spalding*

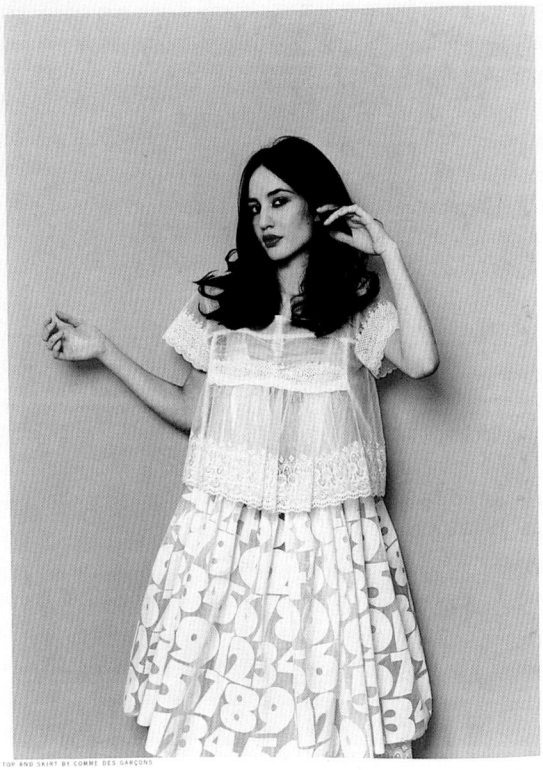

TOP AND SKIRT BY COMME DES GARÇONS

NYLON

THE HOMEFRONT
GOOD FASHION IS SIMPLE, ACCORDING TO LONDON'S DARLING DESIGNER LUELLA BARTLEY. GOOD FASHION IS CLOTHES THAT MAKE YOU FEEL ATTRACTIVE AND WARM. BABY ENOUGH THIS SPRING, THANKS TO THE COMFORTABLE, RELAXED STYLES AND BRIGHT, BLISSFUL SHADES FROM SUPERSTAR DESIGNERS SUCH AS CHANEL, YOHJI YAMAMOTO, AND JEAN PAUL GAULTIER. THE BEST PIECES WORK AS "DOUBLE SHIFT," AM. AND P.M., WORK AND PLAY. THIS MONTH, PHOTOGRAPHER DIRK SEIDEN SCHWAN EXPLORES THE NEXT GENERATION OF PALE SHADES, SOFT COLORS (FROM PINK TO BEIGE) THAT PACK THE VISUAL PUNCH OF WHITE. SHANNAN ROUSS INVESTIGATES THE CULT OF COLLECTING, IN "BEST OF SHOW." PHOTOGRAPHER DUC LAMC CAPTURES A CLOSE LOOK AT THE HIGH-IMPACT DETAILS OF HAUTE COUTURE, AND FOR THIS MONTH'S "21 QUESTIONS," BARTLEY TELLS *NYLON* THAT HOME IS WHERE HER ART IS.

nylon month *may* year *2002* page *099*

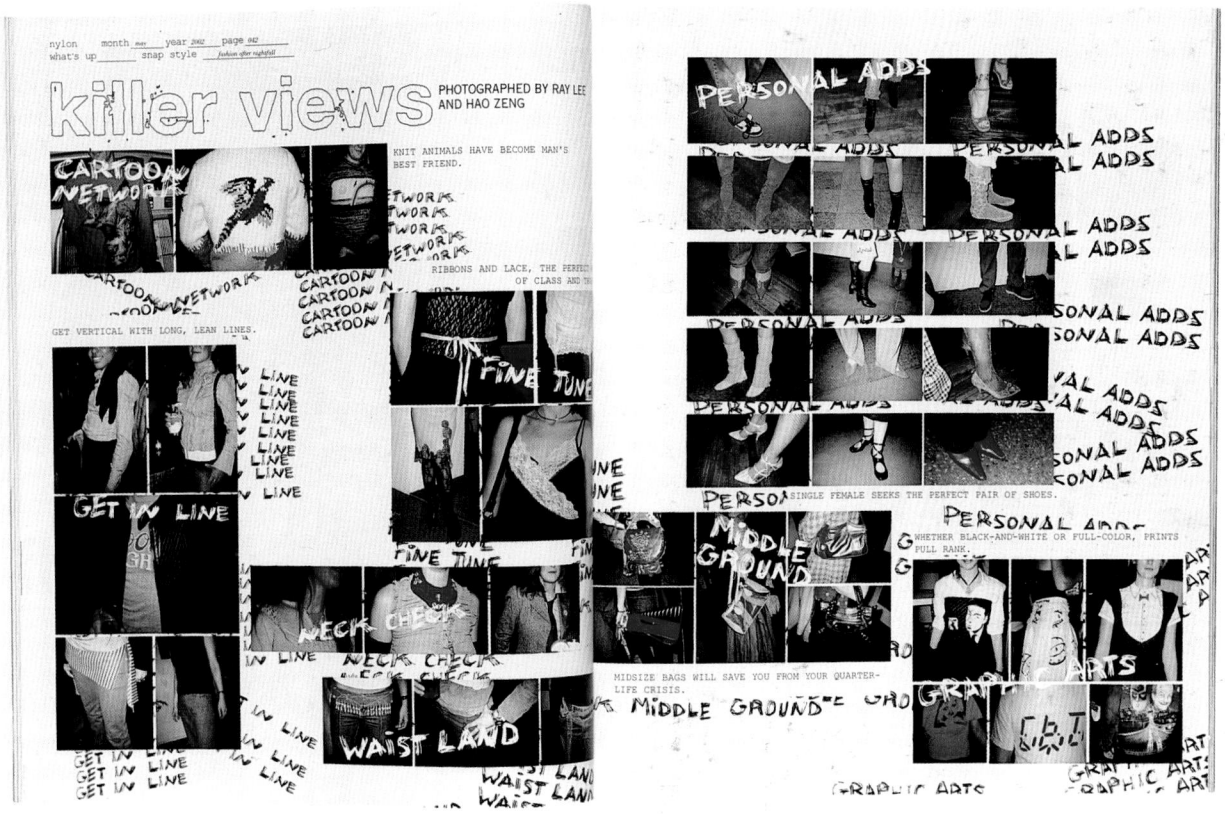

Nylon *(USA, May 2002) 230 x 274mm/9 x 10 7/8 inches*
The type elements here have been both handwritten and printed, rescanned and auto-traced to achieve this loose, distressed effect.
Art director *Lina Kutsovskaya*

Non Serious.

Hide! Join the Network. Information and communication technology devices and services permanently connect you to virtual networks of your choice but alienate you from your direct physical surroundings. Simultaneously, public space is transformed into an unclaimed territory, a wasteland where social exchange partners have given up responsibilities, engrossed in incomprehensible dialogues on mobile phones, exchanging data that never receives public significance. Join the Network. Hide!

By Daniel van der Velden.

'Hide!'

Go Away!

Page 24 out of 84

ok.

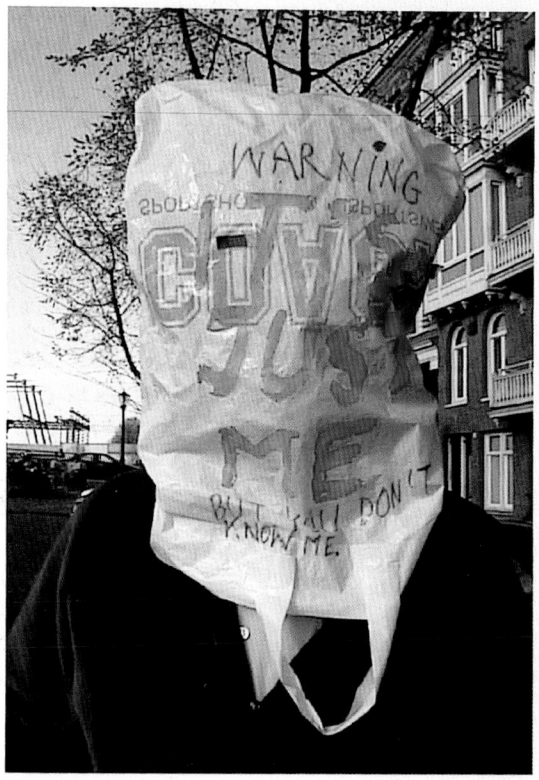

Page 25 out of 84

Thank you Post-It.

Freestylin': an analysis by Wilfried Nijhof and Jop van Bennekom.
Photography by Maurice Scheltens.

Not!

FreeStylin' Looking at forms of boredom. Creating clouds of text.

Page ~~15~~ 16

Notes

Page 17 out of 84

Re– *(The Netherlands, Issue 4, Summer 2000) 220 x 297mm/8 3/4 x 11 3/4 inches*
'The Boring Issue' featured handwritten notes and marks written across the pages, as if doodled on by a bored reader. These two spreads show two different ways the doodles were used to emphasize content. The first uses a heavy circular pattern all but obliterating the headline, echoing the headline 'Creating clouds of text'. The second features a feeble crossing out of the headline, 'Hide!', implying that hiding is all but impossible.
Design *Jap van Bennekom*

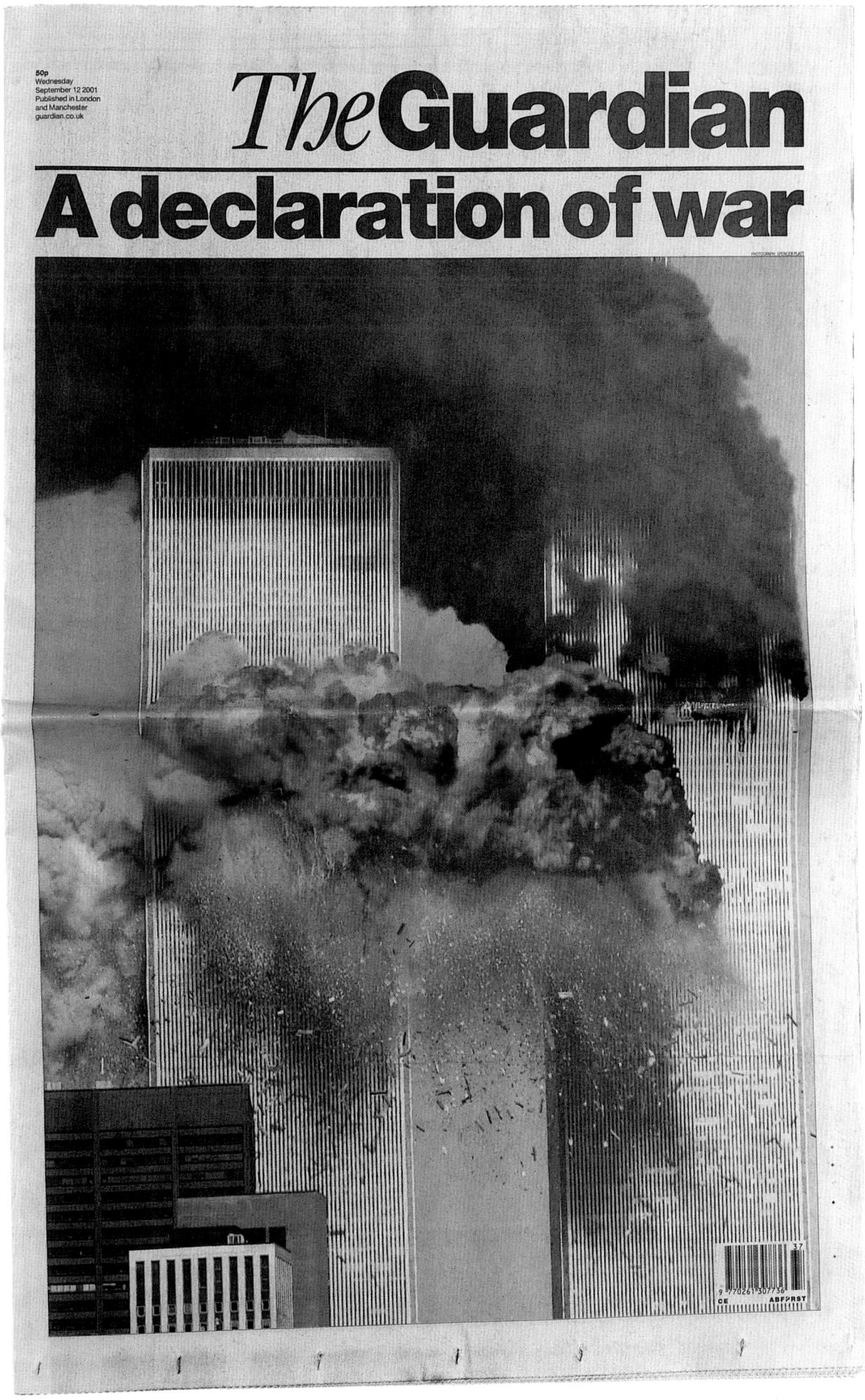

50p
Wednesday
September 12 2001
Published in London
and Manchester
guardian.co.uk

The Guardian

A declaration of war

PHOTOGRAPH: SPENCER PLATT

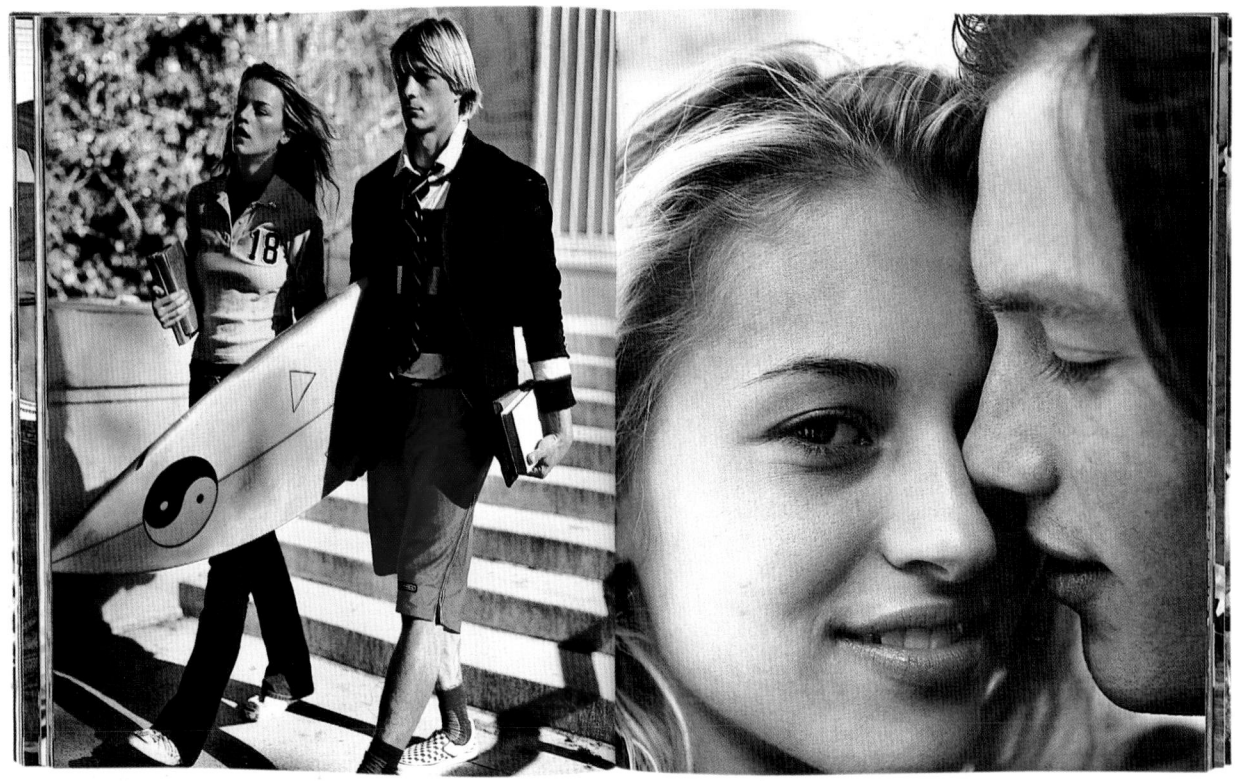

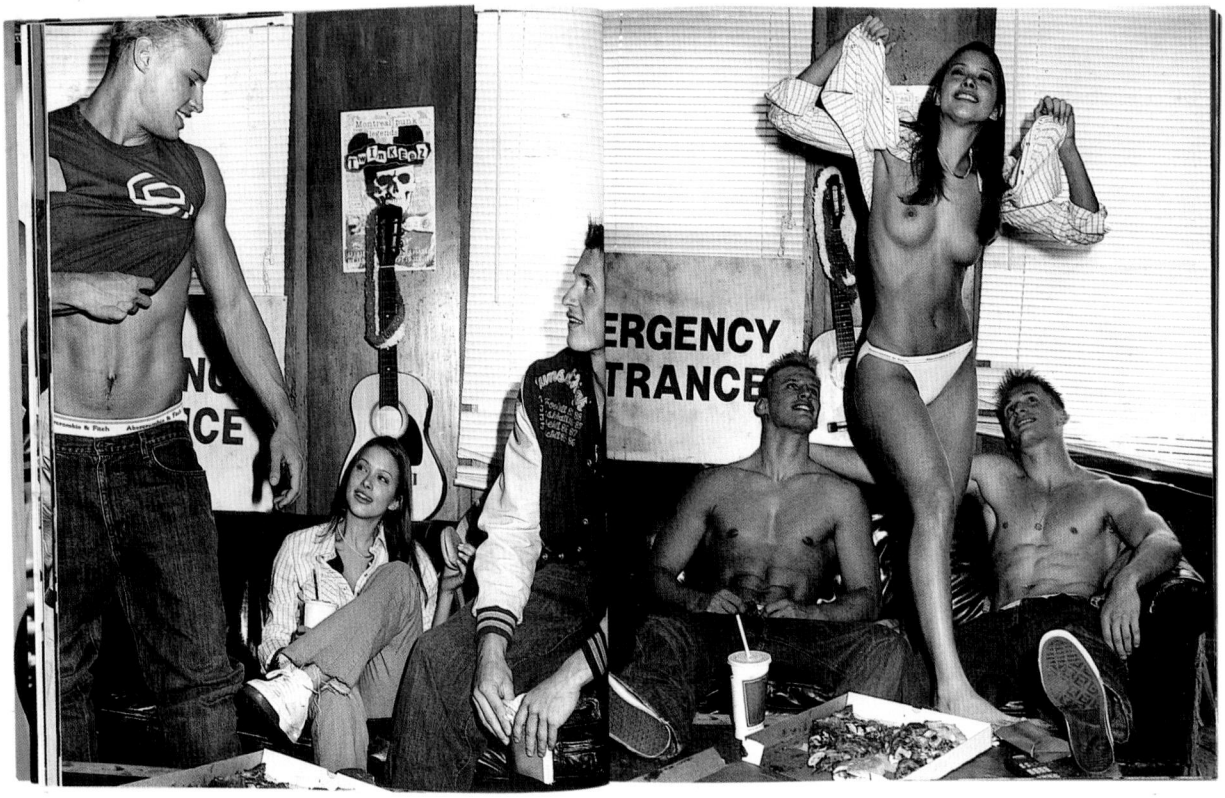

A&F Quarterly *(USA, Back to School Issue, 2001) 230 x 275mm/9 x 10 7/8 inches*
Fashion company Abercrombie & Fitch added an editorial element to their catalogue and relaunched it in a magazine format. This particular issue caused panic among America's religious right with its sexually provocative images of college life.
Photographer *Bruce Weber*

GQ *(UK, April 1998)*
220 x 285mm/8 3/4 x 11 1/4 inches
Such stories were once the mainstay of news magazines and newspaper supplements, but have become increasingly rare as they are squeezed out by celebrity interviews and fashion. In a curious turnabout, a magazine best known for its celebrity and fashion content, published this extraordinary 16-page photo essay about US gun culture.
Art director *Tony Chambers*
Photographer *Zed Nelson*

It is the medium that shapes and controls the
scale and form of human association and action.
— *Marshall McLuhan*

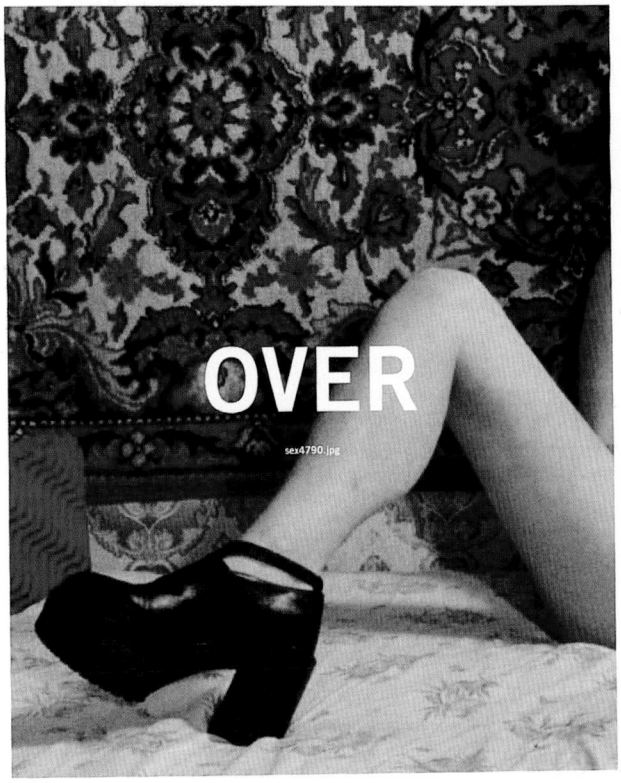

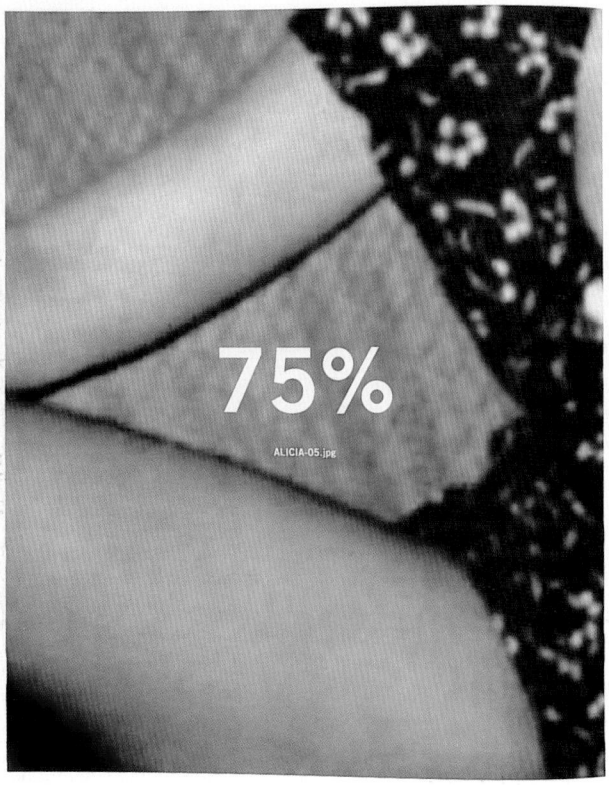

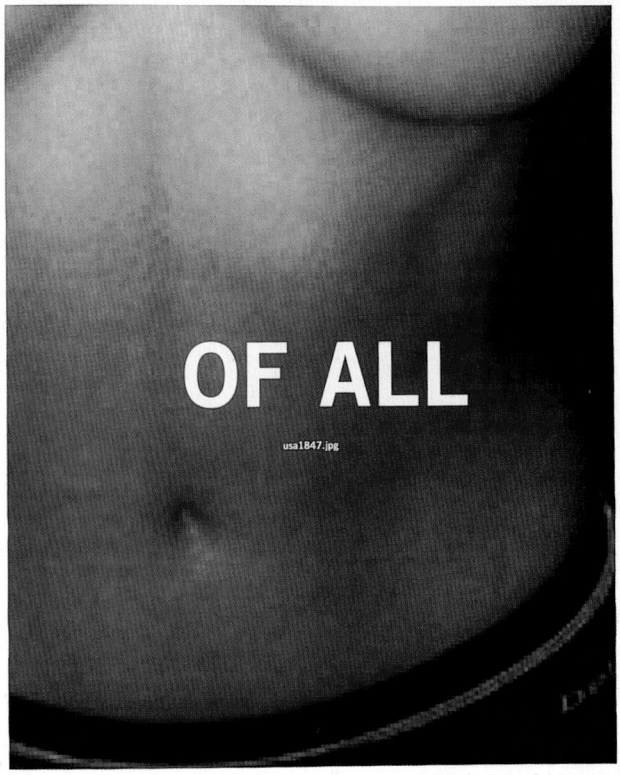

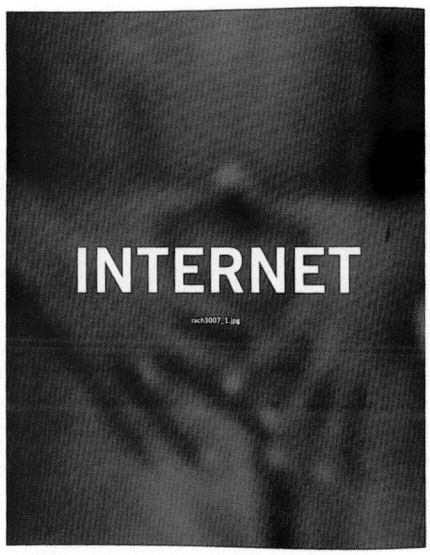

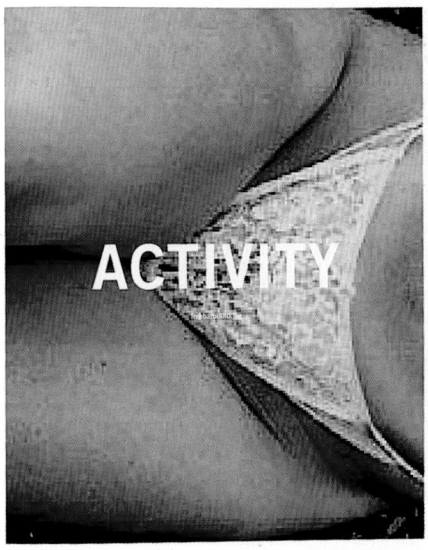

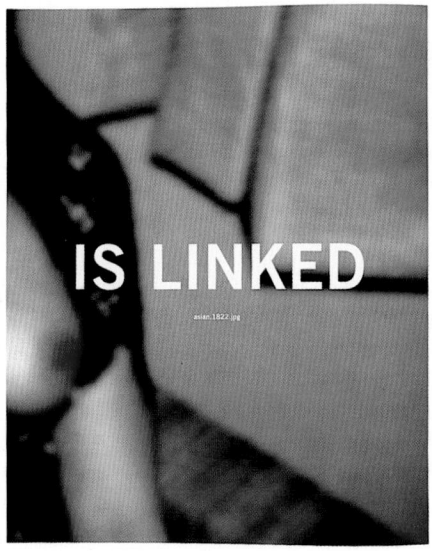

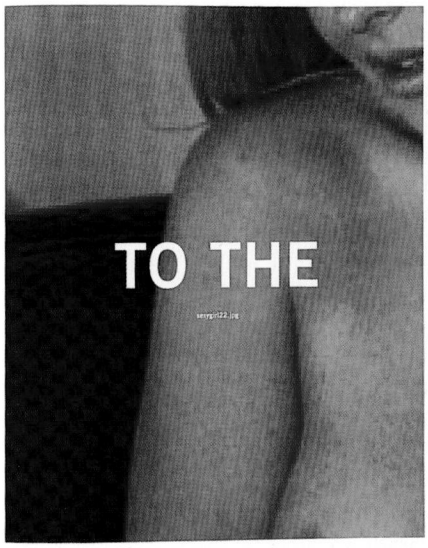

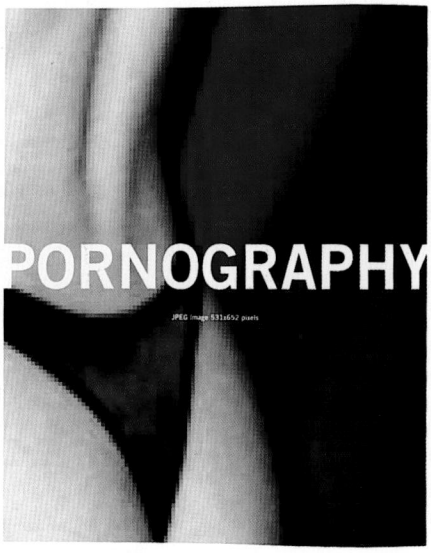

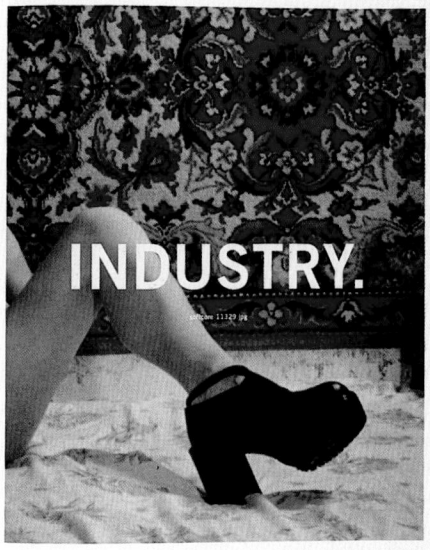

Coupe *(Canada, Issue 1, 1999) 245 x 293mm/9 3/4 x 11 1/2 inches*
A ten-page 'installation' uses a statement about internet usage and runs it across a selection of massively enlarged pieces of downloaded porn site JPEGs, to illustrate a quotation from Marshall McLuhan.
Art direction *The Bang*

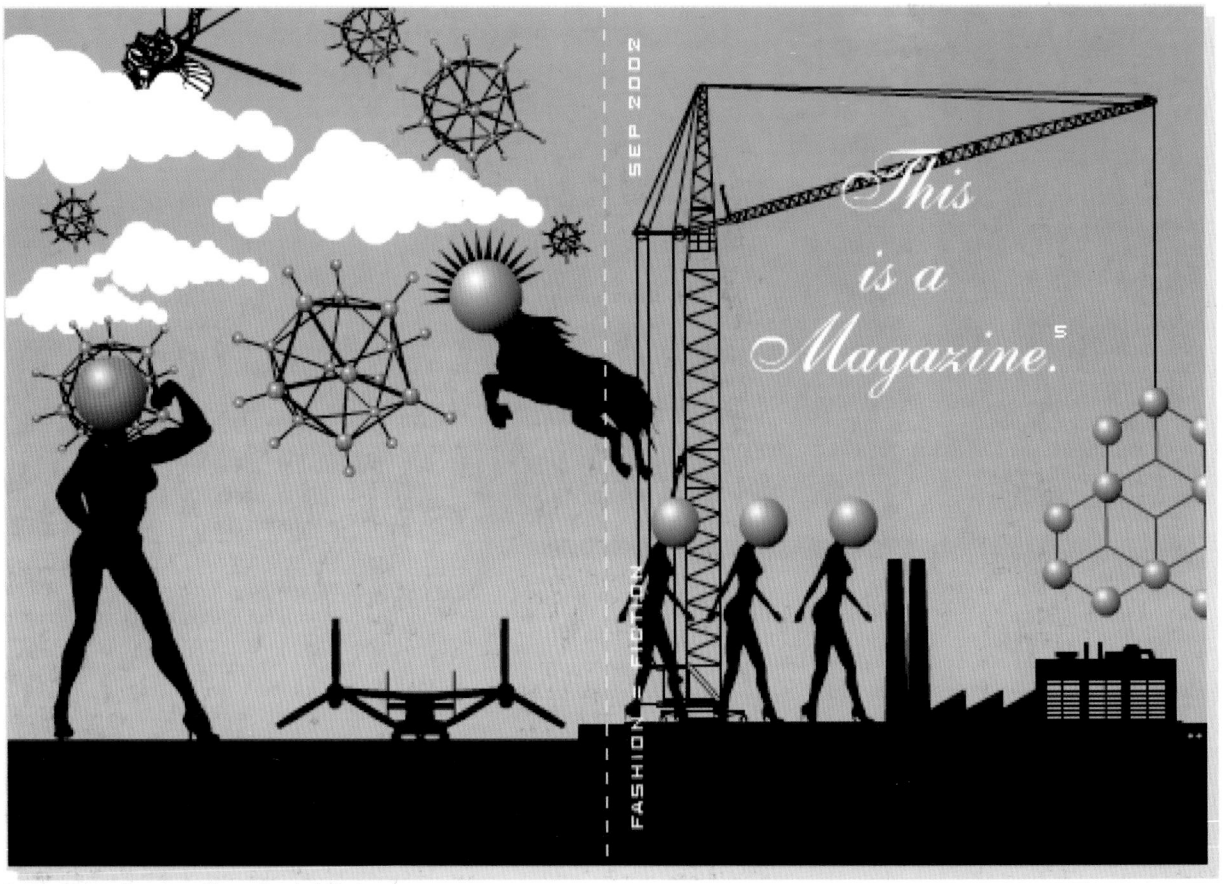

Issue 5, September 2002. Illustration *Andy Simionato*

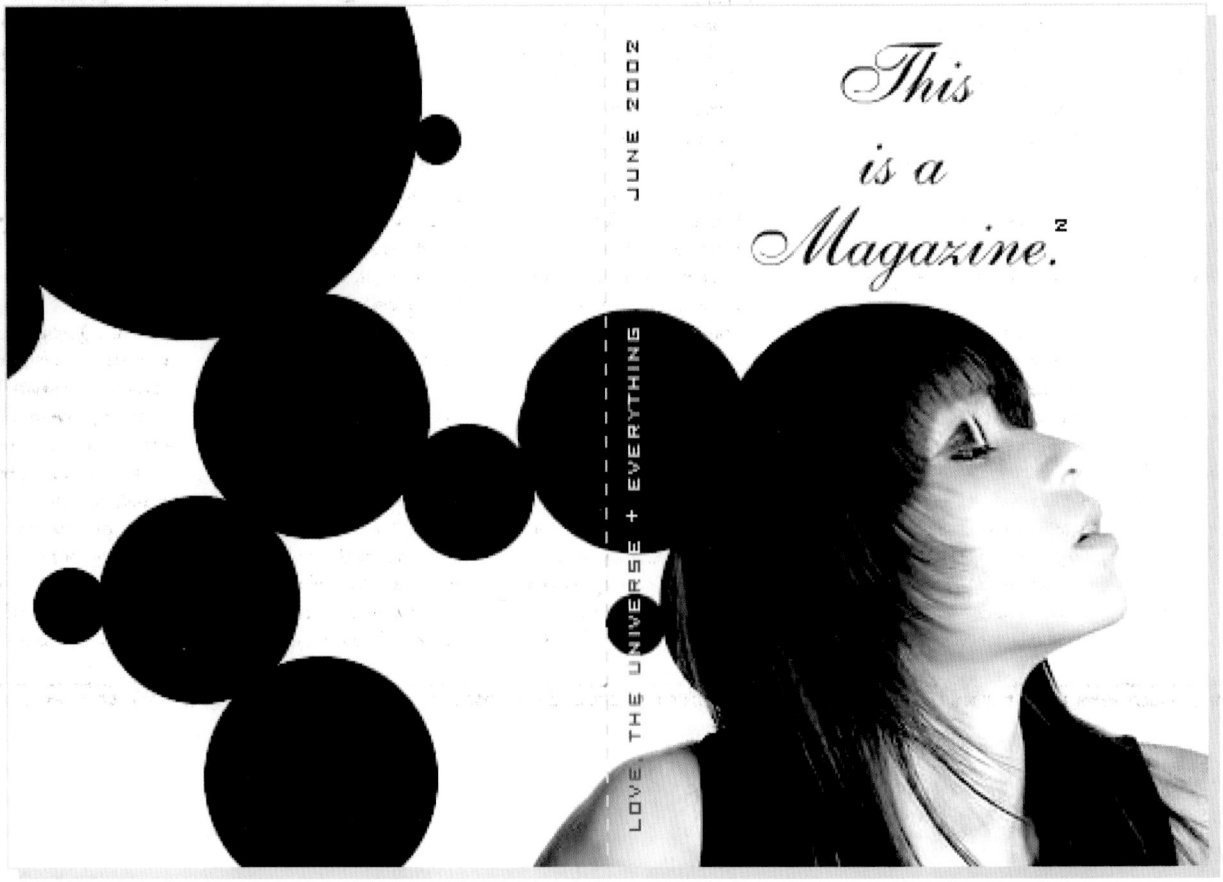

Issue 2, June 2002. Photography *Karen Ann Donnachie*

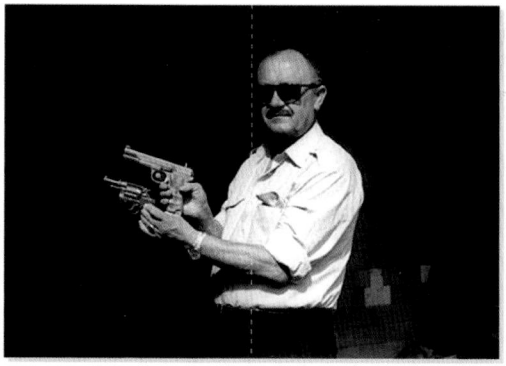

Issue 4, August 2002. Photography *Boogie*

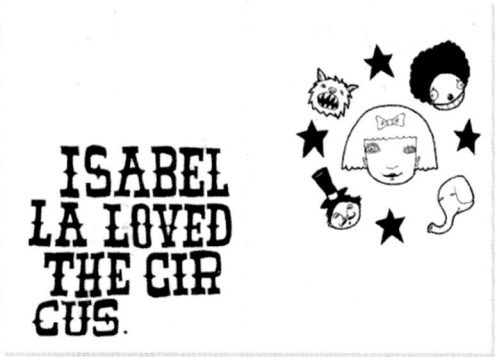

Issue 4, August 2002. Illustration *Wonder Wagon*

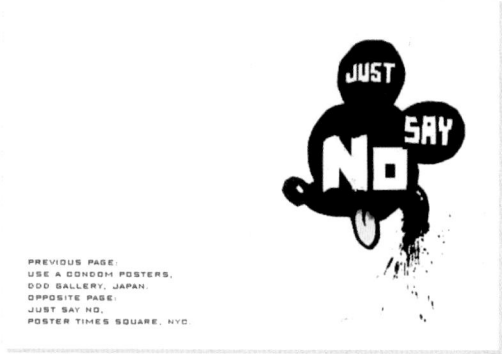

Issue 4, August 2002. Illustration *James Victore*

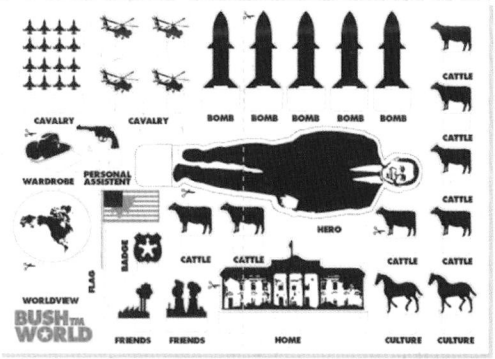

Issue 4, August 2002. Illustration *Our Machine*

Why does thisisamagazine (TIAM) use a print magazine format to display its pages?
Initially I was not really concerned with making a magazine-like interface; it simply suited our needs. I wanted a design that removed much of the conscious choice of mouse-clicking, that allowed the reader to return to absorbing the artwork. Moving left or right is already such a universal 'language' of magazines that it is no longer a conscious act.

Compared to most websites, magazines are so simple in structure, a product of cut pages stitched or bound together into a form that is both volume of work and a collection of articles, images and text. It minimizes the reader's decisions, in order to better perceive the artworks and articles. I believe it frees the artists to communicate with the greatest liberty, each one contributing to an overall effect.

In the same way, with our website you can start to read from the cover, or flip to the back and read from there. (Use the keys 'a' and 'z' respectively.) We are also developing a random key, where the reader can 'flick open' the online magazine at a random page.

Why do you also produce a printed edition?
Because you can't touch a pixel for quality. We sell the printed magazine online and through art galleries and bookstores. The profits (if any) will contribute to part of the expenses of the project. We are not interested in carrying advertising or commercializing the project in other ways.

How similar is the printed edition to the web edition?
The web edition is published once a month, and the print edition is published every three months as a compendium that contains almost all the original artists, but not every page is reproduced as it is in the online magazine. Instead, we reinterpret the articles with print considerations, such as through using fluorescent and metallic inks, forced mis-registration, and sometimes taking a completely new approach to the original story.

What are the differences between creating a magazine for print and for web?
Technically, the two processes are almost identical, even more so now that print design heavily uses CTP (computer to plate) and therefore remains digital practically to the printing press. What is different? The web magazine involves combining pixels and sound, the print magazine combines paper and ink. These physical differences involve different and important considerations: the screen involves projected light and moving pixels, which are transitory but infinitely reproducable. Print uses reflected light, and fixed ink, and its physical permanence has a finite life. Web / Print. A kind of Yin / Yang.

The web page pulses away forever, the print magazine is slowly consumed, and ages through use. Therefore, in our case we like to contrast or highlight these differences, allowing animation to contaminate the still images, to create a web magazine with 'inks' that dissolve and disappear, and a print magazine that has 'pixels' that jump (for example by using fluorescent inks or mis-registration).

In creating a magazine for print we must consider the element of consuming, owning. A pixel is infinitely reproducible without loss in quality, a printed page will have unique elements and be limited in distribution. It also immediately forms part of a consumer system. Whereas the web version is freely available (given the neccessary equipment and technology required to view it). We encourage the copying and distribution of the web version; it's only around 2MB so can be readily emailed.

The web version is owned by a single person, kept on a hard-drive, and 'read' only by that person, generally all in one sitting. Whereas there's a public

Interview

Andy Simionato
Art director
www.thisisamagazine.com

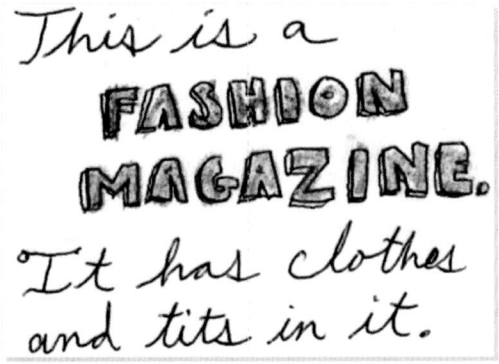

Issue 5, September 2002. Illustration *Reilly P Brennan*

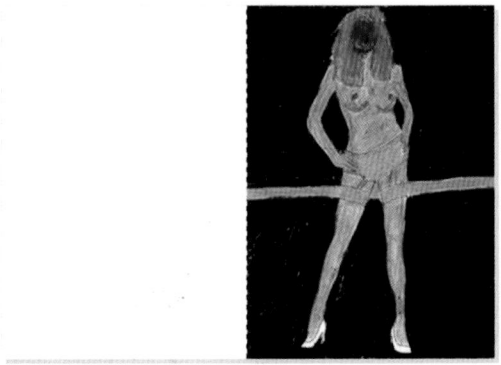

Issue 5, September 2002. Illustration *Reilly P Brennan*

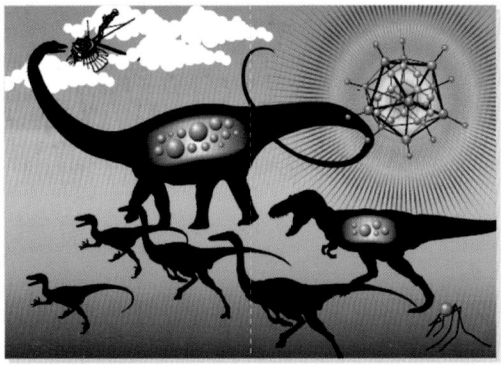

Issue 5, September 2002. Illustration *Andy Simionato*

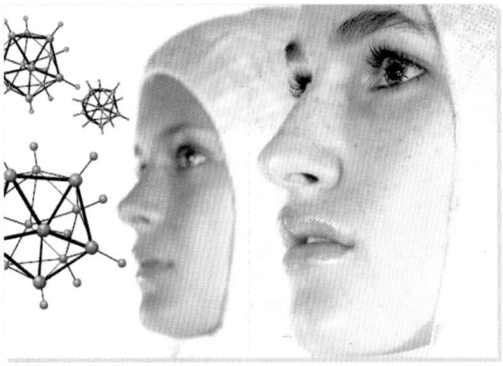

Issue 5, September 2002. Photography *Karen Ann Donnachie*

element to print to consider – the print version will be read in multiple sittings, in different places and by more than one person. People like to keep art-magazines on display, so visitors can browse them.

These considerations are what make the difference in creating the two objects. So I need to consider design elements, and editing choices respectively. In particular, difference in rhythm, density of information/detail, negative space and legibility issues, size and proximity of text to image. That's apart from more basic editorial choices in content. There are some analogies between the two however. For example, I 'read' animation online as special inks or punch-cuts on the printed page.

Ultimately I would like the two media to simultaneously inform and deconstruct each other, to connect and form new visual languages.

Who are your contributors?
Many of our contributors have been published elsewhere; for others this is the first time. Some are (in)famous: James Victore has produced some of the most polemic poster art in north America, such as the Disney Go Home series in Times Square, NYC. Others include Yanick Dusso, designer for Lord of the Rings, Anthony Burrill, Wonder Wagon and Takeshi Hamada who is already well known for producing his own independent magazines.

For me, what is important is the combination of artists. Each acts as a kind of lightning rod, and through placing them near to each other connections start to form. Artists are invited to contribute. Sometimes we provide a brief, other times I go from a suggestion by the artist him/herself. We collect and filter the artwork. Many articles are developed as collaborations, using our Milan studio as a base. We do a layout then test the results – posting the work online for a private contributor's viewing – and finally make the issue public. We announce the new issue to subscribers via email, along with secret sections and keys.

Who are your competitors?
There are many noteworthy online magazines (and I mean projects that are using magazine-style formats or languages of multiple page layouts) but my favourite is Tiger magazine (www.tigermagazine.org), which deals more with the art gallery world. When I saw it I immediately invited its creator Takeshi Hamada to contribute to TIAM. His beautiful drawings will also be featured in the printed version.

TIAM can only be unique through its content. There is a homogenization happening in mainstream magazines, brought about mainly by the competition for increasingly restricted markets and publicity motivated editing. The large number of similiar magazines on the market does not neccessarily indicate that the market is satisfied with what they offer. We continue to produce magazines because, ultimately, despite all the perfume/cell phone/leathergoods advertising financed material we want to have a means for one group of people to communicate something to another group of people. While we have stories to tell, there will always be magazines. They are store-houses (in italian the word for a warehouse is 'magazzino') for our culture.

What kind of response have you had to TIAM?
Issue 1 received more than 55,000 unique visitors, which knocked us out since we didn't even register the magazine in the search engines. We are currently on about 30,000. I start an hour earlier each day so I can respond to all the emails.

Emails and messages have been extremely supportive, as if we are doing something strange or unique but I think this is an exaggeration. We just made a toy, and others enjoy playing with it too. Perhaps there is simply a need to play more.

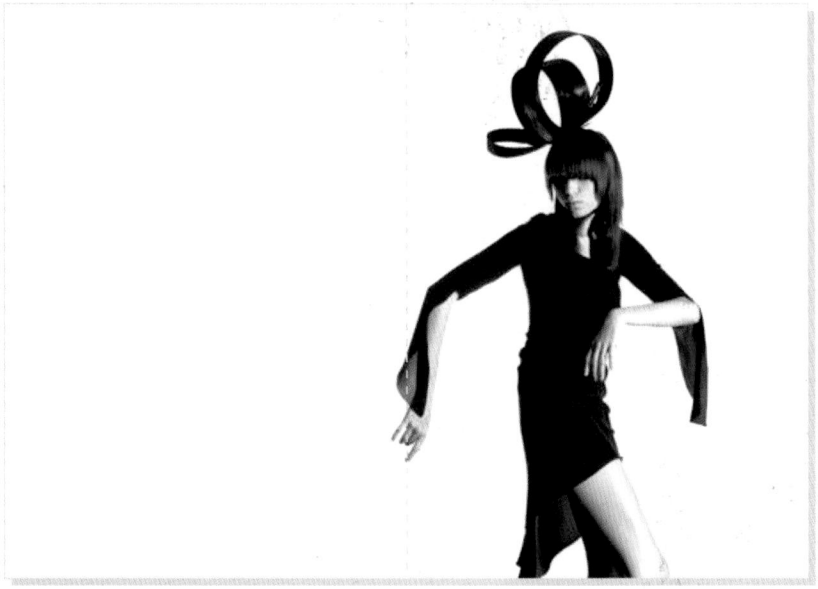

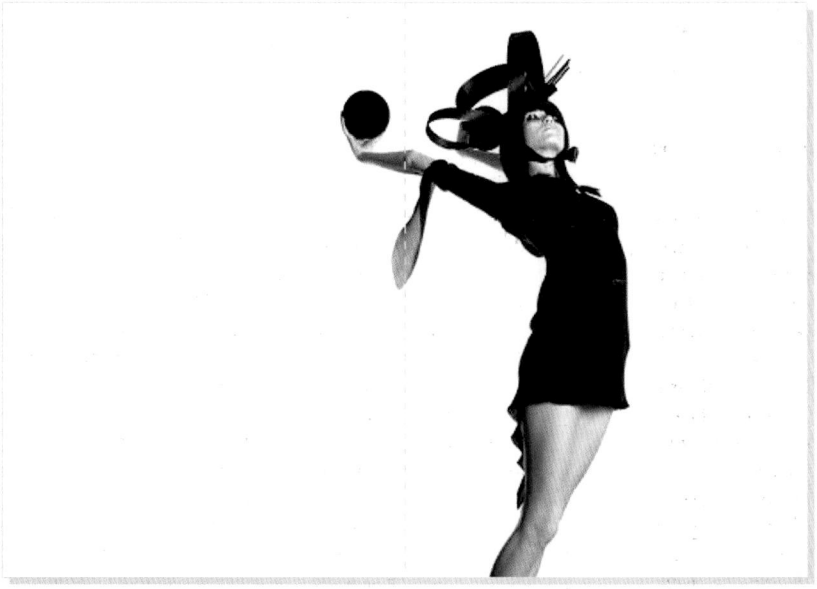

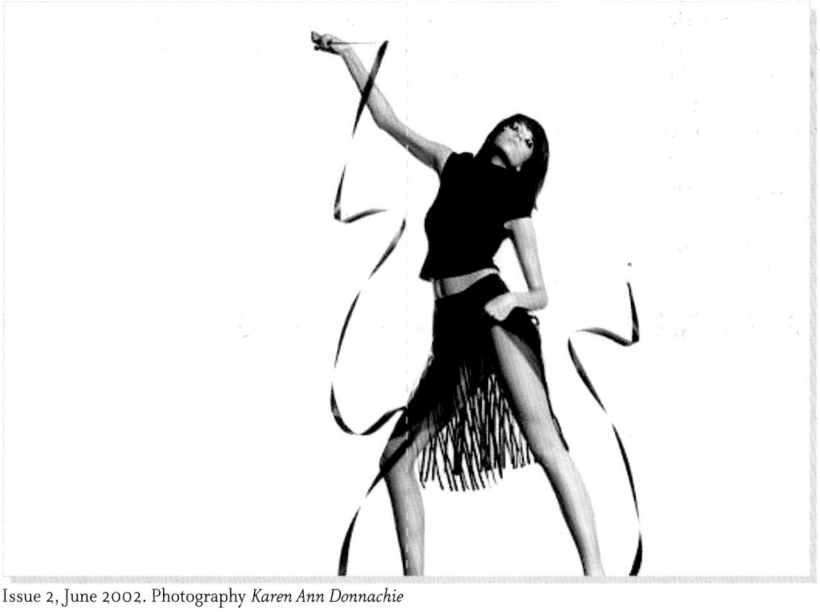

Issue 2, June 2002. Photography *Karen Ann Donnachie*

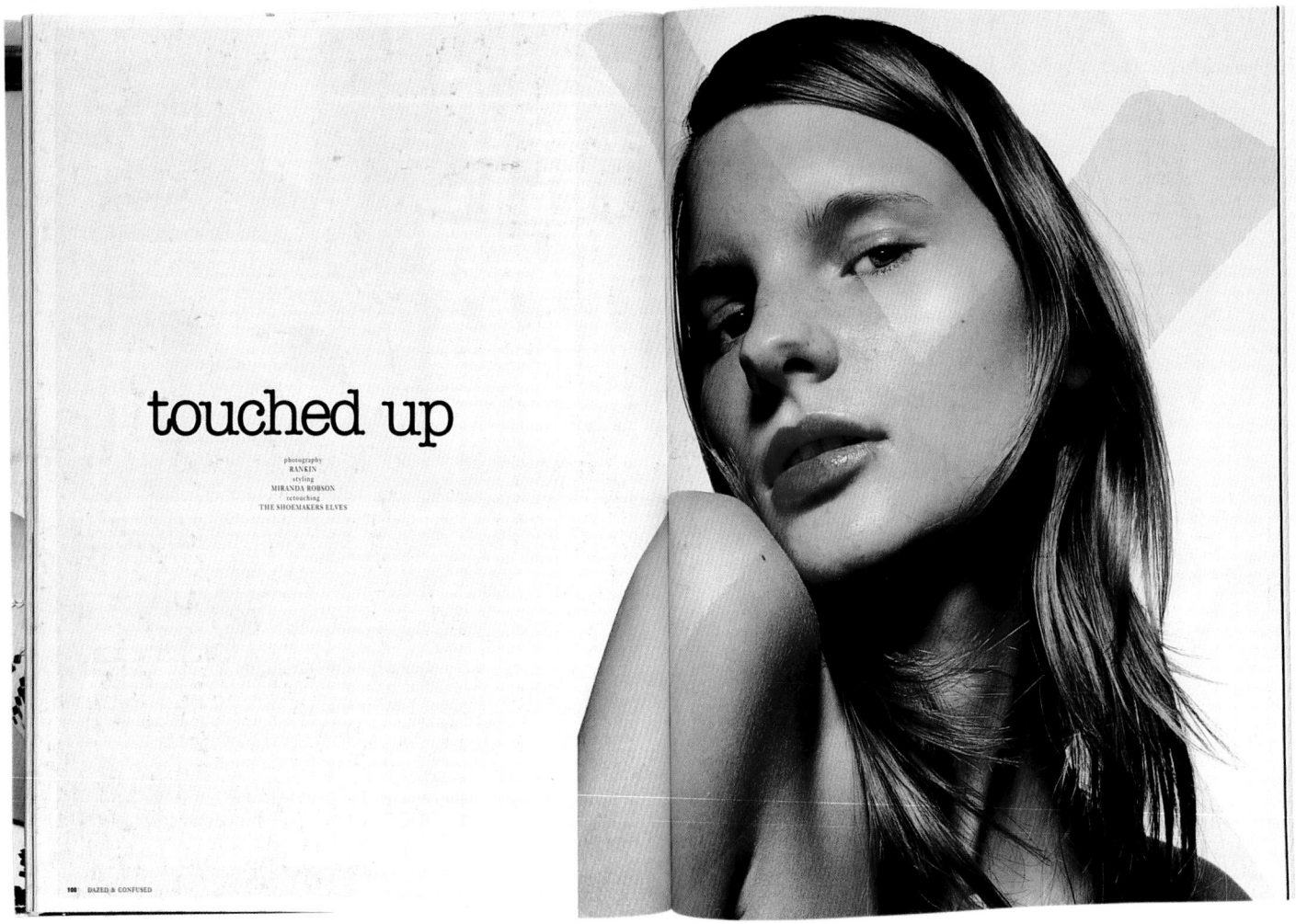
touched up
photography
RANKIN
styling
MIRANDA ROBSON
retouching
THE SHOEMAKERS ELVES
100 DAZED & CONFUSED

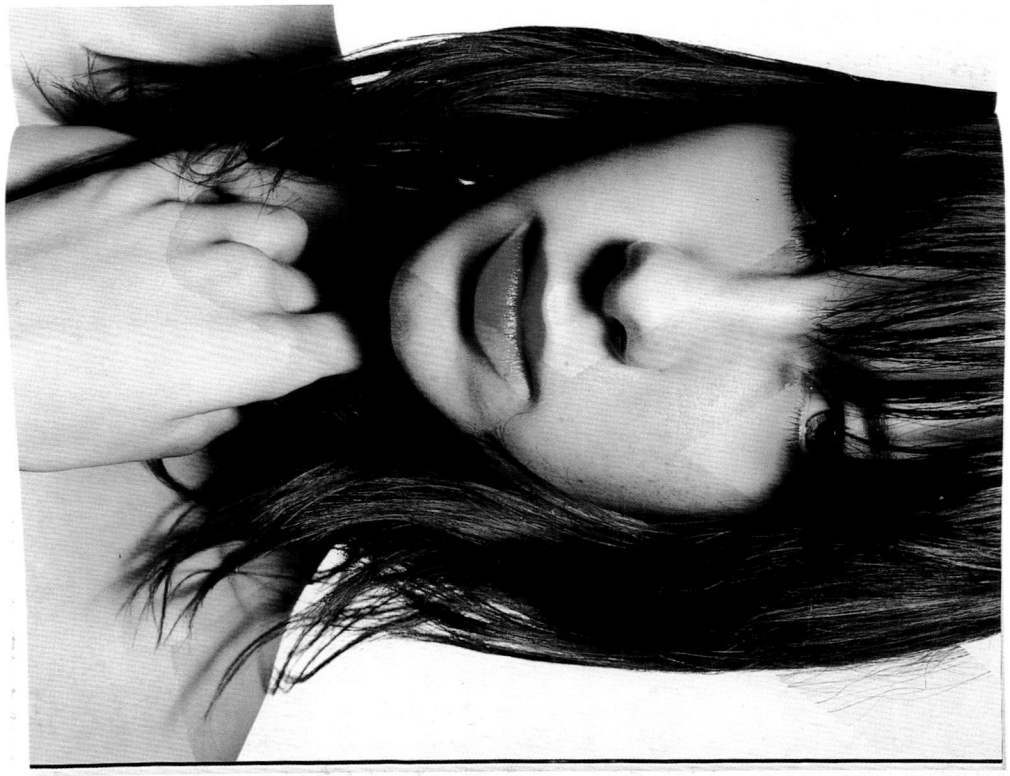

Dazed & Confused *(UK, Issue 85, January 2002)*
230 x 300mm/9 x 11 7/8 inches
This fashion story was demonstrating the extent of retouching now routinely carried out on fashion pictures. The images have been heavily retouched but the areas behind the large crosses have been reproduced un-retouched.
Art director *Suzy Wood* Photographer *Rankin*

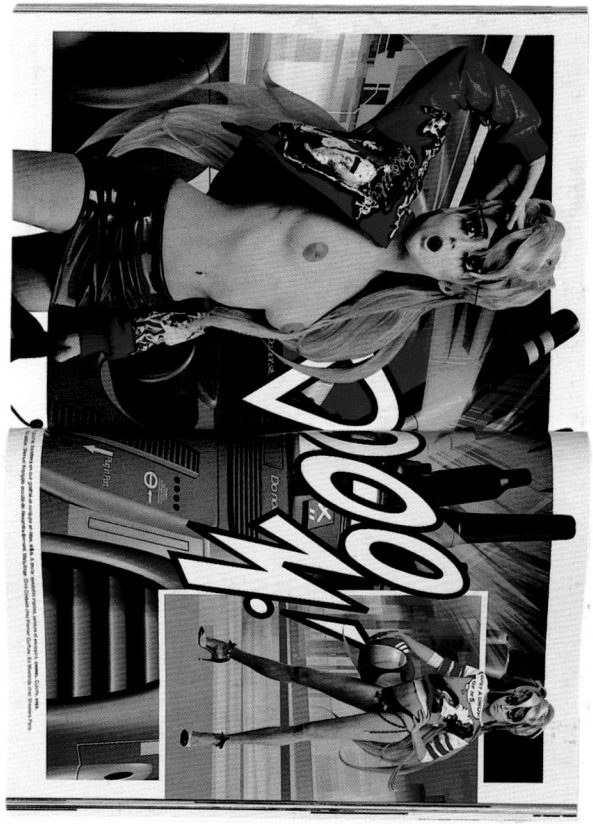

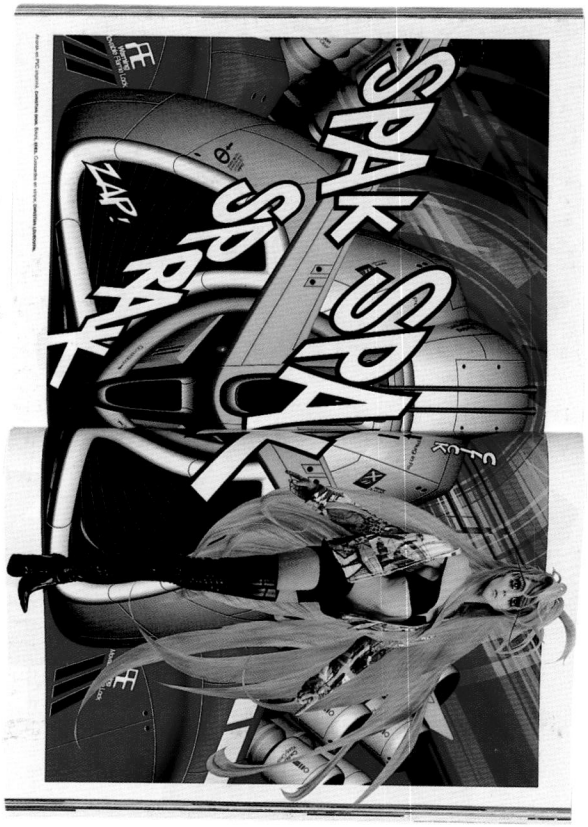

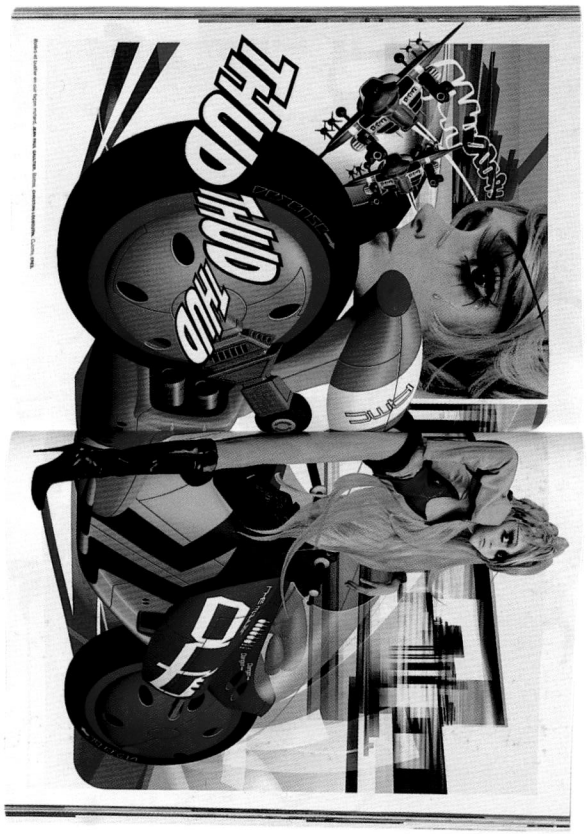

THIS PAGE **Details** *(USA, Issue 2, November 2000)*
230 x 275mm/9 x 10 7/8 inches
Photography and illustration combine in lo-tech style: a fashion story drawn by a young artist, based on photographs by his father.
Art director *Rockwell Harwood* Drawings *Riccardo Sorrenti, based on photographs by Mario Sorrenti*

OPPOSITE **Numero** *(France, Issue 26, September 2001)*
230 x 300mm/9 x 11 7/8 inches
Photography and illustration combine with digital technology in this manga-style fashion story created by Me Company.
Art director *Emma Wizman*

It's 2pm on a brisk Belgrade afternoon as I meet Madonna at the Serbo-Croat Virtual Mothering Institute where she is taking a break from undergoing a simulated birth to meet me. She is smaller than she seems in her ads for her spray-on lingerie collection. Her hair is scraped back into a long grey ponytail and she wears a turquoise bio-sensory boiler suit, which I immediately recognise as one of only a handful made by Gligoroy Ljubco, *enfant terrible* of the Macedonian fashion world.

Nova: 'Hello.' **M:** 'Hi. Have a pod. Drink? Wait. Don't get up. Let the help do it. Britney, Christina...' **N:** 'So, your move to Belgrade – nobody anticipated that.' **M:** 'Yeah, I know. But there's something about this town. It's not just the fashion, the fractured sense of history, the turn-of-the-century architecture... It's the artistic vibe. It's like London was 20 years ago... urban, gritty and real and, you know what, less clone-infested than other parts of the world. I mean the last time I was in the States, I had, like, double vision.' **N:** 'Yes, I heard San Francisco just broke the record for the highest number of Madonna clones inhabiting a city.' **M:** 'Yeah – they're all still in their teens, but, yeah, there are 37 of the things stomping around over there.' **N:** 'So you regret having promoted your last-but-one album, *Genealogy*, by cloning yourself 20 times over?' **M:** 'Well, it was a groundbreaking thing. Besides, all 20 of those clones were allocated good homes in stable gay families before we went ahead.' **N:** 'Madonna, you're about to make your own contribution to world under-population.' **M:** 'Yeah – I had these eggs frozen 16 years ago and just kind of held on to them. But now that most people don't have time to have kids any more and since Guy went off to direct *Mange* – I thought, "I'm going to have one of these things fertilised."' **N:** 'Who's the lucky sperm donor?' **M:** 'Well, I was looking to give birth to a brainy, good-looking sort of a kid. Lysander [Kate Moss's son by her marriage to Noam Chomsky] just seemed the obvious choice. His parents gave him permission. It's not like he doesn't produce the stuff by the gallon-load. Fifteen-year-old boys will be fifteen-year-old boys...' **N:** 'What about your other children? There's talk of a rift between you and Lourdes...' **M:** 'It's not really the nun thing [Lourdes enrolled in a convent at 16]. It's just that I was so hurt when she refused to duet with me on a cover of *Mistletoe and Wine*.' **N:** 'And your son?' **M:** 'He can't sing.' **N:** 'But your relationship...?' **M:** 'It's good. In fact, he was the one who persuaded me to buy up London Underground and turn it into a tourist attraction.' **N:** 'And it's been a success, along with the Floppy-Go-Slippy™ solar-powered flip-flop and your reinterpretation of the Mrs Robinson role after Jerry Hall's 18-year run. Any other projects up your sleeve?' **M:** 'A photographic study: Sixty Nudes at *Sixty*, and I'm playing Gertrude in the CD-Rom adaptation of *Hamlet*.'
MELANIE HOWARD, TREND PREDICTOR FOR THE FUTURE FOUNDATION

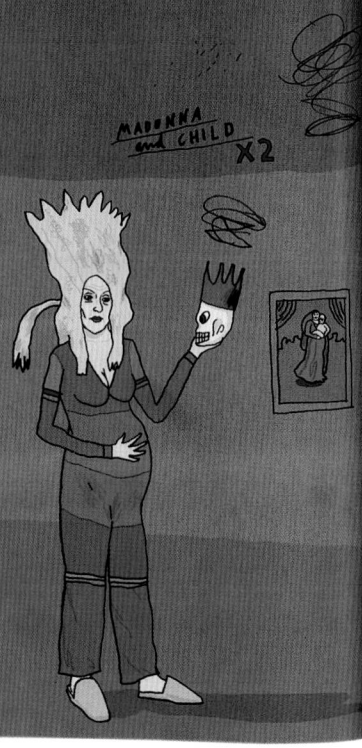

We're two journalists aged 10 and 12 and today *Nova* has asked us to interview Madonna at a beauty parlour for the magazine. We are living in 2020. Madonna is 62 and looks young for her age but not so pretty. She is wearing glasses disguised as sunglasses because of her poor eyesight. Her body is slim and she has no flab because she goes to the gym every day. She is wearing a lot of mascara on her face and a lady is plucking her eyebrows quite thin. She is having her hair dyed light ginger and put into ringlets. She is having her nose and eyebrows pierced. She is wearing the latest clothes, a lot of leather, a tight top and a big floppy parka jacket. She has a mobile phone with a colourful cover.

Men still like her, especially those in their 40s: they think she's sexy. Men in their 30s think she looks good for her age. She takes getting old well and was happy to retire because it meant people stopped mobbing her when she went out.

She lives alone in the country because she is old and needs more fresh air. She is seen driving round in different cars and has one that is able to turn into a boat and an aeroplane just like James Bond. She also likes to ride around on motorbikes.

Madonna asks the woman plucking her eyebrows to put on some music. She is still involved in the world of music. She makes guest appearances with Robbie Williams and Craig David, but her main job is managing young pop bands. She shows up at big awards parties but isn't in the charts anymore.

Madonna is on television and in newspapers because she still goes to posh dancing clubs. Her children are famous singers, dancers and in films. Older people remember her songs but there are a whole new generation of kids and bands that don't know her. She doesn't care though because she's really cool.
LOUISE MARIE ELKANS, 12, AND CINDY CROME, 10

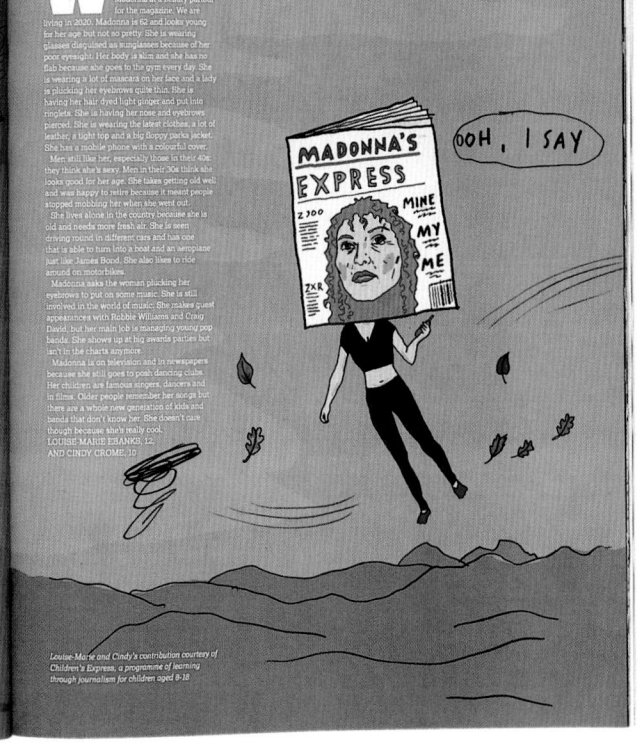

Louise-Marie and Cindy's contribution courtesy of Children's Express, a programme of learning through journalism for children aged 9-18

There is something unsettling about meeting Madonna in her new house. Maybe it's because her new house is the Kremlin, which she picked up when Russia became part of The United States of the World. But what is really unnerving is the lady herself, who has gone through so many reincarnations it is impossible to predict who she will be next. Last month it was Pepe le Pew, before that Mahatma Ghandi.

Madonna sits upright on the edge of a Regency chair. Her hair is light brown and coiffed into a solid mass – it resembles a helmet. She wears flesh-coloured tights, a woollen navy blue skirt and a matching jacket. Her hands are folded onto what appears to be a brick nestling in her lap – it turns out to be a handbag. 'Do sit down,' she says. Her accent is unmistakable: an American take on British upper class. Of course! It's so obvious. This month Madonna is Margaret Thatcher.

As she is now the world's richest woman, few people risk critiquing Madonna's metamorphoses. Indeed, nobody batted an eye when she turned up at Patsy Kensit and Leo Blair's engagement party, a pair of giant black ears pasted to her head (Mini Mouse). Nor did anyone comment when, having spent an alleged £1 million on the outfit, she presented the Oscars from inside an aluminium case (the Tin Man).

Each new 'style' has generated a financial whirlwind. It was Madonna who extended the concept of a fashion accessory to include everything from aeroplanes to real estate. 'You can't get the look without the detail' has been her mantra ever since her Abraham Lincoln phase, during which she bought Mount Rushmore and popularised the use of testosterone among women in a bid to grow a beard. Her stovepipe hat sits on the sideboard as a reminder.

But who is the real Madonna? 'Good question,' she says wavering between today's English accent and the Urdu twang she likes to adopt with close friends. 'To be honest, I lost my identity a while back and I can't seem to find it. I mean, one minute I'm working on a cover version of the *Waltons* theme tune and the next... I look in the mirror only to find Pope Jean-Paul I staring back at me. At first it scared the shit out of me but after a while I thought, "Hey, white really is your colour."'

Madonna looks the picture of relaxed, right-wing elegance. At 60 her body has reached its physical peak. And half the world knows it intimately – thanks to the range of 'salt and pepper' shakers she had made in her likeness last year.

So what next for this makeover junkie? 'Well it's either Jean-Paul Belmondo or I set up my own fashion line as myself circa 1982. Now that fashion has become so stuffy, I think this could be the right time. I mean, look at Alexander McQueen – Siamese twins on the runway? How terribly bourgeois.' Any clues as to what she might be including in her first collection? 'Think fingerless lace gloves,' she twinkles mysteriously.
DAVID WOLFE, FASHION EXPERT

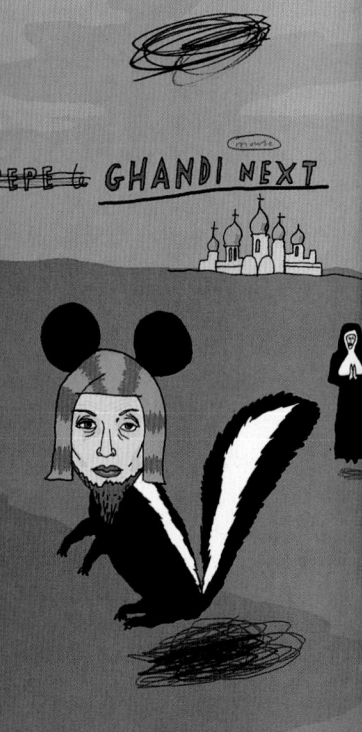

Guru, poet, publishing magnate Madonna, the world's most influential businesswoman-cum-spiritual leader, sits atop her rattan chair and picks up her pan pipes. Just over a million people have made the pilgrimage to see her here today, live in Hyde Park, and although for most of them she is but a tiny speck on the womb-shaped stage, it was worth the journey. 'She changed my life,' whispers Lourdes, a 60-something female fan from New Mexico who changed her name by deed poll 24 years ago when Madonna gave birth to her first daughter. A hush descends upon the crowd. 'She's going to read from *Touched for the Very First Time*,' squeals 55-year-old Bart from Oslo.

As Madonna begins to read, members of the crowd assume The Noose, the beads wrapped around their neck yoga position that she first championed in the belatedly acknowledged classic film, *The Next Best Thing*. 'Open your heart to me,' she says in the voice that has graced a thousand audio-tapes. 'Beautiful strangers – if I ran away I'd never have the strength to go very far.' Her mane of white hair tumbles down her back, her pale billowing garments swirl about her neat frame, her pale limbs are adorned by countless rings and bangles, and her unmade-up face is partly framed by the chiffon drape that erupts from the medieval cone she wears on her head. All of this is set off by Madonna's trademark Bruce Ivory cane, that has become such a must-have since she first modelled at the launch of Stephen Hawkins' 22nd tome, *A Brief History of Pop*.

It's been a tricky ride to the top for the queen of karma, whose role models include Clarinda McUgly, Teresa and, more controversially, God. 'Well, she's a woman isn't she?' Madonna famously quipped in an interview with *The Catholic Herald* five years ago. Having taken a public vow of celibacy in her late 50s, Madonna had to work hard to convince her public this was not just another publicity stunt and enlisted the help of Rabbi Macauley Culkin. It was Culkin who convinced her to donate her entire £1 million high-heeled shoe collection to charitable projects in Asia and invest the next few years helping to raise funds for disadvantaged children and the politically oppressed – earning her the title 'The High Priestess of Hearts'. No wonder, then, that when, last year, she experienced what she describes as a 'vision', there was speculation that Madonna and The Madonna had finally met.

The change in image has meant a change in her circle of friends. Gone are the Gwyneth Paltrows and the William Orbits – instead Martin Amis, Camille Paglia and the actor-turned-UN Secretary BA Baracus take turns to meditate and read each other's auras in the VIP box. As Madonna launches into her Celtic interpretation of *The Rind*, they pause, perhaps awed by her command of the harp. Madonna in her sixties is a breathtaking sight – a teacher, a leader but, most important, a friend.
KIM FARNELL, ASTROLOGER

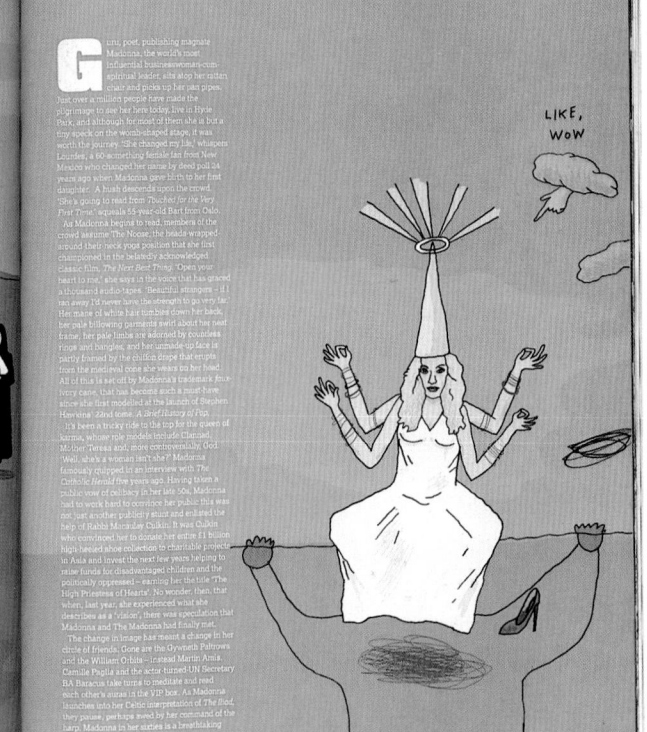

Nova *(UK, Issue 5, October 2000) 230 x 290mm/9 x 11 ½ inches*
Another example of the combined methods of working with analogue and digital: these images of Madonna were hand-drawn, scanned and coloured on the computer and supplied to the magazine as a digital file.
Art director *Gerard Saint* Drawings *Paul Davis*

LIBRARY & RESOURCES AREA EPSOM CAMPUS
THE SURREY INSTITUTE OF ART & DESIGN

Credits, Index

Thank you...

All the art directors, designers, editors and publishers whose co-operation and advice made this book possible

Richard Dean for photographing the magazines

Zoe, Jo, Laura and Felicity at Laurence King Publishing

Steve Martin for help from Japan, Lewis Blackwell for help with the title, Marc Vialli and Montse for opening Magma, a store capable of sating my magazine addiction

Lesley, Cameron and Ewan for putting up with me working evenings and weekends

And Jean Baisier, Lucas Badtke-Berkow, Jop van Bennekom, Peter Bilak, Marion Bouchard, Josefin Brink, Anthony Burrill, Simon Esterson, Fernando Gutierrez, Jessica Gysel, Andreas Hoyer, Warren Jackson, Mayumi & Daisuke Kawasaki, Nigel Kendall, Andreas Lange, Martin Lilja, Jarno Luotonen, Anja Lutz, Sandra von Mayer-Myrtenhain, Lionel Moinier, Dave Niddrie, Andrew Pothecary, Christopher Sanderson, Brian Saffer, Astrid Stavro, Gijs Stork, Winnie Terra, Daniel van der Velden, Jan Walaker, John L Walters and Clare Watters

www.magculture.com
Like the pictures? The real things are even better. Visit *www.magCulture.com* for magazine stockists and links to web magazines

Page numbers in *italics* refer to captions.

032c (Germany) 15, *53, 129*
10 (UK) 15, 16
10,000 Maniacs (Italy) *55*
55 (Brazil) *50*

A&F Quarterly (US) 14, *158*
AA Magazine (UK) 12, 14
Adbusters (US) 7, 15, 17, *55, 84, 136*
Aggugini, Kinder 17
Al Fayed, Mohamed 9-10
Almond, Darren *93*
AM7 (Germany) 15, *65*
Anderson, Pamela 74
Another Magazine (UK) 15, 17, *120*
Antoni Cases Associats 25
Apple Macintosh 6-7, 8, 22
Archis (The Netherlands) 15, *63, 149*
Arena Homme Plus (UK) *71*, 73, *118*
Army (UK) 13
Axis (Japan) 99

Bare (UK) *77, 86, 112*
Baron, Fabien 10, 25
Beach Culture (US) 10
Beast (UK) *19*, 20
Bell, Nick 145-6
BEople (Belgium) *60*
Big (US) 15, *93*
Black Book (US) *85*
Black, Roger 25
Blah Blah Blah (UK) 9
Blommers, Anuschka *39*
Boston Globe (US) 23
Brainheart (Sweden) *108*
Brand Eins (Germany) *67*
Branquinho, Veronique *41*
Brody, Neville *10*
Brutus (Japan) 100-1
Bulgaria (Finland) *28-9*
Burgoyne, Patrick 18-21
Business, The (UK) 24, *57*

Caldwell, Nemone 19, 21
Carl's Cars (Sweden) 15, *139*
Carson, David 7, 9, 10, 16
Carter, Lee 20-1
Catalogue (The Netherlands) 15, *45*
Chambers, Tony 73-4
Chicago Tribune (US) 23
Coca-Cola *123*
Composite (Japan) 99
Condé Nast 14, 73, 74
Copenhagen Living (Denmark) *115*
Cosmopolitan (International) 9
Cosmo Girl (US) 13
Coupe (Canada) 15, *58, 161*
Cowles, Andy 8-11
Cre@te (UK) *77*
Creative Review (UK) 19, 21
Cyzo (Japan) *69*

D (Italy) 24, *116*
Dagens Nyheter (Denmark) 24
Dahl, Sophie *77*
Dawson, Richard *93*
Dazed & Confused (UK) 7, 17, *167, 171*
Deliciae Vitae (France) 15, 16, 17
Details (US) *132, 168*
Dimanche.ch (France) 24-5
Doing Bird (Australia) 15
Domus (Italy) *48*
Dornbracht *41*
Dot Dot Dot (UK) *55, 148*

Dune (Japan) 100
Dutch (France) 15

Eat (Japan) *47, 80,* 100
Eichler, Sandra 125
Elle (Japan) 99
Emap 8
Empire (UK) 8
Esquire (UK) 74
Estampa (Brazil) 24
Esterson, Simon 24
Exit (UK) 15, *53*
Eye (UK) *19,* 20, *89,* 144–7

Face, The (UK) 10, 11, 15, 16, 17, *95*
FHM (UK) 8, 9, 73
Financial Times (UK) 24, *57*
Fleckhaus, Willy 23
Ford *111*
Fortune (Japan) 99
Frame (The Netherlands) 7, *139*
Frankfurter Allgemeine Zeitung (Germany) 23, 25
Froelich, Janet 24
Frost, Vince 24
Fujimoto, Yasushi 100

Garcia, Mario 22, 25
GettyImages *58*
Gill, Eric 10
Good Book, The (UK) *97*
GQ (UK) 73, 74, *75, 159*
Guardian, The (UK) 23–4, 25, *156*

Harper's Bazaar (US) 10, 15, 16
Harvey Nichols Magazine (UK) *119*
Hillman, David 23
Hint (US) 20–1
Holtzman, Joseph 16–17
Holzer, Jenny 24
Horse & Pony (UK) 8
Hot Air (UK) *82*
Hot Rod (Norway) *58*

Idea (Japan) 99
IdN (Hong Kong) *141*
IKEA Room (UK) 14
Illustrated Ape, The (UK) 15
Illustrator 7
Independent, The (UK) 24
Intersection (UK) 15

Jacovides, Michael 15–17
Jetzt (Germany) 124–7

Kalman, Tibor 24
King, Dave 23
Klotzeck, Tom 125
Knight, Nick 20, 21

Lab (UK) 15
Label (Italy) *120, 154*
Laeufer, Andreas 17
Leftfield (UK) *85*
Leslie, Jeremy 12–14
Levi's *42*
Liberation Style (France) *88*
Licko, Susanna 146
Lippa, Rami 13
List (US) 15, *148*
LivingEtc (UK) 9
Loaded (UK) 9, 74
Loaded Fashion (UK) 13
LördagSöndag (Denmark) 24

M (Brazil) *89*
M-real (International) 7, 13, 14, *82, 153*
Magazine (France) 15, *113*
Marie Claire (Japan) 100
Martin, Steve 99–100
Maxim (UK) *9*
Maxim (US) *9,* 11
Maxim Fashion (US) 13
McCullin, Don 23
Melody Maker (UK) 8
Metropoli (Spain) 24
Mined (UK) 7, 15, 17, *42*
Mini International (Germany) *115*
Minogue, Kylie 73
Mob (UK) *122*
Mojo (UK) 8
Monstermob *122*
Moss, Kate *77*
Mundo, El (Spain) 24
Museo-Teo (Italy) *40*
Mute (UK) *143*

National Geographic (US) 7, 16
National Magazine Company 13, 14
National Post (Canada) 23
Needham, Ed 11
Neo2 (Spain) 15, *120*
Neon (UK) 9
Nest (US) 15, 16–17, *140*
Neue Zürcher Zeitung (Switzerland) 25
New Statesman, The (UK) 10
New York Times (US) 24
New York Times Magazine (US) *121*
New Yorker, The (US) 7, 16
newspapers 22–5
Newsweek (US) 22
Nice Magazine (UK) 15, 17, *50*
No.A/B/C... (Belgium) 48
Nova (UK) *77, 173*
Numero (France) *168*
Nylon (US) 7, 15, *85, 151*

O (UK) 12, 14, *87*
Oyster (Australia) 15, *108*

På Stan (Denmark) 24
País, El (Spain) 24, *117*
Palmer, Ally 25
Philadelphia Inquirer (US) 23
Photoshop 7, 73
Plus Eighty One (Japan) *86*
Pop (UK) 7, 17, 73, *150*
Popbitch (UK) 19–20
Popischil, Hans-Georg 23
Porter, Mark 22–5
Premium (Germany) *111*
Punch (UK) 10
Purple (France) *15*
Putt (UK) 15

Q (UK) 8, 11
QuarkXpress 7, 19, 22

Rand, Michael 23
Raygun (US) 7, 9, 10
Re - (The Netherlands) 7, 15, *16*
Reforma (Mexico) 25
Relax (Japan) *82*
Repubblica delle Donne, La (Italy) 24, *116*
Ritz (Japan) 100
Roberts, Kevin 12
Rolling Stone (US) 11
Ryuko-Tsushin (Japan) 100

Salon (US) 21
San Francisco Chronicle (US) 23
Saville, Peter 20
Schumm, Niels *39*
Scotsman, The (UK) 24
Scott, Jeremy *41*
Sec (The Netherlands) *103*
Self Service (France) 15, 16, *131*
SexyMachinery (UK) 7, *34*
Shift! (Germany) 15, *17*
ShowStudio (UK) 20, 21
Silverstein, Lou 24
Simionato, Andy 163–4
Simons, Raf *41*
Sky (UK) 12, 14
SleazeNation (UK) 19, 20, 21, *78*
Smith, Alex 19, 21
Sony Style (US) *13,* 14
Spector Cut + Paste (Germany) 15, *31, 96*
Spektacle (UK) *32*
Spice Girls 74
Sports Graphic Number (Japan) 99
Sports Illustrated (Japan) 99
Statements (Germany) 14, *41*
Stockholm New (Sweden) 19, *60*
Street Fashion (Japan) 15
Süddeutsche Zeitung (Germany) 24, 124–7
Suhonen, Paola *29*
Sunday Times, The (UK) 23
Surface (US) 7, 15, *132*

Tages Anzeiger (Switzerland) 25
Taiyo (Japan) 100
Tank (UK) 7, 15, 16, 17, *58, 172*
Tentaciones (Spain) 24
Thisisamagazine (TIAM) (Italy) 126, 162–5
Tiger (Germany) 126
Time (US) 22
Time Out (UK) *80*
Times, The (UK) 24
Total Sport (UK) 11
Typographic (UK) *37*

USA Today (US) 22, 23
Useful Photography (The Netherlands) *91*

Valor (Brazil) 24
Very (US) 15
Viewpoint (UK) 15, *154, 171*
Visionaire (US) 15, 16
Vogue 74, 99
Vogue (Italy) 15, 73
Vogue (UK) 10
Vogue Teen (US) 13
Volvo (US) 13, *14*

Waitrose Food Illustrated (UK) 14, *115*
*Wallpaper** (UK) 8, 9, 15, 99
Walters, John L. 20
Watts, Bob 21
websites 18–21
Weekend (UK) 23–4, 25, *156*
Wilhelm, Bernhard *41*
Wired (US) *53*
Wish You Were Here (US) 15, *154*
Woche, Die (Germany) *23,* 24
Woman's Journal (UK) 73
Woodward, Fred 11

Young Blood (France) *60*

Zeit, Die (Germany) 25